The Ornament of the Middle Way

A Study of the Madhyamaka Thought of Śāntarakṣita

The Ornament of the Middle Way

A Study of the Madhyamaka Thought of Śāntarakṣita

Including Translations of Śāntarakṣita's *Madhyamakālaṃkāra* (*The Ornament of the Middle Way*) and Gyel-tsab's *dbU ma rgyan gyi brjed byang* (*Remembering "The Ornament of the Middle Way"*)

by James Blumenthal

Snow Lion Publications
Ithaca, New York ✦ Boulder, Colorado

Snow Lion Publications
605 West State Street
P.O. Box 6483
Ithaca, NY 14851
(607) 273-8519

www.snowlionpub.com

First edition USA 2004

Library of Congress Cataloging-in-Publication Data

Blumenthal, James, 1967-
The ornament of the middle way : a study of the Madhyamaka thought of Śāntarakṣita : including translations of Śāntarakṣita's Madhyamakālaṃkāra (The ornament of the middle way) and Gyel-tsab's dbU ma rgyan gyi brjed byang (Remembering "The ornament of the middle way") / by James Blumenthal.— 1st ed.
p. cm.
In English and Tibetan; translated from Tibetan.
Includes bibliographical references and index.
ISBN 1-55939-205-3 (cloth : alk. paper)
1. Śāntarakṣita, 705-762. Madhyamakālaṃkāra. 2. Mādhyamika (Buddhism — Philosophy. 3. Dge-lugs-pa (Sect) — Doctrines. I. Śāntarakṣita, 705-762. Madhyamakālaṃkāra. English & Tibetan. II. Rgyal-tshab Dar-ma-rin-chen, 1364-1432. Dbu ma rgyan gyi brjed byang. English & Tibetan. III. Title.

BQ3187.B58 2004
294.3'85—dc22

2004042887

Printed in Canada on acid-free, recycled paper.
Text design by Gopa & Ted2, Inc.

ISBN 1-55939-205-3

Contents

Acknowledgments

I WOULD LIKE TO THANK a number of people who have made this work possible in an assortment of ways. My deepest thanks must first go to my graduate advisor and teacher Geshe Lhundup Sopa. It is difficult to express my profound gratitude for having had the opportunity to study closely with Geshe-la for many years. Scholars of his caliber are truly rare, but with Geshe-la scholarly acumen is only the beginning. He is a teacher in all the best and most meaningful senses of the word. He has dedicated his life to communicating to others the Buddhist tradition he not only knows intellectually, but so thoroughly embodies. I am but one of many who have been fortunate enough to receive his expert instruction and guidance. I feel particularly fortunate to have been among the last of his doctoral students at the University of Wisconsin. Every aspect of my association with Geshe-la has been one in which I have benefited and it is with great humility that I offer these words of thanks.

Among the other faculty members at the University of Wisconsin who assisted me with this project and have influenced my intellectual development, Professor David Knipe stands out. I have benefited greatly from his probing questions and his vast understanding of the religious traditions of South Asia, including his ability to contextualize Buddhism within this larger tradition from which it is all too often disassociated in scholarly analysis. Professor Narayana Rao, Professor Joe Elder, Professor Robert Bickner, Professor Minoru Kiyota, Dr. Gautam Vajracarya, Dr. Krishna Pradhan, and Dr. James Powell all gave important critical feedback and offered important suggestions and insights which have contributed to the successful completion of this project.

A significant portion of the early stages of research involved in this project was completed in India with the support of a grant from the Social Science Research Council with Federal funding granted under the NMERTA

(Near and Middle East Research and Training Act) program during the academic year 1997-98. During this stay in India, I studied at The Central Institute of Higher Tibetan Studies in Sarnath. Thanks must first go to Ven. Samdong Rinpoche, then Director, for welcoming me and assuring that I received the accommodations and assistance necessary to make my visit a successful one. During this stay, I had the great fortune of studying with the first of several Tibetan scholars (after Geshe Sopa) who assisted me with this project in a variety of ways. While in Sarnath, I met with Geshe Jigme Dawa on a daily basis. He generously read through and commented upon the entirety of Śāntarakṣita's *Madhyamakālaṃkāra* in conjunction with Gyel-tsab's *dbU ma rgyan gyi brjed byang*. In many ways Geshe-la opened the door to Śāntarakṣita's thought for me through his explanation of the terse verses and complex arguments of the root text. While in Sarnath, I also studied with Geshe Ngawang Samden (now Director of the Institute). We had numerous conversations about Śāntarakṣita's ideas and he clarified many difficult points for me as well. In addition, he went over an early draft of the translations included in this volume and made a number of fruitful suggestions. Several others aided this work and became great friends during my stay in Sarnath, including Tenzin Namgyal, Pempa Tsering, Pema Wangchen, Tashi, Ram Chandar, Tiina Hyytiainen, and Barbara Clayton.

In addition to the time I spent in Sarnath, I have been very fortunate in being able to study these materials with several other top Tibetan scholars both in America and in India. I will mention them in the chronological order according to when we studied these materials together. I read and studied the entirety of Śāntarakṣita's *Madhyamakālaṃkāravṛtti* with Yangsi (Geshe Ngawang Gendun) Rinpoche who was unendingly patient with my questions, many of which must have seemed quite unorthodox. It was truly a blessing to have the opportunity to study Tsong-kha-pa's *dbU ma rgyan gyi zin bris* on a daily basis with the great Sera Je scholar Gyume Khensur Lobsang Tenzin Rinpoche. His scholarly erudition and skill at communicating subtle philosophical concepts, combined with his kindness and patience, make him a real tribute to his tradition and a living example of a scholar-adept. His brilliant teaching illuminated many difficult points for me. In addition to formal studies, I spent countless hours in more informal conversation and good spirited debate with Ven. Geshe Tenzin Dorje, also of Tsangpa House at Sera Je. Geshe Tendo helped bring into focus many of the subtleties of the texts and also suggested several additional materials, including specific monastic textbooks (*yig cha*), which aided my study of these subjects. Finally, I would like to thank Geshe Kelsang Damdul of Drepung Loseling Monastery and the Institute of Buddhist Dialectics in Dharamsala whom I had the good fortune of meeting this past year since he moved to Portland, Oregon to be the resident teacher at the Center for Tibetan Buddhism and spiritual director of the Northwest Tibetan Cultural Association. He has graciously read the final draft of the translations included in this book and made several suggestions which undoubtedly have improved the translations as they now stand. Geshe-la also clarified some of my final questions on difficult passages in the texts.

While at Oregon State University, I have received generous support for this project from several sources. I have received two separate grants from the Hundere Endowment For Religion and Culture which have afforded me time off from teaching commitments to work on this project both in India and in Oregon. These grants came at pivotal points in the final research and writing stages of the book and were essential to its completion. I would particularly like to thank Dr. Marcus Borg, who holds the Hundere Chair in Religion and Culture, for his ongoing support of my work. In addition, I received a College of Liberal Arts Research Grant which also afforded me time away from teaching to work on this project. A Library Research Travel Grant from the Valley Library at OSU funded my research in the Tibetan collection at the Memorial Library at the University of Wisconsin in the summer of 2002. Finally, this past fall, I was supported by a grant from the Center for the Humanities at Oregon State University. This gave me three months of solid writing time and enabled me to complete the draft of this book.

Several friends and colleagues graciously agreed to read drafts and chapters of this book and give their valuable feedback. Adam Pergament read through two complete drafts of this volume and gave detailed comments and feedback which have greatly improved the quality of the final product. I am deeply appreciative of his selfless and expert efforts. Roger Jackson read significant sections and his comments on those were invaluable. Sara McClintock read through most of an early draft of the book and her comments inspired me to consider Śāntarakṣita and his Geluk commentators in fruitful ways that had not previously occurred to me. Ven. Lhundup Jampa (Alicia Vogel) also read sections of an early draft and our many lengthy conversations about Buddhist thought and Buddhist scholarship have greatly influenced my understanding and approach to them. Thanks also to Joanna

Donovan, who proofread parts of an early draft. Steve Rhodes at Snow Lion Publications deserves huge thanks for meticulously reading through the final draft and offering many important suggestions and corrections. He was also both patient and encouraging during the various stages of this project. In spite of the expert guidance I have received and all the feedback from friends, colleagues, and teachers on this project, there are bound to be errors still present in a study of this size. All such errors are certainly my own and do not reflect on the teachers and others who have offered input into this project.

Portions of this book have been published elsewhere in articles and I would like to thank those publishers for allowing me to reprint them here. These include:

"Remarks on the dGe-lugs-pa Analysis of Śāntarakṣita's Views on the Status of Hīnayāna Arhats." IIJBS 3 (2002): 33-56.

"Multiple Provisionalities: Dynamic Aspects of Yogācāra-Madhyamaka Synthesis in the *Madhyamakālaṃkāra* of Śāntarakṣita." In *Contributions to the Study of the Thought of Śāntarakṣita,* ed. by Marie Friquegnon. Binghamton: Global Scholarly Publications (forthcoming).

"Remarks on the dGe-lugs-pa Analysis of Śāntarakṣita's Views on the Two Truths" In *Contributions to the Study of the Thought of Śāntarakṣita,* ed.by Marie Friquegnon. Binghamton: Global Scholarly Publications (forthcoming).

Many others deserve thanks for reasons too numerous to recount. These include: Richard Anderson, Jim Apple, Tom Blumenthal, Jim Bradbury, Bob Bremmer, Steven Brence, Bill Breunig, Maureen Burkett, Courtney Campbell, Rich Chao, Chris Chekuri, Ven. Thubten Chodron, Ven. Chökyi Nyima Rinpoche, Hartzog Clamon, John Coltrane, Roger Dammeral, Mark Dennis, Paul Donnelly, Ven. Sera Je Khen Rinpoche Geshe Donyo, John Dunne, John Duvall, Duke Ellington, Amato Evan, Paul Hackett, Ann Hubbard, Neil Hyytinen, Ven. Jen-kuan Shih, Ven. Kelsang Tsering, Roscoe Mitchel, A. K. Narain, John Newman, Lalji Shravak, Ven. Lhundup Damcho (Dianne Finnegan), Ven. Lhundup Dechen, Ken Liberman, Flo Liebowitz, Peter List, Kathy Moore, Lance Nelson, Joseph Orosco, Su-jei Own, Craig Preston, Lani Roberts, Dennis Rohatyn, Michael Scanlan, Rod Stevenson, Sonny Thammasouk, Ven. Tulku Urgyen Rinpoche, Bill Uzgalis, Ya-ling Tsai, Greg Thoming, Ven. Thubten Tsultrim (George

Churinoff), Ven. Sherab, Cecil Taylor, His Holiness Tenzin Gyatso, Dalai Lama XIV, Ven. Thabkay, Ven. Geshe Thabkay, Sam Van Laningham, Diana Vélez, Sean Weber-Small, Bob Weddel, and Sara Winkelman.

Finally, I owe an enormous debt of gratitude to my parents, Susan and Jack Blumenthal. They have always believed in me and my work and encouraged the pursuit of my goals. When these pursuits have taken me half way around the world and back, their love and support have always been there. This work certainly would not have been possible without them. They are among my greatest teachers.

This work is humbly dedicated to all my teachers. May their highest aspirations be fulfilled.

List of Abbreviations

ASA	*Abhisamayālaṃkāra*
BIS	*Berliner Indologische Studien*
D	*Derge Tripiṭaka*
EA	*Études Asiatiques / Asiatische Studien*
GOS	*Gaekwad Oriental Series*
GRS	*dbU ma dgongs pa rab gsal*
IIJ	*Indo-Iranian Journal*
IIJBS	*International Indian Journal of Buddhist Studies*
JAOS	*Journal of the American Oriental Society*
JBy	*dbU ma rgyan gyi brjed byang*
JIABS	*Journal of the International Association of Buddhist Studies*
JIBS	*Journal of Indian and Buddhist Studies*
JIP	*Journal of Indian Philosophy*
KNG	*dKa' gnas brgyad kyi zin bris*
LRCh	*Byang chub lam gyi rim pa chen mo*
LSN	*Drangs nges legs bshad snying po*
MA	*Madhyamakālaṃkāra*
MAV	*Madhyamakālaṃkāravṛtti*
MA/V	*Madhyamakālaṃkāra* and *Madhyamakālaṃkāravṛtti* when considered together.
MAP	*Madhyamakālaṃkārapañjikā*
MMK	*Mūlamadhyamakakārikā*
OLZ	*Orientalistische Literaturzeitung*
P	*Peking Tripiṭaka*
PV	*Pramāṇavārttikakārikā*
RG	*Rig pa'i rgya mtsho*
SDVP	*Satyadvayavibhaṅgapañjikā*
SDVV	*Satyadvayavibhaṅgarvṛtti*

SII	*Studien zur Indologie und Iranistik*
TJ	*Tibet Journal*
Toh	*A Complete Catalogue of the Tibetan Buddhist Canons,* edited by Hakuju Ui *et al.*(Sendai, Japan: Tohoku Imperial University, 1934)
TS	*Tattvasaṃgraha*
TSP	*Tattavasaṃgrahapañjikā*
TS/P	*Tattvasaṃgraha* and *Tattavasaṃgrahapañjikā* when considered together.
TTC	*sTong thun chen mo*
VÖAW	*Verlag der Österreichischen Akademie der Wissenschaften*
WSTB	*Wiener Studien zur Tibetologie und Buddhismuskunde*
WZKS	*Wiener Zeitschrift für die Kunde Südasiens*
WZKSO	*Wiener Zeitschrift für die Kunde Süd- und Ostasiens*
ZBr	*dbU ma rgyan gyi zin bris*

Technical Note

TIBETAN PROPER NAMES appear in Wylie transliteration in parentheses at their first appearance following a phonetic rendering. All subsequent appearances of names will follow the phonetic rendering. The aim is to make the names and the book more accessible to a non-Tibetan-reading audience. When technical terms are provided in parentheses after an English rendering, Wylie transliteration is utilized as well as the standard Sanskrit transliteration. When the term comes from a Tibetan source, the Tibetan is given first, followed by the Sanskrit equivalent when appropriate. When the source is Indian, the Sanskrit is given first, followed by the Tibetan when appropriate. On occasion, only the Tibetan will be given for a term originating in an Indian source. This is due to the lack of an extant Sanskrit version of the text. This is often the case with Śāntarakṣita's *Madhyamakālaṃkāra* for which there is not a complete Sanskrit text extant. Some Sanskrit words are available due to the use of some of the stanzas of *Madhyamakālaṃkāra* in other extant Sanskrit texts. Others are gleaned by use of Shoko Watanabe's *Glossary of the Tattvasaṅgrahapañjikā: Tibetan-Sanskrit-Japanese.* Since the same translators, Śīlendrabodhi and Yeshe De (*Ye-shes-sde*), translated both Śāntarakṣita's *Tattvasaṃgrahapañjikā* (which is extant in Sanskrit) and *Madhyamakālaṃkāra,* it is safe to presume that they utilized the same equivalents for technical terms.

Introduction

OVER THE COURSE of the 1500 years following the enlightenment of the historical Buddha, Śākyamuni (b. 563 B.C.E.),[1] several distinct schools and systems of Buddhist philosophical thought and a rich intellectual history emerged on the Indian subcontinent. The variance in interpretations of the Buddha's teachings and in the subsequent schools of thought was more than just a response to the fact that the canon of Buddhist *sūtras,* considered to be the words of the historical Buddha, publicly emerged over the course of centuries and portrayed the Buddhist presentation of reality in a variety of ways. The various Indian Buddhist systems also emerged in response to the views and tenets of one another and to the writings of prolific scholar-adepts whose canonized texts represented the foundational standpoints of these schools. As the Buddhist tradition evolved in South Asia and spread throughout other parts of Asia, these schools of thought were interpreted, represented, and systematized in a variety of ways by the various inheritors of the Indian Buddhist tradition. One of the many unique qualities of the Tibetan Buddhist tradition is the marked emphasis placed on the treatises of these Indian scholar-adepts and on the intellectual history of their Indian Buddhist predecessors.[2] This study takes as its central subject one such treatise, *The Ornament of the Middle Way* (*Madhyamakālaṃkāra*, *dbU ma rgyan*) (hereafter *MA*), and the Madhyamaka thought of its author, Śāntarakṣita (725-788 C.E.).[3] *MA* is considered to be one of the most important Indian Buddhist *śāstras* (for reasons which will be discussed below), and Śāntarakṣita's Madhyamaka system is a key contribution in the history of Indian Buddhist ideas. This study takes on two tasks: first, an examination of the text and its ideas on their own terms and in the context of the history of Indian Buddhist thought, and second, to further examine them in the context of the interpretive framework of the Geluk (*dGe-lugs*)[4] School[5] of Tibetan Buddhism. By first engaging in an examination of Śāntarakṣita's ideas and text on their own, further examination of the way they are understood and interpreted by major thinkers from a Tibetan sect which inherited this Indian tradition not only illuminates key components of Śāntarakṣita's thought, but equally reveals much about the interpretive process at work in the receiving tradition.

Thus, there are two principal projects in this study. We have the first book length investigation of Śāntarakṣita's Madhyamaka thought as portrayed in *MA* in which all the major themes of the text, and each individual stanza, are closely examined. Śāntarakṣita's contribution to Indian Buddhist philosophical history was enormous. He was responsible for what correctly can be considered to be the final major development in Indian Mahāyāna thought on the subcontinent, the synthesis of Yogācāra, Madhyamaka, and the Buddhist logico-epistemological traditions (*pramāṇavāda*[6]). While certain aspects of his philosophical thought, particularly the details of his thoughts on logic, are treated more extensively in other texts, the foundations of his Madhyamaka thought and the syncretism of the three traditions are presented most clearly here in *The Ornament of the Middle Way* and in his own *Autocommentary on "The Ornament of the Middle Way"* (hereafter *MA/V* when considered together). Given that this is the case, it is surprising that this sort of study has not been undertaken before now. Perhaps this is because complete texts of *MA* and his *Autocommentary on "The Ornament of the Middle Way"* (*Madhyamakālaṃkāravṛtti, dbU ma rgyan gyi rang 'grel*) (hereafter *MAV*) are no longer extant in Sanskrit and many scholars of Indian Buddhist thought do not have the requisite skills in Classical Tibetan, the language in which the texts survive today. This study includes a complete translation into English of the verses of *MA* and translations of substantial sections from *MAV*.[7]

The examination of the themes of the text and of each individual stanza is done in conjunction with Śāntarakṣita's own *MAV* and his disciple Kamalaśīla's *Commentary on the Difficult Points of "The Ornament of the Middle Way"* (*Madhyamakālaṃkāravpañjikā, dbU ma rgyan gyi dka' 'grel*) (hereafter *MAP*). I rely as much as possible simply on Śāntarakṣita's own words in *MA* and *MAV* as I proceed through a descriptive examination of Śāntarakṣita's Madhyamaka thought. Kamalaśīla's *MAP* is utilized primarily when it is felt that *MA* and *MAV* could use further clarification.[8] The particular use of sources will be discussed in more detail below.

The second principal project of this study is an investigation into the treatment of these texts and Śāntarakṣita's ideas by Tibetan recipients of the

Indian Buddhist traditions. Specifically, I will examine the way in which scholars from the Geluk school of Tibetan Buddhism have interpreted, represented, incorporated, and ultimately criticized Śāntarakṣita's ideas in the various genres of their own philosophical literature. Gelukpas consider Śāntarakṣita's presentation of Madhyamaka to be less subtle and less accurate than their own. At times the Geluk presentation of Śāntarakṣita's views is curious in that they attribute views and tenets to him which he does not explicitly state in his own writings. This is the first study to closely examine the curious way in which Geluk scholars have dealt with these competing Madhyamaka views.[9] This is carried out by engaging in a detailed examination of the Indian sources from which the Gelukpas draw to formulate their representation of those views, in addition to a broad based survey of Geluk materials from several genres of their philosophical literature. Examining the way in which scholars from the Geluk School grapple with a rival Madhyamaka perspective not only reveals a great deal about the philosophical process of the receiving Buddhist tradition, but their critiques draw our attention to the pivotal issues on which both their own and Śāntarakṣita's Madhyamaka systems turn. It is our hope that investigating the Geluk treatment of Śāntarakṣita's system not only illuminates insights into the Geluk philosophical project, but that by placing Śāntarakṣita's ideas under the critical eye of fellow, yet competing, Mādhyamikas, we come to understand his own philosophical project better as well. This study will also include a complete translation of the only Geluk text which comments specifically on every stanza of Śāntarakṣita's *MA*, namely Gyeltsab's (rGyal-tshab) *Remembering "The Ornament of the Middle Way"* (*dbU ma rgyan gyi brjed byang*) (hereafter *JBy*).

Madhyamakālaṃkāra

The Buddhist *paṇḍita* Śāntarakṣita and his major text *MA* (along with its auto-commentary, *MAV)* hold an important place, as mentioned above, in the history of Buddhist philosophical doctrine and in the evolution of Mahāyāna thought. Considered by Tibetans (Gelukpas in particular)[10] as the foundational or root text of the sub-school of Madhyamaka thought known among Tibetans as Yogācāra-Svātantrika-Madhyamaka,[11] the text contains several key characteristics which signal its importance to Buddhists in both India and Tibet. First, as briefly mentioned above, Śāntarakṣita's *MA/V*[12] is an important syncretic text and the first clear exposition of a system which integrates all three of the most important developments in later Indian Buddhist philosophy into one coherent system of thought.[13] Specifically, Śāntarakṣita fuses together the two major Mahāyāna philosophical schools, Yogācāra and Madhyamaka, while maintaining his ultimate stance as a Mādhyamika and likewise incorporating the logico-epistemological developments of Dignāga, Dharmakīrti, and their followers. The Yogācāra position of rejecting the existence of objects external to consciousness was accepted by Śāntarakṣita as an accurate presentation of conventional truth and a useful philosophical step on the way to an ultimate Madhyamaka position. Having first understood that entities lack having a nature independent of, or external to, the consciousness perceiving it, Śāntarakṣita argues that one can then proceed to a Madhyamaka analysis of the ultimate and find that the mind also has no independent, enduring, or inherent nature of its own. This dynamic process will be discussed further in this introduction under the subheading "Śāntarakṣita's Yogācāra-Madhyamaka Synthesis," but for now allow me to summarize this synthesis by quoting Śāntarakṣita's ninety-second stanza of *MA* which states:

> By relying on the Mind Only (*cittamatra, sems tsam pa*) [system], know that external entities do not exist. And by relying on this [Madhyamaka] system, know that no self at all exists, even in that [mind].[14]

Mādhyamikas during Śāntarakṣita's time in the eighth century needed to respond to the growth of the Yogācāra School, which had been present in India since the late fourth century. In addition, the logico-epistemological developments with which the Yogācāra tradition was arguably related (particularly in the thought of thinkers such as Dharmakīrti) had gained widespread prominence as well. Thus, integrating the two with a fundamentally Madhyamaka ontology and worldview was an approach which several of the major later Mādhyamikas in India found quite satisfactory. These included, most prominently, Śāntarakṣita's own disciples, Kamalaśīla and Haribhadra. When considering Śāntarakṣita's integration of both major streams of Mahāyāna thought, Yogācāra and Madhyamaka, together with the syncretic inclusion of the *pramāṇavāda* traditions, his innovations can arguably be seen, as mentioned above, as the final *major* development in Indian Buddhist thought before the demise of Buddhism in India in the late twelfth and early thirteenth centuries.

Not only does Śāntarakṣita integrate Yogācāra and Madhyamaka thought with the logico-epistemological traditions into one coherent system, but he also valorizes the importance of studying what are considered to be "lower" Buddhist schools. These were seen as integral stepping stones on the ascent to his presentation of what he considered to be the ultimately correct view of Madhyamaka. The influence of this in Tibet can clearly be seen today in the standard Geluk curriculum, which also emphasizes study of what it considers to be "lower" schools as an appropriate foundation on which one can come to understand the higher ones. This hierarchy of Buddhist philosophical views is explicit in the doxographies and monastic textbooks of the tradition where the tenet systems are presented in a graded organized system from lower to higher. Both in his valorization of the study of lower philosophical systems and in his integration of the *pramāṇavāda* and Madhyamaka, it is clear that Śāntarakṣita was an enormously influential figure on Tibetan philosophical traditions, including those that ultimately criticized aspects of his thought, such as the Geluk.

In addition to these points, the importance of *MA/V* is also signaled by several other methodological and doctrinal factors, two of which I would like to discuss here. The first sixty-two stanzas of *MA* make up the most famous rendering and extensive application of the well-known and key Madhyamaka reasoning, the neither-one-nor-many argument (*gcig du bral kyi gtan tshigs*)[15] demonstrating the lack of an inherent nature in entities. This, along with the "diamond sliver" argument (*rdo rje gzigs ma'i gtan tshigs*), is one of the classical Madhyamaka logical formulations aimed at establishing the emptiness of all phenomena. The neither-one-nor-many argument is the primary argument used by Śāntarakṣita to establish the Madhyamaka position which holds that all persons and phenomena are empty of having any enduring nature and thus are best characterized by the descriptive, technical term *śūnyata* or emptiness. The neither-one-nor-many argument states that no phenomena have any sort of inherent nature because they have neither a singular nature nor a manifold nature. Since the two are exhaustive of all possible alternatives for phenomena that would have an inherent nature, this argument is considered to be valid proof for the lack of any inherent nature in phenomena, thereby establishing the fundamental tenet of the Madhyamaka view. Śāntarakṣita renders this argument as follows in the first stanza of *MA*:.

> Those entities, as asserted by our own [Buddhist schools] and other [non-Buddhist] schools have no inherent nature at all because in reality they have neither singular nor manifold nature – like a reflected image.

In the following sixty-one stanzas, Śāntarakṣita applies this reasoning in individual cases specifically to those entities that his Buddhist and non-Buddhist philosophical rivals claim do have some sort of inherent nature. Thus, by the end of the text Śāntarakṣita feels he has successfully refuted his opponents' views with valid reasoning, establishing the emptiness of inherent existence of all phenomena as an accurate description of reality. Many of the arguments that Śāntarakṣita uses to refute the positions of his opponents later become examples of standard Madhyamaka refutations of lower schools found throughout Tibetan philosophical literature.

The final major point in Śāntarakṣita's text which signals its importance and uniqueness is the fact that he argues in support of two tenets concerning the nature of consciousness which were uncommon among Mādhyamikas to this point in India. First, he accepts the doctrine of self- cognizing cognition (*svasaṃvedana, rang rig*), a tenet no Mādhyamika before him asserted.[16] This is the idea that consciousness is reflexively conscious, that it is conscious of being conscious. Second, he argues that consciousness is not utterly distinct from its objects. Certainly these stances are taken by Śāntarakṣita in part due to, or in reflection of, the syncretic nature of his system that fuses Yogācāra and *pramāṇavāda* views with his own ultimate Madhyamaka position. It is, however, of significant interest to note the unique way in which Śāntarakṣita defines the term self-cognizing cognition. Often in Yogācāra presentations, self-cognizing cognition is defined as a separate part or aspect of consciousness which is observing consciousness. This is the view that is rejected by the Gelukpas in their discussions of this issue. Śāntarakṣita defines it as the very nature of consciousness. That which is conscious is itself self-conscious. The difference is subtle but important and may impact the relavence of certain Geluk criticisms. Although Śāntarakṣita does not go into elaborate detail, his presentation is unique enough and important enough to warrant consideration.[17] This issue will be discussed further in Part I and Part II of this study.

Śāntarakṣita

Prior to going into further detail on the texts and philosophical ideas, I would like to give some brief background on Śāntarakṣita, his life, and his other writings in order to historically contextualize the ideas and texts which are the centerpiece of this study. It is difficult to determine with certainty many of the details of Śāntarakṣita's life in India because historical records simply do not exist. According to tradition, Śāntarakṣita was born into a family of royal lineage in Bengal, in eastern India.[18] We can presume from his literary output and the degree of seriousness with which his ideas and texts were treated by his contemporaries, both Buddhist and non-Buddhist,[19] that he held a high status as a scholar in India.

With regard to his activities in Tibet, it is perhaps best to begin with the legendary account of one of Śāntarakṣita's previous lives attested to in *The Blue Annals* (*Deb ther sngon po*). Therein it says that Śāntarakṣita, Trisong Detsen (*Khri-srong-lde-btsan*) (c. 740-798) and the minister Ba Salnang (*dBa' gSal-snang*)[20] made a commitment to one another during the time of the previous Buddha, Kāśyapa, when they were the three sons of a poultry keeper. At that time they committed themselves to preach and propagate the dharma in Tibet in future times.[21]

There are somewhat more detailed records of Śāntarakṣita's activities in Tibet than of those in India, where, as one of the key figures in the early transmission of Buddhism from India to that country, he spent the latter part of his life teaching. Śāntarakṣita in fact made two visits to Tibet during the reign of King Trisong Detsen when Ba Salnang was one of the king's ministers. His first visit to Tibet in 763 was relatively short, although on his second visit which followed shortly thereafter he remained in Tibet for fifteen years, until his death in 788.[22] During his first visit, at the request of Ba Salnang Śāntarakṣita went to meet with Trisong Detsen so that the king could examine both the character and the teachings of the invited master. At first the king did not recall the commitment they had made with one another many lifetimes before during the time of Buddha Kāśyapa, but according to *The Blue Annals* Śāntarakṣita blessed the king, who then was able to remember his previous lives.[23] He then proceeded to teach many doctrines to the king, but apparently it was not long before "...the great gods and demons of Tibet became wrathful. Lightning struck the palace on the dMar-po-ri [Red Mountain], the royal palace of 'Phang-thang was carried away by water. Harvest was damaged and a great epidemic took place."[24] Ministers who were opposed to the spread of Buddhism told the king that this was all a result of the Indian teacher who was attempting to spread a new religion in Tibet and that he should be expelled from the country. Rather than back down in fear, and on the suggestion of Śāntarakṣita, who only remained in Tibet for four months[25] on this initial visit, the king invited Padmasambhava, the great tantric master, to come and do battle with these demons and to help the flourishing of Buddhism in Tibet. Traditional Tibetan religious histories and hagiographies record that Padmasambhava did just that, converting these demons to Buddhism and enlisting them as protectors of the dharma (*dharmapāla*, *chos skyon*). Soon after the hindrances were removed, Śāntarakṣita was invited to return to Tibet to teach. Padmasambhava became the great teacher of tantra or *mantrāyāna* in this early period, and Śāntarakṣita went on to become the most prominent teacher of philosophy and other aspects of *sūtrāyāna*.

Among his historically important activities in Tibet, Śāntarakṣita is noted for ordaining the first seven Tibetan monks and establishing Samye (*bSams yas*) Monastery, the first Buddhist monastery in Tibet. He served as its first abbot and is thus often referred to by the epithet "Khenchen" or "Great Abbot" among Tibetans. In addition, in anticipation of a controversy over whether to follow the Indian gradual approach or the Chinese sudden approach[26] to enlightenment, as both methods were being taught at this early stage of Buddhism in Tibet, Śāntarakṣita recommended that upon his death his disciple Kamalaśīla be invited from India to teach and to defend the Indian gradualist approach in what would be the famous Debate at Samye.[27] At this debate, Kamalaśīla is reported in Tibetan accounts to have defeated the Chinese master Mo-ho-yen. Generally speaking, the Indian gradual approach was from that point on to be the state patronized form of Buddhism and the sudden or immediate approach of the Chinese was no longer to be taught in Tibet.

As the first major teacher of Buddhist philosophy in Tibet, Śāntarakṣita's interpretation and presentation of Buddhist thought was the dominant system during the period of the early dissemination (*snga dar*) of Buddhism in that country, particularly in central Tibet in the eighth and ninth centuries. His presentation of Madhyamaka thought, known in early Tibetan doxographies as Yogācāra-Madhyamaka,[28] and later known in Tibet as Yogācāra-Svātantrika-Madhyamaka, was taken by most to be Buddhism's highest explanation of the nature of reality and, therefore, the correct interpretation of Madhyamaka. This stood in opposition to Bhāvaviveka's view, which at that time was a rival Madhyamaka position in Tibet known as Sautrāntika-Madhyamaka. In later Tibetan classifications, it became known as Sautrāntika-Svātantrika-Madhyamaka. Karen Lang notes that, "Śāntarakṣita and Kamalaśīla's oral transmission of Yogācāra-Madhyamaka views, in addition to their literary works, undoubtedly attracted many students and made their teachings widespread throughout Central Tibet."[29] Prāsaṅgika-Madhyamaka was yet unknown in Tibet.

It was not until the major works of Candrakīrti were translated in the period of the later dissemination (*phyi dar*) of Buddhism in the eleventh and twelfth centuries[30] that Śāntarakṣita's interpretation of Madhyamaka thought began to be called into question.[31] Actually, Atīśa (982-1054) may have subtly implied problems with the Yogācāra-Svātantrika-Madhyamaka view of Śāntarakṣita and Kamalaśīla when in his *Commentary on "The Lamp for the Path to Enlightenment"* (*Bodhimārgadīpapañjikā*) he listed a Madhyamaka lineage and mentioned all the major non-synthesizing Mādhyamikas, that is Mādhyamikas who did not synthesize Madhyamaka ideas with Yogācāra ideas, such as Nāgārjuna, Āryadeva, Candrakīrti, Bhāvaviveka, Śāntideva, and even Bodhibhadra, but not Śāntarakṣita, Kamalaśīla, or Haribhadra. Although Atīśa is counted among proponents of Prāsaṅgika-Madhyamaka in Tibet, he did not explicitly teach that system there. Rather he taught Bhāvaviveka's Sautrāntika-Madhyamaka. It was not until the time of Patsab (*sPa-tshab Nyi-ma-grags*) in the twelfth century that the Prāsaṅgika-Madhyamaka view began to be widely taught and the privileging of Śāntarakṣita's system began to encounter serious opposition. Patsab studied in Kashmir for twenty-three years[32] and on his return to Tibet translated three of Candrakīrti's major works which had not yet been available in Tibetan: *Madhyamakāvatāra*, *Prasannapadā*, and the *Bodhisattvayogācaryacatuḥśatakaṭīkā.* He became a popular teacher among followers of the Kadam School, which was founded by Atīśa's disciple Dromtonpa (*'Brom-ston-pa*). This is whence the Prāsaṅgika view initially spread in Tibet, particularly among students of the reknowned Kadam scholar, Sharwapa (*Shar-ba-pa*) (1070-1141). Of course the dominance of the Prāsaṅgika-Madhyamaka view in Tibet approached new heights during Tsong Khapa's (1357-1419) time, approximately two centuries after Patsab. It has been the dominant view since then, but by no means the only or unquestioned view in Tibet. Although it is likely that Tsong Khapa's Prāsaṅgika-Madhyamaka is somewhat nuanced, even in relation to Candrakīrti, he does trace his oral lineage through the two Kashmiri scholars that Patsab invited to Tibet, Hasumati and Kanakavarman.[33] Since the time of Tsong Khapa, it has been his Prāsaṅgika-Madhyamaka system to which all rival positions in Tibet have had to answer.

Śāntarakṣita's Writings

There are eleven texts attributed to Śāntarakṣita in the Tibetan collection of translations of canonized treatises and literature not attributed to Śākyamuni, the Tengyur (*bsTan 'gyur*), although only three survive in Sanskrit. The Tibetan Tengyur is divided into sections and sub-sections and Śāntarakṣita's writings are found in several of these. They include the sections containing collections of praises (*bstod tshogs*) and commentaries on tantras (*rgyud 'grel*), including his relatively well known *Tattvasiddhi* in the tantric section. While a close study of all these texts would certainly be important and of interest, the praises and the tantric materials largely lie outside the scope of this study. The texts we are most concerned with here are the philosophical writings of Śāntarakṣita.

The texts which are at the center of this study are of course Śāntarakṣita's *MA* and *MAV*. Here is where he outlines and explains the basic framework of his Madhyamaka thought. These texts appear to be among his latest works since, in the section of *MAV* commenting on the ninety-sixth stanza of the root text, he refers to two of his other philosophical works, *TS* and *Paramārthaviniścaya* (*Don dam pa gtan la dbab pa, Investigation of the Ultimate*).[34] *TS* is his encyclopedic tenet system (*siddhānta, grub mtha'*) style text which surveys a host of Buddhist and non-Buddhist views, offering criticism of opposing views throughout. This text, along with his *Vipañcitārthā,* which comments on Dharmakīrti's *Vādanyāya,* is appropriately considered to be the locus of Śāntarakṣita's *pramāṇavāda* thought.[35] The fact that Śāntarakṣita borrows several stanzas from *TS* for inclusion in *MA* lends further credence to the assessment that it pre-dates *MA*. *Paramārthaviniścaya* is unfortunately no longer extant in any language and as such is a great loss to those interested in the philosophical thought of Śāntarakṣita! One can only speculate as to its contents. No complete edition of *MA* or *MAV* exists in Sanskrit, although select stanzas can be found in extant Sanskrit editions of texts from which he quotes including his own *TS* and Dharmakīrti's *Pramāṇavārttika.* In addition, Prajñākaramati's *Bodhicaryāvatārapañjikā,* which cites *MA,* is extant in Sanskrit. Complete texts of the Tibetan translation are readily available, as are useful critical editions of *MA/V* and *MAP* (Ichigō 1985) which serve as the primary basis of this study and my translations included herein.

Three other works are worthy of mention. According to Ruegg, Śāntarakṣita's *Saṃvaraviṃśaka* and *Saṃvaraviṃśakavṛtti* are also associated with Candragomin's *Bodhisattvasaṃvaraviṃśaka* and are noteworthy as examples of literature on the activities of bodhisattvas written from a Yogācāra-Madhyamaka perspective.[36] Ruegg has also observed that these texts are closely related to the *Bodhisattvabhūmi* and as such may rightfully be considered to belong to the Yogācāra tradition rather than the Madhyamaka.

The final philosophical treatise of Śāntarakṣita which deserves mention is his *Satyadvayavibhangapañjikā* (*Commentary on [Jñānagarbha's] "Distinction Between The Two Truths"*). The attribution of authorship of this text to Śāntarakṣita has been questioned by Tibetans such as Tsong Khapa as well as modern scholars. Tsong Khapa offers two reasons in *Drang ba dang nges pa'i don rnam para phye ba'i bstan bcos legs bshad snying po* (hereafter *LSN*) for why he doubts that the person who authored *Satyadvayavibhangapañjikā* is the same as the person who authored *MA/V*.[37] The first of these two reasons seems to be the more convincing. In his commentary (*TSP*) on Śāntarakṣita's *TS*, Śāntarakṣita's direct disciple Kamalalśīla attempts to refute the purpose of the composition given by the author of *Satyadvayavibhangapañjikā*. While it is not unheard of for students to stray from the views of their teachers, and by all accounts it seems as though Śāntarakṣita did stray to some extent from his own teacher, Jñānagarbha, it is too far outside of the teacher-student etiquette of eighth century India for the student to criticize the view of the teacher while composing a commentary on one of the teacher's texts.

Tsong Khapa's second argument concerns the conventional existence of subject-object duality, which Jñānagarbha accepts. If the author of the commentary also accepts this, then it would contradict positions explicitly stated in *MA* which reject subject-object duality conventionally and thus would lead to the conclusion that the author of the commentary is different or has different views from the author of *MA*. This argument seems less convincing as it is not uncommon for a commentary to simply aim to illuminate the meaning of the text on which it comments. Gyel-tsab's commentary on *MA* is a perfect example of this. We do not presume, for example, that he accepts self-cognizing cognition and contradicts his teacher, Tsong Khapa, simply because he does not criticize Śāntarakṣita on this point. The author of the commentary on *Satyadvayavibhanga* may have merely been attempting to remain faithful to the source text. Tsong Khapa's first reason seems more convincing than his second, and perhaps that is enough to seriously doubt the attribution of this text to Śāntarakṣita.[38] Thus, while this text is attributed to Śāntarakṣita, the accuracy of that attribution is highly questionable and its utility for our understanding of Śāntarakṣita's particular Madhyamaka views is therefore dubious. Its utility for the purpose of this study is all the more questionable since, regardless of its authorship, its aim is to illuminate Jñānagarbha's thought, not Śāntarakṣita's.[39]

A Survey of the Literature

It has been noted periodically over the past thirty years by scholars of Madhyamaka thought that there has been relatively little research done on Śāntarakṣita or the Yogācāra-Svātantrika-Madhyamaka school of thought.[40] While some important work has certainly been carried out on *MA/V* and the Madhyamaka thought of Śāntarakṣita, no extensive book-length study examining each verse of the root text with its auto-commentary has heretofore been executed. There have been numerous short descriptions of *MA* and its contents along with overviews of the fundamental ideas of Śāntarakṣita's Madhyamaka. Examples include the various histories of Indian Buddhism and Buddhist thought, including David Ruegg's *The Literature of the Madhyamaka School of Philosophy in India* and Hajime Nakamura's *Indian Buddhism: A Survey with Bibliographic Notes,* among others. There have also been studies on related subjects, including Donald Lopez's *A Study of Svātantrika* and David Eckel's *Jñānagarbha's Commentary on the Distinction between the Two Truths*.

Individual articles have addressed specific topics of his thought. Tom Tillemans's three articles on the neither-one-nor-many argument (Tillemans 1982, 1983, 1984) are important contributions to our understanding of its most famous application in Śāntarakṣita's *MA*. His forthcoming article, "What are Mādhyamikas Refuting? Śāntarakṣita, Kamalaśīla, *et alii* on Superimpositions (*samāropa*)," investigates the object of negation for those Mādhyamikas in question. Matthew Kapstein takes up the concept of personalistic vitalism, heretofore a category of Western philosophical analysis, and examines Śāntarakṣita's critique of the notion and his subsequent effect on Nyāya philosophers in his essay "Śāntarakṣita on the Fallacies of Personalistic Vitalism." Paul Williams's *The Reflexive Nature of Awareness: A Tibetan Madhyamaka Defence* goes into some detail on Śāntarakṣita's ideas on the notion of self-cognizing cognition or reflexive awareness. Yuichi Kajiyama's article "Later Mādhyamikas on Epistemology and Meditation" investigates a number of the arguments Śāntarakṣita puts forth in *MA* against his opponents and presents stages of epistemological investigation which he argues Śāntarakṣita aims to place into the meditative sphere. I think that Kajiyama's ideas are quite insightful and they have influenced my own analysis of Śāntarakṣita's syncretic tendencies. Sara McClintock's recent articles include "The Role of the 'Given' in the Classification of Śāntarakṣita and Kamalaśīla as Svātantrika-Mādhyamikas," which analyzes the role various forms of logic play and the way in which they are utilized in the Madhyamaka thought of Śāntarakṣita, and "Knowing All Through Knowing One: Mystical Communion or Logical Trick in the *Tattvasaṃgraha* and *Tattvasaṃgrahapañjikā,*" which examines arguments about what it means to be omniscient by drawing primarily from Śāntarakṣita's other major treatise, the encyclopedic *TS,* and from Kamalaśīla's commentary on it, *TSP.* Her dissertation, "Omniscience and the Rhetoric of Reason in the *Tattvasaṃgraha* and *Tattvasaṃgrahapañjikā,"* is an important contribution to our understanding of Śāntarakṣita's broader philosophical project, but is not primarily concerned with *MA/V* or many of the Madhyamaka issues dealt with in this study. Kennard Lipman wrote a dissertation based on Mipham's ('Ju Mi-pham) commentary on *MA*. His translation of *MA* included in the dissertation is problematic at several points and is not of great use. Marie Friquegnon wrote a brief synopsis of Śāntarakṣita's thought for a Wadsworth series on great philosophers entitled *On Śāntarakṣita.* She seems to have relied heavily on informants from the Nyingma School of Tibetan Buddhism. Thomas Doctor has an article forthcoming on Mipham's interpretation of *MA* entitled "Five Extraordinary Assertions: Mi pham's Commentary on the *Madhyamakālaṃkāra.*"

Probably the most extensive work on *MA/V* has been carried out by Masamichi Ichigō. His short article "A Synopsis of The Madhyamakālaṃkāra of Śāntarakṣita" is a brief topical outline of the arguments made in *MA*. His book *Madhyamakālaṃkāra of Śāntarakṣita* includes excellent and quite useful critical Tibetan editions of *MA*, *MAV*, and *MAP* based on the Tibetan editions and extant Sanskrit fragments. It also includes a translation into English of the root verses of *MA* and a thirty-eight page introductory essay which discusses many of the main themes of the text. Ichigō's subsquent article, "Śāntarakṣita's Madhyamakālaṃkāra" (in Luis Gómez and Jonathan Silk's *Studies in the Literature of the Great Vehicle: Three Mahāyāna Buddhist Texts*), includes a slightly revised though less detailed critical edition of *MA* as well as a revised translation of *MA*. It also includes an introductory essay which summarizes the main themes of the text. Although I am not always in agreement with Ichigō's analysis, I find his approach insightful and an invaluable contribution to Śāntarakṣita studies. His translations can be cumbersome at times. Finally, Georges Dreyfus and Sara McClintock have edited a volume entitled *The Svātantrika-Prāsaṅgika Distinction: What Difference Does a Difference Make?* which includes several articles of interest to this study.

Geluk treatments of Madhyamaka thought have been studied extensively and there is too much available to mention it all here. Some of the works which have been particularly important or relevant to this study have been Cabezón (1988, 1990, 1992), Cozort (1998), Hopkins (1983, 1989, 1992, 1996, 1999, 2002), Jinpa (2002), Klein (1994), Lopez (1987), Magee (2000), Napper (1989), Newland (1983), Ruegg (1980, 2000), Sopa and Hopkins (1989), Thurman (1984), Tillemans (1982,1983, 1984, 1988), Tillemans and Lopez (1998), and Yotsuya (1999), among others. None of these has critically analyzed the Geluk delineation of the Yogācāra-Svātantrika-Madhyamaka in light of the primary Indian sources on which it is said to be based or has looked at the treatment of Śāntarakṣita's ideas in Geluk literature based on a close examination of his texts and the commentaries on those texts by his disciple Kamalaśīla.

The Scope of the Study

Having briefly reviewed the relevant secondary literature on Śāntarakṣita's Madhyamaka thought and related Geluk materials, I will proceed to describe the scope and contents of the present study. First, as has been mentioned, this study is interested particularly in the Madhyamaka thought of Śāntarakṣita, and directs its focus to the expression of that thought in his texts *MA* and *MAV*, the primary sources where he puts forth his Madhyamaka positions. In examining Śāntarakṣita's Madhyamaka thought I primarily confine myself to descriptive rather than interpretive analysis. To date, as mentioned above, no modern scholar has conducted a thorough verse-by-verse study of the entirety of *MA*; thus, a descriptive approach is well suited for the examination of these materials. Although personal and subjective biases, often unconscious, are unavoidable in the reading of any text, I have attempted to approach his materials in light of the historical Indian context in which they were composed and on their own terms as much as possible.[41]

Śāntarakṣita was an author who wrote on a number of topics and within a number of genres of Buddhist literature. As I mentioned above, we must set aside the tantric materials and the praises he composed since they lie outside the scope of this project. Among his other philosophical materials, while he and his disciple Kamalaśīla appear to have been significantly influenced by Dharmakīrti and his followers from the *pramāṇavāda* tradition and, in many senses ought to be considered part of that tradition as well, we are largely setting aside this aspect of his thought, found to a greater extent in *TS* and *Vipañcitārthā*, and confining ourselves specifically to his Madhyamaka discourse. Although logic and epistemology play an extremely important part in Śāntarakṣita's thought, it is necessary to draw a line in order to keep this study a manageable size. Thus, by and large Śāntarakṣita's *pramāṇavāda* thought also remains outside the scope of this study. Of course, it would not be appropriate to overly compartmentalize, and so there are exceptions. Important epistemological points come up in *MA*, particularly in connection with the issues concerning knowledge of external objects, the nature of consciousness, and self-cognizing cognition, and they are addressed in these contexts. In addition, when examining the question of the use of autonomous inferences (*svatantrānumāna, rang rgyud kyi rjes dpag*) by proponents of Madhyamaka tenets, a prospect which Śāntarakṣita's Geluk commentators find highly objectionable, issues concerning logic and epistemology will be considered. When these issues relate directly to Śāntarakṣita's Madhyamaka thought, when they are discussed in *MA/V*, and when they are brought to bear by Geluk scholars in their analysis of Śāntarakṣita as an opponent Mādhyamika, they will be addressed in this study.[42] Thus, while not all aspects of his *pramāṇavāda* thought will be exhaustively covered, those which are particularly relevant to Śāntarakṣita's Madhyamaka thought certainly will be. Due to the contested authorship of *Satyadvayavibhangapañjikā*, that text is not considered in this study.

In addition to the focused examination of Śāntarakṣita's Madhyamaka thought, this study will also examine the Geluk analysis, interpretation, representation, and criticisms of his thought. This will be based on commentaries written in whole or in part on Śāntarakṣita's works, the larger philosophical treatises of Tsong Khapa and Kaydrub, as well as on Geluk doxographies and monastic textbooks where his ideas are often represented as the "Yogācāra-Svātantrika-Madhyamaka" system, for which his *MA/V* is considered to be the quintessential source. I chose to examine Śāntarakṣita's thought within the context of the Geluk tradition of Tibetan Buddhism for several reasons. Because Śāntarakṣita is such an important crossover figure between Indian and Tibetan Buddhism, examining a vibrant Tibetan philosophical tradition which did not emerge until five centuries after Śāntarakṣita's time in Tibet reveals the enduring influence he has had on the course of philosophical development in that country. Additionally, a primary factor in my decision to juxtapose Śāntarakṣita's own presentation with the Geluk School's presentation of this philosophical system is the strong contrast apparent in the two perspectives. Although both are Mādhyamikas, the Geluk interpreters of Śāntarakṣita's thought don't consider his understanding to be quite as subtle as their own. By comparing contentious issues and the critiques leveled, we are naturally drawn to pivotal points on which the systems of both Śāntarakṣita and his Tibetan interpreters revolve, thus illuminating both sides a bit better. Furthermore, the Geluk inheritors of Śāntarakṣita's thought seem to treat his ideas in a very curious manner. They attribute ideas to him which he never explicitly states or which are stated by those who Gelukpas consider to be like-minded, notwithstanding the fact that Śāntarakṣita never declared such an allegiance. Investigating how and why they went about this reveals a great deal about appropriate ways in which to understand Buddhist philosophical traditions in context. And it offers an opportunity to penetrate the Geluk philosophical process and project in ways that have not yet received due consideration. While it would certainly be worthwhile to conduct an extensive study of Śāntarakṣita's thought throughout Tibetan intellectual history, we are confining ourselves to examining his thought within the context of the Geluk tradition alone in the interest of space.[43]

This volume is divided into three parts following this introductory essay. It is envisioned that this be a study of Śāntarakṣita's Madhyamaka thought in both its Indian and select Tibetan contexts and that it can thus be read either as a monograph on this subject, where each section builds on the previous one, or as a reference work where the reader can access specific stanzas, topics, or sections as needed. Taken in its entirety as a monograph, Part I provides a descriptive presentation of the ideas conveyed in each stanza of Śāntarakṣita's text utilizing his own autocommentary as the primary tool of interpretation. This is compared with Gyel-tsab's explanation in *JBy,* which also comments on each stanza. Where significant variances exist between the two, they are noted. With this basis in Śāntarakṣita's own presentation and in the most significant Geluk commentary offering explanation of the verses of the text, Part II examines the broader Geluk presentation and criticisms of Śāntarakṣita's thought on specific doctrinal issues. Part III contains complete translations of Śāntarakṣita's *MA* and Gyel-tsab's *JBy*. When used as a reference book on Śāntarakṣita's Madhyamaka thought, if the reader wants to see Śāntarakṣita's treatment of self-cognizing cognition, for example, s/he can go directly to stanza16 and those immediately following it where he addresses this issue in *MA/V*. The stanzas are presented in order in part for this purpose and for ease of access. Or if s/he is specifically interested in the Geluk criticisms of self-cognizing cognition and the way Geluk authors handle Śāntarakṣita's specific stance, s/he can reference this in Part II. If the reader prefers to go directly to the complete translations, uninterrupted by explanation or analysis, s/he can turn directly to Part III. The details of each part are summarized in more detail below.

Part I: Analysis of Texts and Arguments is the largest section of the study. It begins by providing an introduction to the basic framework and philosophical arguments of *MA/V*. We move from there to offer a narrative account of the text and its philosophical arguments by proceeding with a stanza-by-stanza account of the entirety of the text. Again, my aim there is to provide a descriptive, rather than interpretive, account of Śāntarakṣita's text. My own translation of each stanza of *MA* is provided in this section and is accompanied by commentary on it from Śāntarakṣita's *MAV* and/or Kamalaśīla's *MAP* for aid in clarifying obscure points. The extensive passages quoted therein from *MAV* appear for the first time in any Western language. The idea behind this aspect of this section is to offer the reader an opportunity to engage the words of Śāntarakṣita (and occasionally those of his disciple Kamalaśīla – see note 8) on their own terms. My own descriptive analysis aims to help illuminate the terse and often cryptic verses.

Analysis of the Geluk treatment of Śāntarakṣita's thought is also an important part of this study. Thus, following the presentation of Śāntarakṣita's stanzas and commentary, I often add passages from Gyel-tsab's *JBy,* which comments on every verse in *MA*, along with occasional extracts from Tsong Khapa's *Notes on "The Ornament of the Middle Way"* (*dbU ma rgyan gyi zin bris*) (hereafter *ZBr*), which discusses select themes in detail. Many times these Geluk commentarial passages are added for clarification of Śāntarakṣita's ideas and can often, when approached with a critical eye, be quite useful.[44] However, in many instances these passages are also added to highlight the often nuanced way in which the Geluk scholar Gyel-tsab[45] treats the ideas of Śāntarakṣita at this stage (that is, as a predecessor to later Geluk tenet system presentations) of commentarial analysis. In this sense, they are at times provided to contrast with the way Śāntarakṣita explains his own ideas. Despite the pretense in Gyel-tsab's *JBy* of simply commenting to illuminate Śāntarakṣita's intended meaning, one can see in many instances how these depictions of Śāntarakṣita's thought anticipate what was to become a normative presentation of the Yogācāra-Svātantrika-Madhyamaka system in later Geluk literature, but which does not precisely mirror Śāntarakṣita's own words. Discrepancies between the two are highlighted whenever they arise to draw the attention of the reader to the often subtle interpretive framework through which these Geluk scholars read Śāntarakṣita's text. Here I also highlight for the reader the ways in which these subtly nuanced readings in the direct Geluk commentaries on *MA* affected, or at least anticipated, the later and more explicit variances between Geluk renditions of Śāntarakṣita's thought (and that of the so-called Yogācāra-Svātantrika-Madhyamaka school of thought he represents) in other philosophical literature from the Geluk School and that of Śāntarakṣita's own presentation of his ideas. This later Geluk philosophical literature would include representations in treatises, tenet system texts (*grub mtha'*) and monastic textbooks (*yig cha*). These variances will be discussed further in Part II. It is indeed my hope that the reader will read this section straight through in order to engage the full richness of Śāntarakṣita's complete text in this narrative account. It is, however, additionally structured in an orderly way so that each verse is analyzed sequentially and can easily be utilized as a reference where the reader can jump to the specific verse for which s/he is searching.

Part II of this study takes a much closer look at the Geluk treatment and criticism of the thought of Śāntarakṣita and the so-called Yogācāra-Svātantrika-Madhyamaka view for which he is considered to be the quintessential exponent. On the basis of both a well grounded understanding of Śāntarakṣita on his own terms from Part I and the accompanying periodic contrast of nuanced Geluk renderings of *MA* from Gyel-tsab and Tsong Khapa's direct commentaries on *MA* we have the foundation for a more detailed investigation into the specific issues which are considered by Gelukpas to separate their views.

After a brief introductory discussion about the discrepancies between Śāntarakṣita's own presentation of his ideas and the presentation of those ideas in the Geluk literature which comments upon it, Part II proceeds to examine five specific areas of contention for these Mādhyamika rivals. The first issue investigated is that of hermeneutics, or in this instance, the manner of determining interpretable (*drang don*, *neyārtha*) from definitive (*nges don*, *nītārtha*) scriptures. Geluk treatment of this issue in regard to rival Mādhyamikas derives primarily from the beginning section of the "Special Insight" (*lhag mthong, vipaśyanā*) chapter of Tsong Khapa's *Great Treatise on the Stages of the Path to Enlightenment* (*Byang chub lam gyi rim pa chen mo*) (hereafter *LRCh*), and *LSN*. As is often the case with these issues of contention between Gelukpas and Śāntarakṣita's views, Śāntarakṣita does not himself discuss this issue explicitly in any of his writings. Thus the Geluk scholars are left with either drawing from thinkers they consider to be like-minded with Śāntarakṣita, or drawing out logical conclusions from related claims he has made. The implications for this type of analysis are discussed in Part II. In this particular case, Tsong Khapa draws primarily from Kamalaśīla and his text *Madhyamakāloka* as representative of the Yogācāra-Svātantrika-Madhyamaka view with which Gelukpas associate Śāntarakṣita.

The remaining four issues are more doctrinal in nature. They include questions about presentations of the two truths, about path system issues (specifically the status of Hīnayāna arhats), about appropriate forms of logic to be utilized by proponents of Madhyamaka tenets (specifically the viability of using autonomous inferences [*svatantrānumāna*, *rang rgyud kyi rjes dpag*]), and, finally, disagreements regarding the status of self-cognizing cognition (*svasaṃvedana*, *rang rig*). Each of these issues, which represent the sources of the divide between the way Gelukpas consider Madhyamaka to be properly understood and presented and the way Śāntarakṣita does, will be investigated in some detail. Given the often curious portrayal of Śāntarakṣita's ideas in Geluk literature, I will look at the Geluk critiques of the Yogācāra-Svātantrika-Madhyamaka positions on each of these issues and raise the question of whether or not that critique aptly applies to Śāntarakṣita's own positions, stated or implied: I will look closely at the relevant statements by Śāntarakṣita on the issues in question and contrast those with claims made about him or about the Yogācāra-Svātantrika-Madhyamaka view he is said to represent. Oftentimes I will argue that these critiques do not specifically apply to Śāntarakṣita's actual positions. At times it seems as though his ideas are much closer to the Gelukpas' own positions than they are portrayed to be in their literature. However, I do not think that this takes away from the power of what is at work within the Geluk philosophical project. In fact, this sort of investigation which gets at the historicity or lack thereof in their claims, I argue, highlights the important creative aspects and important innovations at work in the Geluk literature which have made their approach to Buddhist philosophy so powerful and vital. In light of all this, Part II will conclude with thoughts about why Geluk authors treat the works of Śāntarakṣita in the manner that they do, and suggest fruitful ways for accurately contextualizing and reading the philosophical literature of these great Tibetan authors.

Part III of this volume comprises my translations. Included are complete translations of Śāntarakṣita's *MA* and Gyel-tsab's *JBy*. As mentioned above, Kennard Lipman included a translation of *MA* in his dissertation, but it has numerous mistakes. He never published it. Ichigō's translation, particularly his revised translation of *MA* (Ichigō 1989), is much more useful but still is problematic in some areas and the English is often awkward. At this early stage in translating Buddhist works where numerous translation issues remain unresolved, including even agreement on how to translate specific technical terms, I think that there is certainly a call for multiple published translations of important texts. In addition, this study really requires the inclusion of a complete translation of *MA* for the reader to utilize as a reference. Also, in order to facilitate coordination of technical terminology between the English version of *MA* and my translation of Gyel-tsab's *JBy*, which is also included here, another translation of *MA* was necessary.

From among the many Geluk materials I chose to include a translation of Gyel-tsab's commentary on *MA,* entitled *JBy,* for several reasons. Śāntarakṣita and the Yogācāra-Svātantrika-Madhyamaka system are treated extensively throughout the body of Geluk philosophical materials – from the major treatises of Tsong Khapa and his disciples, through the tenet system texts of later scholars such as Jang-gya (lCang-skya), Thubkan (Thu'u-bkwan), Jamyang Shayba ('Jam-byangs-bzhad-pa), etc., as well as in the textbooks of the major Geluk monastic colleges at Sera, Drepung, and Ganden. However, there are only two texts in the Geluk literature which are dedicated commentaries on *MA*. These are Tsong Khapa's *ZBr* and Gyel-tsab's *JBy*.[46] Tsong Khapa's text deals primarily with larger theoretical issues concerning *MA,* but does not address the text in its entirety. In fact, his text diverges from *MA* at some points in discussions about logical issues and seems at times to draw as much from Kamalaśīla and Dharmakīrti as it does from Śāntarakṣita. In these instances it appears as though Tsong Khapa is simply using his commentary on *MA* as a forum to discuss related issues about logical method. As noted above, Gyel-tsab's *JBy* is the only Geluk source which comments on every verse of *MA* and thus suits the purposes of this study perfectly as it offers an opportunity to examine in detail how the earliest Geluk scholars may have read and understood Śāntarakṣita's text and ideas and thus have impacted later Geluk treatments of these ideas. While these commentaries and Śāntarakṣita's text are not explicit parts of the Geshe curriculum, the ideas contained therein are certainly found throughout the standard Geluk course of monastic study. In addition, this is the first translation of *JBy* in any Western language.

Sources

As discussed earlier, the focus of this study is the Madhyamaka thought of Śāntarakṣita. While numerous auxiliary Indian sources are utilized during the course of this study, the Indian sources used for the specific documentation of Śāntarakṣita's ideas are in fact quite few, with the intention being to keep the focus on Śāntarakṣita's own words. The two major sources for Śāntarakṣita's Madhyamaka thought are of course *MA* and its autocommentary, *MAV*. Other sources however were also useful at various points in the study. Kamalaśīla's *MAP* was frequently utilized to clarify tersely written verses or unclear points in *MA/V*. Śāntarakṣita borrows several stanzas in *MA* from his own *TS*. Oftentimes in these instances, Kamalaśīla's commentary (on *TS*) in *TSP* was also quite useful. Kamalaśīla's *TSP* can be regarded in much the same way as *MAP* (that is, as a generally reliable commentarial source on Śāntarakṣita's root verses), as long as it is approached with a critical eye. It appears as though Kamalaśīla remains quite faithful to the words of his teacher.[47] Specifically on issues regarding the path system, the status of Hināyāna arhats, and the state of Buddhahood, other parts of *TS* and *TSP* were also useful in this study.

The quantity of materials available relating to the Geluk treatment of Śāntarakṣita's Madhyamaka thought was much more plentiful than the

Indian sources, partly because we are dealing with a tradition rather than with an individual. Geluk authors have treated Śāntarakṣita's ideas in several genres of philosophical literature. It is best to begin to describe these texts with those closest in commentarial proximity to the Indian source materials. To my knowledge, Geluk authors have composed two texts commenting directly on Śāntarakṣita's *MA*: Tsong Khapa's *ZBr* and Gyel-tsab's *JBy*. As mentioned above, Tsong Khapa's text does not deal with the whole of *MA/V*, but rather takes up specific theoretical issues in detail, some of which seem peripheral to the thrust of *MA*. Gyel-tsab's *JBy* (which is based on lecture notes from Tsong Khapa's oral teachings[48]), examines each stanza of *MA*, commenting with the apparent goal of illuminating Śāntarakṣita's intended meaning of each stanza. In addition to these two texts commenting specifically on *MA/V*, Tsong Khapa's other major Mahāyāna treatises including *LSN*, the *lhag mthong* chapter of *LRCh*, and *dbU ma la 'jug pa'i rgya cher bshad pa dgongs pa rab gsal* (*Illumination of The Thought: Extensive Explanation of* [*Chandrakīrti's*] *"Entrance To The Middle Way"*) (hereafter GRS), and Kaydrub's (mKhas grub) *sTong thun chen mo* (hereafter *TTC*) all address to greater or lesser extents Śāntarakṣita's Madhyamaka thought and the Yogācāra-Svātantarika-Madhyamaka system they consider him to represent.

The next layer of Geluk materials, after the direct commentaries on *MA* and the major Mahāyāna treatises, are the numerous tenet system texts (*grub mtha', siddhānta*) which systematically present the views of the major Buddhist and non-Buddhist philosophical systems. The view of the Yogācāra-Svātantrika sub-school of Madhyamaka thought is routinely portrayed in these texts (as in the treatises described above) as the view of "Śāntarakṣita and his spiritual son [Kamalaśīla]". *MA* is considered to be the fundamental source[49] for this system of thought and Śāntarakṣita its key exponent. The major tenet system texts that are well known throughout the Geluk monastic system[50] include Könchog Jigme Wangpo's (dKon-mchog-'jigs-med-dbang- po) *Grub pa'i mtha'i rnam par bzhag pa rin po che'i phreng ba (Precious Garland of Tenets*), Thubkan's *Grub mtha' thams cad kyi khungs dang 'dod tshul ston pa legs bshad shel gyi me long (Mirror of the Good Explanations Showing the Sources and Assertions of All Systems of Tenets*), Jamyang Shayba's *Grub mtha'i rnam bshad rang gzhan grub mtha 'kun dang zab don mchog tu gsal ba kun bzang shing gi nyi ma lung rigs rga mtsho skye dgu'i re ba kun skong (Exposition Of Tenets Brilliantly Illuminating All of Our Own and Others' Tenets and the*

Meaning of the Profound [Emptiness]), and Jang-gya's *Grub mtha'i rnam bzhag/ gsal bar bshad pa thub bstan lhun po'i mdzes rgyan (Presentation of Tenets/ Clear Exposition of the Presentation of Tenets, A Beautiful Ornament for the Meru of the Subduer's Teaching*).

The final layer of Geluk literature relating to Śāntarakṣita's Madhyamaka thought and his *MA/V* are the monastic textbooks (*yig cha*) for the major Geluk colleges. Sera Je and Ganden Jangtse utilize the texts authored by Jetsun Chökyi Gyeltsen (*rJe-btsun-chos-kyi-rgyal-mtshan*). Ganden Shardze and Drepung Loseling utilize the textbook literature of Panchen Sönam Drakpa (*Pan-chen-bsod-nams-grags-pa*). Drepung Gomang utilizes those of Jamyang Shayba. Sera Me uses those of Kaydrub Tanba Dargyay (*mKhas-grub-bstan-pa-dar-rgyas*). And finally, Drepung Dayang uses those composed by the Fifth Dalai Lama, Ngawang Lobsang Gyatso (*Ngag dbang blo bzang rgya mtsho*). In addition to all of these Geluk written sources, oral commentary on these texts by qualified teachers within the tradition represents a key way in which understanding of the ideas is passed down from generation to generation.[51]

Śāntarakṣita's Yogācāra-Madhyamaka Synthesis

I would like to conclude this Introduction by making some comments on the nature of the syncretic tendencies in Śāntarakṣita's text for consideration as one reads further in this study. Perhaps the clearest and most significant reason one may argue for the importance of *MA* lies in its synthesis of the three major trends in Mahāyāna philosophical discourse in the late period of Indian Buddhism. As mentioned above, these three are: the Madhyamaka tradition first espoused by Nāgārjuna and Āryadeva, the Yogācāra tradition first systematized by Asaṅga and Vasubandhu, and the logico-epistemological tradition delineated by Dignāga and Dharmakīrti.[52] Śāntarakṣita wove these three critical intellectual movements into one integrated and coherent system. This Mahāyāna syncretism is summarized most succinctly in the famous ninety-third stanza of *MA* when he writes:

> Therefore due to holding the reigns of logic as one rides the chariots of the two systems [Yogācāra and Madhyamaka], one attains [the path of] the actual Mahāyānist.

Put briefly, the common understanding and presentation of Śāntarakṣita's brand of Madhyamaka[53] takes its cue from the above concise statement as follows: Because he rejects the existence of any ultimate nature or essence in phenomena while accepting some form of conventional existence of those phenomena, he is a Mādhyamika. Because conventional truths are described as not being utterly distinct entities from the mind perceiving them and because he accepts self-cognizing cognition conventionally (two fundamental Yogācāra tenets[54]), he is seen as accepting a Yogācāra position conventionally. Because he advocates the use of autonomous inferences (*svatantrānumāna*), he is representative of a certain type of Madhyamaka view known by the appellation coined in Tibet at least two centuries after his death as "Śvāntantrika-Madhyamaka." Despite the prevalence of this sort of understanding of Śāntarakṣita's syncretic ideas,[55] such an understanding is oversimplified.

There are complexities and dynamic movements at work in Śāntarakṣita's syncretism which such an understanding does not recognize. I argue that when reading *MA,* there are two basic operational frameworks at work which are best kept in mind when attempting to understand properly issues concerning the integration of Yogācāra and Madhyamaka and Śāntarakṣita's philosophical syncretism in general.[56] The first operational framework is found throughout the first sixty-two stanzas of *MA* in which Śāntarakṣita leads the reader through a dynamic engagement with a host of philosophical views, some of which are provisionally accepted. This will be discussed in detail below. The second framework, which is largely grounded in his presentation of the two truths, appears in the final third of Śāntarakṣita's text and is the most common lens of analysis through which glosses of, and investigations into, Śāntarakṣita's Madhyamaka thought take place. I will describe this second (second in terms of the order in which it appears in *MA*) operational framework first since it is the one most commonly recognized by both Tibetans and modern scholars. The first is a bit more complex and will necessitate a more detailed explanation (to be found in the following section, "Shifting Provisionalities in *Madhyamakālaṃkāra*").

Although varying in the details, a presentation of the two truths is common to all Mādhyamikas and is an obvious framework through which to begin to investigate a particular Mādhyamika's views. One would not be ill advised to *begin* the study of the ideas of virtually any Mādhyamika thinker in this way. Within this two truths framework, Śāntarakṣita's descriptions of conventional truths (*saṃvṛtisatya, kun rdzob bden pa*) *can* accurately be understood largely in Yogācāra terms. After all, he does argue in the ninety-first stanza of *MA* that, "That which is cause and result is mere consciousness only."[57] He describes conventional truths as those phenomena which are impermanent, functional, and dependently arisen, further qualifying those things which are dependently arisen, or "cause and result," as phenomena which are of the nature of the mind. Since he goes on to reject the existence of any ultimate nature in phenomena, it seems fair to summarize his Mahāyāna syncretism by saying that Śāntarakṣita advocates a Madhyamaka perspective when describing ultimate truths, and a Yogācāra perspective when describing conventional truths. However, this is only the beginning point for understanding his syncretism. There is another clear operational framework at work in Śāntarakṣita's text which functions side-by-side with the two truths framework for engaging and understanding his ideas.

The other primary operational framework for understanding Śāntarakṣita's philosophical project, which is found in the first sixty-two stanzas of *MA*, is not commonly acknowledged and concerns his urging of his reader to provisionally accept several distinct Buddhist philosophical views in the ascent to the Madhyamaka view. The careful reader is drawn to notice as s/he proceeds through *MA* that Śāntarakṣita feigns acceptance of several variations of Sautrāntika and Yogācāra thought as he analyzes and criticizes the opponent positions (views considered to be lower or less subtle than those he provisionally advocates). In a sense, entrance into his "Madhyamaka" project is an invitation into meaningful engagement with a number of Buddhist views and perspectives, provisionally accepted in stages, for the soteriological purpose of leading the practitioner to the highest understanding of reality (i.e., that of the Madhyamaka). These multiple levels or stages of provisionality mark a much more fluid and dynamic philosophical enterprise at work than is commonly presented.[58] To simply say that Śāntarakṣita uses a Yogācāra perspective in his ontological description of conventional truths is true, but it misses much of what is happening (as will be described below). In the course of guiding the reader through a host of Buddhist philosophical views, Yogācāra views here are meant to be provisionally accepted as accurate, not simply to be taken as descriptions of conventional truths (*saṃvṛtisatya*). When he argues as a Yogācāra in the early portions of the text, his feigned acceptance of these views seems aimed to convince his reader of the correctness of such a position. It is only later in the text, when he has shifted to his final Madhyamaka framework, that he encourages his readers to accept this fundamental Yogācāra analysis of objects as merely correct for describing conventional truths as opposed to being a description of the ultimate (as it seems to be in the earlier portion of the text where the acceptance of this view was feigned).

As mentioned above, a large percentage of *MA* comprises an extensive application of the neither-one-nor-many argument, which aims at demonstrating that all entities asserted by Śāntarakṣita's philosophical opponents to have an inherently existent essence or nature in fact do not have such a nature because they lack either a singular or manifold nature.[59] The ultimate aim of this logical argument is to lead the reader to an understanding of reality which knows that all entities are empty of any inherent nature, the fundamental tenet of the Madhyamaka view which Śāntarakṣita considers to be the highest philosophical explanation of reality. Throughout the first sixty-two stanzas of the root text, and periodically later in *MA*, Śāntarakṣita applies this reasoning to specific views put forth by both his Buddhist and non-Buddhist philosophical adversaries. In each instance where an opponent proposes some entity as having a truly existent nature, Śāntarakṣita examines that entity in light of this argument, and from the ascending provisional perspectives, to demonstrate that in fact it does not have such a nature or essence.

As Śāntarakṣita makes his way through an assortment of rival tenets, the careful reader is drawn to notice that he actually is shifting his perspective or framework of analysis as he goes.[60] The neither-one-nor-many argument can be utilized from several different philosophical perspectives and is in fact employed from various Sautrāntika and Yogācāra perspectives by Śāntarakṣita in his ascent to an ultimately Madhyamaka perspective. While all of his arguments can certainly be understood from a Madhyamaka perspective, he provisionally adopts several philosophical viewpoints and thereby encourages his readers and his rivals to do the same, gradually ascending a hierarchy of views which culminates in a Madhyamaka view.[61]

One must pause for a moment here to consider what it means to feign acceptance of a philosophical view in this context. Certainly, in provisionally feigning acceptance of Sautrāntika or Yogācāra positions, Śāntarakṣita does not want his readers to just stop there. This sort of graded ascent of philosophical views is pragmatic in that if one does not follow Śāntarakṣita to the end (i.e., to the Madhyamaka view), s/he still is on the right track, in his opinion, by following one of the lower Buddhist views which serve as rungs on the graded ladder of philosophical systems. I think, however, that Śāntarakṣita's project here is probably more grounded in polemics. Without explicitly saying it, he seems to be asserting for example that, "X perspective can even be rejected by the Sautrāntikas," or "Y can even be rejected by Yogācāras." In a sense he exaggerates the gravity of the fallacy of the positions he criticizes by demonstrating that they can *even* be rejected by lower schools, much less by his own superior Madhyamaka perspective. By doing this in the context of leading his readers through a host of views which appear to be provisionally accepted, he offers his arguments in a way which can be read on two levels or in two ways, pragmatically or polemically. It is pragmatic in that it leads the reader gradually to his own view via what are thought to be increasingly more subtle "lower" Buddhist tenet systems. He also valorizes study and knowledge of "lower" Buddhist philosophical positions as important steps on an ascent to the highest view and as important models in their own right with which to contrast and illuminate higher views. This is a method Tibetan inheritors of this tradition continue to utilize in their doxographical and other philosophical literature. It is polemical in the exaggerated tone of the criticism and this increases the force of the arguments.

Thus, when analyzing the assertions of non-Buddhists and Vaibhāṣikas, Śāntarakṣita takes on the role of a Sautrāntika. He feigns acceptance of a Sautrāntika position, argues against his opponents as if he were a Sautrāntika, utilizes such Sautrāntika methods as autonomous inferences, and attempts to convince his opponent to accept his Sautrāntika positions. When arguing against Sautrāntika positions, he takes on the role of a Yogācāra, feigning acceptance of that position and encouraging his opponents to accept this perspective as well, superseding the previous provisional view.[62] Thus, it is not simply that Śāntarakṣita accepts Yogācāra tenets as an accurate description of conventional truths in his basic presentation of the two truths, but that he actually feigns unqualified acceptance of a Yogācāra position at this point in the text as an ultimate position as he continues his ascent up a hierarchy of views. Thus, the Yogācāra view functions in two ways in the philosophical enterprise of Śāntarakṣita. On the one hand, he (provisionally) feigns acceptance of the view and encourages his opponents to accept the same when arguing against Sautrāntikas. On this level he demonstrates the utility of the Yogācāra view on its own terms and utilizes it as a step on the graded ladder of philosophical tenet systems. At this point in the text, the reader does not know that this as yet unqualified advocacy of Yogācāra is provisional. On the other hand, from the perspective of the two truths operational framework, which is described in the latter third of *MA*, he defines conventional truths in Madhyamaka analysis in part on the basis of the Yogācāra position of rejecting external objects. This is largely a different enterprise from his earlier utilization of the view where it functions to reject specific tenets in the Sautrāntika position. Moreover, this occurs much later in the text. The first perspective takes place in the context of the neither-one-nor-many argument in the first sixty-two stanzas in which Śāntarakṣita refutes what he considers to be false notions of ultimate existence. We know from his description of conventional truths in the latter third of the text that he does also consider dependently-arisen objects to be in the nature of the mind – much as a Yogācāra would assert ultimately.

With regard to Śāntarakṣita's ascent of views, in the final analysis he takes on the role of a Mādhyamika, the position he actually *does* consider to be the highest Buddhist philosophical understanding of the nature of reality. This ascent through provisional views can be seen to have a soteriological purpose in that it aims to lead the reader gradually on a movement through philosophical positions to the ultimate view that is considered necessary for the attainment of liberation. There is however a sense in which the presentation of the two truths also has a soteriologically based movement in Śāntarakṣita's brand of Madhyamaka that is not found in the writings of other Mādhyamikas who utilize the two truths primarily as a vehicle for presenting their ontological positions. In Śāntarakṣita's thought on the two truths, the conventional Yogācāra position not only has its descriptive ontological utility, but also has this soteriological dimension in that the rejection of external objects on a conventional level is seen as a step in the direction of the ultimate Madhyamaka view, the one he considers necessary for liberation from cyclic existence. Understanding that conventional truths are not utterly distinct from consciousness represents an approach, or important step, on the ascent to that realizing entities ultimately have no nature at all. For example, Śāntarakṣita writes in the ninety-second stanza of *MA*:

> By relying on the Mind Only (*cittamatra, sems tsam pa*) [system], know that external entities do not exist. And by relying on this [Madhyamaka] system, know that no self at all exists, even in that [mind].

Thus, the Mind Only description of conventional truths, which shows that external objects do not exist, not only functions as an ontological marker for designating the conventional status of entities, but also fulfills a soteriological purpose in that it takes the student part of the way toward realizing that entities have no nature at all.

Shifting Provisionalities in Madhyamakālaṃkāra

Let us now examine some of the specific ways in which Śāntarakṣita has gone about these shifts in perspective in the actual text of *MA* and its autocommentary, *MAV*. The second through fifteenth stanzas of *MA,* and accompanying autocommentary, investigate several positions held by non-Buddhists, as well as by Vaibhāṣikas. While Śāntarakṣita does not explicitly state that he is arguing from a Sautrāntika perspective, all of the arguments made are of the type a Sautrāntika might make when arguing against such opponents, as for example Vasubandhu does when he criticizes Vaibhāṣikas from a Sautrāntika perspective in his *Abhidharmakośabhāṣya*, and all could lead one to Sautrāntika-type conclusions. In these sections, Śāntarakṣita seemingly accepts external objects since he draws no attention to any fallacy one might find in accepting them. And, as mentioned above, he utilizes autonomous inferences as his primary form of reasoning, just as a proponent of Sautrāntika tenets would do. This seems to presume that there are empirically real objects of knowledge external to the consciousness which form the basis of the arguments, again just as Sautrāntikas would assert. He also utilizes autonomous inferences when arguing from a Yogācāra perspective (as Yogācāras would, although for them the valid subject is not considered external to the mind), but does not do so when criticizing Yogācāras from a Madhyamaka perspective.

The first shift in perspective, the shift from a Sautrāntika perspective to a Yogācāra perspective, begins with the sixteenth stanza of *MA*, when Śāntarakṣita introduces the topic of self-cognizing cognition (*svasaṃvedana, rang rig*), a basic tenet held by both Sautrāntikas and Yogācāras. He begins by defining self-cognizing cognition in the sixteenth and seventeenth stanzas, and then shifts from the Sautrāntika basis upon which he had been arguing throughout the text thus far to a criticism of the specifics of the Sautrāntika manner of accepting self-cognizing cognition. He seems to consider his arguments up to this point in the text to have refuted non-Buddhists and Vaibhāṣikas and convinced them (or his readers) to accept a

Sautrāntika perspective. Now, examining the Sautrāntika perspective, particularly the acceptance of external objects and various related Sautrāntika epistemological positions, Śāntarakṣita shifts to a Yogācāra perspective in his criticism and encourages his Sautrāntika opponent to do the same. This shift becomes evident in the eighteenth and nineteenth stanzas of *MA* and continues in the following stanzas where Śāntarakṣita criticizes his Sautrāntika opponent for only getting the issue of the self-cognizing nature of cognition, or consciousness, partly right. That is, they understand correctly that self-cognizing cognition is an appropriate tenet to hold, but mistakenly still accept it in the context of accepting external objects, an unacceptable tenet for Yogācāras.

> (18) Therefore, this [consciousness] is capable of self-consciousness (*bdag shes*)since this is the nature of consciousness. How [though] could that cognize the nature of objects from which it is distinct?
>
> (19) [Since] its nature does not exist in external objects (*gzhan*), given that you assert that objects of consciousness and consciousness are different, how could consciousness know objects other than consciousness?

Śāntarakṣita proceeds in his autocommentary and in the verses that follow in *MA* to give a more detailed and extensive criticism of the acceptance of external objects in general and with particular reference to the acceptance of self-cognizing cognition. It is outside the scope of the present discussion to dwell on the details of this here. The point illustrated here is that Śāntarakṣita has shifted his perspective from that of a Sautrāntika to that of a Yogācāra, one which he maintains for the following twenty-five stanzas in the root text *MA* as he refutes various Sautrāntika positions concerning the existence of external objects and other topics. At this point in the text he also encourages his opponent to accept a basic Yogācāra framework in an unqualified way. There is no discussion of this being a mere description of conventional truths. This is argued just as a Yogācāra would if s/he were trying to convince an opponent of the correctness of his/her particular Yogācāra position. In other words, Śāntarakṣita argues for acceptance of this position, which we find out later will only be provisional since he will ultimately criticize important aspects of it from a Madhyamaka perspective.

The next major shift in *MA* occurs in the forty-fifth stanza and accompanying autocommentary. Śāntarakṣita begins this shift by praising the many excellent qualities of the Yogācāra view, but then raises some qualms. This is the point where he turns to a Madhyamaka framework and Madhyamaka mode of analysis of his opponents as he makes his way through several variant Yogācāra positions, particularly concerning whether images (*ākāra, rnam pa*) are true or false.

> (45) Although their view (i.e., the Yogācāra view) is virtuous, we should think about whether such things [as the images known by consciousness accepted byYogācāras] actually exist or if they are something contentedly accepted only when left unanalyzed.

And from the related section of *MAV*:

> Since this [Yogācāra] system is known by means of valid knowledge (*pramāṇa, tshad ma*) and very clear scriptures and since it is also an antidote to the endless, negative, exaggerated grasping of sentient beings, it should be considered to be very pure. Likewise, [this system is virtuous] because it rejects the existence of subtle [partless] particles and the valid knowledge previously explained shows the contradictions [with regards to the Sautrāntika position which distinguishes between the] characteristics of the experiencer and the object of experience. [In addition,] this system is very clear and is also backed up by scriptural quotations.[63]

In the autocommentary, this is followed by a quote from the *Laṅkāvatārasūtra* used to demonstrate a scriptural backing for the Yogācāra position. That quote is followed by the following commentary in *MAV* which highlights more of the virtues of this view, but again raises qualms:

> By relying on this system, scholars remove the impurities of erroneous divisive concepts such as "I" and "mine" and "object" and "apprehender [of objects]". However there is still a small issue which needs to be investigated with regard to this system. Are these images [known byconsciousness] real or will they only be comfortable to accept when left unanalyzed, like a mirror reflection.[64]

In discussing this Yogācāra view, Śāntarakṣita is not doing so in the context of presenting his position on conventional truths within the framework of the traditional Madhyamaka presentation of the two truths. He is doing so in the context of leading his readers on an ascent of philosophical views for which the various Yogācāra positions are considered to be steps along the way.[65] Thus, as he begins his ultimate Madhyamaka analysis he takes seriously the sorts of positions he advocated earlier and argues against these only as he takes on his final view. Thus, once the Madhyamaka shift has taken place, his attention to the Yogācāra position largely revolves around criticism of its faults.

Additionally, it is only after this shift to Madhyamaka that he presents his own version of the normative Madhyamaka division of the two truths, and it is here that we see Yogācāra tenets integrated into his definition of conventional truths. The first evidence of this is alluded to in the *MAV* section quoted just above commenting on *MA* 45 when he praises Yogācāras for removing "divisive concepts such as 'I' and 'mine', and 'object' and 'apprehender'." It is not until the sixty-fourth stanza of *MA* that he begins to more clearly define his view on what constitutes a conventional truth:

> Those phenomena which are only agreeable when not put to the test of [ultimate] analysis, those phenomena which are generated and disintegrate, and those which have the ability to function are known to be of a conventional nature.

He elaborates further in his autocommentary by explaining that a conventional truth is known by conceptual thought or designated with worldly conventions. In the ninety-first stanza he clarifies the mind-only component of this definition:

> That which is cause and result is mere consciousness only. Whatever is established by itself abides in consciousness.

Conventional truths are thus functional, impermanent, agreeable when not investigated with an ultimate analysis which searches for an unchanging essence, and are things which are indistinct from consciousness. This two truths framework can largely be analyzed independently from the dynamic movement through the assortment of philosophical positions investigated previously throughout the text. It is part of the final shift to Madhyamaka and the presentation of his Madhyamaka view. This shift to a Madhyamaka framework and mode of analysis is the final shift in *MA*, as realization of the meaning of this view represents the pinnacle of the soteriological ascent of Buddhist philosophical views in Śāntarakṣita's writings. It is the conclusion of a dynamic philosophical treatise which leads the reader on a *tour de force* of Buddhist philosophical analysis where the various views function in a variety of ways along the way. Śāntarakṣita's philosophical enterprise is far from static and it never ceases to lose sight of its soteriological purpose. I think keeping both of these operational frameworks, 'the two truths framework' and 'the sliding scales framework,' in mind when reading *MA* will result in a more comprehensive and accurate understanding of the text and of the dynamic aspects of Śāntarakṣita's philosophical work in his Yogācāra-Madhyamaka synthesis.

Part I

Part I: Analysis of Texts and Arguments

Introduction

Part I of this study examines the arguments made by Śāntarakṣita in the ninety-seven stanzas of *MA* along with Geluk analysis of those stanzas and arguments. It does so by drawing from and comparing the verse arguments made in *MA* (and supplemented by the commentary in *MAV* and *MAP*[1]) with the two primary Geluk sources which comment directly on *MA:* Gyel-tsab's *JBy* and Tsong Khapa's *ZBr*. I consult Tsong Khapa's *ZBr* on several issues, but, as mentioned above, that text does not follow the structure, or comment on the whole, of *MA* as Gyel-tsab's *JBy* does. For that reason I principally rely upon Gyel-tsab's *JBy* for Geluk commentary on each stanza. My primary purpose here is to provide a narrative account of Śāntarakṣita's text and its arguments. This is supplemented with the Geluk presentation of those through juxtaposition of Śāntarakṣita's own words from *MA* and *MAV* with those of the Gelukpas who composed commentaries directly on *MA*. Śāntarakṣita's root text *MA* is, as mentioned above, commonly regarded in Geluk accounts of Madhyamaka as the foundational text of the Yogācāra-Svātantrika subschool of Madhyamaka thought. Thus examining the primary Geluk commentaries on *MA* here before going on to examine the general presentation of the Yogācāra-Svātantrika-Madhyamaka school in the larger body of Geluk philosophical materials in Part II will hopefully provide a sufficient and useful foundation for the task.

Śāntarakṣita's arguments presented in *MA* will be analyzed in this section in conjunction with his own autocommentary, *MAV,* in an attempt at presenting Śāntarakṣita's views on their own terms, in his own words, and, as much as is possible, in light both of the context within which he wrote and of the probable intended audiences. On certain issues which are taken up both in his *MA* and *TS*, *TS* is consulted as well for a more complete presentation of his view. Kamalaśīla's *MAP* is consulted to clarify points when passages from *MA* and *MAV* seem a little ambiguous. Kamalaśīla's *TSP* is also consulted when commenting on verses which Śāntarakṣita borrowed directly from his other text, *TS,* for inclusion in *MA.* At times *TSP* aided in the clarification of obscure passages. On some relevant issues Kamalaśīla's *Sarvadharmaniḥsvabhāvasiddhi* and *Madhyamakāloka* also are consulted.

As mentioned above, the clearest and most thorough direct commentary on *MA* in the Geluk tradition is Gyel-tsab's *JBy.* This text comments on every verse in *MA,* primarily in the form of tri-modal inference, in an apparent attempt to clarify for the reader the often difficult points Śāntarakṣita makes in *MA.* Gyel-tsab's *JBy* is the most important Geluk text for this portion of the study since it is the only so-called "meaning commentary" (*don 'grel*) from the Geluk tradition which, as mentioned above, directly comments on each argument made in the root text. It appears as though Gyel-tsab earnestly attempts to remain as close to the author's intentions as possible. Gyel-tsab, like Tsong Khapa in *ZBr*, refrains from any criticism of Śāntarakṣita's views even when Śāntarakṣita is arguing for positions which run contrary to his own, such as Śāntarakṣita's arguments for self-cognizing cognition (*rang rig*, *svasaṃvedana*) and his rejection of external objects. This is not to say Gyel-tsab acts solely as a mirror of Śāntarakṣita's views. Indeed part of the aim of this chapter is to draw forth divergences between Śāntarakṣita and Gyel-tsab in their presentations of the arguments before us and to suggest that what later became a mainline Geluk understanding of Yogācāra-Svātantrika-Madhyamaka seems to be informed by Gyel-tsab's understanding, or at least presentation, of Śāntarakṣita's arguments here. Certainly Gyel-tsab's *JBy* gives us a glimpse into how early Geluk thinkers such as himself and his teacher, Tsong Khapa, read the text they considered to be the root text of the Yogācāra-Svātantrika-Madhyamaka School.

Tsong Khapa's commentary, *ZBr*, is not as comprehensive as *JBy* in the scope of its project of explaining *MA.* Tsong Khapa goes into detail on issues of importance to Śāntarakṣita such as the insistence on the need for well reasoned arguments establishing the ultimate lack of an inherent nature in phenomena, in addition to examining some of the larger theoretical issues concerning logic and the application of arguments. For example, there is an extensive discussion of the problem of non-existent or unestablished bases (*gzhi ma grub*, *āśrayāsiddha*) and their coherence within the use of autonomous inferences.[2] On this issue Tsong Khapa draws on not only Dignāga and Dharmakīrti but more primarily on Kamalaśīla's *Madhyamakāloka*.[3] While the purpose of the extended discussion of this key issue is to establish the validity of the manner in which Śāntarakṣita applies the neither-one-nor-many argument to non-Buddhist and Buddhist opponents, this section does not refer to Śāntarakṣita's own *MA* or *MAV*. While it may be reasonable to presume that Śāntarakṣita would agree with Kamalśīla's defense of the use of autonomous inferences with unestablished bases, it is important to note that Tsong Khapa chooses to extensively develop this position here. Gyel-tsab does not discuss this or any other such theoretical issues in his commentary, which functions more as a commentary the meaning of the specific arguments Śāntarakṣita's actual text.

On occasion I have brought in other Geluk materials to highlight certain points, but the primary purpose of this chapter, once again, is to offer a narrative account of Śāntarakṣita's views and to compare Śāntarakṣita's presentation with the primary (and earliest) Geluk attempts at illuminating those. Other forms of Geluk treatment of Śāntarakṣita found in the major treatises of Tsong Khapa such as *LSN*, *GRS*, and in the final chapter of *LRCh*, as well as Kaydrub's *TTC* and tenet system literature[4] for the most part will be further investigated in Part II. They will however, occasionally be cited here when it appropriately supplements the topic at hand. Though often what is found in the Geluk literature is a nuanced presentation of a more generic Yogācāra-Svātantrika-Madhyamaka view rather than a specific characterization of the philosopher Śāntarakṣita, he is nonetheless the figure most commonly associated with that view. Certainly those texts are more widely studied in the Geluk curriculum and are the primary sources which inform the more mainline or normative Geluk understanding of Śāntarakṣita. Nevertheless, in order to lay down the groundwork for engaging in the presentations of those Geluk sources, we need first to examine Śāntarakṣita's texts on their own and the Geluk works which comment directly upon them.[5]

Let us now proceed to the narrative account of the texts.

The Text
Title, Homage, and Introduction

The Tibetan version of the root text begins by giving both the Sanskrit and Tibetan titles of the text. According to the Tibetan tradition, the Sanskrit name is given for several reasons. First, it is considered by Tibetans to be auspicious to hear the Sanskrit name and to have that imprint (*pag cha*) planted in the disciple's mindstream. Second, Tibetan lamas, when orally commenting on an Indian *śāstra,* often point out that the Sanskrit title demonstrates that the teaching and lineage come from India and are therefore authentic. The Indian origins of the text legitimized the source for many Tibetans. This was probably particularly the case during the first centuries of the transmission of Buddhism to Tibet. However, in later times, the voice of Tibetan authors such as Tsong Khapa carried as much authority as the earlier Indian *paṇḍitas*.

The root text, *MA,* then continues and Gyel-tsab's commentary similarly begins with prostrations or homage to Māñjuśri, the Buddha of Perfect Wisdom. The homage to the youthful Māñjuśri in the root text is actually the prayer of Yeshe De and Śīlendrabodhi, who according to the colophon translated the text from Sanskrit into Tibetan. It is traditional for the translator of Buddhist texts to offer homage or prostrations to the appropriate Buddhas in order to clear away any obstacles to successfully completing the translation. This was a tradition which began in Tibet during the reign of Trisong Detsen (*Khri-srong-lde-btsan*) (740-798). When the main topic of the text to be translated is wisdom or related to the *Abhidharma* section of the *Tripiṭaka* then the homage is offered to Māñjuśri. Translations of *sūtras* begin with the translator's homage to the Buddha and the bodhisattvas, and *vināya* texts begin with homage to the All-Knowing One (i.e., Buddha) (*thams cad mkhyen pa*). In his commentary, Gyel-tsab likewise offers homage to Māñjuśri and to his lama, Tsong Khapa, whom he does not name specifically until the end of the text.

After homage to the youthful Māñjuśri in the Tibetan version of the autocommentary, which is actually the homage of the translators, then Śāntarakṣita himself offers homage. For Śāntarakṣita, homage goes to all those who have had the direct realization of emptiness that takes place on the first bodhisattva ground (*bhumi*, *sa*) and who additionally possess the "superior aspiration" or bodhicitta (i.e., the altruistic wish to attain perfect enlightenment in order to most effectively benefit all sentient beings). Śāntarakṣita writes in *MAV*:

> I pay homage continuously to those residing on [bodhisattva] grounds who possess the pure and stable minds seeing to the other [shore], who are like an ocean of the profound way of the dharma

> – to those unsurpassable residers who possess superior aspiration, who meditate in completion [on emptiness] and who take it to heart well.[6]

Śāntarakṣita proceeds from here to state the purpose of composing this text. According to him, the ultimate purpose is to assist followers on the path to the attainment of Buddhahood. This aid is achieved by demonstrating, through logical reasoning, the lack of an inherent nature in phenomena. According to Śāntarakṣita, this realization is a key ingredient in the removal of the obstacles which keep sentient beings bound in *saṃsāra*, and thereby from attaining Buddhahood.

> When one realizes that in reality there is no inherent nature, then all disturbing emotions (*kleśa, nyon mongs*) and stains of knowledge obstacles (*jñeyāvarana, shes bya'i sgrib pa*) will be abandoned.[7]

This clearly demonstrates the close relationship in the Buddhist tradition between philosophical learning and contemplation and the soteriological goals of the path. Study and contemplation of philosophy for Śāntarakṣita are integral to the achievement of Buddhism's highest religious goals in that it helps facilitate an experiential realization leading to the removal of the obstacles to Buddhahood. Śāntarakṣita explicitly relates the direct realization of the Madhyamaka philosophical position to the removal of obstacles to liberation from saṃsara and also to perfect Buddhahood outlined in the Mahāyāna path system literature.[8] Śāntarakṣita continues his explanation as follows:

> Therefore always exert great effort toward realizing the lack of inherent nature in all phenomena by use of reasoning and scriptures.[9]

> With regard to that point, scriptures without inference derived from the power of cogent evidence will not completely satisfy even those disciples following entirely by faith. Thus [I] will explain [the lack of inherent nature] with inferential reasoning.[10]

Logical analysis with specific evidence is described here by Śāntarakṣita as being an imperative part of a disciple's coming to the realization of the emptiness or lack of an inherent nature in all persons and phenomena, a realization which is necessary on the path to Buddhahood. By the eighth century, the use of specific guidelines for the establishment of inferential knowledge for the purpose of refuting opponent's views and illuminating one's own view had become an integral part of Mahāyāna discourse in India.[11] Because the realization of emptiness is necessary for salvation and mere reliance on scripture, even with strong faith, will not accomplish this, Śāntarakṣita announces that he will explain the meaning of emptiness with reasoned argument.

The Neither-One-Nor-Many Argument: Demonstrating That Entities Have No Ultimate Nature

Following the statement of the Tibetan and Sanskrit titles of the text along with the requisite payment of homage and statement of purpose in *MAV* is the first stanza of the root text, *MA*, wherein Śāntarakṣita presents his concise inferential rendering of the famous neither-one-nor-many argument (*gcig du bral kyi gtan tshigs*), one of the primary vehicles through which he will execute the stated purpose of the text. As it is applied to the specific views of a variety of opponents, this will serve as the basis for the first sixty-two of the ninety-seven stanzas which comprise *MA*.[12] The aim of the neither-one-nor-many reasoning, as presented by Śāntarakṣita, is to demonstrate that all phenomena[13] lack an independent, unchanging nature of their own and thus are properly characterized as being empty (*śūnya*) of any inherent nature. This is done by analyzing various phenomena asserted or implied by his opponents to have such a nature and then determining that they do not have a nature since they have neither a truly single nor truly manifold nature. Śāntarakṣita's reasoning begins by searching for a truly single nature in phenomena. When it is established that there is nothing that is truly single in nature, it follows according to this reasoning that there is also no truly manifold nature in phenomena, since "many-ness" is dependent on the aggregation of those which would be truly single, but no such truly single nature exists. Since singleness and "many-ness" are mutually exclusive and exhaustive of all possible alternatives, the establishment of the lack of any singular or manifold nature in phenomena also estabishes that they have no nature at all, and thus are properly described as empty of any inherent nature.

The neither-one-nor-many argument is one of the five major logical arguments Buddhists employ as logical proofs demonstrating the selflessness of persons and phenomena.[14] An earlier form of this argument was put forth by Śrigupta, Jñānagarbha's[15] teacher, who is himself commonly considered to have been the teacher of Śāntarakṣita. He puts forth the argument as follows:

> In reality everything, both inside and out, is empty, because it is neither one nor many, like a reflection.[16]

The basic argument asserted by Śāntarakṣita is similar to that put forth by Śrigupta in that it aims to establish the emptiness of all phenomena by the neither-one-nor-many reasoning. The distinction between the two is that Śrigupta takes as the subject of his reasoning all internal and external phenomena, whereas Śāntarakṣita uses those entities put forth by his philosophical opponents. Jetāri puts forth a version of the neither-one-nor-many argument in his *Sugatamatavibhaṅga-kārikās* and *Bhāsya*.[17] Dharmakīrti also utilizes neither-one-nor-many reasoning in his *Pramāṇavārttika*. Sara McClintock argues that Śāntarakṣita and Kamalaśīla hold such reasoning, even in Dharmakīrti's writing, as "ineluctably leading to a Madhyamaka perspective" although she does not maintain that they see Dharmakīrti as a Mādhyamika.[18] Kaydrub summarizes the argument as put forth by Śāntarakṣita and Kamalaśīla in his *TTC*.[19] Śāntarakṣita puts forth the argument as follows:

> (1) Those entities, as asserted by our own [Buddhist schools] and other [non-Buddhist] schools, have no inherent nature at all because in reality they have neither a singular nor a manifold nature – like a reflected image.[20]

The neither-one-nor-many argument presented here by Śāntarakṣita aims to do precisely what he says in *MAV*: namely to establish with reasoning the lack of an inherent nature in entities. He specifically aims to fulfill this task by applying the argument to all those phenomena considered to have some type of nature of their own by his Buddhist and non-Buddhist philosophical rivals. Thus in the fifty-nine stanzas that follow, he scrutinizes such phenomena in an attempt to find a truly singular nature in them. In stanza sixty-one he argues that if there are no phenomena of a truly singular nature, there can be no phenomena with a truly manifold nature since "manyness" depends on the aggregation of true singularities. Since anything which has its own nature must have either a singular or manifold nature according to Śāntarakṣita's reasoning, if his philosophical rivals are correct in asserting such an ontological status for phenomena, then he should be able to discover such a nature in them. Ultimately he finds this endeavor to be fruitless, thus concluding that entities have no inherent nature of their own. Therefore, he concludes that all phenomena must ultimately be characterized by emptiness. The neither-one-nor-many argument is therefore considered to be an expedient way for Mādhyamikas to show that entities or phenomena do not have an ultimate nature. Śāntarakṣita demonstrates what he considers to be the fallacies involved with each attempt on the part of his Buddhist and non-Buddhist opponents to establish singular, partless entities. This argument itself becomes at many points part of a method for revealing his view by way of refuting actual and hypothetical competing views, not only in the context of demonstrating the lack of a nature in all phenomena, but also in specific instances of investigation where his own views on topics such as self-cognizing cognition (*svasaṃvedana*, *rang rig*) emerge from his criticism of other views.[21]

The Application of the Neither-One-Nor-Many Argument

Analysis of Objects

The Refutation of Unitary Objects Asserted by Non-Buddhists

Śāntarakṣita begins his application of the argument to specific views by taking as his object of refutation, the notion of an unchanging, truly singular, uncaused cause of various effects. His specific target here is the *Prakṛti* (*gTso bo*) put forth by the Sāṃkhya School,[22] although the reasoning could be applied more broadly to similar entities asserted to be truly singular, permanent, and causally efficacious. According to Śāntarakṣita, the *Prakṛti* is said to be the permanent, absolute cause of all that exists although it itself is causeless. Śāntarakṣita considers such an entity to be untenable and contradicting reason. He briefly states his argument in the root text as follows.

> (2) Because they contribute to [the production of] successive effects, permanent [causal] entities are not themselves singular. If each successive effect is distinct, then [the argument in support of]

permanent [causal] entities [that are truly singular] degenerates.

The basis of his argument is that if the *Prakṛti* is the singular, permanent, unobstructed cause of phenomena as Śāntarakṣita contends the Sāṃkhya School asserts, then all its phenomenal effects should exist at all times and there should be no periodic arising and ceasing of objects because the cause of their being would always exist and not ever change. It would be fallacious for the effects to only sometimes arise and fallacious for them not to persist because the unchanging, unobstructed cause of such effects would always be present. But we know from direct perception that phenomena arise and cease periodically over time.

Śāntarakṣita elaborates in his autocommentary. One of his primary arguments here rests on the unobstructed quality of the primary cause, the *Prakṛti*. He writes:

> Since the fruits would [only] be delayed if the cause were not complete, when causal efficacy is not obstructed, how would such a gradual arising of those [effects] be possible?[23]

In other words, if the cause is truly singular and unobstructed as a causal agent which is absolute and permanent, then the periodic arising of effects would be impossible because there would be no incomplete causes which may await completion for production of effects. And if the cause is permanent, singular and unobstructed, distinct effects could not arise because the cause is always the same and always present. Multiple distinct effects cannot arise from a truly single cause. Śāntarakṣita goes on to offer an additional argument to add to his critique of the Sāṃkhya system (and unchanging, truly single causes in general) by highlighting what he sees as the contradictions their system presents with the way beings normally perceive reality. He explains that normally primary causes are thought to be accompanied by conditions. For example a seed is thought to be the primary cause of a sprout, but there are also necessary conditions such as soil, sunlight, and water. If, according to the Sāṃkhya position, effects only depend on the primary cause, then the accompanying simultaneous conditions ordinarily thought to be necessary requisites accompanying the primary cause would not actually be necessary according to their view. This is because all that is necessary is the *Prakṛti*. Śāntarakṣita argues against such a view by claiming that if that were the case:

> . . . then the simultaneously produced conditions only exist due to the power of force, like [an animal with] a rope around its throat, and the ceaseless continuum of effects would be unopposed.[24]

In other words, the simultaneous conditions would have no part to play. Contrary to our direct experience of causality, those conditions would only be like animals dragged around by a leash for the apparent purpose of misleading. For example, a seed may be the primary cause for a plant sprouting, but as mentioned above, necessary conditions also include soil, sunlight, and water. According to Śāntarakṣita's critique, since the Sāṃkhya system holds that the only requirement for the production of effects is the primary cause (*Prakṛti*), all other simultaneous conditions are actually present for no purpose.

Finally Śāntarakṣita responds in his autocommentary to the assertion that, by definition, the ability of the *Prakṛti* is the ability to produce periodic effects, a question Gyel-tsab addresses, but not as directly as Śāntarakṣita does here:

> Some would assert that this "spontaneously produced cause" is itself a designation of an ability and that [ability] is asserted to be a gradual production of effects. To them [I] offer this reply: How do you come to this kind of mistake? If you say that the nature of those gradual effects periodically [changes] from one to another, then you must give up the assertion of its permanence because the nature of each of the earlier and later effects is to arise and disintegrate.[25]

Śāntarakṣita considers that he logically compels his Sāṃkhya opponents here to abandon any notions of true singularity with regard to the *Prakṛti*. Śāntarakṣita argues this case by pointing out that because *Prakṛti* is said to be related to different effects at different moments in time, that therefore it must have parts which are related to those different effects and different moments separately. This must be the case since it has already shown that they it cannot have that causal relationship with all effects at all times. If for example *Prakṛti* is the cause of rain, and it is truly single and unchanging, then it must always be the cause of rain and thus it must always rain. Otherwise there must be a part that causes rain and a part that does not and they must change over time and be related to distinct moments. Thus Śāntarakṣita feels he has correctly demonstrated the absurdity of maintaining the existence of a permanent and truly singular cause of a multiplicity of periodic effects.

Gyel-tsab's explanation of this stanza reads as follows:

> . . . If one were to use an autonomous inference: the subject, all mere fruits, [must] arise simultaneously because all arise from the one unobstructed, capable direct cause, [*Prakṛti*]. If you accept this, then it is made clear by direct perception [that all effects do not in fact arise simultaneously]. Since such a fallacy comes, therefore the mere cause, the subject [of the inference,] is not truly singular because it aids in the production of many successive fruits. Therefore having refuted the true, singular existence of the mere cause, the truly existent *Prakṛti* is refuted.[26]

Gyel-tsab's explanation elaborates in slightly more detail than what is specifically stated by Śāntarakṣita. He argues that this *Prakṛti* must either have the ability to produce effects over time or not have that ability. If it does not, then all effects must arise simultaneously, which clearly they do not. Since the *Prakṛti* must therefore have an assortment of abilities to produce successive effects at various moments in time, this clearly contradicts its true singularity and permanence.

> . . . if one says that although *Prakṛti* is truly singular, it would not be contradictory to claim that it aids in the production of periodic fruits, then is it that the *Prakṛti* must have the ability to produce results successively [over time] or not? If not, then it must produce [all] fruits simultaneously because that which produces fruits would not have the ability to gradually produce [them over time]. If so, then truly *singular* permanence is contradicted because [*Prakṛti*] has many different abilities to produce successive fruits..[27]

Tsong Khapa adds in *ZBr* that permanence and the ability to function as a causal agent are incompatible:

> Since functionality is pervaded by impermanence, [the existence of] both permanence and functionality [together] are shown to be incoherent.[28]

The Refutation of Unitary Objects Asserted by Buddhist Schools

The next subject to which Śāntarakṣita applies the neither-one-nor-many argument are those objects asserted by Buddhists to be uncompounded, permanent and truly singular. He does not specifically label his opponent in either *MA* or *MAV*, although Kamalaśīla does identify the opponent as Vaibhāṣikas in *MAP*[29] and Gyel-tsab follows Kamalaśīla on this point in his own *JBy*. Like many of the objects subjected to this reasoning by Śāntarakṣita in this section of the text, there may be specific tenet holders he has in mind, but the arguments are worded sufficiently broadly so that they may be applied to similar related positions. The pertinent next stanza in *MA* regarding the logical untenability of asserting truly singular, uncompounded moments of consciousness reads as follows:

> (3) Even those uncompounded objects of knowledge [known by] the knowledge which arises in meditation [for an *ārya*], according to the system [of the Vaibhāṣikas],[30] are not unitary because they are related to successive moments of knowledge.

Śāntarakṣita illuminates this point in his autocommentary by highlighting a contradiction similar to the one for which he criticizes the Sāṃkhya system. Specifically, entities which are of a single nature must be permanent and yet the entities which his opponent here wants to assert as inherently singular and uncompounded cannot be either permanent or singular given their relationship with an impermanent consciousness. Śāntarakṣita explains the crux of the rejection very clearly in his autocommentary, *MAV*:

> Because they are subject and objects, although the [objects] are related with a changing consciousness (*rnam par shes pa rim can*) [which is the subject], if one were to ask whether they may nonetheless be of a single nature, [the answer is,] "No."[31]

The crux of the argument is that if the object of this wisdom of the meditative equipoise of an *ārya*, as asserted by the Vaibhāṣika School, is permanent and singular, then it cannot be related to various moments of consciousness because consciousness is impermanent and in a constant state of flux. If it were related to more than one distinct moment of consciousness, then it cannot be singular since there must be a part which is related to moment A of consciousness and another part which is related to moment B of consciousness. Therefore even uncompounded phenomena such as the wisdom which arises from meditative equipoise cannot be permanent and singular as asserted by the Vaibhāṣikas, but must be impermanent since it is related to various moments of consciousness.

Gyel-tsab explains the argument in the form of an autonomous inference and adds a point to the reasoning which he feels further demonstrates the irrationality of the Vaibhāṣika position, although this point is not explicitly argued by Śāntarakṣita. Gyel-tsab argues the idea that the normal flow of moments of time would be incongruous with the experience of moments of meditative equipoise if that wisdom were truly singular:

> The subjects, the three non-compounded phenomena, objects of knowledge established by the wisdom of the meditative equipoise of an *ārya*, which the Vaibhāṣika system asserts to be truly singular, are necessarily not truly singular because they are related as subject and object with the various successive [moments of] knowledge which arise in meditation. The pervasion is established since the wisdom which is known in such meditative equipoise would be [cognized] out of order, and the three uncompounded phenomena are necessarily momentary.[32]

Successive moments of consciousness would be cognized out of order according to Gyel-tsab because they would all be known at once.[33] In other words, what is known at a later time can also be known at an earlier time since the known object is said to be truly singular. Put yet another way, if consciousnesses at moments A, B, and C all have as their object the same wisdom and if that wisdom is truly singular, then since the truly singular wisdom cannot be related to different moments in time, the wisdom known by those three moments of consciousness must all be known at once and could not be ordered according to successive moments.

The fourth stanza of *MA* and then Śāntarakṣita's own autocommentary (*MAV*), followed by the fifth stanza of the root text, clarify Śāntarakṣita's basic argument. I have presented the sequence of root text stanza, commentary, and root text stanza here exactly as it appears in *MAV*. It can also be seen by close examination that Gyel-tsab's rendering of the argument described above parallels Śāntarakṣita's more elaborate argument here.

> (4) If the nature of the object known by a previous consciousness continues to exist subsequently, then the previous cognition would still exist in the latter [and], similarly, the latter would exist in the former.

> If that were not the case, then the nature of the uncompounded object known by the previous consciousness would still exist at a later time even though the previous consciousness would not exist [at that later time]. Likewise the object known by the later consciousness would exist at the earlier time even though the later consciousness does not exist [at that earlier time]. Thus stated, [the strength of such a position] deteriorates.But if the nature of the later consciousness does not abide in the earlier time and the object known by the earlier consciousness does not abide in the later time, then if that is the case:

> (5) Since the nature of the [latter] object does not arise in the earlier [time] and [the earlier object] does not arise at the latter time, uncompounded phenomena like consciousness must be objects known to arise momentarily.[34]

Śāntarakṣita goes on to argue in his autocommentary that since consciousness is impermanent and disintegrates moment-by-moment, so too should the nature of its objects to which it is related, including those so-called uncompounded phenomena such as the wisdom arising from the meditative equipoise of an *ārya*, also be impermanent and disintegrating moment-to-moment. It is important to keep in mind that this analysis is happening within the larger framework of the neither-one-nor-many argument, which serves as the basis on which Śāntarakṣita aims to refute all competing views by first demonstrating that entities asserted by his Buddhist and non-Buddhist philosophical rivals to be of a single nature are, in fact, not of a single nature. At the end of the argument he proceeds to show how they also lack a manifold nature and thus must have no nature at all.

In his analysis of the single nature of uncompounded phenomena as asserted by Vaibhāṣikas, to which Śāntarakṣita devotes a lengthy discussion, the next angle from which he approaches the analysis of these supposed uncompounded phenomena is from the perspective of the cause of their arising and abiding. The following quotation from the autocommentary includes both the sixth and seventh stanzas from the root text (*MA*) along with Śāntarakṣita's own commentary on them (indented) and takes up this argument as follows:

> (6) If the previous [uncompounded object] arises from the power of [the causes and conditions of the uncompounded object of] an earlier moment, then this would not [actually] be uncompounded, like minds (*citta, sems*) and mental states (*caitta, sems las byung ba*).
>
> > If one were to argue that [objects] of later moments arise independently, that could not be the case.
>
> (7) If you accept that these momentary [objects] arise independently because there is no dependence on others, then they must either exist permanently or not exist at all.
>
> > Because they arise periodically, they will clearly be known as dependently co-arisen, like those arising from minds and mental states.[35]

Gyel-tsab's commentary on this argument follows Śāntarakṣita's line of reasoning in inferential form. He argues that the uncompounded phenomena which Vaibhāṣikas want to assert to be singular must arise from their own power because if, as Śāntarakṣita points out, they arise by the power of a previous uncompounded phenomena, then they would not be independent and uncompounded by definition but must be dependent. However, if they arise from their own power, they must either exist permanently, "because this is an entity which does not cease after the cause ceases [since it would not depend on causes] or it never exists because it is a phenomenon which does not follow after a cause."[36] Entities which are said to not be dependent on causes must be either permanent, according to Madhyamaka analysis, or not exist at all because that which does not depend on causes for its arising will not cease to abide by virtue of the removal of a cause or will not arise at all by virtue of no cause bringing it into existence. There would be no logical explanation for the cessation of its abiding or for any change in its ontological status. Therefore, since there would be no explanation for its change in ontological status, if it did not exist permanently, it would not exist at all. In his discussion on this issue, Tsong Khapa adds that the fallacy of holding these permanent, singular, uncompounded entities is logically not significantly different from asserting the existence of the *Prakṛti* of the Sāṃkhya School. His point is that the reasoning which rejects the *Prakṛti* and that which rejects the uncompounded phenomena asserted by the Vaibhāṣika School are practically the same:

> . . . if one does not reject that there are singular uncompounded entities [which exist at] previous and subsequent [times] as asserted by our schools, then since you must therefore accept other school's *Prakṛti*, etc. which produces periodic effects, you would similarly not be able to reject any singular, permanent entities because the two reasonings appear to have a single meaning.[37]

Śāntarakṣita does not specifically address the other two uncompounded phenomena asserted by the Vaibhāṣikas, but Tsong Khapa does mention that they too would incur the same logical problems when investigated thoroughly:

> Since the other two uncompounded phenomena (i.e., space and partless particles) are also asserted to be known periodically by distinct consciousnesses, they also would be rejected in a similar way as the previous one.[38]

Śāntarakṣita goes on to say that in many respects these arguments have been put forth merely out of pride in that the subjects themselves do not actually exist. Thus, they are hardly worthy of investigation were it not for the fact that people think that they exist.[39] Śāntarakṣita is revealing part of the enormous debt he owes Dignāga and more significantly, Dharmakīrti. Dharmakīrti categorized objects into two types: generalities/universals (*sāmānya, spyi*), which are permanent and non-functioning in the way that they appear, and particulars (*viśeṣa, khyad pa*), which are impermanent and are functional entities. Universals are mental concepts which do not truly exist and are actually non-entities (*abhāva, dngos med*). It is these universals to which Śāntarakṣita refers when he makes these comments regarding the fact they are hardly worthy of investigation in *MAV* since they do not have the ability to meaningfully function (a primary characteristic of entities). In fact, he follows that comment in *MAV* with the eighth verse of *MA,* which is borrowed directly from Dharmakīrti's *Pramāṇavārttika*, chapter 1, stanza 211:[40]

> (8) What is the purpose of investigating objects which have no meaningful ability to act? What is the purpose of a lustful person inquiring as to whether a eunuch is attractive or not?[41]

Tsong Khapa deals extensively with the topic of the tenability of utilizing unestablished bases (*gzhi ma grub, āśrayāsiddha*), objects which do not exist, such as the Sāṃkhya system's *Prakṛti* for example, as the subject of inquiry in a logical argument in *ZBr,* although he does so in dependence on Kamalaśīla and Dharmakīrti rather than on Śāntarakṣita.[42]

The Refutation of Unitary Persons

Śāntarakṣita follows his application of the neither-one-nor-many argument refuting truly unitary entities asserted by Buddhist schools with the refutation of truly unitary persons. The view he chose as his target of refutation appears to be that held by the Vātsīputrīyans, although he does not explicitly name his opponent.[43] They accept an inherently existing person (*pudgala*) but assert that such persons are neither permanent nor impermanent and neither one with nor different from the five aggregates. Gyeltsab's summation of the Vātsīputrīyan position in *JBy*, which aims at the target of Śāntarakṣita's argument, describes the view they are said to maintain as follows: "There are intrinsically singular persons which are inexpressibly [neither] permanent [nor] impermanent."[44] It seems apparent that this is an accurate description of the view Śāntarakṣita is aiming to refute. Śāntarakṣita states in the *MA,* in accordance with the neither-one-nor-many argument through which he is operating, that those persons asserted to exist in such a way actually have no nature since they have neither a singular nor a plural nature due to their being neither momentary nor non-momentary. His inference in the *MA* is below. I have also included Śāntarakṣita's own autocommentary immediately following the *MA* stanza on this point for further clarification of his reasoning:

> (9) It is clearly understood that a person [of the type asserted by Vātsīputrīyans] has neither a singular nor a manifold nature, since

> [such a person] cannot be explained as momentary or non-momentary.
>
> > Regarding this subject, persons which are accepted by our outsider opponents: the root of the proof demonstrating their lack of a unitary or plural nature is easy to establish. If they were momentary then they would have a manifold nature because another nature would arise in each moment [due to its relationship with distinct moments]. If they were not momentary then they would have a singular nature because their single nature would be stable and permanent. Since they do not assert [either way], there is no difficulty in establishing their emptiness of a singular or plural nature.[45]

It is of interest to compare here the commentary Śāntarakṣita makes explaining his root text argument with the commentary of the Geluk scholar Gyel-tsab. Gyel-tsab is famous within his tradition as a master of logic and this mastery is evident throughout his commentary on *MA*. He uses the same form of tri-modal autonomous inference utilized by Śāntarakṣita to explain his arguments, but he has also expanded this argument into two separate inferences and explained the pervasion in order to present an argument which seems to amplify the clarity of the point Śāntarakṣita is attempting to make:

> The subject, persons, would not be truly singular because they are not expressed as permanent. [And] they would not be truly many because they are not expressed as impermanent. There is a pervasion because if an entity does not have a manifold nature, it must be singular [and] if entities are of many natures, they must be manifold. In brief, they must not be truly singular because they are not expressible as impermanent or permanent.[46]

The Refutation of Unitary Pervasive Entities

In the tenth stanza of the root text, Śāntarakṣita attacks two distinct positions. He uses the first two lines of the stanza to formulate a question aimed at refuting the first position, namely truly singular pervasive entities such as the abstract concept of space. Space is generally defined by Buddhists as the lack of obstructive contact. The third and fourth lines are used to refute the second position, the existence of singular, gross, non-pervasive entities. Thus in Gyel-tsab's commentary the stanza is also divided along these lines as he elaborates on their meaning. Śāntarakṣita however offers the four lines[47] as one cohesive stanza in the root text:

> (10) How can pervasive [entities such as space] be unitary given that they are related with a variety of directions? Gross [non-pervasive entities] are also not unitary since [some parts] of such entities can be visible [while other parts] are not visible.

When Śāntarakṣita explains the lines refuting singular pervasive entities such as space in the first half of this stanza, he argues in the accompanying explanation in his autocommentary that if singular pervasive entities such as space are related with other entities in distinct directions, then those entities with which space is related, such as trees for example, must also by virtue of their relationship with single-nature space be of that same singular nature. This is the case because something with a truly single nature cannot be related with something having a different nature. If it were, then its nature would not be truly single because it would have a part which was in a relationship with something different. Śāntarakṣita explains it as follows:

> What is the nature of those singular entities such as space and so forth which are related to trees, etc. of different directions if they are also related with others? Because they (i.e., trees) are related to that [relator] which is itself singular, similarly these other [relatees such as trees] also should not be distinct from that [singularity].[48]

In his commentary Gyel-tsab again explains the root text verse by offering a clearly presented proof but also again by shifting the parts of the argument of Śāntarakṣita's autocommentary explanation while apparently maintaining the same meaning. The reason for Śāntarakṣita that singular pervasive entities such as space could not be singular is because if this were so, then entities of various directions such as trees would also have to be singular due to their relationship with singular space. His reason is that entities of a singular nature cannot be related with anything which is of a different nature, and clearly trees do not have a singular nature. Thus, if trees for example were related with singular pervasive space, then they must be of a single nature. Since we know that is not the case, we must therefore conclude that there is no such thing as truly singular or unitary space. Gyel-tsab draws out this point by a simple inference emphasizing again that unitary, pervasive entities such as time and space cannot in fact be unitary, and thus cannot exist as they are claimed to exist by Śāntarakṣita's opponents. This is because these unitary entities are said to exist in relationship with other entities which are of a manifold nature and thus must have manifold parts themselves to correspond with the parts of the manifold objects to which they are related:

> The subject, [pervasive] time and space, etc., would not be truly singular because a tree, etc., which belong to different directions like east and the like, are simultaneously collected [in one place] and dispersed [over many].[49]

Kamalaśīla's explanations of this verse from both *MAP* and *TSP* illuminate the same points.

The Refutation of Gross, Unitary Entities

Śāntarakṣita proceeds to argue in the second half of the tenth stanza that gross entities which are said to be made up of the accumulation of partless particles also are not of a singular nature. Here he argues that if gross objects are merely the accumulation of partless particles, and if those building blocks are of a truly singular nature, then the gross object must also be the same singular nature. This would be the case because if the particles which serve as the building blocks are of a single nature and are related to one another (as they must be to accumulate into gross objects), then they must all have the same nature because truly single entities cannot be related with other entities of a different nature. Thus the gross objects (which are made up of the accumulation of these truly single, partless particles which must all be of the same unitary nature) also must have that same unitary nature.

Therefore, he argues that Buddhist tenet holders such as Vaibhāṣikas and Sautrāntikas[50] must make two incompatible assertions. The want to accept gross objects which are the accumulation of parts. And yet they must also accept that these gross objects are of a singular nature. They must accept that gross objects are of a unitary nature because the building block parts which combine to form gross objects, these truly unitary particles, must all be of the same single nature. Since entities such as these partless particles which are of a truly singular nature cannot be related with objects of a different nature, all the particles which combine to form the gross object must be of the same singular nature. It is incoherent to accept a gross object composed of parts yet which is truly singular. While Vaibhāṣikas probably would not come right out and claim that gross objects are truly singular, Śāntarakṣita argues that they cannot avoid that claim if they accept that what goes into the formation of gross objects is truly singular, partless particles. If they have a single nature, the accumulation must combine to have that same singular nature or else the smallest partless singular building blocks would not be truly single or partless due to being related to things which are different from them. Yet due to their acceptance of gross objects having the ability to possess conflicting qualities, such as part of a pot being visible to an eye consciousness while another part is not, there is a contradiction in its being truly singular yet possessing parts.

Gyel-tsab outlines an organized approach to explaining the contradictions associated with the Vaibhāṣika view as presented in this Mādhyamika rendition of it. In his outline he describes three contradictions with holding the Vaibhāṣika view of saying that a gross object such as a pot is intrinsically single. Here he elaborates on contradictions alluded to by Śāntarakṣita in *MAV*. The first contradiction has to do with a pot having the qualities of being capable of being both unobstructed to the visual consciousness and obstructed to the visual consciousness at the same time. If it is intrinsically single, Gyel-tsab argues that it should be either all visible or be completely obstructed from visibility; part of a singular entity could not be visible while another part is obstructed because the existence of parts would contradict its singularity. The second contradiction draws on a similar line of reasoning in that an intrinsically singular gross entity should not have distinct parts. Here Gyel-tsab emphasizes gross entities in which part is mobile while other parts are not. The common example given in oral explanation by Geluk lamas is that of a tree with branches. If a tree is intrinsically single yet its branches can be moving while the trunk is stable, then a tree must have parts and therefore not be truly single. The final contradiction mentioned by Gyel-tsab is the contradiction regarding color. If one takes a gross single object like a cloth and paints one side one color and another side a different color, then we see a contradiction emerging with reference to the qualities the object possesses. A singular object should not have a multitude of qualities if it is truly singular. Gyel-tsab is specifically concerned with the idea of gross objects being truly singular and not with the preceding step in reasoning which argues that if one accepts that if gross objects are made up of truly singular partless particles, then the gross object must be accepted as truly singular as well.[51]

The Refutation of Unitary, Partless Particles

The next topic in Śāntarakṣita's root text is the refutation of truly unitary, partless particles and follows logically from the previous one (the second part of stanza ten). Śāntarakṣita introduces this topic in *MAV* out of a discussion of the issues concerning the assertion that gross, unitary objects are made up of unitary, partless particles.[52] From this discussion in *MAV*, Śāntarakṣita proceeds to cite the eleventh and twelfth stanzas back-to-back in *MAV*, then comments and follows that with the thirteenth *MA* stanza. Gyel-tsab notes that the eleventh through thirteenth stanzas of the root text all pertain to this argument. If one were to name the main target of Śāntarakṣita's argument here, it appears to be a view held by both the Vaibhāṣika and Sautrāntika Buddhist schools that there exist the minutest particles which are actually partless and, therefore, of a truly single nature. Neither Śāntarakṣita, Kamalaśīla, nor Gyel-tsab specifically names their opponent here, but the views of the above two schools would certainly be among the targets of this argument. According to this position held by Vaibhāṣikas and Sautrāntikas, and as discussed above with regards to the previous topic, the smallest essential building blocks for the physical world are these partless particles which are of a single nature and which combine to form gross objects. The eleventh through thirteenth root text stanzas aim to disprove the reasonability of asserting such truly unitary, partless particles and read as follows:

> (11) What is the nature of the central [partless] particle which faces singly towards [another] particle yet abides [with other partless particles in various directions] either [around and] joining with it, or around it [with space between them, or] around it without space between?

> (12) If it is asserted that [the central particle] also faces entirely toward another such [unitary, partless] particle, then if that were so,

wouldn't it be the case that [gross objects such as] land and water and the like would not be [spatially] expansive?

(13) If you accept [partless particles with sides] which face other such particles [in different directions], then if that is the case, how could [even] the most minute particles be singular and partless?

In order to refute the notion of the existence of partless particles, the argument put forth here questions basic assertions and assumptions of the type held by both the Vaibhāṣika and Sautrāntika philosophical schools.[53] The first of these three stanzas questions what the nature of such a particle would be which is related in one of three possible ways with other particles abiding in the ten directions around it. If the central particle is related with multiple particles surrounding it in any of the three possible ways (these being exhaustive of all possible ways to combine to form gross objects), then it must have parts related to the various particles around it and therefore not be truly single. The second of these three stanzas from the *MA* questions how such particles of singular nature could combine to form gross objects. If they do in fact combine to do this, then that first or central partless particle must have other inherently singular partless particles with which it combines surrounding it in one of the three possible ways, as Śāntarakṣita states in the first stanza, in order to form gross objects. A contradiction arises here however because if other particles abiding in the ten surrounding directions combine with the central particle, then the central particle must have sides facing each of those particles in ten distinct directions. Either that, or it must have some sort of relationship with those directions and therefore would not be truly singular due to its having parts related with different directions, as Śāntarakṣita questions in the thirteenth stanza of the *MA*. If it were truly singular and could only have one side (i.e., not have spatial extension) and face and combine in one direction, then gross objects such as land and water or even earth *maṇḍalas,* as Śāntarakṣita writes in his autocommentary, could not be spatially expansive. This of course runs contrary to our direct perception, which knows all sorts of gross expansive objects such as the ones mentioned. Gyel-tsab explains this point very briefly in the form of an inferential proof:

The subject, a particle which abides in the center of the ten directions, would not have a different place [of abiding from] the particle to the east and in the nine other directions because the part of

> the subject facing to the east and the parts of the subject facing the other nine directions are one. If you accept this, then it would not be possible to develop into gross forms like earth due to accepting that [previous inference]. If you accept each of the [ten] faces, then that subject (i.e., the particle in the center of the ten directions) must not be singular and without parts because the subject would have ten different faces facing the [surrounding] particles in the ten directions.[54]

Gyel-tsab therefore offers two alternatives to those who assert partless particles, both of which are unacceptable. The first is that gross forms could not develop if their position were correct because particles, being truly singular, could not combine in the so-called ten directions as would be necessary for gross form to take shape, but could only combine in one place. If a single partless particle were to combine with particles in a variety of directions around it, then it would not be truly single and partless since it would be related with other particles in a variety of directions and have multiple parts related with each other particle in each distinct direction. Therefore, the only other alternative for proponents of partless particles, according to Gyel-tsab, is to accept that those partless, singular particles which they assert to be the building blocks of gross form are not truly partless or truly singular and that in fact there are no truly singular partless particles; they do not exist. Kamalaśīla discusses this topic in his *Sarvadharmaniḥsvabhāvasiddhi*, emphasizing the physicality or the material quality of the particles while making essentially the same point:

> If particles are physical, then they should be known to have distinct directions. If that were not the case, then [gross physical objects such as] mountains and the like would not [be able to take form] as the accumulation [of particles] because there would certainly be no distinct directions such as east and north, etc.[55]

Śāntarakṣita proceeds from here, in the following stanzas and commentary on them, to summarize and elaborate on the arguments he has just made. His autocommentary following this stanza from the root text additionally reveals indirectly Śāntarakṣita's own high regard for the soteriological value of Buddhist philosophical inquiry and logical inference. Not only does he argue that this philosophical exercise, engaged upon in the application of the neither-one-nor-many argument, aids in the understanding of the philosophical system Śāntarakṣita maintains, but more fundamentally, the philosophical inquiry itself facilitates an understanding of emptiness, the realization of which is central to the attainment of Buddhahood in Mahāyāna Buddhism. Thus, philosophical investigation is inseparably part of the path to the soteriological goal for Śāntarakṣita. Reason is a tool for the religious.[56] He summarizes in the fourteenth stanza and accompanying autocommentary as follows:

> (14) Particles have thus been established to have no inherent nature. Therefore it is evident that eyes and [other gross] substantial [entities], etc., which are asserted [to be real] by many of our own [Buddhist] schools and other [non-Buddhist] schools, are directly known to have no inherent nature.
>
> If we are certain that subtlest particles do not exist, then the eyes and form and consciousness of that asserted to be real [by our schools] and the substantial [phenomena] and qualities, etc. asserted by the Vaiśeṣikas and the like will effortlessly be known to be empty of inherent existence. Thus, one may ask if this [teaching of the five aggregates (*skandha, phung po*), twelve constituent elements (*āyatana, skye mched*) and eighteen sources (*dhātu, khams*)][57] is the teaching of the Conqueror or not?[58]

Śāntarakṣita argues that as a result of the understanding that particles do not have a single, inherently existing nature, the holders of such a view would come to know that those grosser objects, which the accumulation of those particles supposedly form, also have no inherently existing nature. Much in the vein of *The Heart Sūtra* (*Prajñāhṛdaya*/ *Bhagavatīprajñāpāramitāhṛdayasūtra*, *Shes rab snying po*/ *bCom ldan 'das ma shes rab kyi pha rol tu phyin pa'i snying po'i mdo*), which similarly negates a host of Buddhist concepts, Śāntarakṣita refutes the true existence of the fundamental components of Buddhist *abhidharma,* including the true existence of the five aggregates, the twelve constituent elements, and the eighteen sources.

Gyel-tsab offers a basic inferential proof as explanation of this verse in which he demonstrates that all of those objects of knowledge, including the five aggregates, the twelve constituent elements, etc., and the substances asserted by non-Buddhist schools, all lack any truly existent nature because there are no truly existent particles.[59] Gyel-tsab notes that the pervasion for the given inference is established by Śāntarakṣita in conjunction with the following fifteenth stanza of *MA*. This stanza immediately follows Śāntarakṣita's hypothetical question (quoted above in the autocommentary on stanza 14) to other Buddhist schools about whether or not those *abhidharma* teachings are in fact the teachings of the Buddha .

> (15) The nature of these [entities] is [said to be] composed of those [particles]. The qualities of these [entities], their own actions, and even their universals (*spyi, sāmānya*) and particularities (*khyad pa, viśeṣa*) are said to be made up of those [particles and therefore must not inherently exist].

If the particles which make up gross entities do not have any inherent nature, then the gross objects also must have no inherent nature. Śāntarakṣita proceeds in his autocommentary, *MAV,* to give a very lucid explanation of his line of reasoning and the logical consequences which evolve out of asserting single, partless particles as truly existent. His argument criticizes the view that all such objects are made up entirely of partless particles on the basis that if partless particles do not exist, then those grosser objects which they combine to form must also not truly exist:[60]

> Our schools assert that the ten types of constituent elements composed of form (i.e., the five senses and five sense objects) are made up of these subtlest particles. If those [subtle particles] do not [truly] exist, it would be unsuitable [to posit] these [ten as truly existent]. It is the same as saying that eye consciousness arises in dependence on [truly existent] form and a [truly existent] eye organ [although those do not truly exist]. Although the five consciousness sources (*rnam par shes pa'i khams lnga*) such as eye [consciousness are said to] depend on those (i.e., form and an eye faculty), if those did not exist, on what would their production rely? If the five constituent consciousnesses do not exist, then the mental consciousness which is actually established by that immediate condition [of the existence of the five constituent consciousnesses] would naturally not be feasible. Likewise if the

> accumulation of the six consciousnesses is not established, then also a thorough explanation of the mind which is just beyond that would be irrational. And likewise, if the mind has no nature, then concomitant mental factors (*caitta, sems las byung ba*) which exist simultaneously with that [mind], such as feeling, discrimination, intention, etc., also will be easily known as having no nature. [The same would] also [be true for] non-associated compositional factors (*ldan pa ma yin pa'i 'du byed rnams*). Since the heroic masters of logical thought have laid out bundles of explanations hundreds of times, there is no need for an additional one.[61]
>
> Therefore, because there are no [truly] existent [particles] in relationship with [other particles], the accumulation of those also does not exist. Since it has already been shown that permanent entities such as space, time, directions, self, and even subtle partless particles clearly have no inherent existence, with this same manner of investigation, the form aggregate and the consciousness aggregate (together with its concomitant factors) are also shown to have no inherent existence.[62]

Analysis of Subjects

Analysis of Mind, Its Objects, and Its Means of Perception As Asserted in Other Buddhist Systems

Śāntarakṣita's next topic of inquiry is the mind, its objects, and its means of perception and is one which (as briefly mentioned in the Introduction) reveals much about the syncretic nature of his thought. It is here that we find that he begins to interweave Madhyamaka thought with mainline Yogācāra tenets such as self-cognizing cognition and the rejection of external objects with some of the epistemological insights of Dharmakīrti. It is specifically in Śāntarakṣita's critiques of the epistemological positions of proponents of Buddhist tenets of several different stripes, from Vaibhāṣika through Yogācāra, by way of demonstrating the lack of a true, unitary nature in all phenomena, that the marriage of the logico-epistemological tradition with Madhyamaka in his thought begins to emerge. Here we see not only an element of the debt Śāntarakṣita owes to Dharmakīrti, but also the innovative quality of his own work in bridging the Buddhist logico-epistemological traditions with Madhyamaka thought. This sort of philosophical bridge became central to many Tibetan Buddhist philosophers, including Tsong Khapa and his followers such as Gyel-tsab.

Self-Cognizing Cognition (svasaṃvedana, rang rig),[63] *External Objects, and Images*

The first issue addressed under this topic in the root text is unique in some very important respects with regard not only to its meaning and implications for Śāntarakṣita's own epistemology and ontology but also in the context of the text itself. The topic of self-cognizing cognition and related issues, which are the subject of the sixteenth stanza and its accompanying explanation in *MAV*, is the only topic in the first two-thirds of the root text, the section where he is applying the neither-one-nor-many argument to his opponents' views, where Śāntarakṣita actually makes an affirmative statement explaining his own view explicitly to the reader. Elsewhere in the application of the neither-one-nor-many argument, his own view slowly emerges only implicitly from an analysis of what he rejects and the way he rejects it. And that slow emergence of his view only becomes fully clear much later in the text. Here however, Śāntarakṣita discusses the proper way of asserting the validity of self-cognizing cognition in detail. This subject is also taken up by Śāntarakṣita in *TS* and Kamalaśīla elaborates both in *MAP* and *TSP*. In fact, the majority of the *MA* verses on this topic as well as the following related topics on the veracity or lack thereof of truly existent images are borrowed by Śāntarakṣita from his own earlier text *TS*.

Śāntarakṣita begins the subject by describing self-cognizing cognition as the very quality which defines sentience. That which is conscious must be self-conscious, by definition. That which is not self-conscious is insentient. The reflexive nature of consciousness avoids any sense of subject-object duality between consciousness and its self-conscious quality or, for Śāntarakṣita, between consciousness and its object. Consciousness of an object is really consciousness of itself, apparently appearing as an object.[64] The acceptance of self-cognizing cognition (Śāntarakṣita only accepts it conventionally whereas Yogācāras accept it as ultimate) and the rejection of being able to know objects which are distinct from consciousness are mainline Yogācāra tenets, but are unique among Mādhyamikas. He goes on further to describe self-cognizing cognition as naturally self-illuminating, much like the flame of a candle. Paul Williams sums up Śāntarakṣita's view in the following manner: "What is meant by '*svasaṃvedana'* is (i) that consciousness does not depend on another thing to be known, and (ii) it is nevertheless known. Therefore, it follows that it is self-known."[65] He notes too that both Kamalaśīla, in *MAP,* and Mokṣakaragupta consider the self-cognizing quality of cognition or consciousness to be so obvious as to be self-evident to even cow-herders.[66] This maintenance of the validity of self-cognizing cognition is an important point upon which Prāsaṅgika-Mādhyamikas such as Tsong Khapa and the Geluk School will later criticize Śāntarakṣita and the Yogācāra-Svātantrika-Mādhyamika School he is considered to represent. (See Part II for a discussion of the Geluk critique.) In Gyel-tsab's *JBy*, commenting directly on *MA*, he offers no criticism however, but only attempts to elucidate Śāntarakṣita's position.

Śāntarakṣita introduces the topic in *MA* by giving a partial definition of the term, but uses a synonym for self-cognizing cognition (*svasaṃvedana, rang rig*), namely self-knowledge (*ātmasaṁvittir, bdag nyid shes pa*). In the section immediately following this *MA* verse in his own *MAV,* however, he uses the technical term "self-cognizing cognition" several times in a manner which clearly suggests it is intended to be considered as synonymous with "self-knowledge." The sixteenth stanza of *MA* opens the topic in this text in the following manner:

> (16) Consciousness is produced in the opposite way from that which is of an inanimate nature. That which is not the nature of being inanimate is the self-knowledge of this [consciousness].

Śāntarakṣita begins by simply defining consciousness as that which is the opposite of being inanimate in the process of attempting to convince dualists[67] (i.e., those who assert external objects) who reject self-cognizing cognition[68] that in fact they should hold the position of self-cognizing cognition. In other words, Śāntarakṣita claims that whatever is animate or conscious is reflexively conscious (i.e., self-aware). The sixteenth stanza of *MA* also appears as stanza 1999 in *TS*. Stanza 1998 is not used in *MA* but gives further explanation of Śāntarakṣita's position on an integrally related issue. Specifically, in *TS* 1998 he rejects the possibility of knowledge of external objects. Śāntarakṣita emphatically states that consciousness can never know an object which is utterly distinct, separate, or external to itself. This is the case for Śāntarakṣita regardless of whether or not the object has images (*akārā, rnam pa*), an issue to be taken up below.[69] If consciousness can never cognize any objects external to itself, it follows then that consciousness must be conscious of itself. Thus, one can clearly see how Śāntarakṣita's position on the conventional status of self-cognizing cognition and his acceptance of a general Yogācāra rejection of external objects are linked in important ways.

In the commentary from *MAV* and the subsequent two stanzas of *MA* (which also correspond to the subsequent two stanzas in *TS*), Śāntarakṣita criticizes a hypothetical dualist opponent who presumably is convinced to accept self-cognizing cognition yet still holds to the problematic epistemological view that persons may nonetheless have an ability to directly cognize external objects, those from which they are different. This is a critical, mistaken assertion according to Śāntarakṣita. First, however, Śāntarakṣita elaborates on his initial description of self-cognizing cognition, describing it as "naturally clear" (*rang bzhin gyis gsal ba*)[70] and "mere cognition" (*rig tsam*).[71] Self-cognizing cognition which has consciousness as its object, and is of course consciousness itself, must therefore be clear with regards to its object since its object is non-distinct from itself. In other words, consciousness is in a non-dual relationship with itself as its object. If its object were external, it would not be clear because consciousness and the object would not have this unmediated non-dual relationship. But Śāntarakṣita argues that his position does not have this fault of claiming objects to be external or separate from the clear consciousness, as do his opponents who accept self-cognizing cognition but also assert objects of consciousness to be external.[72] He then goes on to explain the fallacies involved with maintaining a consciousness which cognizes external objects. Knowledge of external objects must not be clear because there would be some distance between consciousness and its objects; it would not be an unmediated form of knowledge.

Much like Dharmakīrti, Śāntarakṣita, in discussing the relationship between consciousness and its objects in the accompanying *MAV* discussion, stresses again the notion that consciousness does not meet with objects which are distinct from itself. This in part accounts for the natural clarity of self-cognizing cognition. Examining Dharmakīrti's own comments on the topic, we can clearly find a major source of Śāntarakṣita's thinking on the topic. For example, Dharmakīrti describes his own position as follows in the first chapter of *Pramāṇāvarttikakārikā*:

> [Excepting consciousness itself], there is nothing to be experienced by consciousness, and [likewise], it has no experience other

> [than self-experience]; since consciousness is deprived of the cognized and the cognizer, it is illuminated by itself.[73]

Gyel-tsab specifically comments on the *MA* stanza in his *JBy* and does so by putting the root text stanza into inferential form. Gyel-tsab remarks that the subsequent seventeenth stanza of Śāntarakṣita's root text establishes the pervasion. It is of interest to note the particularities of Gyel-tsab's presentation of the argument here because it specifically addresses the means of production of self-cognizing cognition. This presentation by Gyel-tsab leaves Śāntarakṣita susceptible to the type of criticism Tsong Khapa levels at holders of self-cognizing cognition in *LSN* and *dKa gnad brgyad gyi zin bris*. Specifically, Tsong Khapa argues that if self-cognizing cognition is dependent only on itself and not on an object for its arising, then it must be self-produced and therefore inherently existent, an obviously unacceptable tenet for any Mādhyamika. Whatever is self-produced is independent and therefore ultimately existent according to Madhyamaka analysis. This is one of the few occasions in *JBy* where Gyel-tsab apparently presents Śāntarakṣita's view in such a way that it will easily fall into a logical fallacy when interrogated in other Geluk philosophical literature, though Gyel-tsab does not embark on criticism here. This of course, perhaps not coincidentally, is also one of the few places in the first two-thirds of *MA* where Śāntarakṣita positively asserts a position and one which (again, perhaps not coincidentally) Gyel-tsab would find objectionable. So we can see that while in general Gyel-tsab is faithful to Śāntarakṣita in his commentary, and that it can be a useful aid for penetrating many of the arguments being made in Śāntarakṣita's text, one needs to read with a discriminating eye. This is particularly true when the text discusses issues with which Gelukpas will ultimately take issue. Gyel-tsab writes,

> [Regarding] the subject, consciousness has the quality of self-cognition because it is produced in the opposite manner from the way inanimate objects are produced. There is a pervasion because an apprehending consciousness which is in the nature of being non-inanimate is the self-cognizing consciousness of that mind. In order to establish the pervasion, the four [lines in the root text beginning with] "Self-cognizing cognition," etc. pertain.[74]

Gyel-tsab's argument that consciousness is self-cognizing because of the way it is produced remains very close to Śāntarakṣita's at a minimum, but the emphasis on the means of production does open Śāntarakṣita to the specific criticism mentioned above – that self-cogniznіng cognition entails entails self-production, which entails inherent existence.

Śāntarakṣita proceeds in the seventeenth stanza of *MA* to criticize his hypothetical dualist opponent whom he feels he has convinced to accept self-cognizing cognition yet who still holds, in his opinion, a mistaken view of note here, that the nature of consciousness is unitary. So while Śāntarakṣita is using this as a forum for establishing the correct way of understanding self-cognizing cognition and rejecting external objects, he is still remaining within the overarching neither-one-nor-many argument as it is applied to all of his opponents throughout the first sixty-two stanzas of the root text. This stanza will also attempt to lead that hypothetical dualist opponent holding self-cognizing cognition into a dilemma regarding the ability to know objects from which conciousness is distinct.

> (17) Self-cognizing cognition is not an entity which [exists as] agent and action [with its object] because it would be incorrect for consciousness, which is of a single, partless nature, to be three (i.e., knower, knowing, and known).[75]

Śāntarakṣita seems to have a strong commitment to the idea that well reasoned arguments can have a transformative effect on a rational mind, steering one correctly towards an accurate understanding of the nature of reality. Thus, throughout this part of *MA* (and throughout *TS*), Śāntarakṣita seems to be sincerely concerned with addressing specifically held views from his time period. Śāntrarakṣita's discussion and criticism of opponents' views from an assortment of philosophical perspectives throughout this text seems to aim at facilitating, for his opponents, a gradual ascent through progressively subtle positions to what he considers to ultimately be the correct and most subtle view, his own Madhyamaka position.

Gyel-tsab asserts that this stanza helps establish the pervasion of the previous stanza. Gyel-tsab comments on the stanza as follows:

> The self-cognizing cognition of that subject (i.e., consciousness) does not exist in a manner of substantive difference from the three (knower, knowing, and known) because the subject is one without

> any substantive parts. This pervasion is established because it would be incorrect to posit three different substances [such as] knower, knowing, [and known] for one which does not have substantial parts.[76]

We find a slight difference between the argument of this stanza in the root text and the way Gyel-tsab explains it in his *JBy*. Śāntarakṣita appears to be addressing his argument here to an opponent who holds that consciousness is partless and truly singular while accepting self-cognizing cognition, but at the same time wants to assert the existence of objects which are utterly distinct from or external to the consciousness perceiving them. Both the singular nature of the mind and the externality of its objects are unacceptable tenets according to Śāntarakṣita. Thus, he seems to have two aims here: the first is to demonstrate that no such truly singular mind exists; secondly, he wants to convince such an opponent that objects are not utterly distinct from the consciousness perceiving them. Gyel-tsab's commentary seems to zero in on the rejection of external objects but not on the rejection of a truly singular consciousness or truly singular self-cognizing cognition. While Śāntarakṣita would certainly be pleased to have convinced an opponent to accept self-cognizing cognition, this is still occurring within the framework of his larger Madhyamaka argument aimed at demonstrating that all entities lack a truly existent nature because they lack either a singular or manifold nature, a point Gyel-tsab seems to have lost sight of here.

Before proceeding into the next *MA* stanza, Śāntarakṣita leads the reader to it in the autocommentary by arguing that because consciousness does not rely on anything outside of itself to be illuminated, it therefore must have a nature which illuminates itself:

> Not relying on others to be illuminated, that which is self-illuminating is called the self-cognizing cognition of consciousness.[77]

The first half of the eighteenth stanza follows from the previous *MA* verse argument concerning the nature of consciousness. Here he essentially defines the nature of consciousness as self-consciousness. This is an extension of his argument against an epistemological standpoint which argues that consciousness can have valid knowledge of objects other than itself, a position which does not make sense if one maintains that all consciousness is self-consciousness. In the second two lines, Śāntarakṣita proceeds again specifically to attack the epistemological standpoint of his hypothetical opponent who posits self-cognizing cognition and an ability to have valid knowledge of objects external to the consciousness. It is once again on epistemological issues such as these concerning self-cognizing cognition that we again see the influence of Dharmakīrti on Śāntarakṣita. Dharmakīrti similarly maintains that consciousness *only* experiences itself and thus knowledge of external objects cannot be considered valid. Śāntarakṣita writes:

> (18) Therefore, this [consciousness] is capable of self-consciousness (*bdag shes*) since this is the nature of consciousness. How [though] could that cognize the nature of objects from which it is distinct?[78]

The first statement of the stanza above draws from the autocommentary, in which Śāntarakṣita argues for self-cognizing consciousness on the grounds that it does not rely on anything else to illuminate itself. An important point in Śāntarakṣita's presentation of self-cognizing cognition is that it is non-dual with its objects and that consciousness therefore does not perceive objects other than, or utterly distinct from, itself. Gyel-tsab organizes the argument into inferential form, wherein he also draws out the relationship between the self-cognizing nature of consciousness and the lack of external objects. He writes:

> That subject (i.e., consciousness) would be correctly posited as self-cognizing consciousness because the subject is the nature of the apprehending consciousness [which is non-dual with its object].[79]

The language of Gyel-tsab's commentary is a little vague and could also be translated as "...could be correctly posited as *having* self-cognizing consciousness."[80] The following two lines of *MA* ("How [though] could that cognize the nature of objects from which it is distinct?"), along with the next stanza, directly attacks the hypothetical opponent's epistemological standpoint, which holds that consciousness knows objects which are external to it. Therefore, fallacies exist for Śāntarakṣita's hypothetical dualist opponent, who holds to self-cognizing cognition while maintaining the existence of external objects and a truly singular consciousness. While

Gyel-tsab comments on the first and second halves of the eighteenth stanza of *MA* separately, the full import of Śāntarakṣita's meaning seems to come across when the stanza is read as a whole. In his criticism of this opponent's explanation of knowledge of external objects, we come to see indirectly Śāntarakṣita's reasoning for utilizing a Yogācāra epistemological perspective on a conventional level, which includes putting forth self-cognizing cognition and the lack of objects with a nature different from the mind. We find an explicit declaration of the non-dual nature of consciousness and its objects according to Śāntarakṣita in *TS* when he says,

> Therefore, that which is the subject of the dispute (i.e., self-cognizing cognition)is considered to be non-dual, since it is devoid of object and subject (*vedyakartṛtvaviyogāt*) because it is the nature of consciousness, like a reflection.[81]

The following *MA* verse furthers the rejection of a consciousness that knows external objects or, more precisely, objects in which its nature does not exist:

> (19) [Since] its nature does not exist in external objects (*gzhan*), given that you assert that objects of consciousness and consciousness are different, how could consciousness know objects other than consciousness?

Śāntarakṣita follows this question in his autocommentary with a multi-layered argument aimed at convincing his opponents to accept that objects do not exist external to the consciousness which perceives them: for it would be impossible to know those objects directly if they are distinct entities. In addition, with regards to the neither-one-nor-many argument, if consciousness is truly singular, then it would be incoherent to assert that it could know objects from which it is different because it would have to be related to objects of a different nature. He is, of course, not arguing for a truly single nature of the mind, but merely pointing out the fallacies entailed by maintaining such incompatible tenets as the truly single nature of consciousness and its ability to know objects distinct from itself. This is an excellent example of how Śāntarakṣita pitches arguments to opponents on their own terms and aims to *gradually* lead them to what he considers to be the correct view (i.e., that of the Madhyamaka). Śāntarakṣita is in fact in the midst of attempting to demonstrate that nothing has a truly unitary nature. Śāntarakṣita does not explicitly state his position regarding the two truths here, as that will come towards the end of the text. At this point the reader may even presume he is attempting to establish the Yogācāra as his final view, a view with which in the last analysis he will have serious problems. But he does begin to give some grounding for his position (to be stated specifically later in the text) of provisionally accepting many components of a Yogācāra framework as a component of his final adoption of the Mādhyamika perspective for analysis of ultimate truth.

Gyel-tsab attempts to explain Śāntarakṣita's point made in the second half of stanza eighteen and in stanza nineteen in his commentary, *JBy*. These stanzas once again criticize the notion that consciousness could know objects from which it is different. Gyel-tsab adds a point at the end which is not specifically mentioned in the *MA* stanza when he claims that it would be a mistake to try to extend this reasoning to self-cognizing cognition in an attempt to refute it as well. This is because what is being refuted here is something asserted to be of a distinct substance from consciousness, whereas that is not the claim with regards to self-cognizing cognition. Gyel-tsab writes:

> It would be incorrect [to posit] directly experienced external objects (*don dngos su myong*) because the object [and] the consciousness are different substances. That is the case because the nature of the object does not exist in the [perceiving] consciousness and the nature of the [perceiving] consciousness does not exist in the object. It would be incorrect [to posit] consciousness cognizing external objects in the same way as [the positing of] the correctness of self-cognizing consciousness because the object of consciousness [and the consciousness] are unrelated different substances.[82]

Śāntarakṣita adds one last point of criticism to the critique of his hypothetical opponent as he segues into the next topic, the refutation of what Gyel-tsab describes as three possible Sautrāntika epistemological standpoints. Kamalaśīla does indicate in *MAP* that the opponent Śāntarakṣita has in mind here is a variety of Sautrāntika.[83] Here Śāntarakṣita, who does not specify by name either opponent, adds that since the opponent he has been discussing asserts that consciousness does not even possess images (*ākāra, rnam pa*), it is therefore even a lower system of thought than the systems he is about to address, which do in fact assert, albeit incorrectly, that consciousness possesses images:[84]

> Moreover, it is taught from that perspective [which we have just finished] that consciousness has no images. Since consciousness has no strong connection with images, it is taught that this school is even much lower [than the ones we are about to discuss].[85]

*Critique of an Epistemology Asserting Valid Cognition of True Images (*satyākāra*) External to Consciousness*

Following the statement above in his *MAV*, Śāntarakṣita proceeds into his refutation of true singularity via a refutation of what, as just mentioned above, appears to be a Sautrāntika epistemological standpoint. Here Śāntarakṣita apparently divides his opponents who accept a truly singular consciousness, external objects, and true images (*satyākāra*) into three distinct sub-schools in a way which closely parallels the way Gelukpa doxographers divide sub-schools of Yogācāra in their tenet system texts. In his commentary, *JBy*, Gyel-tsab specifically names the three primary opponents he thinks Śāntarakṣita addresses in the following twenty-three stanzas as corresponding to three divisions of Sautrāntikas, namely: Non-Pluralists (*sna tshogs gnyis med pa*), the Half-Eggists (*sgo nga phyed tshal ba*), and Proponents of an Equal Number of Images and Consciousnesses (*rnam shes grangs mnyam pa*). Again, it is Gyel-tsab, not Śāntarakṣita, who specifically names these divisions of Sautrāntika in accordance with what will later become normative Geluk designations for divisions of Yogācāra in their doxographical presentation. Śāntarakṣita simply puts forth the views one at a time and then criticizes them merely by referring to each school in succession as "others."

While he is applying the neither-one-nor-many argument here to refute the true singularity of either consciousness or its images, it seems as though the primary concern of Śāntarakṣita is the continuing topic of presenting a correct epistemological standpoint. The underlying refutation seems to be a critique of what he considers to be erroneous epistemologies as he argues against the component parts of these positions These opponents of Śāntarakṣita may in fact be hypothetical and not represent actual schools of thought or individual thinkers existent in India during his time. It is possible that they were set up to be refuted by Śāntarakṣita in order to once again help illuminate his view in a dialectical fashion.

In the first *MA* stanza pertaining to the epistemological standpoint he is addresssing, Śāntarakṣita proposes a general proposition which would be applicable to all Sautrāntikas and perhaps others in order to begin to put forth his opponent's view so that the reader has a clear idea of what is to be refuted:

> (20) According to the position [of some], consciousness knows images, in spite of the fact that in actuality the two (i.e., consciousness and images) are distinct. Since it is just like a mirror reflection, it can be suitably experienced by mere imputation.[86]

Śāntarakṣita explains that according to this position, one directly experiences images of objects because the gross imputed object is like a mirror image of the gathered actual images of the external object. He further elaborates on his own *MA* stanza dealing with the way of knowing external objects according to this position in his autocommentary, *MAV*. There, Śāntarakṣita states that the position of his opponent holds that the mirror-like image of the object which is known by the consciousness is in the nature of the object and that, therefore, the consciousness which knows the mirror image of the object also knows the object itself.[87] Since consciousness is still only conscious of the images and not the actual external objects, according to this view (which appears in line with Sautrāntika thinking), its proponents feel they can maintain external objects, true images, and self-cognizing cognition.

Gyel-tsab however explains this *MA* stanza slightly differently,[88] emphasizing the Sautrāntika assertion that one can validly know external objects because they assert images of objects in a different manner than Vaibhāṣikas. According to Gyel-tsab's presentation, as opposed to the Vaibhāṣikas who hold the validity of knowledge of objects because objects do not have images, Sautrāntikas maintain that they do not fall into the fallacies of Vaibhāṣikas because they do accept the existence of true images of objects. Here, Gyel-tsab seems to be basing his commentary more on what later evolved into the normative Geluk presentation of tenets than specifically on the words of Śāntarakṣita's root text. Gyel-tsab explains the Sautrāntika position in the following manner is his commentary:

> According to Sautrāntikas, when one analyzes objects, even though objects and consciousness are of different substances, s/he may hold the validity of the experience [of objects by the consciousness perceiving them] because s/he accepts [mirror-like reflections of] images of the object.[89]

Gyel-tsab explains that the previous inference and the one that follows constitute a two stanza analysis of the differences between the two "lower" Buddhist philosophical systems which postulate external objects. The previous inference (stanza 20) demonstrates the validity of experiencing external objects according to the system of analysis explained by Śāntarakṣita (which Gyel-tsab considers to be Sautrāntika) and then the following root text stanza (stanza 21) "demonstrate[s] the incorrectness also of analyzing them according to the system of the Vaibhāṣikas."[90] Geluk doxographers such as Thubkan (*Thu'u bkvan blo bzang chos kyi nyi ma*) and Jamyang Shayba (*'Jam dbyangs bzhad pa*) consider Śāntarakṣita to be a proponent of true images (*rnam bden pa*), but more in line with the Yogācāra position on true images than that of the Sautrāntikas.[91]

The rejection of the three varieties of proponents of external objects with images which are known by a singular consciousness follows over the course of several stanzas after the brief dismissal of the position previously discussed (asserting external objects without images). The *MA* rendition of this dismissal of what Gyel-tsab describes as the Vaibhāṣika position on the valid cognition of external objects is explained as follows in the twenty-first stanza of the root text:

> (21) However, there cannot be externally cognized images for those who do not assert a consciousness which reflects images of objects.[92]

Śāntarakṣita expands on this argument in his autocommentary by explaining that because such opponents do not accept that images of objects are known, the knowledge of gross objects must in their view actually extend further than the total knowledge of its parts or images. This is seen as incoherent. From there he argues along Sautrāntika lines that since the opponent does not accept the relationship between objects, their mirror-like reflections, and consciousness (a relationship which Sautrāntikas accept), that it is wholly illogical to posit externally cognized objects at all:

> Since [images] are the nature of being uncognized, the entities which are objects of cognition would be [cognized] more extensively than [the actual] objects themselves. Since they also do not accept that there are causal relations [between objects and] mirror reflections [known to consciousness as Sautrāntikas accept, such] knowledge also would not exist. If that is the case, consciousness knowing images would itself be unsuitable.[93]

Gyel-tsab does not add much in his commentary beyond restating that the Vaibhāṣika epistemological explanation which he takes this argument to be addressing is incorrect because they do not accept images. Gyel-tsab then proceeds into what he describes as the refutation of the three subdivisions of Sautrāntika, which, as mentioned above, he names as Non-Pluralists, Half-Eggists, and Proponents of an Equal Number of Images and Consciousnesses. According to him, each gives a slightly more subtle (yet still incorrect according to Śāntarakṣita) explanation than the previous one. All three of Śāntarakṣita's opponents here can be labeled appropriately as proponents of real or true images (*satyākāra-vādins, rnam bden pa*).

Due to this ascending level of subtlety in the order of presentation, Śāntarakṣita begins with the rejection of the grossest. That is, the position of one who asserts the existence of a truly singular consciousness which can cognize a multiplicity of images at once. Gyel-tsab labels this opponent as Sautrāntika Non-Pluralists. Throughout his discussion of consciousness and its cognition of images as interpreted by various unnamed opponents, Śāntarakṣita applies the neither-one-nor-many argument to his opponents' ontological assertions about the status of consciousness and its objects while simultaneously critiquing the accompanying errors he sees in these opponents' related epistemological positions. It would be a mistake to underemphasize the importance these epistemological concerns carry for Śāntarakṣita.

> (22) Since [images] are not different from the unitary consciousness, there cannot be a multiplicity of images. Therefore one would not be able to establish the knowledge of [external] objects with the force of that [image].[94]

Śāntarakṣita argues that because images of objects are manifold and the consciousness which is asserted by his opponent here is said to be truly singular, that consciousness would be incapable of knowing external objects. This is because the cause of a consciousness knowing objects, namely the manifold images which make up the object such as colors, shapes, etc., could not be established by a singular consciousness. A truly singular consciousness cannot be related to a multiplicity of images because that would undermine its claim to being truly singular. If it were related to a multiplicity of images, it must have a part related to image A and another part related to image B, etc. If it has such a multiplicity of parts, it is not truly singular. It is interesting to note the way Gyel-tsab explains this because although his argument is similar, his emphasis is subtly different. His emphasis is not on convincing the opponents he describes as Sautrāntika Non-Pluralists that according to their view they could not know external objects, but rather on logically coercing them to accept objects as being one substance with the consciousness and thus needing to all be the same due to their identity with a singular consciousness. This line of argumentation moves very close to a Yogācāra epistemology and the sort of framework Śāntarakṣita will want to incorporate provisionally later in the text:

> At the time that a multiplicity of images such as blue, yellow, white, and red are known to a single consciousness, these images could not be substantially distinct from one another because they are all indistinct from the one partless consciousness. If you accept this, then having appeared as images of the object, it would be incoherent to accept the establishment of the object as substantially different from the [consciousness which apprehends the images of the object] because those images are not of a different substance.[95]

Śāntarakṣita continues his argument in the next *MA* stanza against a similar opponent, but this time apparently a Yogācāra, or at least one who rejects external objects while still maintaining that a singular consciousness can know a multiplicity of images at once. His point is that even for those who reject external objects, it does not make sense to talk about a unitary consciousness knowing a multiplicity of images. Here we find a more direct appearance of the neither-one-nor-many reasoning. He implores his opponent to realize that it is logically impossible for a singular consciousness to be one with, or even related as perceiver and perceived with, a multiplicity of images. He challenges his opponents to explain how this would be possible if it is in fact the case. This line of argumentation, which suggests again Śāntarakṣita's incorporation of aspects of a Yogācāra epistemological standpoint, including a rejection of external objects, is more akin to the way Gyel-tsab commented upon the previous stanza. Later Geluk doxographers would probably label this opponent as a Yogācāra Non-Pluralist, one of the three divisions of Yogācāra Proponents of True Images. Here however, Gyel-tsab does not use this label. The specifics of the opponent become more clear in Śantarakṣita's autocommentary which follows this stanza in the *MAV*. Śāntarakṣita's autocommentary, below, on the twenty-third stanza of the root text explains that either there is a contradiction in the way in which images and consciousness exist, since one is unitary and the other is manifold, or else they must be completely distinct and unrelated and therefore the consciousness would not perceive images or the objects which are established on the basis of knowing images:

> (23) Consciousness cannot be unitary since it is not separate from images. If that were not the case, then how would you explain the two (i.e., images and consciousness) as unitary?[96]
>
> > If the consciousness is a body which is not different from the multiplicity of images, then the [consciousness] would be manifold like the particularities of those images. If consciousness were of only a single nature and there were a multiplicity of images, then at that time a contradiction would ensue since the subject (i.e., consciousness) would exist in a manner contradicting [the many images] if the two, consciousness [and images,] were not distinct.[97]

The above is one of Śāntarakṣita's major critiques of the Proponents of True Images of the Yogācāra School. Both Kamalaśīla in *Madhyamakāloka* and Haribhadra in *Abhisamayālaṁkārāloka Prajñāpāramitāvyākhyā* use similar lines of argumentation, particularly in their utilization of this neither-one-nor-many reasoning in their own refutations of Yogācāra Proponents of True Images.[98]

According to Śāntarakṣita, the object and subject (or consciousness) are conventionally of the same nature. A blue object and an eye consciousness perceiving blue arise together because they both arise in dependence on previous latent potentialities (*vāsanā, bag chags*) and this explains how objects can be validly cognized. According to Sautrāntikas, they are distinct entities working in a cause-and-effect relationship. But if a multiplicity of images is a cause for a truly singular consciousness, then the effect must not be related to the cause. This would be irrational. So for Śāntarakṣita there are two major logical fallacies in the reasoning in the text as stated thus far. It is illogical for consciousness to be truly singular given that it is related to a multiplicity of images and it is illogical for that single consciousness to directly perceive external objects from which it would be distinct. For Śāntarakṣita objects are not of a different nature from the consciousness perceiving them and nothing is truly singular. Gyel-tsab follows Śāntarakṣita's line of reasoning here.

The next opponents are quite similar to the previous one according to Śāntarakṣita. However, they claim that they avoid the fault of the previous opponent because according to their system, images arise one at a time in rapid succession, so consciousness actually only perceives and is only related to one image at a time. This position is stated in the twenty-fourth stanza of *MA* and is that of the opponents Gyel-tsab labels as Sautrāntika Half-Eggists. Once again, Śāntarakṣita does not name his opponents specifically and simply allows the asserted tenets to suffice. Whether there were actual proponents of this view in India at the time of Śāntarakṣita or if he was simply constructing this potential view for its value as an object of refutation is not clear. Regardless, as it is presented in *MA,* and as mentioned above, the current opponents claim to avoid the fault of the previous ones who claim the existence of a truly unitary consciousness which perceives many images at once. These opponents attempt to avoid such a fault by claiming that it is actually an extremely rapid succession of consciousnesses, each perceiving one image and deceiving the person into thinking they are all being perceived at once, which accounts for what appears to be a single consciousness perceiving a collection of images such as blue, green, round, etc. simultaneously:[99]

> (24) [Colors such as] white and the like arise in succession to the consciousness, yet because of arising quickly, foolish people think that they arise simultaneously.

Gyel-tsab summarizes this position, which will ultimately be rejected by Śāntarakṣita, as follows:

> First, regarding the four [lines in the root text beginning with]

> "[Colors such as]," etc., [the Half-Eggists] claim, "We do not have those faults because when numerous images such as blue and yellow, etc. appear to one consciousness (*shes pa*), even though the images such as white, etc. [actually] appear successively to the consciousness, because of the rapidity with which they are engaged, the foolish person mistakenly thinks that they have appeared simultaneously. For example, it is like thinking that the circle of light appears all at once even though [such a circle of light made by rapidly twirling] the burning end of a stick [forms] gradually.[100]

Śāntarakṣita's autocommentary on this statement of the opponent's position given in the preceding *MA* verse, along with the examples this opponent gives (according to Śāntarakṣita) to support his/her position, segues in his autocommentary directly into the critique beginning with the twenty-fifth root text stanza. This stanza is embedded in Śāntarakṣita's autocommentary, *MAV*:

> Like [an arrow] piercing a hundred petals of a blue lotus flower, because it happens so quickly, although they [are pierced] successively, [this opponent] still struggles to claim that people think it happens simultaneously. [Or] for example, they say that it is like when one sees a wheel of fire, the sight of which is the result of rapidly [twirling] in a circle the burning end of a torch. If that is the case then,[101]

> (25) Why, when the mind which hears the sound of such words as *latā*[102] [and *tāla*] arise very quickly, does it not hear [the two syllables] as if they were arising simultaneously [thus rendering the two words indistinguishable]?[103]

Śāntarakṣita's argument attacks this position which asserts that multiple images of a single object are simply known by consciousness one at a time in rapid succession, and thus this position does not have the fault of asserting a singular consciousness knowing a multiplicity of images. He does so by questioning the examples his hypothetical opponent gives to justify the meaning of their explanation and by offering counter-examples which, in theory, should support their position but in actuality seem to reveal its shortcomings. Śāntarakṣita's opponent's examples illustrate that images appear one at a time in rapid succession to a consciousness and not simultaneously as the previous opponent asserted. Thus, when consciousness perceives many images, such as the many colors of a painting, it does not actually perceive them all at once, but rather a series of moments of consciousness perceive images one at a time in rapid succession. They appear in so rapid a succession in fact that the continuum of consciousnesses does not even realize that they are not arising simultaneously. Thus, ordinary individuals think that they perceive all the images or aspects (*akārā, rnam pa*) of a painting simultaneously, but actually they perceive each individual image one at a time in rapid succession. Describing the process in this way, Śāntarakṣita's opponent here believes that s/he avoids the faults of the previous opponent, who asserts that a truly single consciousness knows a multiplicity of images simultaneously, since s/he merely asserts one consciousness knowing one image, yet in an extremely rapid succession. Śāntarakṣita counters that this position also has fallacies of its own which are difficult to overcome. The common example or metaphor which this opponent (whom Gyel-tsab identifies as a Sautrāntika Half-Eggist) gives to defend his/her position likens the way an ordinary person's mind perceives a multiplicity of images with the example of a burning torch, which when twirled very rapidly in a circle gives the appearance of a wheel of fire in the dark night. Although it is not an actual wheel of fire, it appears that way due to the rapidity with which the succession of images of flame appear to the consciousness. And this same mistake is made with regard to images of all objects, such as the various colors of a painting which appear to be cognized all at once but in actuality are claimed to be cognized in rapid succession according to this position.

Śāntarakṣita's counterargument directs attention to sense faculties other than the eye consciousness. He specifically targets the ear consciousness. He questions why aural images arising to the ear consciousness would not seem to arise simultaneously in the same way that visual images appearing to the eye consciousness do. In other words, Śāntarakṣita asks why visual images seem to appear instantaneously while aural images do not? To make his point, the twenty-fifth verse of *MA* and accompanying commentary in *MAV* give a specific counter-example using two pairs of Sanskrit words, *latā* and *tāla,* and *sara* and *rasa,* in which the sounds are the same but the syllables are reversed. If the images of the sounds of these words were heard as if they arose simultaneously like the wheel of fire, then confusion would arise as to which word was heard and it would be impossible to differentiate them since the aural images "la" and "tā" would be seem to be heard simultaneously to the ordinary individual. Since the order in which the syllables arise would deteriorate, the words would thus be indistinguishable. That is, if the process for aural images were the same as that of this opponent's description of visual images (and we have no reason to believe s/he thinks otherwise according to Śāntarakṣita), then a seemingly simultaneous appearance of aural images would occur and this would make words such as *latā* and *tāla* indistinguishable to ordinary individuals. Since this is not the case (i.e., these words are not indistinguishable), Śāntarakṣita makes his point that multiple images of a single object do not appear to moments of unitary consciousness in a rapid succession as his opponent claims. This, according to Śāntarakṣita, is made clear by direct perception since the words *latā* and *tāla* are distinguishable. Thus, this opponent has still not solved the problem of a unitary consciousness knowing a multiplicity of images because its own solution is contradicted by direct perception according to Śāntarakṣita. He explains this in *MAV* in the following manner:

> If it were the case that words such as *latā* and *tāla* and *sara* and *rasa* and the like were made up of single syllable mental objects which also arise extremely rapidly, then why do these [aural images] not [also seem to ordinary individuals to be] known simultaneously like individual [visual images such as the colors of] a painting, etc.?[104]

Śāntarakṣita proceeds to add an additional argument to his criticism of the current opponent's position by arguing that even a conceptualizing mind, which one could argue makes such mistakes out of ignorance, could not cognize in the way this opponent claims. This is the case because as with the way images arise and disintegrate moment-by-moment, so too does the conceptual consciousness perceiving them. If the consciousness itself does not abide for any duration of time, such a conceptual consciousness could not hold a direct perception of a succession of images arising over time in the mind and could not even erroneously consider them to exist simultaneously. It would only be possible if the images were enduring and thereby many could appear to a single consciousness. But then one falls back to the same fallacies as the Non-Pluralist, in addition to having to accept the true existence of images due to their enduring nature.

> (26) Even if we were to consider only conceptual minds, [the images] would still not be known in succession. Since they do not remain for a long time, all minds are similar [to images] in the rapidity with which they arise.[105]

> (27) Therefore, all objects are not apprehended gradually. Rather, just as they appear, [they] are apprehended simultaneously as distinct images.[106]

Gyel-tsab reiterates Śāntarakṣita's point when he explains the inappropriateness of asserting that a rapid series of individual images appear to a momentary conceptual consciousness as though they were simultaneous. He points out that just as with images, consciousness also is momentary and does not abide for any duration. Therefore a conceptual consciousness could not hold previous images in any way which would lead to the conclusion of a simultaneous appearance, since it itself only abides for a moment. He writes in his commentary on these stanzas as follows:

> [The opponent argues that] all minds mistakenly [think that they] apprehend objects simultaneously without knowledge that they are actually apprehended successively because the apprehension is very quick. An absurd consequence would entail [if that were the case] because it does not abide for long [as would be necessary to hold this series of images as appearing simultaneously] and yet it is not momentary, like for example the images which you assert.[107]

In other words, the opponent wants to claim that the consciousness is momentary like the images it perceives, yet must also make the contradictory claim that consciousness also abides for some duration of time in order to erroneously piece together the distinct consecutive images and to come to the incorrect conclusion that they are perceived simultaneously. According to Gyel-tsab's explanation of the argument Śāntarakṣita is making, if a conceptual consciousness were momentary, it could not even erroneously piece together such images. This is because the previous momentary image known to a previous momentary consciousness would not abide for any duration so as to be erroneously conceptualized as being known simultaneously with other related images.

The following argument in *MA,* which continues to target the opponent which Gyel-tsab calls a Sautrāntika Half-Eggist, does so with further elaboration on the issue of memory, which seems to naturally follow at this point. Here Śāntarakṣita continues his argument in which he rejects the idea that the mistaken appearance of a group of images arising simultaneously is the result of joining memories of distinct, successive perceptions. According to Gyel-tsab, in stanzas twenty-eight through thirty Śāntarakṣita's arguments are positing the *absurdum* and establishing the pervasion of the present critique:

> (28) Even with regard to [the example of] a burning torch, the arising of the mistaken instantaneous appearance of a wheel [of fire] is not [a result of] joining the boundaries between [memories of distinct] perceptions because it appears very clearly.[108]

Śāntarakṣita's argument maintains that his opponent here is making contradictory assertions. They claim that the eye consciousness sees the wheel of fire clearly and that it joins the sequential appearances by memory. That is why the sequential images of a twirling burning torch appear as a wheel or why the gradual perception of many colors appear as a painting, a single object with many images. At the same time as stating that this perception of the wheel of fire appears clearly, they maintain that the distinct appearances are joined by memories. Śāntarakṣita's point is that unlike mental consciousness, which has the ability to remember and thus to join memories, the five sense consciousnesses (including the eye consciousness) do not have the ability to remember or join memories. Sense consciousnesses are direct, non-conceptual, non-mistaken appearances. If the perception is clear, it must be made by the eye consciousness, but if formed by the joining together of memories, then it must be an act of the mental consciousness, which would by virtue of its formation by memory not be "clear." Memories by definition are not clear because they are not direct and non-conceptual consciousnesses. This accords with the general presentation of Svātantrika-Madhyamaka tenets found in Geluk literature that claims that Svātantrikas hold that perceptions of sense consciousnesses are non-mistaken (in contrast with the Geluk Prāsaṅgika position which holds that all conventional perceptions are mistaken). According to the Geluk presentation of Svātantrika-Madhyamaka tenets, it is the mental consciousness that is mistaken with regard to imputing true existence onto objects. Śāntarakṣita follows stanza twenty-eight in his *MAV* with this brief synopsis:

> In general is it a contradiction for clear appearances to be joined together? Yes, it is a contradiction.[109]

Gyel-tsab highlights the same contradiction in his *JBy* by pointing out that the conceptual mental consciousness is that consciousness which can join earlier and later consciousnesses and that is, by definition, *not* clear. Nevertheless, Sautrāntika Half-Eggists, as he calls them, claim earlier and later moments are joined *and* are perceived clearly. This is in spite of the fact that such clear perception is considered to be the sole domain of the non-conceptual sense consciousnesses. Śāntarakṣita states this very clearly in the twenty-ninth verse of *MA*:

> (29) This joining of boundaries is done by the memory [of the mental consciousness], not by the seeing [of an eye consciousness], because that [eye consciousness] cannot apprehend past objects.[110]

The argument therefore is that if the perceptions of the eye consciousness are clear, and they occur in a series of successive perceptions, and are not all perceived simultaneously, then examples like the wheel of fire clearly appearing as a wheel as a result of its rapidity would be incorrect as Śāntarakṣita's opponents assert it. This would be the case because it would be a result of memory which is a product of the mental consciousness and thus not a clear direct perception such as is the case with any of the five sense consciousnesses. The mistake of an eye consciousness and the mistake of a mental consciousness are two totally different types of mistakes. An eye consciousness can make a mistake by seeing something which is not there such as an hallucination, but conceptual thought itself is a mistake of a mental consciousness for Śāntarakṣita. Mental consciousness with its memory can join conceptual thoughts, but an eye consciousness cannot do that because an eye consciousness is only conscious of the present according to Śāntarakṣita. Since an eye consciousness cannot apprehend past objects, it cannot join them either. It therefore could not create the perception of the wheel of fire as his opponents would assert. In the thirtieth stanza Śāntarakṣita reiterates his point:

> (30) Since the object of that [memory] has passed, it is not clear.
> Therefore, the appearance of the wheel [of fire] is of a type which
> is not clear.

Śāntarakṣita adds in the immediately following section of the *MAV* for emphasis on this point, that, "Even for entities residing directly in front of [the sense consciousness], the memory could not conceptualize them very clearly."[111] Gyel-tsab defends this point made in the *MA* by explicitly establishing the pervasions in a series of inferences. His arguments here are again aimed at the Sautrāntika Half-Eggist:

> If one replies, "There is no pervasion," [they are wrong]; there would be a pervasion to that [inference] because if it is a mind which joins the boundaries of earlier and later [images], then there must be memory. The subject, a non-conceptual consciousness, could not join the boundaries of the former and later [images by means of memory] because it could not apprehend past objects. [For this position to be coherent] there would have to be [past] objects clearly appearing to the subject, and a mind which joins the boundaries of former and later [images] because it apprehends past objects, [yet it is impossible for there to be clearly appearing past objects]. The subject, a mind which misapprehends the burning end of a stick as a circle, would not be a mind which joins the boundaries of former and later because if it is, the object would not clearly appear to it, but [you say] that the object does appear clearly.[112]

Having completed his argument against this opponent, Śāntarakṣita moves on in an ascending order of subtlety to the opponent who argues that a singular consciousness and a multiplicity of images are compatible because there are as many consciousnesses as there are images and so there is a one-to-one relationship between them. Although Śāntarakṣita does not identify his opponent by name, Gyel-tsab labels this opponent the Sautrāntika Proponents of an Equal Number of Consciousnesses and Images.[113]

Śāntarakṣita begins by describing their solution to the problems found in the previous two opponents' assertions of a single consciousness perceiving manifold images. He explains that this opponent argues that there will arise as many types of a common consciousness at one time as there are distinct images in the object. Thus, they avoid the various faults arising from positing one consciousness perceiving many images, as is the case with the first opponent's position, because there is truly only one consciousness for each image cognized. They avoid the related epistemological faults of the second opponent with regards to issues concerning memory because they do not claim that a consciousness remembers a rapid succession of past images.

When they claim here that as many types of a common consciousness will arise as there are images, the word "common" (*mthun*) refers to the six types of consciousness. Thus, two eye consciousnesses are considered to be of a common type, but an eye consciousness and an ear consciousness are of uncommon (*mi mthun*) types. Śāntarakṣita in the following combined stanzas explains the position succinctly and then proceeds to launch into an immediate critique:

> (31, 32) If one were to claim that when someone sees the base of the images of a painting, as many minds will arise simultaneously as there are images in that [painting], then if that were the case, even when cognition is of a single image type such as the color white, etc., since there is a distinct beginning, middle and end to that, there will be a variety of objects of observation [within that cognition of a single image].

This opponent aims to avoid the problems of the previous two opponents by asserting that numerous consciousnesses, one for every aspect or image, arise simultaneously, thus avoiding the problems incurred by Śāntarakṣita's previous opponents regarding a truly singular consciousness knowing many images. Throughout this discussion of consciousness and its means of knowing, Śāntarakṣita skillfully maintains the discussion of appropriate epistemological positions within the framework of the neither-one-nor-many argument investigating the ontological status of entities his philosophical opponents claim have a truly existent nature. Thus his present critiques all center around the rejection of a truly singular or unitary nature for consciousness as claimed by some of his Buddhist opponents. Śāntarakṣita's critique here draws on a similar line of reasoning to that which he employs against those who hold partless particles. His argument zeros in on the question of how one holding this view will precisely define a truly single image for which a truly single consciousness abides. This presentation implies a necessary reduction of images to a true singularity, given the relationship images are said to have with a truly singular consciousness. Images could not be manifold in such a circumstance because then they would require more than one consciousness to apprehend them. And if the Proponents of an Equal Number of Images and Consciousnesses wish to describe images as singular, then a similar critical examination such as was applied to proponents of truly singular partless particles would hold. Truly unitary images could not have multiple sides or face multiple directions. They could not exist in relation to other distinct and different images or with moments of time. And, defining spatial parameters such as its beginning, middle and end could not exist for a truly unitary image. Śāntarakṣita explains this in his autocommentary in the following manner:

> Likewise, the many images such as blue, white, and the like which you assert to be single also have many images themselves, each with the nature of having a number of parts like this side and that side. And with respect to those [parts of images], knowledge of the nature of those also must be manifold. If you would claim that they are manifold, well then, what is unitary? [In order to defend your position asserting a truly unitary consciousness for every image, consciousness would ultimately have to be] apprehending objects which are particles without limbs. Even those with very precise wisdom would not be able to finely distinguish with certainty the limbs of those objects [so as to be able to distinguish singular images for which a single consciousness must arise]. This sort of view [with such subtle acumen] is said to be inexperienceable.[114]

Śāntarakṣita argues that to hold a view that maintains an equal number of consciousnesses and images, those images must be truly singular, like the consciousnesses they are related to, and one must be able to cognize and define the precise limits of an image. If there is a singular consciousness and a singular image, they must be definable or at least the single image must be identifiable by consciousness so that there may be a one-to-one relationship between the consciousness and that image. A consciousness which knows a truly singular image must know its boundaries. Images must finally be reducible to true singularity, otherwise they would require more consciousnesses. And if they are related to a consciousness which is singular, then they too must be singular. For images to be truly singular they would have to be reduced to partless particles. Śāntarakṣita argues that there is no wisdom so acute that it could distinguish a partless particle, and the point itself is moot as such particles have already been shown to be absurd. In other words, Śāntarakṣita's argument here aims at refuting this view by demonstrating that one cannot actually find a distinct, singular image for which there would be a single consciousness because every image can always be broken down into smaller parts, thus undermining its true singularity and requiring an endless number of consciousnesses (for each part). Gyel-tsab explains this point in a succinct inference:

> The subject, a consciousness perceiving a unitary image of [the color] white, must be perceiving many images because that white image would have many different [parts which are also individual images such as the one facing] north, south, etc. If you accept this, then there could be no consciousness apprehending only one image.[115]

Śāntarakṣita reiterates his position on this point in his next root text stanza and its accompanying explanation from the *MAV*:

> (33) I honestly do not feel that [an image] such as the color white, etc., which is like the nature of a particle which is a partless singularity, has ever appeared to any consciousness.
>
> In all sincerity, I have never seen a particle which is void of any parts. Without having seen a [partless particle], you still accept it, which seems self-deceiving. If the cause for accepting an object's existence by intelligent people is a visual [valid cognition], then since [such a valid cognition] does not exist, [single, partless particle] are unacceptable.[116]

Śāntarakṣita bases this argument on the Sautrāntika-type assertion that although partless particles appear, they cannot be individually perceived, except as aggregations which form gross objects. The argument aims to push further the absurdity of accepting an equal number of consciousnesses and images by once again questioning the rationality of the claim that it is possible to find an image or particle which is truly singular as would be necessary in order for the view to hold true according to Śāntarakṣita. Gyeltsab reiterates the same point by further explaining that although partless particles appear according to the Sautrāntika view, they still cannot be perceived, and thus there seems to be no reason to accept that they actually exist. Certainly there is no way for an individual consciousness to distinctly apprehend a truly singular image which must be like a partless particle. Mādhyamikas, like Śāntarakṣita, hold that even according to the Sautrāntikas' own assertion, there can be no inherently existing partless singularity because if there were, it would be perceivable by valid cognition. Partless singularities are not perceivable by valid cognition, even according to the Sautrāntikas' own assertions. If truly singular particles or images do not exist, then what could a truly single consciousness cognize?

The next *MA* stanza completes the argument against these opponents by making clear that the arguments against the feasibility of a truly unitary nature for sense consciousnesses also holds for the sixth consciousness, the mental consciousness. This is the case because the mental consciousness is established in conjunction with the five sense consciousnesses. The five sense consciousnesses do not have single partless entities as their objects, but rather gross objects which are the accumulated aggregation of parts. In that same way, the mental consciousness does not have a single partless entity as its object, but rather manifold cognition and mental states:

> (34) [According to our opponent,][117] the sources of the five [sense] consciousnesses are images of objects [made of] accumulated [partless particles]. Minds (*citta, sems*) and mental states (*caitta, sems byung*) are objects established in the sixth [source of perception].

In other words, Śāntarakṣita argues that just as the five sense consciousnesses have gross objects made of an accumulation of partless particles as their sources of perception, thereby undermining the feasibility of perception of a truly singular object, so too does the sixth consciousness (i.e., the mental consciousness) have manifold objects of observation. According to the Sautrāntikas, its objects are the accumulation of minds and mental states, and thus are also not unitary.

Analysis of Mind, Its Objects, and Its Means of Perception As Asserted in Non-Buddhist Systems

Critiques of Views Maintaining Unitary Consciousness

Śāntarakṣita proceeds at this point to address a series of views on the mind, its objects, and its means of perception that were current among non-Buddhist schools during his time. Each of these systems, in various ways, asserts the existence of a truly singular mind or consciousness. Śāntarakṣita proceeds to critique them by application of the neither-one-nor-many argument to the specifics of the way in which they assert the mind to exist. In his commentary on each of the five critiques, Gyel-tsab establishes that the thesis to be proven in each case is "a consciousness apprehending only one object could not exist." This despite the fact that consciousness must only have one object if it is truly unitary. The following *MA* stanza offers a succinct summation of Śāntarakṣita's argument against two classical Indian schools concerning the nature of mind:

> (35) Even according to the scriptures of non-Buddhists (*phyi rol pa*) [such as the Vaiśeṣikas], the appearance [of gross objects] as singular would not occur because its objects are substances which have qualities (*guna, yon tan*), etc.

Śāntarakṣita's rejections of non-Buddhist schools in *MA* tend to be concise; the only exception is his reasonably detailed treatment and rejection of the Sāṃkhya system. In contrast, his *TS* treats many of the non-Buddhist systems in great detail. Śāntarakṣita does not specifically name his opponent in the thirty-fifth stanza of *MA,* but in the *MAV* he indicates the schools by mentioning Kaṇāda, who was the founder of the Vaiśeṣika School and Kapila (*Ser-skya*), who is a famous Sāmkhya philosopher.[118] Kamalaśīla also identifies Kaṇāda in *MAP*, but makes no mention of Kapila or the Sāṃkhya School until his commentary on stanza thirty-seven.[119] Gyel-tsab identifies the opponents as Vaiśeṣikas (*bye brag pa*) and Naiyāyaikas (*rigs pa can*). Geluk School representatives, such as the doxographer Könchog Jigme Wangpo, do not consider the differences between the Vaiśeṣikas and Naiyāyikas significant enough so as to warrant separate treatment. He explains this point in his *Precious Garland of Tenets*:

> The Vaiśeṣikas [Particularists] and the Naiyāyikas [Logicians] are followers of the sage Kaṇāda and the Brāhmaṇa Akṣipāda respectively. Although these two schools differ a little in the features of some of their assertions, their general tenets do not differ.[120]

As can be seen above, Śāntarakṣita's treatment of his opponents here is brief in comparison with the extent of his treatment of Buddhist opponents. Gyel-tsab also summarizes the point with two succinct inferences which indicate how, according to these systems, it would be incorrect to maintain the existence of a consciousness which apprehends only a truly singular object as would be necessary for a consciousness to be truly singular. This true singularity, with regard to subjects and objects, will remain the main object of negation in regards to the following non-Buddhist tenet holders to be addressed as well.

> Even according to the non-Buddhist system [of the Vaiśeṣikas], the existence of a consciousness apprehending only one object would not be possible because all minds have many images . . . . According to the system of the Vaiśeṣikas and the Naiyāyikas, a mind which apprehends only one object could not exist because substances and the like which have parts must be apprehended with the qualification of qualities, actions, collections, and particularities, etc.[121]

Gyel-tsab echoes Śāntarakṣita's argument here. Śāntarakṣita also adds that not only is a mind apprehending only one object impossible according to these non-Buddhist systems because they hold that objects must be apprehended with their qualities, but he also notes that numerous objects (each with numerous images) may appear to one consciousness according to this opponent. Thus, not only are many images of one object apprehended by the consciousness, but many objects with their many images are apprehended by the consciousness.

Śāntarakṣita proceeds in the next stanza to demonstrate the lack of a mind apprehending only a single object according to the positions of two other non-Buddhist schools, the Jains and the Mīmāṁsakas. Śāntarakṣita treats these two non-Buddhist schools with one sweeping argument and a brief explanation in his autocommentary. The criticism is very similar to the previous one. Because, according to Śāntarakṣita, Jains and Mīmāṁsakas maintain that objects of perception are like gems emitting many colorful rays and that the multiple images of a single gross object are apprehended by a single consciousness at once, it is irrational according to Śāntarakṣita for Jains and Mīmāṁsakas to maintain that the consciousness apprehending such a multitude of images is truly singular.

> (36) [According to the views of the Jains and the Mīmāṁsakas], all entities are [manifold] like the nature of a gem [emitting colorful] rays. It would be irrational for the mind which apprehends those [entities] to appear in the nature of singularity.

Gyel-tsab's explanation echoes Śāntarakṣita's argument by explaining by inference the argument in the thirty-sixth stanza. He argues quite simply that since entities have parts and emit manifold images like the rays of a gem, and consciousness apprehends an entire object, including its manifold images, simultaneously, that the consciousness itself cannot be of a truly single nature by virtue of its relationship with manifold objects or images.

Śāntarakṣita identifies his opponent in the thirty-seventh stanza as "the followers of the views of Suraguru,"[122] a famous proponent of the Lokāyata (Hedonists) system. Śāntarakṣita's argument in the following root text stanza maintains that a consciousness apprehending a singular object would be impossible according to their system because the Lokāyatas maintain that all subtle and gross level objects, including all sense faculties and sense objects, are compounds of the four elements. As compound objects they cannot be singular, so a consciousness which apprehends them also cannot be singular by virtue of its relationship with those manifold compound objects.

> (37) Even for proponents of the [Lokāyata] system, which accepts the establishment of all sense faculties and objects as compounds of [the four elements] such as earth and the like, [consciousness] is still incompatible with a singular [manner of] engaging entities.
>
> > Since the basis on which [knowledge which] establishes the images of a compounded object is a manifold compound, it would be irrational for such a consciousness apprehending compounded phenomena to [be thought of as] engaging compatibly with singularity.[123]

Gyel-tsab argues along the same line of reasoning, pointing out that since the objects of the consciousness are composed of a combination of the four primary elements, it is of course illogical for the consciousness perceiving that object to perceive a single entity or to perceive such an entity as truly singular. Thus it is logically untenable as well for that consciousness to be truly single given its relationship with manifold objects. Gyel-tsab comments on the root text stanza in the following manner:

> Even according to the system of the Lokāyatas [Hedonists], the previous thesis (i.e., "a consciousness apprehending only one object could not exist") [would hold true] because they accept that all forms, etc. such as objects, and organs such as the eye organ, etc. are in the nature of a collection of the four elements.[124]

Śāntarakṣita then proceeds to demonstrate the logical untenability of maintaining a consciousness perceiving a single object according to the assertions put forth in the Sāṃkhya system. Śāntarakṣita explicitly names the famous Sāṃkhya proponent Kapila in *MAV,*[125] and Kamalaśīla identifies these arguments, and Kapila, with the Sāṃkhya School in the *MAP*[126]. Here his argument targets the Sāṃkhya assertion that the five mere existences (*pañca tanmātrāṇi, de tsam lnga*) which comprise all objects of consciousness are all in the nature of the three qualities (*guna, yon tan*). Given this position concerning objects, it is untenable to posit a consciousness perceiving a single object since all objects are marked with these three qualities to greater or lesser degrees. The reasoning is very similar to those we have seen given earlier against the views of other non-Buddhist opponents. Śāntarakṣita explains this very clearly in the thirty-eighth and thirty-ninth stanzas of *MA* as follows:

> (38) Even according to the position [of the Sāṃkhyas, which claims that the five mere existences] such as sound, etc. are [the nature of the three qualities such as] courage (*sattva, snying stobs*) and the like,[127] a consciousness of the appearance of a unitary object is illogical because objects appear in the nature of the three [qualities].

> (39) Regarding the trifold nature of entities, if the appearance of that [type of entity] is incompatible with a consciousness, which

> is of a single nature, how could it (i.e., the consciousness) be asserted to apprehend that object?[128]

Gyel-tsab echoes this argument in his *Remembering "The Ornament of The Middle Way"*:

> Even according to the Sāṃkhya system, that thesis (i.e., "'a consciousness apprehending only one object could not exist") would be correct because of accepting that the five mere existences – form, sound, and the like which are the nature of the three qualities (*guna, yon tan*): particles (*rajas, rdul*), darkness (*tamas, mun*), and courage (*sattva, snying stobs*) – are objects appearing to the mind. If one says, "There is no pervasion," [then in order to establish the pervasion, we argue that] the subject, a consciousness apprehending those five mere existences, would not apprehend the reality of the object because the five mere existences are in the true nature of the three [qualities]: happiness, suffering, and equanimity, and only one [of the three] objects would appear to it.[129]

Śāntarakṣita continues his line of argumentation from *MA* by addressing a potential response on the part of Sāṃkhya adherents. He supposes that the Sāṃkhya reply would be to argue that since only one of the three qualities of any particular object really dominates, and that since only that dominating quality would be perceived, therefore a single object of a consciousness is still a tenable assertion for holders of Sāṃkhya tenets. Śāntarakṣita answers such an argument by countering that if two of the three qualities of an object are not perceived, then one could not even establish direct experience of such an object. Gyel-tsab maintains this same line of reasoning against a potential Sāṃkhya response in his commentary on the two root text stanzas addressing Sāṃkhyas. He also states that, "the reality of the object" would not be apprehended if two of the three qualities of that object were not perceived. In other words, there would only be a total of three potential objects of perception if only one were perceived in any given object. All objects of perception would be reducible to only one of the three qualities.

The final non-Buddhist school to be addressed by Śāntarakṣita is the Vedānta School (*rigs byed gsang ba'i mthar smra ba*) which, at this time in Indian history, probably refers to Śaṅkara (c. 788-820).[130] He and his teacher, Gaudapāda, were important rivals to Buddhists at this time. As an Indian school positing a form of non-duality (*advaita, gnyis med pa*), and also as active critics of Buddhist thought while remaining the closest to Buddhism doctrinally among non-Buddhist Indian schools, theirs was a position which one would assume Śāntarakṣita needed to take quite seriously. He nonetheless is a bit flippant with his treatment in *MA*, remarking in his autocommentary about the ease with which their position is rejected and how unbelievable it is that someone could actually accept such views. Although Śāntarakṣita agrees with the Vedānta position that the universe is ultimately non-dual and thus there are no distinct external objects, the notion that there is an unchanging consciousness existing in a non-dual relationship with manifold images, and to which manifold images appear, is sharply criticized. Once again, this argument takes place in the context of the neither-one-nor-many argument in which Śāntarakṣita attempts to demonstrate that there are no truly singular consciousnesses as asserted by other tenet holders. His argument is similar in reasoning to those he has used earlier in this text against other opponents. Śāntarakṣita explains this in the fortieth stanza of his root text and accompanying explanation in his *MAV*:

> (40) [Since] they do not even assert the existence of external objects, [Vedāntas ask] why the suitability of maintaining a permanent consciousness, which is said to arise either simultaneously or successively with various appearances, is so difficult [to accept].

> Even with regard to those who maintain such a position, [a unitary consciousness apprehending] various [appearances] is still easy [to refute].A consciousness to which many images such as blue and yellow, etc. simultaneously appear would itself be manifold like the nature of those images because it is not different from the many images....The position of gradual arising also has the same faults.[131]

Gyel-tsab is quite brief in his summation of the argument into a simple inference. This is common to the Geluk treatment of non-Buddhist schools in general:

> That [thesis, "a consciousness apprehending only one object could not exist,"] would hold true, even for the system put forth by the Vedāntas (*rigs byed gsang ba'i mthar smra ba*), because the consciousness to which an assortment of objects appears is gross (i.e., has parts related to the assortment of objects appearing to it).[132]

It seems as though neither Śāntarakṣita nor Gyel-tsab, in his attempt to illuminate Śāntarakṣita's argument, is giving Vedāntins a fair shake. They seem to be conflating ultimate and provisional descriptions of reality in Vedānta. According to the Vedānta of Śaṅkara, while under the influence of *māyā*, a world of multiplicity is said to appear. But, to the ultimate, unchanging consciousness of Brahman, no dualities are said to appear.[133] Mādhyamikas such as Śāntarakṣita may have other valid criticisms of Vedānta, but the treatment here does not seem to deal with a Vedānta position as they might present their own ideas.[134]

Analysis of Mind, Its Objects, and Its Means of Perception As Asserted in Other Buddhist Systems (Cont.)

Further Critiques of Views Maintaining a Unitary Consciousness

Śāntarakṣita swiftly moves from his critique of various non-Buddhist positions which hold a unitary consciousness that cognizes manifold images to a critique of related Buddhist positions. Here he begins with an investigation of a Buddhist opponent asserting a single consciousness which cognizes the three unconditioned (*asaṃskṛta, 'dus ma byed*) phenomena such as space. Śāntarakṣita argues that even when a consciousness cognizes unconditioned objects like space, it still has as its object the sound generality (*śabdasāmānya, sgra spyi)* of the mere name which is composed of conceptual images of individual letters and so, due to the compounded nature of its name, if nothing else, it is still not singular and therefore the consciousness cognizing it is not singular either. Śāntarakṣita outlines his argument in the forty-first *MA* as stanza follows:

> (41) Even for the cognition of [the three non-compounded phenomena such as] space and the like, because of the appearance of many [conceptual images of] letters for the appearance of the mere name, there are many clear appearances.

Gyel-tsab reiterates this point quite clearly in his commentary on Śāntarakṣita's *MA* stanza:

> The subject, an awareness apprehending non-compounded phenomena, would hold images of an assortment of objects because many generalities, [such as] sound generalities of letters, appear to it.[135]

Śāntarakṣita presses further against his opponent[136] in the next two root text stanzas by pointing out the logical inconsistencies which emerge as a consequence of maintaining that there can be some unitary consciousness to which even non-manifold objects such as uncompounded space appear. He argues that even those phenomena which his opponents (such as Sautrāntikas) consider to be uncompounded have parts, such as the generalities of the sounds of letters in the identifying word images of conceptual minds. And since these parts are not completely separate from the object, to say that the object is not manifold contradicts its image's appearance to the mind according to Śāntarakṣita's critique. On the other hand, he argues that to claim that these images do not exist, in an attempt to avoid this philosophical problem, would be to deny the existence of the object since an object is not distinct from the images to which it is related. Śāntarakṣita is arguing here that if there is a consciousness cognizing a truly single object, logical inconsistencies would ensue both with regards to examination of the consciousness and examination of the object. He explains this in the following *MA* stanzas and autocommentary:

> (42) Although there are some who assert consciousnesses to which manifold [images] do not appear, still it is not suitable to establish their existence from the perspective of the ultimate because it has already been shown that there is a logical fallacy [in asserting] the existence [of such] with these characteristics.

> (43) Therefore it is established from all perspectives that consciousness occurs with the appearance of manifold images, and thus like the [many] distinct images [themselves,] cannot logically be of a single nature.

Śāntarakṣita uses fingers and a fist as an example in the autocommentary to illustrate the logical fallacies of attempting to separate parts or images from the compounded objects themselves with regard to epistemological issues concerning a single consciousness cognizing them.[137] This follows Śāntarakṣita's earlier refutation of the non-compounded phenomena asserted by the Vaibhāṣikas and Sautrāntikas, etc. from an ontological perspective. He concludes that even if there were a partless phenomenon, it could not be separated from its images (including the sound generalities of its verbal designation) for the consciousness apprehending it, and thus must be an accumulated or compounded thing after all:

> There are no subtle entities which are not included among the accumulated things. Therefore how does one analyze a mind which is a knower of one object? How is a gathering of mental states the single object of a mind?[138]

Critiquing the Yogācāra Views

Yogācāra Proponents of True Images

Śāntarakṣita proceeds from here to address Yogācāra/Vijñaptivāda/ Cittamātra views of various stripes over the course of the next seventeen *MA* stanzas and accompanying *MAV* explanation.[139] He begins his treatment of Yogācāras by briefly stating a portion of their view and mentioning that there are some problems with it. Śāntarakṣita then, in the forty-fourth *MA* stanza and accompanying autocommentary from *MAV*, writes in the first person, as a Yogācāra expressing his own view.[140] In this way, from the perspective of a Yogācāra, Śāntarakṣita illustrates their view by way of a Yogācāra critique of various Sautrāntika positions. According to Śāntarakṣita and the Yogācāra position he is feigning, the primary problems with holding the Sautrāntika position hinge on their view that there is a separation of the object of experience from the characteristics of the experiencer. In addition, Sautrāntikas misunderstand the role which latent potentialities (*vāsanā, bag chags*) play in our experience. It is explained as follows in *MA* and its related autocommentary:

> (44) Images are manifest due to the ripening of latent potentialities of a beginningless [personal] continuum. Although they appear, since it is the result of a mistake, they are like the nature of an illusion.

> … Even these images appearing to the consciousness which you assert to be truly existent, appear [to the consciousness] by the power of thoroughly ripened latent potentialities arisen as a result of exaggerated grasping at entities since beginningless existence.[141]

Śāntarakṣita explains the Yogācāra view by means of their criticism of Sautrāntikas in his autocommentary before and after the forty-fourth stanza. This critique contends that a knower must by definition not be separate from the object known or there would be no difference between that and the cognizing of an apparition. Yogācāras deny a total separation of knower and known. Gyel-tsab summarizes Śāntarakṣita's expression of the Yogācāra viewpoint below in much the same manner as, although in a far more abbreviated fashion than, Śāntarakṣita in his *MAV*:

> Although from beginningless time the appearances of objects which are produced by manifestations resulting from the ripening of latent potentialities (*vāsanā, bag chags*) appear as objects which have come forth, they are said to be like the nature of magical illusions appearing as objects while there are no objects.[142]

The first half of the next stanza and corresponding commentary begins by praising aspects of the Yogācāra view which share many commonalities with Śāntarakṣita's own Madhyamaka standpoint. Of course both put forth Mahāyāna philosophical positions, but Śāntarakṣita, although he is technically classified as a Mādhyamika, has such a strong affinity for the Yogācāra position of rejecting external objects that it is integrated into his own explanation of conventional truth later in the text. I have chosen in this section on Yogācāra to include particularly extensive quotations from Śāntarakṣita's *MAV* for two reasons. First, as I stated at the beginning of this chapter, the text has never been translated into a Western language. Thus, these quotes offer a first glimpse into Śāntarakṣita's own line of presentation and argument on these issues. Second, these passages are also of particular note here because Śāntarakṣita goes into extensive detail in *MAV* on the Yogācāra view, a position so critical to his Mahāyāna syncretism. In fact, this section becomes the foundation for his Yogācāra-Madhyamaka synthesis later in the text. We should take note that he now shifts to speaking from the perspective of his own actual Madhyamaka voice. Thus he begins here with his praise of the Yogācāra view and some questions regarding specific issues:

> (45) Although their view (i.e., the Yogācāra view) is virtuous, we should think about whether such things [as the images known by consciousness accepted by Yogācāras] actually exist or if they are something contentedly accepted only when left unanalyzed.

Since this (i.e., Yogācāra) system is known by means of valid knowledge (*pramāṇa, tshad ma*) and very clear scriptures and since it is also an antidote to the endless, negative, exaggerated grasping of sentient beings, it should be considered as very pure. Likewise, [this system is virtuous] because it rejects the existence of subtle [partless] particles and, with the valid knowledge previously explained, shows the contradictions [with regards to the Sautrāntika position which distinguishes between the] characteristics of the experiencer and the object of experience. [In addition], this system is very clear and is also backed up by scriptural quotations.

[For example], the *Laṅkāvatārasūtra* states, "Since the beginningless mind is infused [with karma and ignorance], even though images of objects appear like a mirror reflection, the mind still does not see objects exactly as they are. Persons, causes, the aggregates, conditions, particles, and Īśvara are all merely designations imputed onto images by the mere mind. There are no existent objects [other than] the mind itself. Seeing external objects is mistaken. If analyzed with logic, [substantially distinct] objects and apprehenders [of objects] will be refuted."

By relying on this system, scholars remove the impurities of erroneous divisive concepts such as "I" and "mine" and "object" and "apprehender [of objects"]. However there is still a small issue which needs to be investigated with regard to this system: are these images [of consciousness] real, or will they only be comfortable to accept when left unanalyzed, like a mirror reflection. [143]

As he comments on the first part of the root text stanza, Śāntarakṣita praises Yogācāras for their skill in exposing many of the faults of the other Buddhist schools both with scriptural quotations, like the one cited from the *Laṅkāvatārasūtra,* and with logical reasoning. While there is no doubt that Śāntarakṣita is sincere in his praise, Geluk commentators have added that this too may be a skillful way of drawing in Yogācāras to read further. This is because Śāntarakṣita later goes on to question some of the faults which he feels also exist in their system. Yogācāras were probably seen by Śāntarakṣita as the most likely converts to his view since there are so many parallels between their systems of thought and his own. Historically, they were also the primary philosophical rivals of Mādhyamikas in the great monastic institutions of India at that time.

The question Śāntarakṣita raises in the forty-fifth stanza of *MA* concerns a general problem he feels may be present in Yogācāra thought. Śāntarakṣita does this before going on to address the particular tenets of the various subdivisions of Yogācāra. According to Madhyamaka analysis, Yogācāras hold that consciousness is truly single and exists in a non-dual relationship with its objects. In other words, the images of an object known by the consciousness are not different entities from the consciousness itself. Yet if there are multiple images, how can consciousness, knowing this multiplicity of objects, be truly singular? According to Śāntarakṣita, the first question that needs to be raised concerns the ontological status of those images. That is, are they real or not? Either response produces problems for Yogācāras according to Śāntarakṣita, who proceeds to examine the claims of several distinct sub-schools of Yogācāra thought that propose distinct solutions to the problem. Gyel-tsab's commentary on this *MA* stanza, which is written in the form of a question, leads specifically into the examination of the division of Yogācāra into Proponents of True Images, and their subdivisions, and Proponents of False Images . However, Gyel-tsab enters the inquiry directly by questioning not the truth or falsity of images but the truth or falsity of consciousness itself:

> Although that view is good and virtuous in that it dispels many of the bad adherences of the Sautrāntika and [other] lower schools, however, is that non-dual consciousness, which it is comfortable to accept as singular when unexamined, true or is it false?[144]

As he turns his attention to various Yogācāra stances on the question of the status of images of consciousness, Śāntarakṣita does so in the context of his general critique of opponents and through examination of epistemological issues viewed through the lens of the neither-one-nor-many argument. Śāntarakṣita begins with those Yogācāras who accept images or aspects (*ākāra, rnam pa*) as true. According to Gyel-tsab's general outline of topics on the examination of Yogācāra tenets, this first topic is the examination of the Proponents of True Images. This he divides into three sub-schools, the first of which is the Half-Eggist.

Neither Śāntarakṣita not Kamalaśīla uses names to designate the three supposed sub-schools of Yogācāra thought. The names used here are attested to in later Geluk tenet system texts; thus we find here some of the earliest Geluk delineations of them. This is not meant to suggest that the views Śāntarakṣita addresses do not correspond with those under the names of the sub-schools Gyel-tsab outlines. This is only intended to point out to the reader an instance of how Geluk doxographical categories and framework get overlaid onto the commentary of a specific Indian text.

The first subtopic within this examination of those whom Gyel-tsab labels as the Yogācāra Half-Eggist is the positing of an *absurdum*. The *absurdum* deals with the problems arising for Half-Eggist Yogācāras who both hold multiple images to be truly existent and a single consciousness to be truly existent, and moreover attempt to maintain some sort of ultimate non-duality between the two despite the contradictions in their mode of existence. Śāntarakṣita will argue that Yogācāras holding images to be true must conclude that consciousness and images are separate, and that it is logically untenable for them to exist in some non-dual way. If they are of one non-dual nature, then if there are many images, the nature of the consciousness must be many. Conversely, if the nature of the consciousness is single, then the many true images must be of a single nature due to their relationship with a single consciousness. Both conclusions being illogical,[145] the only alternative is to argue that they are separate (i.e., not non-dual), which contradicts the entire Yogācāra epistemological as well as ontological framework. He explains this quite clearly in the forty-sixth *MA* verse and accompanying autocommentary:

> (46) Since contradictions would ensue for those unitary [images] *even if* the actual consciousness is manifold, [consciousness and images] are undoubtedly distinct entities.

> Since if [consciousness] is not different from actual images, then as with the nature of these [many] images, consciousness must be manifold. Or on the other hand, if these images are not different from a singular consciousness, the proposition that their [i.e., the many images] nature is one [and the same] like the nature of that consciousness would be difficult to oppose. Since contradictions remain [either way], ultimately images and consciousness must themselves be different.[146]

Since consciousness is held to be single and truly existent, and since images of objects are clearly manifold (because there are many of them), there is an incompatibility problem for the Yogācāra Half-Eggists who want to claim that such a single consciousness is of the same nature in a non-dual relationship with the many images of its objects. The argument is similar to that which critiques the corresponding Sautrāntikas except that, rather than the fault being that a singular consciousness is simply related with a multiplicity of images, here it is actually asserted to be in a *non-dual* relationship with those images. Gyel-tsab clearly sums up this argument with similar reasoning. He succinctly outlines the contradictions which arise with either of the two alternatives: maintaining a singular consciousness or a manifold consciousness with regard to its non-duality with truly existing images:

> [If there exists a truly existing consciousness which is non-dual with the images of objects it perceives], that consciousness would have to be [the nature of] many, because it is truly one with many images. Otherwise the images would be truly singular because they are truly substantially one with the [truly singular] consciousness. If you say, "There is no pervasion," then those two would be separate substances because the images are truly many and the consciousness is [truly] singular.[147]

Śāntarakṣita continues to address his Yogācāra opponent who maintains that a truly singular consciousness can exist in a substantially non-dual relationship with the multiplicity of images of objects it perceives (the opponent Gyel-tsab calls "Half-Eggist") in the forty-seventh stanza of the *MA*. Here Śāntarakṣita utilizes arguments demonstrating absurd consequences (*prasaṅga, thal gyur*) which he argues directly follow from the position these Yogācāras are trying to maintain. The argument centers on the position that both images and consciousness are asserted to be truly existent and have a non-dual relationship. This is despite the fact that the images of a cognizing consciousness could be numerous according to the Yogācāra Half-Eggists, whereas the consciousness is singular and unitary.

He gives examples to demonstrate the absurdity of maintaining a non-dual relationship between a truly singular consciousness and truly manifold images. The example mentioned in the forty-seventh *MA* stanza below concerns the images of an object of which part is moving and part is at rest. If a tree, for example, were in a non-dual relationship with a singular consciousness, it would necessarily be single. However, a consciousness can perceive the tree's branch as moving while its trunk is at rest. That being the case, the tree must have parts (the part that is moving and the part at rest) and if they are knowable simultaneously by the consciousness, the consciousness must not be singular. This is another way of emphasizing the incompatibility of a truly singular consciousness cognizing a multiplicity of true images with which it is in a non-dual relationship. In other words, all the images of an object in a non-dual relationship with a single consciousness must be single and of the same single nature as the consciousness. If this were not the case, the consciousness itself would not be single. Thus if one part of a tree is moving, the entire tree must be moving and if one part of the conscious image of a painting is yellow, it all must be yellow:

> (47) If images are not different from [the singular consciousness], then it will be very difficult to respond to the following consequence: that with regard to moving and rest and the like, due to the movement of one, all would move.
>
>> Yet their teaching says that they are not different, that they are of that [single] nature. If that is the case, then if one image is engaged in the action of moving, etc., or if one is the nature of yellow, etc. then all [related] remaining images will also be like that. If that is not the case, then they must definitely be of various natures (i.e., not one).[148]

Gyel-tsab and Śāntarakṣita explain this verse in an almost identical manner:

> When we see the movement of one object, all would move, and when one is yellow, all would be yellow because all images are one.[149]

Śāntarakṣita moves from here to an attempt at rejecting the position of the previously mentioned Sautrāntika opponent. Such Sautrāntikas hold views which are quite similar to the Yogācāras just examined (the so-called Yogācāra Half-Eggists) except that they claim objects to be external from consciousness. They also claim that a truly singular consciousness knows many images of objects. Śāntarakṣita argues that they would be unable to avoid the same faults as those Yogācāras who do not accept external objects:

> (48) Even according to the system of those maintaining external objects, if images are not separate [from each other], then they would all also certainly be engaged as a single phenomenon and not other than that.

Here Śāntarakṣita argues that even if objects are external to the consciousness and do not fall into the fallacy of having the same nature as a singular consciousness (as the Yogācāras do), there is still a problem with holding images as truly existent. If images were to truly exist, and if those images are not separate from each other, then since they are also truly single, they must all be one and engaged as such. This is because the truly single images would be related to each other and truly singular things cannot be related to something from which they are different. For example, if one were yellow, all would have to be yellow. If one part were moving, the whole would have to be moving. A truly single consciousness could not engage a gross object composed of many distinct images. And a gross object could not be observed via the accumulation of many different and singular images which are related with one another.[150]

Śāntarakṣita proceeds to another proponent of Yogācāra tenets who attempts to solve this logical dilemma as his hypothetical Sautrāntika opponents did earlier. Śāntarakṣita does not label the present view as a specific sub-school of Yogācāra. But Gyel-tsab does label them in correspondence with the way this view would later be treated in Geluk tenet system literature, namely as the view of the Proponents of an Equal Number of Subjects and Objects (*gzung 'dzin grangs mnyam pa*). Like the Sautrāntikas before, in order to avoid this problem of a truly single consciousness cognizing a multiplicity of images, these Yogācāras assert that there are an equal number of consciousnesses as images. Thereby, they avoid the fallacy of a truly singular consciousness being in a non-dual relationship with a multiplicity of images. There is a one-to-one relationship between consciousnesses and images. Here Śāntarakṣita maintains that the argument refuting such a position would in fact be quite similar to the argument criticizing the true existence of single, partless particles. The *MA* verse makes this point before Śāntarakṣita elaborates in his autocommentary:

> (49) If you accept an equal number of consciousnesses and images, then it would be difficult to overcome the same type of analysis as is made regarding particles.
>
> If, like the nature of subtle particles which abide [around a central particle] without intervals, there also arise many corresponding consciousnesses, then like the earlier analysis of subtle particles, it would also be difficult to overcome that criticism with regard to consciousness.
>
> As with this [particle], if we were to [hypothetically] claim that the consciousness is asserted to be [like the particle] in the center surrounded by [other] particles, then what is the nature of that [central consciousness] which is in front of one [image] and also in front of another?[151]

As Śāntarakṣita states, the line of argumentation here takes a parallel line of reasoning with that against partless particles. If a consciousness is conscious of only one image and is truly singular, then the question would arise as to what the relationship is between the consciousness of the central image and the other consciousnesses of other images surrounding it. If there is a relationship with the other consciousnesses of other images, then it is not truly single. Or, if it is truly single, then the other consciousnesses of other images must not be of another nature but actually of the same nature. This is contrary to their position.

Śāntarakṣita then proceeds to a critique of the next variety of Yogācāra interpreters in the fiftieth and fifty-first stanzas of the *MA*. Gyel-tsab labels this opponent as Non-Pluralist. The opponent addressed here maintains that a variety of different images can all exist with the same nature as the singular consciousness. Here Śāntarakṣita compares the faults of these Buddhists with those of non-Buddhists such as Jains. In *JBy*, Gyel-tsab comments on the following two *MA* stanzas together in the process of explaining Śāntarakṣita's critique:

> (50) If one [consciousness experiences] a variety [of images], wouldn't that be like the system of the [Jain] Sky Clad (*Digambara*)? A variety [of images] is not the nature of singularity just as manifold precious [gems] and the like [are not the nature of singularity].
>
> (51) If the variety [of images] exists in a single nature, how could they appear in the nature of many, and how could parts such as those being obstructed and those which are unobstructed, etc. be distinguished?

Gyel-tsab's explanation begins by restating the Non-Pluralist position and then comparing it, not only to the Jains (*Nirgranthas*, *gcer bu pa*)[152] as Śāntarakṣita does[153], but also to the Vedāntists. He explains that it would be logically untenable for numerous images together to be of the same nature as a single consciousness. This is because if numerous images appear to a single consciousness, either the consciousness is not truly singular or these different images could not actually be distinguishable since they would be of a single nature. Gyel-tsab writes:

> If one asserts that a variety of images would be truly in the nature of a singular consciousness [as the Non-Pluralists assert, it would be] like the system of theVedāntas and the Nirgranthas. If that truly singular consciousness to which various objects appear is asserted, then there is a pervasion, because if various images appear [to it, it] would not be truly singular, like a heap of a variety of precious [gems]. There is also the appearance of various images to the consciousness. If you accept the singularity of images, then it would be impossible for many different images to appear, such as "visible" and "invisible," etc. and images of various sorts such as blue and yellow, etc., because the various images are truly singular.[154]

Gyel-tsab echoes Śāntarakṣita's argument by pointing out that if the so-called Non-Pluralists wish to maintain, as they must, that the variety of images and the consciousnesses perceiving them are truly singular, then all the images perceived must have the same nature as the perceiving consciousness. Therefore, all the many images of an object must have the same nature since they all are singular and of one nature with the consciousness. For example, one object cannot be the nature of blue while another has the nature of yellow because that would require a perceiving consciousness with a manifold, not single, nature because it has parts (i.e., the part conscious of blue and the part conscious of yellow). Therefore such a position entails internal contradictions.

Yogācāra Proponents of False Images

Having completed his refutation of the three variations of what Gyel-tsab calls Yogācāra Proponents of True Images, Śāntarakṣita continues arguments against Yogācāra views with his criticism of the so-called Yogācāra Proponents of False Images (*Yogācāra-alīkākāravāda, nal 'byor spyod pa'i rnam brdzun pa*). Once again, this is the name Gyel-tsab gives to the positions and not a designation Śāntarakṣita himself uses. This topic is divided into two subtopics according to Gyel-tsab: first, putting forth their assertions and then, refuting them. In the following stanza from *MA*, Śāntarakṣita explains their assertions:

> (52) Some say that [consciousness] does not naturally possess images of these [objects]. In reality, images do not exist but appear to the consciousness by virtue of a mistake.

Gyel-tsab sums up this view by saying that the Proponents of False Images claim not to have the faults ascribed to the Proponents of True Images because, rather than holding images to be truly existent and singular, the Proponents of False Images hold that images merely appear without actually existing in reality. According to Śāntarakṣita's *MAV,* they claim that, "consciousness is ultimately clear like a crystal,"[155] and that, "images appear due to the ripening of mistaken imprints since beginningless time."[156] Śāntarakṣita then proceeds into the first of a series of eight *absurdums* used to demonstrate what he considers to be the faults of this view. This first *absurdum* raises epistemological questions about the viability of clearly experiencing objects if there are no actual images or aspects:

> (53) If [images] do not exist, how can consciousness clearly experience those [objects]? That [clear, non-dual consciousness] is not like a consciousness which is distinct from the entities, [and those entities must possess images which appear to it].

This first *absurdum* aims to demonstrate the fallacies in the assertions of Yogācāras who claim images are not real. It does so by claiming that according to their view, the *absurdum* would follow that they would not be able to clearly experience objects or entities. Consciousness is not distinct from entities, according to Yogācāras, and entities are experienced as inseparable from their images or aspects. Therefore the deluded experience of images would always be present with any moment of consciousness of entities. Thus, there can be no clear experience of objects which is not accompanied by the deluded experience of the images or aspects of that entity. The experience of entities would always be clouded by the faulty experience of images which do not actually exist. Proponents of False Images maintain that there are no real images and thus their view entails the *absurdum* that all perceptions of entities inseparable from images must necessarily be deluded. This is because although consciousness does not actually perceive the images, it thinks it does.

The second *absurdum*, the incorrectness of experiencing images at all, argues in a similar vein as the first. Consciousness could not correctly experience images at all because there are no actual images. Śāntarakṣita argues that just as there is no real white experienced in non-white, there can be no correct experience of images when there are no images. One would not be able, for example, to experience the blueness of a blue chair in the experience of such an object without images. This is absurd according to Śāntarakṣita. The *MA* stanza explains as follows:

> (54) Likewise, that [image, such as yellow,] will not be known as that [yellow image] by anyone if entities are without [yellow images]. Likewise bliss is not experienced in suffering and non-white is not seen in white.

Gyel-tsab reiterates the argument, with similar language, to make the point that it would be absurd for there to be a correct experience of the aspects or images of an entity if the aspects do not actually exist. In other words, if the image of the blueness of a blue chair does not actually exist, one could not correctly perceive that blueness, and that would be absurd according to Śāntarakṣita.

Śāntarakṣita then proceeds to the third *absurdum,* which Gyel-tsab labels as "[the *absurdum* showing] the incorrectness of direct experience."[157] Here he argues on the basis of direct experience in order to demonstrate another example of the fallacies entailed by maintaining the mainline Yogācāra position which argues that images or aspects are ultimately false or unreal. He argues that because Yogācāras maintain direct knowledge of objects is possible, and since objects are considered to be of the same nature as consciousness, the claim for the unreality of images must in fact be faulty. This is the case because images do not actually exist in their view and so they must not be of the same substance as the consciousness, which is real. Since direct knowledge for Yogācāras consists of objects which are not separate from consciousness itself, and yet the images of those objects are not real and thus are distinct from consciousness, it would not be correct to even describe the perception of these faulty images as "knowledge." Since being one substance with consciousness is a prerequisite for direct knowledge, there must be no direct knowledge of images. Therefore, rather than direct experience, these Proponents of False Images (as Gyel-tsab calls them) are left only with illusions and the *absurdum* demonstrating the incorrectness of direct experience. This is so because, despite the fact that they claim images do not exist, they would also claim that images are known directly. If images are mere illusions, like flowers in the sky, direct perception of them, of something which does not actually exist, would be absurd. This is particularly true given that Yogācāras maintain direct perception based on the fact that consciousness and objects are of the same nature. Śāntarakṣita expresses this succinctly in the following manner in the fifty-fifth root text stanza:

> (55) With regard to images, "knowledge" (*shes pa*) is not actually the correct term because [the image] is distinct from consciousness itself (*shes pa'i bdag*), like flowers [growing] in the sky, etc.

Gyel-tsab attempts to clarify this argument by reorganizing the tri-modal inference:

> Images, the subject, would not be correctly experienced directly because they are not of the [same] substance as consciousness, like flowers [growing] in the sky.[158]

The fourth *absurdum* Śāntarakṣita uses to refute Yogācāras who assert the unreality of images is what Gyel-tsab calls "[the *absurdum* demonstrating] the incorrectness of experience having examined [the image]."[159] This is meant to demonstrate that because images are false and do not actually exist, it is absurd to maintain that the image would have the causal efficacy necessary for it "to produce itself as an image known to consciousness."[160] Śāntarakṣita explains this *absurdum* in the following manner in the fifty-sixth stanza of *MA:*

> (56) [Consciousness] is incapable of experiencing [images] even when they are examined because non-existent [images] have no [causal] ability, like the horn of a horse. [To assert that] a non-existent [image] has the ability to [cause the] generation of an appearing consciousness of itself is irrational.

Gyel-tsab remains extremely close to Śāntarakṣita in his rendering of this argument:

> The subject, consciousness, would be incorrect in its experience of the image, having examined it, because the image does not have the ability to produce itself as an image known to consciousness, for example like an impotent horse.[161] There is a pervasion, because if it does not exist in reality, it (i.e., the image) would not have the ability to produce the consciousness to which it appears.[162]

Gyel-tsab goes on at this point in his commentary to make an argument, which is tangential to the topic, regarding the proximity of partless particles in various directions to a singular consciousness. Gyel-tsab argues that if a particle in the east appears farther from the consciousness than one in the west, then if they both have the same nature, the one in the west should also appear farther. This of course would contradict direct perception. This argument against a single consciousness knowing many truly singular particles, while in line with Śāntarakṣita's thinking in arguing against

Vaibhāṣikas, is out of place in the context of the *absurdums* he is presenting here against Yogācāras who describe images as unreal. One is drawn to wonder whether this was mistakenly inserted at this point in the text as a result of a printing error, since it seems to be so clearly outside the context of Gyel-tsab's topic (i.e., the eight *absurdums*) according to his own outline.

The fifth *absurdum* used to demonstrate the incorrectness of the so-called Yogācāra Proponents of False Images deals with the relationship between images and the consciousness. Śāntarakṣita ought to be considered part of the *pramāṇavāda* tradition of Dharmakīrti et al., who explained that there are only two possible relationships between related objects: causal relationships and relationships of identity. For a Yogācāra who denies the reality of images, it would be absurd for images and consciousness to have either of these two types of relationships, yet they are asserted nonetheless to be related according to this system. They cannot have a causal relationship, because if images do not actually exist, they cannot, by definition, have any causal efficacy. And images and consciousness cannot have a relationship of identity because, according to the Proponents of False Images, consciousness has a real nature while images do not. Śāntarakṣita explains this in the fifty-seventh *MA* stanza and related autocommentary:

> (57) What reason is there which would account for a relationship between those [images] which are definitely experienced and consciousness? It is not the nature of that which does not exist and does not arise from it.
>
> Images are not the nature of consciousness because, if so, they would have the fault of existence, like consciousness, or [consciousness] would have the fault of non-existence, like images. The nature of non-existence also does not arise from consciousness.[163]

Gyel-tsab summarizes the crux of Śāntarakṣita's argument here very succinctly in his commentary:

> When the consciousness is experienced, it would be incorrect to experience various images, because there is no relationship between

> consciousness and images. That is so because there is no causal relationship or relationship of identity.[164]

Śāntarakṣita thus proceeds to the sixth *absurdum,* which Gyel-tsab calls "[the *absurdum*] of the incorrectness of being occasionally arisen."[165] Here Śāntarakṣita questions Yogācāras who assert the unreality of images on the basis of the occasional or periodic arising of images. Since images are not real, they should not have a cause for their arising. And if they do not depend on causes, it does not make sense that they would arise only occasionally or be impermanent. Normally in Buddhist thought, if something has no cause, it is argued that is must either permanently exist or permanently not exist. This is because the existence or non-existence of an entity depends on the causes of its arising. But images in this case must rise and disintegrate without causes since they do not actually exist. And absurdly, they are experienced to do so in a timely manner corresponding with the objects with which they are related. Śāntarakṣita argues this point against his Yogācāra opponents in the fifty-eighth stanza of the *MA* and its accompanying autocommentary in *MAV*:

> (58) If there were no cause [for images], how is it suitable that they arise only on occasion? If they have a cause, how could they not have an other-dependent nature (*paratantra-svabhāva, gzhan gi dbang gi ngo bo*)?
>
> > Because images do not really exist, there is no real cause. If there is no cause, there should be no periodic arising because there is no reliance [on causes for arising]. Such faults are said to occur [due to holding this view]. If you accept that [images] possess causes, then according to that you must immediately accept [images] as existent. If there is no [cause], then there would be no arising [of images] from other powers. How would you be able to respond to this? Arising from other powers is nothing other than dependent origination. Existence due to the nature of arising from conditions also is not other than this.[166]

The fifty-ninth stanza of Śāntarakṣita's *MA* deals with what Gyel-tsab calls "the *absurdum* of being a mere subjective image (*'dzin rnam, grāhaka-ākāra*)." Here the *absurdum*, as outlined in Śāntarakṣita's *MA,* maintains that if images do not exist and yet objects are perceived by means of images, then since there could not exist a consciousness connected with images (being that images do not exist), consciousness could not experience objects either. This is because objects are never experienced without images, and thus consciousness would merely be self-consciousness without an object.

> (59) If [images] do not exist, then consciousness [with images] also [would not exist] due to the non-existence of the images. Consciousness then, like a clear, round crystal, would not really experience [objects].

Gyel-tsab adds that consciousness would only experience itself since it would be impossible to experience objects without experiencing their images or aspects. He also illustrates the analogy with the metaphor of a clear crystal. His commentarial inference reads as follows:

> If someone claims that there are no images of apprehended objects, then the subject, consciousness, would merely consist of images of the apprehending subject (i.e., its own self-cognition) due to being a consciousness without images of objects (*gzung rnam*). If you accept this, then for apprehension which is like a clear, round crystal which is void of the images of the object, there would be no image for the apprehender because [images] are not perceived although they should be perceived.[167]

The eighth and final *absurdum* used to refute the so-called Yogācāra Proponents of False Images is referred to by Gyel-tsab as "the *absurdum* of being a dependent entity." Here Śāntarakṣita argues that even if the perception or consciousness of images is erroneous, it still must arise in dependence on others even if that which it depends on is an illusion. Yogācāras thus must concede that this would fall into the category among the three natures (*trisvābhava, ngo bo nyid gsum*) of the other-dependent nature. And if this is the case, then they must be real according to Yogācāras since Yogācāras claim other-dependent natures are real. This point is illustrated very clearly by Śāntarakṣita in the sixtieth *MA* stanza:

> (60) If they say that this [eye consciousness which sees a mirage] is known as such as a result of a mistake, then why does it rely on mistakes? Even if it arisesby the [power of delusion], still then that [consciousness of a mirage is] dependent on the power of others.

Gyel-tsab also echoes this point as he comments on Śāntarakṣita's sixtieth stanza by showing how, even if in reality there are no images, that since they are perceived, they still must be dependently-arisen. And dependent phenomena are real functional entities according to Yogācāras.

> If one says that, although in reality there are no [images of] objects, images appear due to a mistake, then the subject, images, would be other-dependent because they depend on a mistake. This is the case because they (i.e., the images) arise from the force of a mistake.[168]

Wrapping Up the Neither-One-Nor-Many Argument: Demonstrating That Phenomena Lack a Manifold Nature

The above refutation of the Yogācāras concludes the arguments directed against specific opponents in the first major section of the text. In accordance with the general statement of the neither-one-nor-many argument made in the first stanza of *MA*, up to this point in the text Śāntarakṣita has extensively examined the entities asserted to be real by competing Buddhist and non-Buddhist schools with regard to a real singular nature. He has argued with inferential reasoning that none of their positions are coherent, as was part of the claim in the first stanza:

> (1) Those entities, as asserted by our own [Buddhist schools] and other [non-Buddhist] schools, have no inherent nature at all because in reality they have neither a singular nor a manifold nature – like a reflected image.

He considers that he has established the first half of the first criterion for establishing the argument in his initial neither-one-nor-many reasoning as valid since he has established that the subject has the property of the reason (*pakṣadharma, phyogs chos*) with regard to singular natures. In each individual case of examining entities asserted by his Buddhist and non-Buddhist opponents to have a truly single nature, Śāntarakṣita has established that the first part of the reason (*liṅga, rtags*), the lack of a single nature, is a property of the subject. In other words, he has demonstrated that none of the entities asserted by his opponents has a truly single nature. He still needs to establish that the second part of the reason, the lack of a manifold nature, is a property of the subject. This task is taken up in a single stanza in the *MA*, but Śāntarakṣita explains its meaning extensively in his *MAV*. The first *MA* stanza to address the issue of entities possessing a nature which is truly many is the sixty-first:

> (61) When analyzing any entity, [we find] that there are none which are truly single. For those for which there is nothing which is truly single, there must also be nothing which is [truly] manifold.[169]

Śāntarakṣita argues that on the basis of establishing that there are no entities of a truly singular nature one must also accept that there are no entities which could be validly established as having a manifold nature, since a manifold nature would depend on the accumulation of singular natures. In other words, if there are no singular natures, as Śāntarakṣita went to great lengths to establish by individually addressing the relevant positions of all the major doctrinal opponents of his day, then there cannot be an accumulation of singular natures (which is seen by Śāntarakṣita to be the necessary condition for an entity with a nature which is truly many). Śāntarakṣita explains this quite clearly in his *MAV*:

> When permanence and impermanence, pervasiveness and singularity, [partless] particles and gross objects, and consciousness, etc., accepted by followers of Buddhist and non-Buddhist views, are distinctly analyzed as to their singularity, there is no amount of perseverance which can endure the heavy burden of such [critical] analysis. Since it would be incorrect to consider anything as being of a single nature, accepting a manifold nature must also be unreasonable because many-ness is characterized by the accumulation of singularities. If there is nothing which is single, there must also be nothing [which is the accumulation of singularities]. It is like if there are no trees and so forth, there also will be no for-

> est. Therefore it says [in Āryadeva's *Catuḥśataka*],[170] "When we analyze any phenomena, there is nothing [found] which is truly single. For those for which no singular nature exists, no [manifold nature] exists either."[171]

Śāntarakṣita strengthens his point when commenting on this by adding supportive quotations from *sūtras* including, most prominently, the *Laṅkāvatārasūtra*. By means of quoting from an authoritative source, his argument is thus defended by both reason and scriptures. This is an important quality of a thorough Buddhist argument, as Śāntarakṣita argues early in the *MAV*.[172] Tsong Khapa also discusses this strategy extensively in *ZBr*.[173] Based on the above refutation of any truly manifold nature, the criterion of the subject having the property of the reason with regards to either a single or manifold nature is considered to be established. This is the first of the three formal criteria (*tshul gsum*) (along with the forward and counter pervasions) for establishing the validity of the argument. The subject has the property of the reason because it has been established that all instances of the subject, entities asserted by his Buddhist and non-Buddhist opponents to have a true nature, are instances of entities which have neither a singular nor a manifold nature, the reason.

Śāntarakṣita then goes on to give a brief explanation of the example (*dṛṣṭānta*, *dpe*) – that entities have no nature like a reflected image. He explains that the erroneous assessment of entities as having a truly existent nature is similar to the way we cognize a mirage of water in the desert due to the intense rays of the sun on a dry surface. Although there is a cause for cognizing in this way, it is not correct to say that the conclusion which we tend to draw, that there is water, is correct.[174] Similarly, it is not correct to draw the conclusion that objects which appear to us to have a truly established nature actually do. They are also like the images of objects in mirrors: they do not actually exist in the way that they appear to exist.

After this, he also extols the value of studying the "lower" philosophical systems. Looking back on his extensive argument, Śāntarakṣita writes that, "having investigated all those systems, it would be incorrect to completely discard them."[175] Śāntarakṣita's statement here is echoed both theoretically and in practice within the Geluk School. There is a functional and practical purpose to the study of the "lower" Buddhist schools which is soteriological in nature, according to Śāntarakṣita, despite their errors. The study of the lower systems progressively ripens the disciple's mind for ascent to understanding the highest view, a necessary requisite for the attainment of Buddhahood. Of course, Śāntarakṣita and Geluk scholars would differ as to what the highest view is, but their insistence on studying and understanding what they consider to be the "lower" Buddhist philosophical systems remains the same. For Śāntarakṣita, it seems as though the movement up the philosophical ladder, in which each "lower" school is evaluated from the perspective of the school he considers to be slightly more subtle, becomes a part of the dynamic philosophical process described in the Introduction, in which the student is encouraged (provisionally) to take on a succession of views in the ascent to the highest. Within the Geluk tradition this is but a part of the larger inclusiveness of Tsong Khapa's vision, where all the Buddha's teachings are incorporated into an internally coherent system, including not only a variety of practices, as in the *lam rim* literature, but also the spectrum of philosophical views. In this sense, Gelukpas incorporate views they consider to be less subtle than their own in their larger philosophical projects. In another sense we can say that Śāntarakṣita is a Mādhyamika, but part of coming to a Madhyamaka understanding is this soteriologically informed movement up through "lower" tenet systems. Geluk philosophical study operates in a similar way.

Establishing the Pervasion: Entities Have No Nature At All

Returning to the arguments at hand, in the following *MA* stanza Śāntarakṣita addresses what Gyel-tsab describes in his initial outline of topics for this text as the establishment of the pervasion. The establishment of the pervasion is one of the criteria by which the validity of a logical argument is insured. Having established the first criterion, that the subject is the property of the reason, the establishment of the pervasion remains. Formally, this refers to the notion that the predicate of the argument is pervaded by the reason. This is traditionally divided into two: the forward pervasion and the counter pervasion. The forward pervasion would be present if all instances of the reason are instances of the predicate. In the case of the neither-one-nor–many argument, this criteron would be present if all phenomena which have neither a singular nor a manifold nature (the reason) are instances of phenomena which have no nature at all (the predicate). The counter-pervasion holds if there are no instances of the predicate which are not instances of the reason. In the case of the neither-one-nor-many argument, this would hold if there are no instances of phenomena which have no nature which are not also instances of phenomena which have neither a singular nor a manifold nature. These two aspects of the establishment of the pervasion are the second and third criteria (the first being that the subject is a property of the reason) in the establishment of a valid argument. Thus, when Gyel-tsab refers to establishing the pervasion, he refers to the initial inferential statement of the neither-one-nor-many argument in the very first stanza of *MA,* which has been extensively explained in the subsequent sixty stanzas. This establishment of the pervasion of the argument is accomplished, and all potential philosophical holes in his argument are closed, according to Śāntarakṣita, in this sixty-second stanza and the accompanying commentary:

> (62) The existence of an entity belonging to a class other than that which has a single or a manifold [nature] does not make sense because the two are exhaustive of all possible alternatives.
>
> > Since a single nature and a plural nature are characterized as being exhaustive of all possible alternatives and mutually exclusive, any other alternative is cleared away.[176]

Śāntarakṣita establishes the pervasion of the neither-one-nor-many argument, after refuting a true singular nature and a true manifold nature, by arguing that if an entity has neither of those two types of nature, it necessarily must not have any nature at all. This is the case because the two alternatives are mutually exclusive and include all possible alternatives for the way a truly existent nature could exist. Gyel-tsab mirrors Śāntarakṣita's reasoning here as he comments on this stanza and on the establishment of the pervasion. Gyel-tsab explains the pervasion of the argument in the following manner:

> If the true existence of one and the true existence of many are not established, then there must be no true existence because there are no entities [with a truly existent nature] that belong [neither] to the class of [entities with a] unitary [nature] nor with a manifold [nature]. That would be the case because it would be contradictory for there to be entities which rely on [a class other than] those of one and many, which are inclusive of all possibilities.[177]

With the establishment of the pervasion Śāntarakṣita completes the largest portion of the text, the neither-one-nor-many argument, which comprises sixty-two stanzas of the ninety-seven stanza text and represents the most well known exposition of the argument within the Buddhist canon.

Examination of Conventional Truths

Utilizing the same commentarial sources and basic methods employed to examine the neither-one-nor-many argument in the first sixty-two stanzas, this section of Part II follows the remainder of Śāntarakṣita's *MA,* stanza-by-stanza, in a continuing attempt at presenting a narrative account of the claims and arguments made in Śāntarakṣita's critical text. In the final thirty-five stanzas of the root text and accompanying autocommentary Śāntarakṣita takes up several issues which are central to his unique rendering of Madhyamaka thought. These include the status of conventional truths, several issues concerning logic and epistemology, and his famous bridging of Madhyamaka discourse with several aspects of mainline Yogācāra thinking, including the rejection of external objects.

At this point in the text, having completed the neither-one-nor-many argument which, according to Śāntarakṣita, clearly establishes that entities do not ultimately exist because they do not have an ultimately existent single nature nor an ultimately existent manifold nature, he then moves on to discuss the way entities do exist. Śāntarakṣita begins with the explicit statement that entities only exist conventionally.After stating that entities do exist conventionally, Śāntarakṣita then ponders what can be done for those who stubbornly accept entities as ultimately existing after the extensive evidence he has given to indicate conclusions to the contrary:

> (63) Therefore, these entities are characterized only by conventionality. If [someone accepts] them as ultimate, what can I do for that person?

Śāntarakṣita explains in his *MAV,* with both reasoning and quotations from scriptures, that while entities do not exist ultimately, it is not the case that they do not exist at all. Such a view would entail falling into the extreme of nihilism or absolute non-existence. In his process of explanation, he first attacks the ignorance which clings to ultimate existence as a result of holding incorrect philosophical views. It is to these people that he questions in the root text as to what he can do for them if they insist on holding such views after the thorough analysis and rejection of ultimate existence in the previous sixty-two stanzas. Śāntarakṣita then attacks innate (*sahaja, lhan skyes*) ignorance which clings to ultimate existence but without a basis in constructed wrong views. He does this with extensive quotations from *sūtras*, citing several instances in which the Buddha states that phenomena do not exist in reality (*yang dag par*) (i.e., ultimately). For example, Śāntarakṣita quotes *The Skillful Elephant Sūtra* as stating the following:

> *The Skillful Elephant Sūtra* says, "Śariputra was wondering [about this question] which he asked [the Buddha], 'Is there consciousness [knowing] the nature of any phenomena? Or is there not?' The Bhāgavan replied, 'This searching for the nature of phenomena is searching for the nature of an illusion.' The Bhāgavan said, 'That [illusion] does not exist just as a [nature of phenomena] must not exist.' If someone asks what the reason is for this, the Bhāgavan taught that the reason is, 'All phenomena are the nature of an illusion.' Anything that is like an illusion does not exist. Likewise, regarding the searching for the nature of phenomena, the searching [itself] does not exist. If one asks for an explanation, the explanation is that there are no phenomena whatsoever which exist in reality." This and so forth was how it was explained.[178]

In his treatment of this section of the text and the topic he describes as "identifying the characteristics of entities," Gyel-tsab simply offers the following inferential proof: "The subject, these entities, must exist in a false manner because their basis is established and the establishment of true existence is [already] refuted."[179] He goes on to state that it would be incorrect to argue that they do not exist at all because their mere existence has been truly established by valid cognition (*tshad ma, pramāṇa*).

Śāntarakṣita's quotation from *The Skillful Elephant Sūtra* is followed with a question from a hypothetical opponent about the nature of conventionally existent entities. S/he questions that if their real existence is so strongly negated, there might easily arise questions as to whether Mādhyamikas such as Śāntarakṣita deny the complete existence of entities altogether. This hypothetical question leads Śāntarakṣita to discuss the precise manner in which entities do conventionally exist and to offer a working definition of conventionally existent phenomena in the sixty-fourth stanza of *MA*. This subject is described by Gyel-tsab as "[identifying the characteristics of] conventional existence."

> Well then, if this is the nature of conventional [phenomena], are there no existent entities? If there exist no entities, then if one says that seeing [them] and [their] functionality would be contradicted, [I must reply that] those [conventional phenomena] are not explained to be like that.[180]

> (64) Those phenomena which are only agreeable when not put to the test of [ultimate] analysis, those phenomena which are generated and disintegrate, and those which have the ability to function are known to be of a conventional nature.

In the sixty-fourth root text stanza and accompanying autocommentary, Śāntarakṣita establishes three criteria for what he calls a conventional truth: 1) they are seen or known by the mind, 2) they are dependently-arisen entities which have the ability to function in the way that they appear, and 3) they are unable to withstand ultimate analysis. He elaborates further in his autocommentary by explaining that conventional truths are known by conceptual thought or designated with worldly conventions.[181]

Ichigō correctly argues that Śāntarakṣita is only referring to true or real conventional truths here in his definition.[182] Śāntarakṣita does not explicitly delineate a distinction between real and unreal conventional truths as Kamalaśīla does in *MAP*. Kamalaśīla clearly distinguishes between dependently-arisen functional entities which can be considered as real conventional truths, and mere conceptual constructs such as the "creator God" asserted by the Sāṃkhyas which are unreal conventional truths. Such false conventionalities, "...do not have as their objects any of the characteristics of those things which arise by dependent origination."[183] But Śāntarakṣita does define real conventional truths (*yang dag pa'i kun rdzob*) (though not unreal conventional truths) explicitly on two occasions in *MAV*. For example, when commenting on the sixty-fourth *MA* stanza he writes:

> "Conventional" is not a nature which is merely the designation of a sound. Because they cannot withstand [ultimate] analysis, dependently-arisen entities which function and are seen are [called] real conventionalities.[184]

And when commenting on the sixty-fifth and sixty-sixth stanzas he writes:

> Entities which are able to function yet cannot withstand [ultimate] analysis are called real conventionalities.[185]

He thus implies that there must also be unreal conventional truths to contrast with these "real" (*yang dag*) conventionalities, although he does not explicitly define them.[186]

Śāntarakṣita further explains that conventional truths are not merely the names or labels, but that the words are references to entities, which are made up of parts, which are the causal basis behind the imputation of the designation. He quotes the Buddha in his autocommentary to stress this point:

> The Protector (i.e., The Buddha) also said, "For example, we wish to call 'a chariot' those [entities] which are the accumulation of the parts [of a chariot]. Likewise, the [accumulation of] aggregates has become the cause conventionally for what we call 'a sentient being'."[187]

When Gyel-tsab comments on this point in his commentary, the argument and its reason take a slightly different shape, yet the essential components remain the same. Śāntarakṣita lists the criteria and describes those entities which meet the three criteria as conventional truths. He explains a reason for their description as conventional only in relation to real conventionalities. There, part of the reason for their being called real conventional entities is given as their inability to withstand ultimate analysis. For Gyel-tsab, the inability to withstand ultimate analysis is listed as one of the criteria, while the reason for their being called conventional entities is their ability to be found by conventional valid cognition. This explanation is more in line with the standard Geluk definition of real conventional truths, which are only real from the perspective of worldly knowledge or conventional valid cognition. Śāntarakṣita uses this language later in discussions of conventional truths in his autocommentary, but not in commenting on this stanza. Gyel-tsab writes:

> The subject, [entities which are characterized by] the three – [1] the inability to endure the examination of final (i.e., ultimate)

> analysis, [2] the character of being produced and ceasing, and [3] the ability to function – [these] are [described as] conventional truths because they are objects found by conventional valid cognition (*tha snyad pa'i tshad ma*).[188]

In the following two root text stanzas, which run together without interruption in the commentary in *MAV*, Śāntarakṣita proceeds into the third subtopic under the larger topic of demonstrating that entities do exist conventionally. This subtopic, which is addressed in the sixty-fifth and sixty-sixth stanzas of the root text, is a refutation of the ultimate existence of the cause of the illusion. While his aim here is to refute the notion that causes ultimately exist, Śāntarakṣita is not rejecting efficaciousness of causes altogether. Because true existence has been refuted, truly existent causes are also refuted, but that does not mean there are absolutely no causal relationships whatsoever. In the root text stanzas on this, Śāntarakṣita argues precisely this point. Although causes do not ultimately exist, because they cannot withstand ultimate analysis, they do exist conventionally and are causally efficacious on a conventional level:

> (65) Although they are agreeable only when not analyzed [by ultimate analysis], since it depends on the earlier cause, the subsequent fruit arises in correspondence with that.

> (66) Therefore, if [one claims] that there is no conventional cause, that is said to be incorrect and is no good. If its substantial cause (*upādāna, nyer len*) is said to be real, then that must be explained.

Śāntarakṣita goes on in *MAV* to give further explanation of the way in which conventional entities exist as causal, functional entities, yet still cannot bear ultimate analysis, which looks for a true nature in things. He does so by repeating explanations he has already given about the way real conventionalities exist. He reiterates that conventionalities are not merely the sounds of imputed labels, but that they correspond with entities which serve as the basis of emptiness and functionality. Still, they simply cannot withstand ultimate analysis, which searches for true existence:

> Entities which are able to function yet cannot bear [ultimate] analysis are called real conventionalities. It is said that beings, etc.

> are not merely the sound [of the labels which designate them]. If those [beings, etc.] arise in dependence on their own cause which is unable to withstand examination by [ultimate] analysis in this expressed way, how could there be no cause [at all]? If analyzed with wisdom and gnosis, intelligent ones will assert the existent nature of the cause.[189]

Gyel-tsab summarizes this argument in a similar manner:

> By saying that it is incorrect if [one holds the view that] there is no true cause of a pot, etc., this statement is not good because even though there is no true cause, subsequent fruits arise from previous similar types. Truly existent causes are impossible because true existence has already been refuted.[190]

Refutation of Dissenting Arguments

Śāntarakṣita moves on from asserting some of the foundational points of his views on conventional truths. He will elaborate in some more detail towards the end of the text on how precisely he incorporates key features of Yogācāra thought into his ideas concerning conventional truths. At this point however he goes on to what Gyel-tsab describes as the refutation of dissenting arguments of other schools. Gyel-tsab lists seven topics here, only the first five of which seem to actually be cases where Śāntarakṣita addresses dissenting views. The final two would more accurately be described as cases where Śāntarakṣita asserts some of the unique features of his own view. Gyel-tsab lists the seven topics as follows: "dispelling the contradictions with direct perception, dispelling the contradictions with scripture, expressing the ultimate truth, dispelling [dissenting] arguments regarding that [ultimate truth], putting forth the nature of conventional truth, showing the way that the nature of the Mahāyāna is more glorious than the others, and [showing how] if one knows this system, [s/he knows] the cause of the generation of compassion and faith."[191] There are two stanzas in the root text which address the first topic, dispelling contradictions with direct perception:

> (67) Regarding the inherent nature of all entities, we have cleared away others' assertions by following the path of reasoning. Therefore there is nothing to be disputed [in our position].

> (68) If they are earnest, those [opponents] will not be able to find any fault in [the view of] those who assert neither existence nor non-existence, nor both existence and non-existence.[192]

Śāntarakṣita argues that by following the path of reasoning, of logical inquiry, he has refuted all other tenet systems that maintain inherent existence or an inherent nature in entities. And he argues that if his opponents are honest and reasonable, they must agree with his thorough and logical rejection of such a nature in entities. When put to the test of ultimate analysis, even by a non-*ārya* (i.e., one who has not had a direct realization of emptiness), it is apparent that no entities can withstand such analysis. His reference to the tetralema, found most famously in Nāgārjuna's *MMK*, seems to be a clear indication of his sense of his views being in strict alignment with Nāgārjuna's

Gyel-tsab explains Śāntarakṣita's point regarding potential conflicts with direct perception when he comments as if from the perspective of Śāntarakṣita himself. Notice too that Gyel-tsab uses the phrase "established as truly existent " (*den par grub pa*) rather than the language of Śāntarakṣita's text to which he refers. Śāntarakṣita's text utilizes the phrase "the inherent nature of all entities" (*dngos po kun gyi rang bzhin*). Use of such replacement terminology leads the Geluk student to read Śāntarakṣita's text in light of what became a normative Geluk reading of the Yogācāra-Svātantrika-Madhyamaka in later doxographical literature.[193] In such later sources, Yogācāra-Svātantrika-Mādhyamikas are purported to reject true or ultimate existence, but to accept inherent existence. This of course was largely informed by the writings of Tsong Khapa and his immediate disciples.

> If one says, " If there are no entities which are established as truly existent, that contradicts direct perception," I respond that there are no faults of contradicting direct perception by virtue of refuting true existence because although entities bearing the investigation by the reasoning examining the final status (*mthar thug dpyod pa'i rigs pa*) [of entities] are refuted, objects found by conventional valid cognition are not refuted. There would be no faults of contradicting direct perception, etc. with that explanation because we do not accept the true existence of the four extremes of existence, non-existence, both, or neither.[194]

The sixty-ninth stanza addresses what Gyel-tsab describes as the dispelling of the contradictions with scriptures. Here Śāntarakṣita quotes extensively from a number of *sūtras* in his autocommentary, but not only to put to rest qualms about contradictions in general with scriptures. In addition, he wants to address the potential qualms of "lower" Buddhist schools that may consider his arguments to be contradicting the Buddha's words. He seems particularly concerned with their reaction to his stance on the non-production of all phenomena. It is argued here by Śāntarakṣita that if phenomena do not truly exist, then they cannot be truly produced, for there cannot be any true cause of their being. Śāntarakṣita begins by linking the argument against the true production and true cessation of entities to the neither-one-nor-many argument by questioning how entities could be truly produced, persist, or cease if they all lack a truly singular or truly plural nature. If there is no true cause of production and no true fruit, there cannot be true production. The argument against true production also can be traced back to Nāgārjuna's *Mūlamadhyamakakārikā* and his four-fold negation of causation:

> Nothing ever arises anywhere from itself, from somewhere else, from both, or from no cause at all.[195]

Śāntarakṣita follows his own root text stanza in his autocommentary with a series of quotations from various *sūtras* to support his view and to demonstrate that his view, which clearly is defensible with logic, is likewise supported by scriptures.

> (69) Therefore, in reality there are not any established entities. Due to that, the *Tathāgatas* taught the non-production of all phenomena.

>> In reality it would be incorrect [to postulate] that even gross or subtle entities are thoroughly established because this explanation presented demonstrates that [entities] lack the nature of one or many. Therefore by what are they actually produced? And [how do they] exist before [production]? And [how are they] impermanent? How also would other such phenomenal entities exist?

In that way, *The Ocean of Intelligent Teachings Sūtra* states as follows, "There is not even the slightest nature in dependently-arisen phenomena. Since they have no nature, those do not arise [in any of the four ways]."

The Skillful Elephant Sūtra says, "If there are not any phenomena which are produced, it is only the childish ones who claim arising for those phenomena for which there is no arising."

The Abiding and Arising of the Jewel Sūtra says, "There is no inherent existence for any [entity]. Since there is no inherent existence,how can there be conditions for another's [production]? And since there is no inherent existence, how can they be produced by another? This reason was taught by the *Sugata*."

Therefore, *The Meeting of the Father and the Son Sūtra* says, "It is taught that by engaging in dependent origination one is also engaging in *dharmadhātu* (i.e., ultimate truth). The Bhāgavan said regarding that, that ignorance does not exist as ignorance in and of itself. If one responds by asking 'Why?,' it is because ignorance does not have inherent existence. Also for any phenomena that do not inherently exist, entities do not exist. For those for whom entities do not exist, there are no thoroughly established existents. Without thoroughly established existents, there is no production. Without production there is no cessation. That which is not produced and does not cease would not aptly be called past nor would it aptly be called present, nor future. For anything which does not exist in the three times, a name does not exist, characteristics [of it] do not exist, a signifier (*mtshan ma*) does not exist, and it, functioning as an imputation, does not exist. They do not exist in any other [way] but merely by name, by mere sign, mere designation, as mere convention, mere assertion, and as mere imputation. Except for the purpose of guiding sentient beings [the Buddha did not teach] that ignorance itself ultimately does not exist. Any phenomenon which ultimately does not exist also does not exist by way of designation and does not exist as something expressible when functioning as an imputation. The Bhāgavan said that in reality, everything from this so-called mere name on up to the mere imputation of those [names] also do not exist."

This sort of teaching arose extensively. Since that is the case, when the [second] wheel of the dharma turned it was taught by the Protector (i.e., the Buddha) that from the earliest times, all phenomena were peacefully free [of inherent existence], not produced, and the nature of *nirvāṇa*. These verses explain it eloquently. They demonstrate completely that all phenomena in the three times are naturally equal [with regards to their lack of inherent existence].[196]

The Meeting of the Father and the Son Sūtra says, "All of these phenomena are equal by way of their being equal in the three times. Even in the past, all phenomena had no inherent existence. Also in the future, and at the time of arising, all phenomena have no inherent existence."

It (i.e., *The Meeting of the Father and the Son Sūtra*) also says, "It is clearly [demonstrated] that all phenomena are empty of inherent existence. Any phenomena which do not inherently exist, did not exist in the past, will not exist in the future, and do not exist at the time of arising. If someone asks, 'Why?,' [we would respond that] one would not say that, functioning as imputations, [phenomena] which do not inherently exist [do not inherently exist only] in the past, etc. Nor would one say, on the basis of imputations, that they [do not inherently exist only] in the future, nor only at the time of arising. Even non-production and the like have been classified as conventional realities."[197]

Śāntarakṣita thus presents extensive support from *sūtras* for his position that there is no inherent production. These Mahāyāna *sūtras* were likely the same sources Nāgārjuna drew from when he refuted real causation in his work. Several important points are made above by referencing these *sūtras*. Śāntarakṣita clearly wants to emphasize that he does not merely talk about the past or future when speaking of a lack of inherent existence of production, but also of the present, of the "time of arising." This eliminates any potential ambiguity about the lack of inherent existence necessitating a relationship to a specific time other than the present, because the lack of inherent existence is the same in all of the three times. Much of the argument against real production, which bases itself on the lack of inherent existence in any phenomena, centers on the notion that if there are no inherently existing phenomena, there can be no inherently existing cause. Without an inherently existing cause there can be no true production. Gyel-tsab summarizes all of this quite succinctly. He argues that if there is nothing which is truly established, then there can be no truly established cause. Gyel-tsab writes:

> There is a reason for stating in the scriptures that all phenomena are not produced and do not cease. It is because there are no entities which are truly established.[198]

Śāntarakṣita continues his argument regarding the lack of production from the previous stanza. In the seventieth stanza and accompanying commentary he explains that with regards to ultimate truth, all verbal fabrications are ultimately eliminated, but that such verbal fabrications are necessary conventionally for ascent to that ultimate view. According to Gyel-tsab's outline of topics, the following topic, "the refutation of the ultimate existence of the cause of the illusion," is addressed by Śāntarakṣita over the course of the next three stanzas (70-72) in his root text. I have also included Śāntarakṣita's own autocommentary here on the seventieth stanza:

> (70) Because they are harmonious with ultimate truths, some call this [non-production] ultimate truth, but in reality they (i.e., ultimate truths) are free from all accumulations of verbal fabrications (*prapañca, spros pa*).

> With regard to the ultimate, entities and non-entities, production and non-production, emptiness and non-emptiness, etc. are all free from the net of elaborations. Because non-production and the like are harmonious with engaging in that

> [wisdom realizing emptiness], we label them as [verbal fabricaions of] the ultimate [truth]. Without the stairs of real-conventionalities, it would be unsuitable for a master to go to the top of the house of reality (i.e., ultimate truth). Why then is it taught directly that that is not ultimate [truth]?[199]

According to the explanation of this stanza given to me by Geshe Jigme Dawa, a leading Geluk scholar, this discussion also revolves around a division of ultimate truth into two categories, the ultimate truth of the object and the ultimate truth of the subject. The ultimate truth of the object is also further divided into the real or actual ultimate truth of the object and the mere designation of the ultimate truth of the object. Thus Śāntarakṣita, according to Geshe Jigme Dawa, is aiming at the actual ultimate truth of the object, which is beyond any elaboration, while noting the necessity of conventional designations in ascent to that.[200] This point is elaborated upon, and the pervasion of the argument is established, in the next two root text stanzas:

> (71) Due to the lack of [ultimate] production, there can be no non-production, etc. Because of the refutation of the nature of that [production], verbal expressions referring to that [non-production] do not exist.

> (72) There is no point in applying [words] of negation to a non-existent object. Even if one relies on conceptual thought, it would be conventional, not ultimate.

Gyel-tsab clarifies this point in the following manner in his commentary on Śāntarakṣita's root text verses:

> The subject, the non-truly existent sprout, would be merely synonymous with the ultimate truth [of the object] because whatever object can be found by inferential knowledge can newly arise as [the object of] non-conceptual wisdom of the equipoise arising from meditation. Ultimately, it would be free from all elaborations, for just as true production is an object of negation, true non-production is [an object which is negated] as well because it does not ultimately exist. If one replies that the reason (*rtags*) is not established, then [in response to that objection we argue that] non-

> production is not ultimately established because there would be no true production of the object of refutation. There is a pervasion because if there is no true production, then in meditative equipoise (*mnyam gzhag*), according to the view [of the wisdom realizing emptiness of a Noble One], there would not be application of the words which refute it. That is so because there would be no application of negating words (*dgag sgra*) without a base of negation. If they (i.e.,Yogācāras) say that there is application of negating words to conceptually designated objects, then that subject would not be established as ultimately real but would be conventional because it would be a negation negating the object of refutation designated by conceptual thought.[201]

Śāntarakṣita proceeds to address further potential objections to his views, the first of which is the argument that unenlightened people of low intelligence could realize emptiness through direct perception. Gyel-tsab describes this fourth topic as, "dispelling [dissenting] arguments regarding ultimate truth," which itself has four subtopics. The first of these is to abandon the *absurdum* that people of low intellectual capabilities will know emptiness through direct perception, which according to Gyel-tsab is addressed in the seventy-third stanza of the root text. The argument questions why everybody could not directly intuit the ultimate nature of entities if they perceive them with direct perception:

> (73) Well then, [what if someone were to say that] since by cognizing those [entities] the nature of them can be directly perceived, why don't non-masters also know [the ultimate nature of] entities in this way?

The argument continues in Śāntarakṣita's *MAV*:

> If they [directly] cognize [entities], then not cognizing the nature of those would be irrational. If we see a ground without a jar, then likewise we know the nature of the ground as being without a jar.[202]

The argument proceeds to claim that if an ordinary person sees an object without an inherent nature, then s/he should directly know that it has no inherent nature, just as s/he would know a ground without a jar is without a jar. This of course is not the position of any Mādhyamika, including Śāntarakṣita. He responds in *MAV* that the difference between the perception of those of low intellect who are unenlightened and the perception of enlightened ones is that in addition to valid cognition of gross objects, those of low intellect also impute inherent existence onto the objects they perceive. Thus they impute an extreme perspective onto objects which do not abide in either of the two extremes. He explains further in the following verse and autocommentary:

> (74) They (i.e., non-masters) do not [know the ultimate nature of entities] because, due to the power of false imputations [of real existence] onto entities by the burdened, beginningless continuums of all sentient beings, [emptiness] is not known directly by living beings.
>
> > Those beings who have been stirred by the poison of strong attachment to entities generated in beginningless existence, since they merely know directly, they are unable to fully engage (*chud par mi nus*) images.[203]

Gyel-tsab explains the argument in a similar manner while stressing the persistence of the delusion in the minds of beings since beginningless *saṃsāra*:

> Even though it is so that there are no truly existent entities, there is a reason why shepherds, etc. do not cognize emptiness by direct perception. It is because from beginningless time [their] mental continuums are bound by the mistaken perception which exaggerates [the reality of] things [and imputes] true [existence].[204]

This leads Śāntarakṣita directly into answering the question regarding who *does* know ultimate truth if it is not known merely by ordinary people with direct perception of entities. The answer he offers is twofold. First, it is known by those inferring emptiness through logical reasoning. Secondly, it is known by powerful yogis through direct perception. Śāntarakṣita explains this point in the seventy-fifth root text stanza and accompanying autocommentary:

> (75) [Those who realize emptiness are] those who know it inferentially with reasons which make [the lack of a real nature] known and that cut superimpositions, as well as those powerful yogis who know it clearly by direct perception.

Gyel-tsab elaborates on this point by echoing the general categories Śāntarakṣita describes of beings who know emptiness. He does so however by also specifying precisely where in the Mahāyāna Buddhist path system these specific beings abide at the time of realization. In this way, he also qualifies the type of realization which those beings are having at the time:

> Even though those of low intellect (*blun po*) do not cognize [emptiness], there are persons who cognize emptiness. Those bodhisattvas on the path of preparation (*sbyor lam*) and the path of accumulation (*tshog lam*) [cognize emptiness conceptually] by relying on reasoning (*gtan tshigs*) into [the nature of] reality. Bodhisattvas abiding on the [ten] grounds realize [emptiness] directly by [relying on] direct yogic cognition.[205]

At this point, Śāntarakṣita segues to a defense of the use of autonomous inferences (*svatantrānumāna, rang rgyud kyi rjes dpag*) in his autocommentary and then in the root text, under the topic which Gyel-tsab describes as refuting the *absurdum* or qualm of his opponent that "there would not be any meaningfully established speech." It is worthy of notice that Gyel-tsab refrains from any criticism of Śāntarakṣita's positions here with regard to logic despite the fact that Śāntarakṣita's position is quite different from Gyel-tsab's on this issue. This issue in fact is a central distinguishing mark between Gelukpas such as Gyel-tsab and their understanding of Svātantrika-Mādhyamikas such as Śāntarakṣita. Details of the discrepancies between the Geluk stance on logic and that of Śāntarakṣita will be discussed at greater length in Part II of this book.

Śāntarakṣita begins the discussion by setting forth a hypothetical two-pronged critique of his own views regarding logic. The first challenge, as explained by Śāntarakṣita, begins with an opponent of his questioning how he could establish valid arguments given his acceptance of the lack of inherent existence of all phenomena. They argue that if everything lacks inherent existence, then even the components of the argument and criteria to be proven would not truly exist:

> If you accept that all entities have no inherent existence, then because the property of the subject criterion, etc.[206] is not established, is it not the case that the inference and the conventional knowledge to be inferred [by the inference] would not be established? Due to that, how could the proponent delineate [any thesis]? If no reason is asserted which establishes the lack of inherent existence of all phenomena, then at that time, since there is no reason established for the lack of [inherent] existence, the meaning of your assertions is not established.[207]

This first criticism seems to come from those opponents whom Śāntarakṣita considers to be from lower Buddhist schools in that they do not accept the Madhyamaka position of the emptiness of inherent existence of all phenomena because they think it falls into the extreme of nihislim. They argue that if everything lacks inherent existence as Mādhyamikas assert, then the components of the arguments lack inherent existence and thus cannot establish an argument for the lack of inherent existence of phenomena.

The second prong of the criticism is one which resembles that of the "lower" Buddhists and also closely parallels the type of criticism Candrakīrti leveled against Bhāvaviveka and which Gelukpas use to criticize the so-called Svātantrika-Mādhyamikas. While there is no evidence of a split of Mādhyamikas into schools divided along the lines of logic in India at this time, it seems as though the issue of appropriate forms of logic to be utilized by Mādhyamika thinkers may have been a contested issue in Śāntarakṣita's mind and one which needed to be addressed. Śāntarakṣita begins to explain the challenge in the following manner in his *MAV*:

> If [a reason] is asserted [which establishes all phenomena as lacking inherent existence], then there is an [inherently] existent reason. If that is the case, then the meaning of your assertions would not be established since the lack of inherent existence of all phenomena would not be established [since you must admit that the reason is inherently existent].[208]

Śāntarakṣita is thus posed with two challenges here. On the one hand, it is argued that his inferences are meaningless since he must consider their parts to lack true existence. On the other hand, if he holds them to be valid, then he must maintain the inherent existence of the parts of the argument.

This would undermine the purpose of logically establishing the lack of inherent existence. Śāntarakṣita responds to these challenges in the following three stanzas of *MA*. A primary problem facing Śāntarakṣita is how to assert meaningful logical arguments establishing emptiness if all the component parts of the argument lack any inherent existence on which to proceed. How can he engage in meaningful debate if there is no substantial nature in the component parts of the argument? He needs to be able to establish subjects and marks of an inference which are meaningful and commonly known to both himself as a Mādhyamika, who maintains that all phenomena lack inherent existence, and to those opponents from lower schools who do maintain real entities. A common subject is a prerequisite for a valid autonomous inference (*svatantrānumāna*) of the type he wants to utilize because, if the subject of the argument is not held in common, then proponent and opponent are not discussing the same topic, and thus their discussion deteriorates into meaninglessness. Yet when the subject of an inference is a book, for example, that designation "book" would mean something entirely different to a Mādhyamika than it would to an adherent of some other philosophical system. The critique is, therefore, that the proponent and opponent would be talking past each other, never really discussing the same subject. His lower Buddhist opponents argue that if he tries to establish the lack of inherent existence with arguments where the components of that argument have inherent existence, then the very use of the argument cancels or undermines its meaning. Later Geluk critics who claim to follow Candrakīrti take this point a step further in terms of subtlety and argue that if there are commonly appearing components of the argument to both the proponent and opponent, then the components, such as the commonly appearing subject, must have some objective inherent nature such that it can be known in precisely the same way by both parties. This is clearly a problematic prospect for a Mādhyamika. Discussion of these arguments can be found in detail in Part II of this study. But, suffice it to say here that Śāntarakṣita responds by arguing that a common subject can be established since there are validly established entities known by all beings:

> (76) Having discarded [views] concerning the way subjects exist based on particular discourses of scriptures, there are entities which are well known by everyone from masters to women to children.

> (77) All these entities, including that thesis and the proof, are engaged as such. If that were not the case, we would have such problems as that of an unestablished base (*āśrayāsiddha, gzhi ma grub*),[209] etc., as has been argued.
>
> (78) Because I have not rejected entities with regard to their possessing the taste (*rasa, ngang*) of appearances, [this position is] unshaken with regard to the establishment of the subject and the thesis.

Śāntarakṣita continues to address this criticism by reinforcing his position that common components of an argument and the criterion for its establishment are valid because those objects of the sense consciousnesses are the objects of the sound referents of the words which make up the inferential statement. This is despite the fact that they ultimately lack true existence. Moreover, Śāntarakṣita argues that he never rejected "entities with regards to their possessing the taste of appearances." He is attempting here to establish a common subject which is 1) known by all, 2) not generated by tenets, and 3) is referred to by the mere sound of the word as a referent of the entity, the reason, and other component parts:

> Some say that all inferential reasoning and the conventional objects [of knowledge] inferred by such reasoning must be given up completely [since they depend on] different subjects generated by incompatible tenets.
>
> Eye, ear, and nose consciousness, etc. of everyone from masters to women to children engage (i.e., come to know) [in subjects for autonomous inferences] by relying on subjects which [correspond with] the sound [of the words pointing to] that which possesses the taste of appearances.[210]

It is a bit ambiguous as to what exactly Śāntarakṣita means when he says that entities "possess the taste of appearances" (*snang ba'i ngang can*). When he claims that he has not rejected the notion that entities "possess the taste of appearances," he seems to fall into precisely the problem that his critics find troublesome for Mādhyamikas, namely that for there to be common subjects in an autonomous inference the subject must be inherently existent. It could be argued by his opponents for example that even accepting that entities possess the "taste" of their appearances conventionally suggests the existence of an inherent nature in those entities that would contradict the most fundamental Madhyamaka position. This is precisely the view Śāntarakṣita has gone to great lengths to reject in this text and thus it is a bit perplexing here.[211] Perhaps his opponents take a commonly appearing subject to mean one known in exactly the same way by both the proponent and opponent in the argument whereas Śāntarakṣita does not feel such rigid precision in their common understanding of the subject and the reason is necessary. Again, this issue will be taken up further in Part II.

Like his unnamed opponent here, this is a topic on which later Geluk scholars will criticize Mādhyamikas who use autonomous inferences, such as Śāntarakṣita. But Śāntarakṣita quickly turns the table on such opponents in his *Autocommentary on "The Ornament of The Middle Way."* He questions how they would be able to establish any knowledge at all given their position on this issue of proper forms of logic. Since he does not grasp at some inherent existence in the object while simultaneously not abandoning utterly the meaning or significance of the characteristics of its appearance, Śāntarakṣita feels that he avoids faults from the perspective of either Madhyamaka or logic. He proceeds to explain then how it is only through this form of logic that one can correctly understand the canonical philosophical commentaries (*śāstras*), implying that it is only in this way that one can ascend through the philosophical views to an understanding of what he considers to be the most philosophically accurate view, that of Madhyamaka:

> If that is not the case (i.e., if there is no common subject), there will be no establishment of the base of the reason for all [arguments] you assert to be established, such as [the argument demonstrating that by] the existence of smoke there is fire and [the arguments about] impermanence, etc., because established subjects are not established as having the nature of the qualities of the parts they possess.[212]

> As is said, as long as we do not rely on polluted grasping, designations will be thoroughly established. If one becomes a master in conventions, s/he will not be obscured in his/her understanding of the meaning of the *śāstras*.[213]

Śāntarakṣita then makes one more pass at his critics who question the suitability of using autonomous inferences while asserting that phenomena lack inherent existence. He does so, before concluding this topic, by claiming that to them, the Madhyamaka view is a nihilistic view which uproots the very virtues of the Dharma:

> In the view of those subjugators who have animosity toward the system of those postulating meaningful [arguments], the view that all phenomena lack any inherent existence is like the view of complete non-existence from the crown to the [lowest part of the] body.
>
> According to that view, causes and conditions will be deprecated. By that wrong view, the virtuous side will be uprooted, the golden crop of the holy Dharma will be like flowers in the sky, and those with excellent aspirations [and the correct view] will be abandoned far away. [214]

Śāntarakṣita goes on in the next three stanzas to argue for the validity of asserting previous lives and to discuss issues concerning the relationship between present and previous lives in a single continuum. In *MAV,* the three root text stanzas (seventy-nine through eighty-one) run continuously and are commented upon together by Śāntarakṣita. Gyel-tsab comments on stanza seventy-nine first, and then remarks that the following two stanzas establish the pervasion. According to Gyel-tsab's outline, this is the *absurdum* that there would be no karma and effects, a common criticism leveled against Mādhyamikas due to their rejection of "real" production and "real" cessation. The first among the three subtopics of this subject is the demonstration of the absurdity of asserting the invalidity of previous and later lives which, according to Gyel-tsab, is addressed in the seventy-ninth stanza of the root text:

> (79) Therefore, the seeds of a similar type, which [stimulate] conception with entities or conception without [entities], etc. in the continuums [of beings] from beginningless existence, are objects of inferential [knowledge].

The above argument, which seems a bit vague and tenuous at first glance, is based on the notion that one can know inferentially that the seeds of consciousness are of a similar or related type in the continuums of beings over multiple lifetimes and, therefore, one can infer previous and later lives. Śāntarakṣita also summarizes the point very succinctly in the following section of his autocommentary:

> Because of conceptualizing entities and the like [in previous lives], at their first arising in this life it is inferred that they are produced from imprints (*bag chags*) with which we have become accustomed and which are similar [to those of the same continuum in previous lives].[215]

Gyel-tsab explains his understanding of Śāntarakṣita's point in *JBy* as follows. He argues that in the same way that one becomes accustomed to objects of desire in one lifetime based upon the seeds of a previous similar type, so too do infants become accustomed to conceptualizing entities, etc. upon birth on the basis of having been accustomed to conceptualizing entities similarly in previous lives.

> The subject, the conception without entities of a newborn baby, is preceded by its similar former type because it is consciousness, like a habituated desire.[216]

As mentioned above, in Śāntarakṣita's autocommentary stanzas seventy-nine through eighty-one are presented successively without any intervening commentary although Gyel-tsab comments on stanza seventy-nine first and then stanzas eighty and eighty-one together.

> (80) Regarding this, they (i.e., the conceptions of entities) do not arise by the force of entities because these [entities ultimately] do not exist. The nature of entities has been thoroughly rejected in an extensive manner.

> (81) Because they arise gradually, they are not sudden. Because they are not permanently arisen, they are not permanent. Because they themselves are similarly accustomed to those [previous habits of conceptualization], they first arise from their own kind.

Śāntarakṣita offers a detailed explanation of his argument in the *MAV*. He argues that these imputed notions of entities and entitylessness which even exist in newborn babies do not arise as a result of external entities. This is verified by the fact that such entities have already been logically rejected in this text. Likewise, they are not sudden and are not permanent since there is nothing that is permanent. Since the consciousnesses of even newborn infants are already accustomed to common modes of consciousness, such as perceiving entities and entitylessness, they must arise from a previous instance of a similar type of consciousness, and thus from one of a previous life.

Gyel-tsab explains this point in a similar manner. It is interesting to note that Śāntarakṣita states in stanza eighty that entities "do not exist," and that "the nature of entities has been thoroughly rejected in an extensive manner" (*dngos po rnams kyi bdag nyid de//rgya cher rab tu bkag pa yin/*), whereas Gyel-tsab refers to "the true existence of entities" (*dnos po bden pa*) as having already been refuted. This movement in technical terminology anticipated, or perhaps more precisely, influenced the later Geluk doxographical depiction of the Yogācāra-Svātantrika-Madhyamaka School as one which rejects true or ultimate existence but accepts inherent existence, existence by way of its own characteristics, or existence from its own side conventionally. This subtle swapping of technical terminology actually has profound implications for the way Śāntarakṣita's ideas will later be represented in Geluk doxographical literature. Although Śāntarakṣita explicitly rejects a *nature* in entities, Gyel-tsab portrays him as rejecting *true existence*. Outside of a context of defining the two truths, such a subtle move is easily overlooked. When I mentioned this to Geshe Kelsang Damdul in personal correspondence, he agreed that this was probably a move which influenced or was used to set up later doxographical distinctions between the Yogācāra-Svātantrika-Madhyamaka position and that of the Gelukpa's own Prāsaṅgika-Madhyamaka. Gyel-tsab writes:

> That subject (i.e., the conception of entities)would not be able to arise by the force of a partless object because there are no partless objects and because the true existence of entities has already been refuted. It would not be causeless because it occurs in succession. [Its] nature would not be permanent because it is not permanently arising. Thus, a previous consciousness [precedes it] because it is consciousness.[217]

Having rejected the true existence of all entities with the neither-one-nor-many argument and having asserted their conventional existence, Śāntarakṣita thus concludes that he has demonstrated that his Madhyamaka view avoids the two extremes of eternalism (*rtag pa*) and absolute non-existence or nihilism (*chad pa*). This despite accusations to the contrary by his critics from other Buddhist and non-Buddhist schools. He explains this in the following stanza from *MA* (and his own accompanying autocommentary):

> (82) Therefore, the views of [the two extremes of] eternalism and absolute non-existence remain far away from the ideas put forth in this text. [Entities arise], change, and become like a seed, sprout, and plant.

Gyel-tsab sums up this point in an interesting and succinct manner:

> The system of Madhyamaka does not have the faults of permanence or nihilism.[There is no fault of] permanence because after the cause is eliminated (*ldog*), the subsequent effect ceases (*log*),[218] and there is no fault of nihilism because fruitsarise[219] from causes like sprouts arise from seeds.[220]

Śāntarakṣita defends his position on how Mādhyamikas avoid the extremes of eternalism and nihilism with a quotation from a *sūtra*. His citation defends this position while also claiming that even bodhisattva training and practices do not exist. Śāntarakṣita clarifies that Mādhyamikas do not fall into the extreme of nihilism due to the conventional acceptance of causes and results:

> *The Cloud of Jewels Sūtra* (*Ratnameghasūtra, dKon mchog sprin gyi mdo*) says, "[Qualm:] If one says bodhisattvas are masters in Mahāyāna, then [how would you reply to the qualm that] among the trainings and all the practices of bodhisattvas, training does not exist, the path of training does not exist, and those who train do not exist?
>
> [Reply:] Due to [the acceptance of the conventional existence of] causes, conditions and bases, this does not constitute a view of [the extreme of] absolute non-existence."[221]

Following this, Śāntarakṣita goes on to argue in the eighty-third stanza of *MA* that liberation from cyclic existence is actually possible. Both the previous argument, about the viability of asserting previous and future lives, and this argument, about the feasibility of liberation from cyclic existence, are taken up by Dharmakīrti in the *Pramāṇasiddhi* chapter of *Pramāṇavārttika*.[222] Śāntarakṣita's treatment of this topic here is explained in the context of demonstrating how "liberation is easier [if one understands the meaning of] this text."[223] "Understanding the meaning of this text" means understanding the lack of inherent existence of all persons and phenomena, which Śāntarakṣita has gone to great lengths to logically establish here. It seems as though his argument claims that by cultivating a realization of emptiness, knowledge of the selflessness of (persons and) phenomena, such an *ārya* eventually attains liberation from cyclic existence through the abandonment of afflictive emotion obstacles (*kleśāvaraṇa, nyon sgrib*) and contrived erroneous views. This is a result of a process of deepening one's understanding of emptiness through meditation and familiarity:

> (83) Masters who know the selflessness of phenomena abandon disturbing emotions, which arise from perverted views, without effort since they have become accustomed to a lack of inherent existence.

Gyel-tsab make two interesting moves in his commentary here on Śāntarakṣita's stanza. When Śāntarakṣita speaks of "masters who know selflessness of phenomena," it is interesting to note that Gyel-tsab refers to them more specifically as "*ārya* bodhisattvas." This is as opposed to Hīnayāna arhats who, according to the Geluk presentation of Svātantrika-Madhyamaka, only know the selflessness of persons. This is worth noting because for Gelukpas both Hīnayāna arhats and bodhisattvas realize the selflessness of persons and phenomena. This subtle shift presents Śāntarakṣita's views in accordance with the way they will later be presented and criticized in other Geluk philosophical materials. Neither in *MA* nor in his autocommentary on this stanza does Śāntarakṣita refer to such persons or imply that such persons are necessarily *ārya* bodhisattvas.[224] (See the discussion of the status of Hīnāyana arhats in Part II.)

The second interesting shift worth pointing out here concerns the technical terms used to describe emptiness. Gyel-tsab's commentary refers to the cause of the afflictive emotions as the grasping at true existence (*bden 'dzin*) and eliminates Śāntarakṣita's use of the term "lack of inherent existence" (*rang bzhin med*) later in the stanza in favor of the more general "emptiness" (*stong nyid*) (Geluk critics say that Śāntarakṣita accepts inherent existence). These changes again lend themselves in subtle ways toward reading Śāntarakṣita's text through a framework which will contribute to later Geluk critiques in other philosophical materials. (These critiques will be discussed in detail in Part II.) Regardless of the subtle implied points made by Gyel-tsab in his comments, the point here for Śāntarakṣita seems to be that liberation from cyclic existence is possible. Gyel-tsab's commentary is as follows:

> *Ārya* bodhisattvas, the subject, abandon afflictive emotions which arise from the cause of grasping at true existence without [much] effort because they are accustomed to emptiness that is already seen.[225]

The following issue addressed by Śāntarakṣita argues for the validity of the doctrine of karma in general, and sees it as the appropriate explanation in accounting for the specific form and conditions beings take upon rebirth. In other words, he argues that people can look to their own previous accumulations of virtuous and non-virtuous karma for an explanation of their present conditions. Śāntarakṣita aims to explain away the misunderstanding of Madhyamaka thought which claims that one need not worry about committing non-virtuous actions because they are all empty of any inherent nature.[226] According to Gyel-tsab's outline of topics, this topic is the *absurdum* of positing the invalidity of afflictive emotions (*kleśas, nyon mongs*). Gyel-tsab frames the topic as a proof establishing that the fruits of afflictive emotions will certainly arise in the mental continuum of the individual who created them. Śāntarakṣita offers entrance into the topic by first asserting that all beings are the specific results of their own previous karma:

> The mark of persons is in exact correspondence with the pleasing and unpleasing results ripened from virtuous and non-virtuous karma.[227]

Śāntarakṣita affirms not only afflictive emotions but also the positive results of virtuous karma. Thus, the scope is a little larger than Gyel-tsab's topical name suggests, but the meaning of the point is the same – karma functions on a conventional level:

> (84) Since entities which are causes and results are not negated conventionally, there is no confusion in establishing what is pure and what is an affliction.

Gyel-tsab separates discussion of afflictive emotions within this topic from discussion of issues regarding the accumulations of merit, which immediately follows. He is once again succinct in his commentary on this stanza as he explicitly connects the relationship between issues of karma and afflictive emotions with tenets propounding the feasibility of attaining liberation from *saṃsāra*:

> There are not faults of distortion or deterioration in [the positions concerning] *saṃsāra* and liberation due to the refutation of the true existence of extremely afflictive emotions (*saṃkleśas, kun nyon*) because causes and results are accepted conventionally.[228]

The following related topic, according to Gyel-tsab's outline, is the *absurdum* of positing the invalidity of the accumulations of merit. This is addressed in the eighty-fifth through ninetieth stanzas of Śāntarakṣita's *MA*. Śāntarakṣita himself begins the topic with three stanzas in his root text before beginning to explain in his autocommentary:

> (85) Since this teaching of causes and results is established, the positing of stainless accumulations [of wisdom and merit] is suitable according to this text.

> (86) Pure results arise from pure causes just as the pure limb of ethics arises from the correct view.

> (87) Likewise, impure [results] arise from impure causes just as sexual misconduct, etc. arise from the power of wrong views.

> Since all effects act under the influence of the isolate (*ldog pa*) of the corresponding causes, pure and impure [causes] result in pure and impure [effects].[229]

The cornerstone for maintaining the validity of the accumulations of merit for Śāntarakṣita rests on his acceptance of the conventional validity of cause and result, of karma and its effects. Rather than regarding the position that all entities are empty of inherent existence as a problem on this issue, because it would seemingly negate the existence of the accumulations of merit, the emptiness of inherent existence of entities is intimately tied to the acceptance of the conventional validity of cause and result. If entities were not dependent on causes and conditions, then they could not ultimately be empty of inherent existence. This is the case because entities which have no cause for their arising also must have no cause for their cessation and thus would be permanent. It is precisely because entities are dependent on impermanent causes and conditions for their existence that they lack any inherent existence or unchanging essence. This is because when the cause of their being no longer exists, the result is the cessation of the entity. Thus it is because phenomena are empty and impermanent that all effects are under the influence of causes. Therefore, according to this line of reasoning, there would be no contradictions. Gyel-tsab similarly stresses the centrality of the conventional establishment of cause and effect in this system, yet additionally ties the view of emptiness to virtuous morality. He comments on stanzas eighty-five through ninety together:

> According to this system, stainless accumulations also are suitable[230] because, having refuted true cause and effect, they are established conventionally. The subject, the merits which arise from the intention of the wisdom realizing emptiness, arise as pure results because the cause is pure, just as the morality which abandons taking life, etc. arises from the intention of the correct worldly view. The subject, the merits which arise from the intentions of grasping at true existence, would have the opposite predicate and reason like [for example] sexual desire arisen from the strength of the wrong view.[231]

Śāntarakṣita proceeds from here to establish the argument by positing a logical connection between the correct view of emptiness and right moral action. The link is argued to be that, if one does not correctly see all phenomena as lacking true existence, then ultimately valid cognition is harmed because one knows objects as truly existent when they actually are not. As a result, strong grasping becomes prevalent, serving as the basis for all sorts of inappropriate actions and intentions. Śāntarakṣita explains this in the next two stanzas and accompanying autocommentary. The first stanza explains how awareness is mistaken. The following stanza connects that mistaken awareness with an inability of individuals under the sway of mistaken awareness grasping at true existence to cultivate great quantities of virtue by activities such as practice of the six perfections:

> If someone were to ask how this is established, I will explain here.

> (88) Since it is harmed by the valid knowledge (*pramāṇa, tshad ma*) [established in this text that demonstrates that entities have no inherent nature], reification of entities is known as a mistaken awareness, like a consciousness of a mirage.

> Since in reality it is incorrect that any entity would be of either a single or manifold nature, [ultimate] existence is harmed by valid knowledge as has previously been explained. The characteristics of the action of knowing and of the knower, as well as of the object itself, are also harmed by valid cognition as has previously been explained. Therefore, saying that [entities] are actually existent is [a form of] strong grasping because the existence of all entities and the giver, etc. are harmed by valid cognition. Thus, that is a mistaken view, like considering a mirage to be water.[232]

Śāntarakṣita proceeds from here to explain how even virtuous activity, such as the six perfections, are of little benefit when executed from the basis of strongly grasping at ultimate existence. While there will be some benefit, the highest goal of attaining perfect enlightenment is certainly not possible.[233]

> (89) Because of that [grasping at inherent existence], accomplishing the [six] perfections with the force arising from that [grasping will be of little power], just as [accomplishments] arising from wrong views [which cling to] "I" and "mine" are of little power.

> When inner (i.e., Buddhist) and outer (i.e., non-Buddhist) philosophical opponents conscientiously practice charity and

> morality, etc. (i.e., the six perfections) on the basis of views which grasp at the gathered perishable [aggregates as permanent] (*'jig tsogs la lta ba*), they will not be [completely] accomplished as limbs of unsurpassable, complete, perfect enlightenment.[234]

> (90) There is a great fruit arising from not seeing entities as [ultimately] existent because they arise from an extensive cause, like a sprout [arising from] a powerful seed, etc.

Gyel-tsab reiterates this point[235] with very little variance:

> The subject, the generosity which arises without the wisdom realizing emptiness, will generate fruits of little power because the cause of giving arises from a perverted view, like the fruits which arise from grasping at "I" and "mine." That is the case because truly established phenomena are harmed by valid knowledge, like grasping at a mirage and considering it to be water [is harmed by valid knowledge].

> [In contrast with the relatively little worth to be found in the performance of the six perfections and other acts of virtue when they are still grounded in erroneous views which cling to "I" and "mine"], the subject, generosity that arises on the basis of the [wisdom realizing] emptiness, produces pure effects because of arising from extensive, thoroughly pure causes of development, like the arising of a sprout of a fresh seed.[236]

Yogācāra-Madhyamaka Synthesis

Here, in the final stanzas of *MA,* we find some of the keys to Śāntarakṣita's Yogācāra-Madhyamaka synthesis. While in many senses, Śāntarakṣita's text has been quite dynamic in its utilization of an assortment of both Buddhist and non-Buddhist views to help illuminate his own view, at this point in the text he is explicit in incorporation of a Yogācāra framework for understanding conventional truth. I think it is important to reflect on what has happened in the text up to this point in order to fully understand his Yogācāra-Madhyamaka synthesis. As mentioned in the Introduction, Śāntarakṣita is engaged in a dynamic philosophical enterprise in this text in which the perspective of his philosophical analysis shifts depending on the views of his opponents. Generally speaking, he argues as a Sautrāntika when criticizing Vaibhāṣika views, as a Yogācāra when criticizing Sautrāntika views, and as a Mādhyamika when criticizing various Yogācāra positions. While in the final analysis he maintains specific views and we can correctly say that he is a Mādhyamika since he rejects the existence of an ultimate nature in phenomena, one might also be inclined to say that he is a "Yogācāra-Mādhyamika" in that he rejects the externality of objects conventionally. However, Śāntarakṣita's philosophical movements are more dynamic than such a static portrayal may reveal, as useful as they may be for taxonomic purposes. By use of "sliding scales of analysis," I think Śāntarakṣita's brand of Buddhist philosophy, far from being exclusive, is much more inclusive of all systems of Buddhist thought. In fact, as discussed in the Introduction, he utilizes multiple provisional views, not only that of Yogācāra, in an attempt to lead followers to a Madhyamaka position realizing the lack of any inherent nature in phenomena.

Furthermore, there appear to be graded stages of provisionality. This is not to say that Śāntarakṣita does not offer standard definitions of ultimate and conventional truths, where his basic presentation of conventional truths rests on the fundamentals of a Yogācāra framework. My point here is that to attempt to understand Śāntarakṣita's philosophical enterprise solely on the basis of those definitions, without a deeper investigation of the dynamic process at work in his philosophical enterprise which additionally integrates multiple provisionalities, is to miss much of the richness.[237] I also think that Śāntarakṣita was enormously influential on Tibetan philosophers, in this respect, as they began to formulate their own styles of doxography and indigenous Tibetan approaches to the study of Buddhist philosophy. All of the major schools of Tibetan Buddhism now utilize doxographical presentations of Indian tenets as a primary method for leading students up a hierarchy of views to the one considered to be the highest and most accurate philosophical presentation of the nature of reality. It is quite possible that this methodological approach is a sign of one aspect of the lasting influence Śāntarakṣita has had on Tibetan philosophical study.

At this point in the text, having now refuted the qualms Śāntarakṣita thinks are commonly brought to Mādhyamikas, he proceeds into the next topic. This Gyel-tsab describes as putting forth the nature of conventional truth. This is where we find the explicit discussion of the Yogācāra-Madhyamaka syncretism. In order to lead into this discussion of conventional truth, which for Śāntarakṣita inevitably leads to epistemological issues, he notes by way of introduction that he has already covered the subject of self-cognizing cognition (*svasaṃvedana, rang rig*). His point is that, because it has been found through ultimate analysis that self-cognizing cognition has neither a singular nor manifold nature and therefore must have no nature, it ought to be regarded as conventional. Like the other Yogācāra tenets he accepts, Śāntarakṣita makes clear that this acceptance is only conventional, unlike Yogācaras themselves, who accept such things as self-cognizing cognition ultimately:

> I have already demonstrated that self-cognizing cognition is classified as conventional truth because it cannot bear an analysis which looks for a singular or a manifold nature. Therefore, because I have already made [this argument], I will not make it again.[238]

Śāntarakṣita begins the discussion which aims at defining his position on conventional truth in the ninety-first root text stanza. Here he boldly claims that all conventional phenomena, those which are dependently-arisen or, in other words, are cause and result, are merely consciousness, just as the Mind Only School ultimately holds. Thus, just as proponents of the Mind Only School maintain self-cognizing cognition ultimately, Śāntarakṣita maintains self-cognizing cognition on the conventional level as an integral part of his epistemological standpoint. At this point in the text, Śāntarakṣita is presenting his final position after moving through several layers of provisionalities. This final position involves the use of a Yogācāra or Mind Only framework for understanding conventional truths and a Madhyamaka framework for ultimate analysis. This stanza is thus one of the pivotal stanzas in the entire text, as it explicitly establishes his philosophical link with the Mind Only School:

> (91) That which is cause and result is mere consciousness only.
> Whatever is established by itself abides in consciousness.

Śāntarakṣita's autocommentary follows this stanza with a short discussion of how knowledge of external objects is untenable. This he has argued earlier in the text from a Yogācāra perspective in relation to the Sautrāntikas and Vaibhāṣikas. If objects were separate from the consciousness, then it is argued they could not be validly cognized. Gyel-tsab succinctly explains this point:

> The subject, all phenomena which are included in cause and effect, are not other than the substance of consciousness because they are established by the mode of experience which knows them by direct valid cognition.[239]

Śāntarakṣita supports his position on the non-existence of external objects by quoting the *Laṅkāvatārasūtra* in addition to his logical argumentation, thus appealing to both reason and scriptures. After quoting the *sūtra*, he then questions whether Yogācāras go far enough with their reasoning. Śāntarakṣita takes a step further than Yogācāras who merely reject the real existence of external objects. By applying ultimate Madhyamaka analysis, which looks for a true nature in entities, to the mind itself, the real existence of the mind also is rejected by Śāntarakṣita. He thus turns a corner here that bridges the two Mahāyāna philosophical systems into one syncretic system. The Yogācāra view is useful for rejecting many of the incorrect assertions of lower schools. By use of a Yogācāra framework for conventional truth, it is also a relatively easy move to a Madhyamaka analysis of the mind that sees that it too does not have any ultimate nature. In effect, Śāntarakṣita is offering a second framework through which to reject the true existence of phenomena. First he analyzes entities by way of the neither-one-nor-many argument. Then here, he states that one can know that external phenomena do not truly exist because they are not of a separate nature from the mind, in other words, by relying on a Yogācāra-type analysis. Then he returns to the Madhyamaka framework of the neither-one-nor-many argument by claiming that the mind itself does not ultimately exist because it has neither a singular nor a manifold nature. This effectively supersedes the overarching Yogācāra position in favor of a Madhyamaka one for final analysis. Śāntarakṣita explains this as follows in *MAV* passages leading to the ninety-second stanza of *MA* and in the *MAV* commentary which follows the ninety-second root text stanza:

> *The Descent into Laṅkā Sūtra* (*Laṅkāvatārasūtra, Lang kar gshegs pa'i mdo*) says, "External forms do not exist. [They only] appear external to our minds."

> They (i.e., Yogācāras) think that this teaching is an excellent explanation. Since even when those powerful minds with strong abiding diligence examine the mind for a singular or manifold nature, they do not see an ultimate nature, they do not assert it to exist in reality. Therefore:[240]

(92) By relying on the Mind Only (*cittamatra, sems tsam pa*) [system], know that external entities do not exist. And by relying on this [Madhyamaka] system, know that no self at all exists, even in that [mind].

> By relying on the system of the Mind Only, [objects] asserted as external from the mind and associated [mental states], such as for example [dichotomies such as] "I" and "mine" or "grasper" and "object of grasping," etc., are known without difficulty as lacking inherent existence.
>
> According to this [Madhyamaka] system, since nothing arises independently, the mind is also already known to have no inherent nature. If one takes this from the perspective of the Madhyamaka path which abandons all extremes, then since the mind has no singular or manifold nature, it has no nature at all. [241]

Gyel-tsab once again sums up the point in a succinct inference explaining that first one knows that all phenomena do not exist but are the mere nature of the mind, and then one realizes that the mind also does not truly exist based on a Madhyamaka analysis utilizing the neither-one-nor-many reasoning. Gyel-tsab comments on the ninety-first and ninety-second stanzas together as follows:

> That subject (i.e., all phenomena which are included in cause and effect) should be known conventionally as merely in the nature of mind because it is void of external existence. Ultimately, the mere mind is not established because it ultimately does not have a singular or a manifold [nature].[242]

Śāntarakṣita relies heavily on the *Laṅkāvatārasūtra,* one of the *sūtras* more widely cited by proponents of the Mind Only School, as scriptural inspiration and support of his views in his autocommentary. For example, at this point in his autocommentary he has three quotes from the *Laṅkāvatārasūtra* supporting arguments he made earlier in *MA/V* regarding the non-existence of external objects, and regarding the position that production and cessation and that which is cause and result are merely mind only. This leads up to perhaps the most well-known stanza of the entire root text of *MA*, the ninety-third, where he briefly summarizes his syncretic view which fuses Yogācāra, Madhyamaka, and the Buddhist logico-epistemological tradition into one coherent system:

> (93) Therefore, due to holding the reigns of logic as one rides the chariots of the two systems (i.e., Yogācāra and Madhyamaka), one attains [the path of] the actual Mahāyānist.

This one stanza in many senses sums up what may be considered the final major development of Indian Buddhist philosophy, the synthesis of the Buddhist logical tradition with the two major trends in Mahāyāna, namely the Yogācāra and the Madhyamaka. This is undoubtedly the most commonly quoted stanza from the entire text.

Śāntarakṣita then goes on with a rather lengthy refutation of several non-Buddhist philosophical school in his autocommentary under the topic heading Gyel-tsab describes as "showing the way that the nature of the Mahāyāna is more glorious than the others." He sums up his feelings about the superiority of the Mahāyāna path in the ninety-fourth and ninety-fifth stanzas of the root text, which explicitly denounce the religious paths of the Vaiṣnavites and Śaivites with respect to their ability to bring about the ultimate goal of Buddhahood. In his own commentary on these stanzas, Śāntarakṣita goes on to indicate the superiority of this Mahāyāna system over those of Hīnayānists such as *śrāvakas* and *pratyekabuddhas*. For Śāntarakṣita, even Hīnayānists realize selflessness, so the key distinction between Mahāyānists and Hīnayānists in this respect seems to hinge on the role Mahāyānists assign to great compassion. Thus we may infer that compassion plays a central role for these Mahāyānists in affording them the capability of removing knowledge obstacles in addition to disturbing emotions and ultimately attaining Buddhahood:[243]

(94) The cause of abiding in the immeasurable is not experienced by the highest of worldly ones, much less experienced by Viṣṇu or Śiva.

(95) This ultimate, pure nectar is an attainment which belongs to none other than the *Tathāgata*, who is motivated by the causes and conditions of great compassion.

> Pure like the light of the moon, this [experience of] the nature of the selflessness of persons and phenomena, this unconfined nectar, is [the experience of] the praiseworthy Protector.
>
> Therefore, the wisdom which knows the supreme [status of] all images (i.e., emptiness) and is the embodiment of gross and subtle compassion which has abandoned and is free from all disturbing emotions and knowledge obstacles will remain in *saṃsāra* for the supreme purpose of all.
>
> Likewise, since they have first realized selflessness, if even *śrāvakas* and *pratyekabuddhas* do not have completely pure minds [like Buddhas], then obviously that is also the case for the great gods Viṣṇu and Brahmā who cling to perverted views of the self.[244]

Perhaps most noteworthy here for our purposes, in addition to the proclaimed superiority of the Mahāyāna, is the way in which Gyel-tsab deals with these stanzas. Unlike Śāntarakṣita, who suggests that *śrāvakas* and *pratyekabuddhas* realize selflessness but suggests that they don't have the completely pure minds of Buddhas due to their lack of great compassion, Gyel-tsab's commentary suggests that Śāntarakṣita would claim that these Hīnayāna arhats do not realize emptiness. This topic is discussed in detail in Part II of this book, but in brief, this commentary aligns the presentation of Śāntarakṣita with other Geluk presentations of path system issues for Yogācāra-Svātantrika-Mādhyamikas in general. Generally speaking, one of the key points on which Gelukpas differentiate their view on Hīnayāna arhats from that of Svātantrika-Mādhyamikas such as Śāntarakṣita is that they claim Svātantrika-Mādhyamikas will say that Hīnayāna arhats only realize selflessness of persons and that this is all that is needed to remove the disturbing emotion obstacles (*kleśāvaraṇa, nyon sgrib*) and attain liberation from cyclic existence. They would go on to say that what Svātantrika-Mādhyamikas think distinguishes the Hīnayānists from Mādhyamikas, in terms of removing knowledge obstacles (*jñeyāvaraṇa, shes sgrib*), is not compassion, but a more complete or deeper realization of emptiness characterized by the realization of selflessness of phenomena as well. This sort of presentation of Śāntarakṣita's view below by Gyel-tsab does not seem to jibe with Śāntarakṣita's own presentation:

> The subject, the wisdom realizing the empty nectar, the actual cause of abiding in the deathless stage for as long as *saṃsāra*'s inestimable duration, is not experienced by any non-Buddhists, including Viṣṇu and Śiva, etc., not by the crowns of worldly existence, and not even by *śrāvakas* and *pratyekabuddhas,* because this is directly, independently experienced only by the *Tathāgatas* who possess the cause of pure compassion.[245]

Those who have realized the meaning of this system and understand emptiness and the way to liberation from suffering see the continuum of suffering of all sentient beings very clearly according to Śāntarakṣita. It is therefore argued that they generate great compassion and the wish to work for the alleviation of all suffering (i.e., the Mahāyāna motivation). Gyel-tsab's outline of topics describes the demonstration of how if one knows this system, s/he knows the cause of the generation of compassion and faith as the final topic of the text. This is summed up in the final two stanzas and accompanying autocommentary:

> (96) Therefore, intelligent beings who follow the system of [the *Tathāgata*] should generate compassion for those believing in tenets which are based on mistaken [views].

>> By generating great compassion for those [bound by] conceptual thinking,without mixing [their own minds] with contrary views and having come to the supreme teaching of suchness after searching for the view, those who accept the family of the lineage of the compassionate teaching of the

> *Tathāgata* take on the heavy burden of beings such as the disciplined followers of mistaken teachings. This is the great compassion which wishes to separate others from suffering. If the cause of the suffering of those [influenced by wrong views] increases, then so too will the generation [of great compassion]; like when one adds kindling, the blaze of a fire increases.[246]

The Mahāyāna motivation becomes so strong, Śāntarakṣita maintains, that as suffering increases it is only fuel on the fire of great compassion working toward its extinction. Śāntarakṣita concludes, in the final stanza of the text, by illustrating that the entrance to the correct view even for non-Buddhists is this generation of great respect for the Buddha:

> (97) Therefore, due to possessing the wealth of intelligence, one sees that there is no essential [worth] to those other systems, and s/he generates great respect for the Protector (i.e., the Buddha).

Part II

Part II:
An Analysis of the Geluk Interpretation, Representation, and Criticism of Yogācāra-Svātantrika-Madhyamaka and the Madhyamaka Thought of Śāntarakṣita

Introduction

The way in which scholars from the Geluk School of Tibetan Buddhism relate to Śāntarakṣita, his writings, and the so-called Yogācāra-Svātantrika-Madhyamayaka system for which in their estimation his texts serve as the fundamental exposition, is a curious one. Those who read Śāntarakṣita's writings, along with those of his Geluk commentators, may be struck by the fact that many ideas attributed to Śāntarakṣita in the various genres of Geluk philosophical literature[1] do not always find direct correspondence with explicit statements made by Śāntarakṣita himself. Often, positions taken to be implied are drawn out and attributed to Śāntarakṣita as if he had explicitly made such claims when in fact he had not. Other positions, asserted by Indian philosophers who are thought to have been like-minded in that they are also considered by Geluk scholars as adherents of the same Yogācāra-Svātantrika-Madhyamaka School (a school none of these Indian Buddhist scholars ever mention by name), such as Kamalaśīla, Haribhadra, Śrigupta and Ārya Vimuktisena, etc., are taken to be the positions of Śāntarakṣita as well.[2]

One of the purposes of this part of my study is to examine the Geluk treatment of Śāntarakṣita's thought, paying particular attention to two primary concerns: the discrepancies between Śāntarakṣita's own presentation of his view and that of the Geluk presentation of the same (primarily as represented by the tenets set forth in their literature as those of the Yogācāra-Svātantrika-Madhyamaka system), and the areas of contention between the two (in other words, the issues where Gelukpas criticize the views of

Śāntarakṣita). It is well known that Geluk scholars who consider Śāntarakṣita's *MA* a quintessential Indian source on Yogācāra-Svātantrika-Madhyamaka also consider that system to be less subtle and profound than their own Prāsaṅgika-Madhyamaka system. Investigating areas of contention and the discrepancies between the two presentations serves our purposes well by focusing our attention on the critical points of the positions and, in the end, helping to clarify the views of both Śāntarakṣita and of his Geluk interpreters. By analyzing these issues closely, the views of both sides are illuminated in much greater detail and our attention is naturally drawn to those issues which are thought to be most critical, those around which the relative unique qualities of the systems revolve. This is certainly true for the Geluk critics who draw attention to these particular points they criticize, but I would argue that it draws us to many of the issues that are critical for Śāntarakṣita as well.

For Gelukpas, as Prāsaṅgika-Mādhyamikas, there needed (and still needs) to be areas where the views of competing Mādhyamikas, such as Śāntarakṣita, fall short if there is to be some important reason to follow their own interpretation of Madhyamaka as opposed to another's. Not only are shortfalls in competing views necessary, but they become a central vehicle for illuminating the Prāsaṇgika-Madhyamaka view by way of contrastive dialectics. In Geluk analysis, there are five primary issues where Yogācāra-Svātantrika-Mādhyamikas such as Śāntarakṣita miss the mark. We will examine them here.[3] The first concerns hermeneutics, the proper manner of determining which Buddhist texts are definitive in meaning (*nges don, nītārtha*) and which require some degree of interpretation in meaning (*drang don, neyārtha*). The other four issues are all more specifically doctrinal. These concern disagreements about the two truths and the status of conventional truths , disagreements about the appropriate form of logic to be utilized by Mādhyamikas, disagreements about the feasibility of asserting self-cognizing cognition, and finally, disagreements about several issues concerning the Mahāyāna path system, particularly as it concerns the status of Hīnayāna arhats. This portion of the study will examine each of these issues closely.

We will look at the Geluk position on each of the above issues, the manner in which they present either Śāntarakṣita's position specifically or, more commonly, a Yogācāra-Svātantrika-Madhyamaka position generally, and the critique they level at that position. We will also compare the common Geluk presentation of each of these views with Śāntarakṣita's own presentation of his views and attempt to determine from a historical perspective whether the Geluk depictions are accurate accounts of Śāntarakṣita's views. There are three specific issues (hermeneutics, the two truths, and the path system) in which the historical accuracy of the Geluk depictions is questionable.On the issue of self-cognizing cognition, it appears that the Geluk critique is aimed at the way that position is held by Yogācāras, rather than the specific way it is asserted by Śāntarakṣita. This will be discussed below. It is also unclear whether Geluk authors, who make blanket statements about the use of autonomous inference among so-called Svātantrika-Mādhyamikas, had a thorough understanding of Śāntarakṣita's use of them. And if they had, it is debatable as to whether they would have found his particular use problematic. When there are discrepancies, we will question how these might affect the strength of the Geluk criticisms and what might have motivated this particular portrayal.

This portion of the study will conclude by reflecting on the discrepancies between Śāntarakṣita's positions and the Geluk representation and ultimate criticism of them. It is particularly the case in Geluk tenet system texts, but also in the general Mahāyāna treatises, that Śāntarakṣita's views are interpreted and codified in conjunction with the views of other Indian writers associated with his philosophical positions (although he in fact may never have thought of himself as so specifically doctrinally aligned with them). The views of Śāntarakṣita and others who were thought to be like-minded, along with what are considered to be logical conclusions drawn out of other tenets they asserted, are presented as a unified philosophical system or school of thought, the Yogācāra-Svātantrika-Madhyamaka system, in contrast with the Prāsaṅgika-Madhyamaka system, etc. Most commonly, this view is simply referred to in Geluk literature as that of "Śāntarakṣita and so forth" or "Śāntarakṣita and his spiritual son [Kamalaśīla]." José Cabezón argues that, "in the scholastic tradition of Tibetan Buddhism, especially in the literature of the dGe lugs pa sect, the *siddhānta* schematization served as a *de facto* canonization of Buddhist philosophy that came to define what was philosophically normative."[4] Indeed, the presentation of the views of the Yogācāra-Svātantrika-Madhyamaka system found in tenet system texts by such important Geluk scholars as Könchog Jigme Wangpo, Jamyang Shayba, Jang-gya, and Thubkan does serve as the basic reference point for the views on Śāntarakṣita and this system of thought. These presentations also define the normative interpretation and understanding of Śāntarakṣita's view more so than do the actual writings of Śāntarakṣita or

Kamalaśīla[5]. Given the discrepancies between Śāntrakṣita's stated views and the representation of his views in Geluk tenet system texts and other philosophical literature, and that the presentations of his views in that literature have come to define a normative understanding of Śāntarakṣita's and other Indian Buddhist philosophical views in the Geluk tradition, questions must be raised as to how those who engage the Geluk tradition's understanding, interpretation, and representation are to make sense of it. What exactly is happening within the interpretive framework of the Geluk School in its presentation of Śāntarakṣita's views? And why is it happening? How does Tsong Khapa's historical and intellectual context differ from Śāntarakṣita's or that of Śāntarakṣita's earliest Tibetan students, and how does that affect his treatment of Śāntarakṣita's ideas?

It will be argued here that several issues need to be considered when evaluating or attempting to understand accurately the way Geluk philosophical texts engage the ideas of Śāntarakṣita and the Yogācāra-Svātantrika-Madhyamaka School. First, we need to properly understand the historical and intellectual contexts in which the writings were produced. We need to know what factors may have influenced the manner and form of their composition. Secondly, we need a sense of the interpretive framework of the Geluk writers. How might their reading of texts, in light of their Prāsaṅgika orientation, have influenced their reading, understanding and presentation of Śāntarakṣita's writings? Finally we need to understand the purpose for composing philosophical treatises in general in the Geluk tradition, and specifically, the purpose behind those which comment on the writings and/or ideas of Śāntarakṣita and others representing the Yogācāra-Svātantrika-Madhyamaka School. It will be argued in the end that pedagogical concerns which are ultimately soteriological in nature have much to do with the Geluk analysis and treatment of Śāntarakṣita's ideas, and that by keeping such pedagogical concerns in mind, we may have a more informed, accurate, and fruitful reading of both the Geluk writings and the primary Indian sources on which they comment. I will return to this in my concluding comments, after examining each of the five issues in some detail.

Geluk Hermeneutics and Śāntarakṣita

> In all the Buddhist traditions, faith is but a way to wisdom, doctrines but prescriptions for practices, and thus Scripture has less

> authority than reason. It should not be surprising therefore that hermeneutics, the science of interpretation of sacred doctrine (*sad-dharma*), should be central in the methodology of enlightenment, the unvarying goal, though variously defined, of all the Buddhist traditions.[6]

The question of how to deal with the vast body of texts which comprise the Buddhist canon has been a daunting one within the tradition for millennia, particularly given that the Buddha is purported to have taught in distinct ways, with differing degrees of subtlety, at different times, for different purposes, and for the propensities of different disciples. Every Buddhist tradition to emerge after the first several centuries of the Common Era, when the Sanskrit Mahāyāna canon which contained several distinct understandings of reality was prevalent, had to develop an interpretive framework for understanding these variances.[7] Perhaps the clearest and most succinct exposition of the Geluk hermeneutical position for our purposes, concerning Śāntarakṣita and the Yogācāra-Svātantrika-Madhyamaka system, comes in the early parts of the "Special Insight" (*lhag mthong, vipaśyanā*) chapter of Tsong Khapa's *LRCh*. Although hermeneutics is certainly a central theme in *LSN*, the central focus of hermeneutics in that text concerns the interpretation of the so-called Yogācāra sūtras, particularly *The Sūtra Unravelling the Thought* (*Saṃdhinirmocanasūtra*). In *LRCh*, Tsong Khapa is concerned with demonstrating the process for determining, among the vast canon of Buddhist sūtras, which are interpretable and which are definitive from the perspective of the Prasaṅgika-Mādhyamikas. Therefore, in setting up the criteria by which one may correctly distinguish canonical texts of definitive meaning from those of interpretable meaning, Tsong Khapa does so by contrasting his approach with that taken by his Mādhyamika rivals.

Knowing which texts are interpretable and which are definitive is an indispensable prerequisite for obtaining the correct view according to Tsong Khapa. By way of introduction to his discussion of the topic, Tsong Khapa frames the dilemma and offers a simple solution. However, his solution requires one to already know what the ultimate truth is to some degree, or what "the ultimate" is to which he refers. He writes:

> Those who wish to realize suchness must rely on the Conqueror's scriptures. However, due to the various thoughts of trainees, the

> scriptures vary. Hence you might wonder in dependence on what sort [of scripture] you should seek the meaning of the profound. Suchness should be realized through reliance upon scriptures of definitive meaning.
>
> Should you wonder, "What sort [of scripture] is of definitive meaning and what sort requires interpretation?" This is posited by way of the subjects discussed. Those teaching the ultimate are held to be scriptures of definitive meaning and those teaching conventionalities are held to be scriptures whose meaning requires interpretation.[8]

In this way Tsong Khapa outlines his basic definitions of interpretable and definitive scriptures. Those whose subjects are the ultimate, meaning those that teach the ultimate nature of reality, are definitive, and those for which the subjects are conventionalities are interpretable. In addition, he argues that some *sūtras* teach both conventional and ultimate truth, but that their principal purpose is to illuminate the meaning of the ultimate and they are thus considered as definitive scriptures (*nges don gsung rab*). Tsong Khapa also describes certain commentarial literature, such as that of Nāgārjuna, which he argues was prophesied in several *sūtras* and *tantras* as being non-erroneous or definitive. He defends this position by pointing out that all the great Mādhyamika commentators, including Buddhapālita, Bhāvaviveka, Candrakīrti, and Śāntarakṣita, consider the works of Nāgārjuna to be non-erroneous commentaries on *The Perfection of Wisdom Sūtras*. The writings of Nāgārjuna's disciple, Āryadeva, hold similar consensus among the great Mādhyamika commentators. The point here is that definitive scriptures require no further interpretation because there is no further meaning beyond them to find. A definitive text is so called not so much because its specific words are to be taken literally as because the meaning it aims to convey is definitive.

Interpretable scriptures (*drangs don gsung rab*) are therefore those which require interpretation of the meaning, those for which there is a "higher" meaning not explicitly expressed in them, those for which the subject is conventional truth, or those for which the subject is the presentation of one of the "lower" Buddhist views. In the Special Insight chapter of *LRCh*, Tsong Khapa quotes Kamalaśīla from his treatise *Illumination of the Middle Way* (*Madhyamakāloka, dbU ma snang ba*) in order to support his own position:

> Kamalaśīla's *Illumination of the Middle Way* states, "Therefore, it should be understood that, 'Only those that discuss the ultimate are of definitive meaning,and the opposite are of interpretable meaning'."[9]

Despite this statement of apparent concurrence with Tsong Khapa's views, Geluk treatments of both subdivisions of Svātantrika-Mādhyamikas (i.e., Sautrāntika-Svātantrika-Madhyamaka and Yogācāra-Svātantrika-Madhyamaka) consider them to diverge from the Gelukpas' own Prāsangika-Mādhyamika position on the issue of interpretable versus definitive scriptures. The primary discrepancy regards texts whose exposition requires interpretation because they are not valid just as they are expressed. Gelukpas consider the meaning conveyed in a text to be of central importance here, whereas they claim that for Svātantrikas the words of the scripture must additionally be acceptable literally as they are written. If any slight interpretation is needed, then according to Geluk authors, a Svātantrika-Mādhyamika such as Śāntarakṣita would find that text interpretable. For example, *Prajñāhṛdaya* (The Heart Sūtra) is considered to be a definitive text for Gelukpas because the meaning it conveys is definitive. Its subject is the emptiness of all phenomena, the ultimate nature of reality. However, according to Geluk authors, it is not considered definitive for Svātantrika-Mādhyamikas because there are so many instances of negation without qualification. Stating that there is "no form, no feeling," etc. without qualifying these statements with terms such as "ultimately existing" or "truly existing" indicates that this text requires further interpretation for them. Tsong Khapa again quotes Kamalaśīla's *Madhyamakāloka* and then comments on it in *LRCh* to support his presentation of the Svātantrika-Madhyamaka position:

> Kamalaśīla's *Illumination of the Middle Way* says, "What is a [sūtra] of definitive meaning? That of which there is valid cognition and which makes an explanation in terms of the ultimate, for it cannot be interpreted by another [person] as something aside from that."
>
> Through this statement one can implicitly understand [scriptures] of interpretable meaning. Those for which the meaning is to be interpreted, or which require interpretation, are those which, their meaning being unsuitable to hold just as it is, must be interpreted

> as some other meaning through explaining [their] thought. Or, they are those for which the meaning, although alright to hold as literal, is not the final suchness, and one must still seek that suchness as something other than that[10] [mere appearance].[11]

Gelukpas claim that Svātantrika-Mādhyamikas demand qualifcation because they accept that one can say entities "inherently exist" (*rang bzhin kyis grub*) conventionally and do "exist by way of their own characteristics" (*rang gi mtshan nyid kyis grub*) conventionally. According to Gelukpas, it would be acceptable for Svātantrikas to simply state that entities actually exist because for Svātantrikas they inherently exist conventionally. Thus the qualification of "conventionally" or "ultimately" is needed. This issue thus begins to overlap with concerns about definitions of the two truths that will be discussed further below. Suffice it here to say that, according to the Gelukpa presentation of Svātantrika hermeneutics, texts must qualify statements about the status of entities or else the texts must be considered as interpretable, or requiring interpretation, since its meaning would not be clear without some degree of interpretation.

It is not clear if this is presented in this way by Gelukpas to illuminate points about conventional truths, to further clarify their own hermeneutical stance, or that perhaps this presentation reflects the position of Bhāvaviveka or another figure (as often the positions of Bhāvaviveka are taken to be the positions of all Svātantrika-Mādhyamikas) and has been generalized to be considered the position of all Svātantrika-Mādhyamikas. The latter does not seem to be the case since Tsong Khapa relies heavily on Kamalaśīla on this issue. It is clear however that Śāntarakṣita does not feel compelled himself to qualify terms such as "not existent" with "ultimately" or "truly" in his own writings. There are numerous instances which confirm this in *MA*. And while Kamalaśīla discusses issues concerning interpretable and definitive scriptures, Śāntarakṣita does not. It seems that the most likely reason for insisting on this position for Svātantrika-Mādhyamikas is to reinforce the Geluk presentation of their own position on conventional truths. This presentation of hermeneutics reinforces their presentation of Svātantrika-Madhyamaka ontological claims, which Gelukpas find problematic.

Śāntarakṣita and Kamalaśīla are commonly grouped together under the common heading of Yogācāra-Svātantrika-Madhyamaka, and when commenting on the writings of Śāntarakṣita in *MAP* and *TSP* it seems as though Kamalaśīla remains faithful to the writings and intentions of his teacher.

However, a close study of *Madhyamakāloka* (the text Tsong Khapa draws heavily from on this point) would be required to determine whether his views remain close to Śāntarakṣita's in his own independent treatise.[12]

In the Special Insight chapter of *LRCh,* however, Tsong Khapa's aim is not to give a historical, narrative account of the views of all Indian Buddhist scholars. Rather, he presents streamlined accounts of general systems of thought which are most likely amalgamations of several authors' views against which he can contrast and draw forth his own views. For a delineation of Svātantrika views on interpretable and definitive scriptures, he relies on Kamalaśīla as representative. Thus, while his presentation of the Svātantrika-Madhyamaka position on interpretable and definitive texts does not seem to correspond with Śāntarakṣita's own style of writing (where, for example, he does not seem to feel a need to qualify a rejection of the existence of an entity with "ultimately"), Tsong Khapa's presentation does have pedagogical utility for the Geluk student as a presentation of tenets which can be used in a contrastive manner to help illuminate their own position.

Path System Discrepancies: The Status of Hīnayāna Arhats[13]

Introduction

This section of my study investigates the way in which Tsong Khapa and his Geluk followers criticize Śāntarakṣita and the Yogācāra-Svātantrika-Madhyamaka School's positions on path system issues concerning the status of Hīnayāna arhats. More precisely, this section examines Geluk criticism of Śāntarakṣita's views on the status of disturbing emotion obstacles (*kleśāvaraṇa, nyon sgrib*) and knowledge obstacles *(jñeyāvaraṇa, shes sgrib*), their definitions, and the timing and manner in which they are removed (or not) on the path to complete Buddhahood. These issues are central to a presentation of the Mahāyāna path system and a key marker which Gelukpas use to differentiate their own Madhyamaka system from that of their Svātantrika-Mādhyamika opponents.

I will begin by presenting the Geluk understanding and criticism of Śāntarakṣita's views (or probably more precisely, those of the Yogācāra-Svātantrika-Madhyamaka system he is said to represent) on these issues. This Geluk presentation and criticism will then be contrasted with actual statements by Śāntarakṣita in his own texts, and those in his direct disciple Kamalaśīla's commentaries on his teacher's work, including *MAP* and *TSP*.[14] Śāntarakṣita did not explicitly discuss his views on the Mahāyāna path system in great detail, although he does make statements in *MA*, *MAV*, and *TS* which offer some insight into his position on these issues. Via this contrastive examination of texts and ideas, I will offer analysis on the seemingly curious Geluk treatment of these issues with regards to the thought and writings of Śāntarakṣita.

Geluk Presentation and Critique of Śāntarakṣita's Positions

The Mahāyāna path system, the map-like description of the states of consciousness and their concurrent obstacles to perfect Buddhahood for adherents on all stages of the Buddhist path, finds its foundational and most extensive exposition in *The Ornament of Clear Realization* (*Abhisamayālaṃkāra*, *mNgon par rtogs pa'i rgyan*) (hereafter *ASA*). This is the primary Mahāyāna canonical source for statements concerning the status of Hīnayāna arhats. While Śāntarakṣita did not himself write a commentary on this text, he makes some important statements in *MA*, *MAV,* and *TS* concerning his views on the Mahāyāna path and the issues at stake concerning Hīnayāna arhats. These are on occasion elaborated upon by Kamalaśīla in his *TSP* and *MAP*. In fact, between *MA/V* and Kamalaśīla's *MAP*, *ASA* is cited eighty-seven times.[15]

Because Gelukpas generally present Śānatarakṣita, Kamalaśīla, and Haribhadra (another student of Śāntarakṣita,[16] who composed two important commentaries on *ASA*: *Abhisamayālaṃkārāloka* and *Abhisamayālaṃkāra-Sphuṭārthā*) as univocal representatives of the Yogācāra-Svātantrika-Madhyamaka School, and the *ASA* as a text composed from the perspective of that school,[17] the tenets established in the *ASA* and the treatises of Kamalaśīla, particularly his three *Bhāvanākrama*s, and in Haribhadra's two *ASA* commentaries are treated as reflecting those of Śāntarakṣita. Kamalaśīla's three texts, and especially Haribhadra's two *ASA* commentaries, are the most widely utilized Indian sources on the Mahāyāna path system among Tibetan Buddhist scholars in general and Gelukpas in particular. On most counts, this fact, and the fact that the Gelukpa's major Indian commentarial sources were written by authors Gelukpas associate with the Yogācāra-Svātantrika-Madhyamaka School, is not problematic for them with regard to their use in their course of study. But there are several critical points with regard to the later stages of the path in Geluk analysis on which Gelukpas, as Prāsaṅgika-Mādhyamikas, disagree with Svātantrika-Mādhyamikas such as Śāntarakṣita or those associated with him. Specifically, Tsong Khapa and his followers take issue with the way in which they take Yogācāra-Svātantrika-Mādhyamikas to understand the manner in which certain obstructions are classified and the place on the path at which they are abandoned. As a result, a major criticism Gelukpas level against Śāntarakṣita, and those associated with him, specifically concerns positions about the status of Hīnayāna arhats. This will be explained in detail shortly. For now let it simply be stated that the implications of their respective positions on these issues are crucial from the Geluk perspective for emphasizing the necessity of ascertaining the precise correct view in the soteriological ascent to the ultimate goal. In the final analysis, Gelukpas maintain that followers of the Yogācāra-Svātantrika-Madhyamaka view will not remove the final knowledge obstacles whose removal is necessary for the attainment of the omniscience of Buddhahood until their view is more in line with that of the Prāsaṅgika-Madhayamaka. Thus, for Gelukpas, philosophical precision is never far removed from the cultivation of the desired religious experience.[18] Their critique regarding the status of Hīnayāna arhats leveled against "Śāntarakṣita and his followers" does not always necessarily reflect tenets actually asserted in texts by Śāntarakṣita. Often they are critiques of positions asserted by Haribhadra or are found in *ASA,* as we will demonstrate in this section.

Let us begin by presenting some of the terms of the debate. In the most general sense, there are two different types of obstacles described in the Mahāyāna path system literature: delusions or disturbing emotion obstacles, which are defined as obstructions to liberation from cyclic existence or *saṃsāra*, and knowledge obstacles, which are defined as obstructions to the omniscience of complete Buddhahood. Geluk literature maintains that both varieties of Mādhyamikas agree on this. The points of contention rest on how these terms are specifically defined (i.e., what sorts of obstacles fit into which category) and when precisely on the path, and by what types of beings, each of these obstacles is removed.

According to the Geluk presentation, adherents of the Yogācāra-Svātantrika-Madhyamaka position hold that grasping at the self of persons (*gang zag gyi bdag 'dzin*) is a disturbing emotion obstacle preventing liberation from *saṃsāra*. On this point Gelukpas, as proponents of Prāsaṅgika-

Madhyamaka would agree, but they would not agree that this is the whole story. We will come to their own position shortly. Svātantrika-Mādhyamikas, according to the Gelukpa presentation, assert in concurrence with Hīnayānists that all that is needed to attain arhatship and attain liberation from *saṃsāra* is to remove all the disturbing emotion obstacles, the basis of which is the grasping at the self of persons. This self of persons (*gang zag gyi bdag*) is defined as a self-sufficient substantially existent person (*gang zag rang rkya thub pa'i rdzas yod*).[19] Just as their Hīnayāna counterparts assert that all that is needed to attain *nirvāṇa*, liberation from cyclic existence, is the abandonment of the grasping at this self of persons, so too do the Yogācāra-Svātantrika-Mādhyamikas, according to the Geluk presentation, assert the same. For the Yogācāra-Svātantrika-Mādhyamikas, disturbing emotion obstacles such as the three poisons, etc. which keep one bound to *saṃsāra* hinge in large part on clinging to self-sufficient, substantially existent personhood. Basically they follow the teachings of the Hīnayāna schools in the way that they describe an arhat's attainment of *nirvāṇa*.

The factor that distinguishes the realizations of a Mādhyamika from those of a Hīnayānist is the grasping at the true existence of phenomena (*chos kyi bden 'dzin*). The Yogācāra-Svātantrika-Madhyamaka School, in Geluk presentations, says that while Hīnayānists can attain arhatship and liberation from *saṃsāra* with the abandonment of grasping at the self of persons, they will not attain Buddhahood until they cultivate the more subtle understanding and realization of emptiness which includes not only abandoning grasping at the self of persons (*gang zag gyi bdag 'dzin*) but also the more subtle grasping[20] at the self, or true existence, of phenomena. This more subtle obstacle to be abandoned is not categorized as a disturbing emotion obstacle by them, but rather as a knowledge obstacle or, in other words, an obstruction to the attainment of the perfect omniscience of Buddhahood.

According to Tsong Khapa, the Yogācāra-Svātantrika-Mādhyamikas assert that the knowledge obstacles which are abandoned after arhatship include the grasping at the more subtle true establishment of persons[21] (as opposed to the self-sufficient substantial existence of persons) and of phenomena (*chos dang gang zag bden par grub pa'i 'dzin pa*). It is this grasping which needs to be abandoned in order to attain perfect Buddhahood, and the grasping at these, which by definition, distinguishes the realizations of an arhat from those of a Buddha. In this presentation of the Yogācāra-

Svātantrika-Madhyamaka position, an *ārya* who enters the path of seeing (*mthong lam, darshanamārga*) has his/her first direct experience of the emptiness of self-sufficient substantially existent personhood (*gang zag rang gyi thub pa'i rdzas yod kyis stong pa*) and has removed all such grasping based on disturbing emotion obstacles from the root at the point of arhatship. In contrast, a Buddha not only has removed that grasping, but also has realized the more subtle emptiness of truly established persons and phenomena *(gang zag bden par grub pas stong pa*) and removed any grasping at the true existence of those.

Prāsaṅgika-Mādhyamikas such as Tsong Khapa and his Geluk followers claim that this distinction in degrees of subtlety between realization of the selflessness of persons and realization of the lack of true existence of phenomena is misinformed. They assert that the only distinction between the two is in the base of what is negated. Therefore, Gelukpas categorize the grasping at the true existence of phenomena along with the grasping at the true existence of the self as mere disturbing emotion obstacles. This is in contrast with the Yogācāra-Svātantrika-Mādhyamikas, who categorize the former as a more subtle knowledge obstacle. Tsong Khapa cites Candrakīrti in defence of his own presentation which distinguishes Madhyamaka positions when he says in *LRCh*:

> Other Mādhyamikas assert grasping at the self of phenomena [to be knowledge obstacles], [whereas] this master (i.e., Candrakīrti) asserts them to be afflicted ignorance (*nyon mongs can gyi ma rig pa*).[22]

And, contrary to the Yogācāra-Svātantrika-Mādhyamikas who claim (according to Gelukpas) that Hīnayāna arhats need only realize the grosser selflessness of persons (i.e., the lack of a self-sufficient, substantially existent self), this realization of emptiness (both of the subtle selflessness of persons and of phenomena) is indeed achieved by Hīnayāna arhats in Tsong Khapa's view and must be, by definition, if they are to attain liberation from *saṃsāra*. But this alone does not equate with attaining the omniscience of a Buddha. Tsong Khapa argues in *LSN* that the Buddha did in fact teach emptiness, including both selflessness of persons and phenomena, in numerous Hīnayāna *sūtras*.[23] And, if a Hīnayānist were an arhat, s/he would by definition have directly realized the subtle selflessness of persons and the selflessness of phenomena. While by definition arhats must have directly realized the selflessness of persons and phenomena in order to have attained liberation from *saṃsāra*, according to the Prāsaṅgika-Madhayamaka system of Tsong Khapa, there are still the more subtle knowledge obstacles. These are obstacles to a Buddha's omniscience which need to be abandoned since they do not consist in the grasping at the true existence of phenomena as asserted by their Madhyamaka opponents.

Because even the grasping at the self of phenomena is eliminated with the removal of the disturbing emotion obstacles, the knowledge obstacles which are removed after arhatship, and which are the key distinguishing factors between arhats and Buddhas, must be something qualitatively different and more subtle for Gelukpas. According to the Prāsaṅgika-Madhyamaka view of Tsong Khapa, they are of two types and are removed on the eighth, ninth, and tenth bodhisattva grounds (*bhumi, sa*). The first of the two types of knowledge obstacles is the mistaken appearance (*snang ba'i 'khrul pa*) of inherent existence, which is much more subtle than the grasping at inherent existence abandoned before arhatship. This mistaken appearance arises to eighth, ninth, and tenth ground bodhisattvas on the path of meditation (*bhāvanāmārga, sgom lam*) when they arise from meditation. The second types of knowledge obstacles are the karmic stains or propensities (*vāsanā*, *bag chags*) of those mistaken appearances and are the result of previously existent disturbing emotions (*kleśas, nyon mongs*) and karmic acts in the past.[24] These latent karmic propensities are purified on the eighth, ninth, and tenth grounds by the profound compassion of bodhisattvas and the ensuing immense amounts of virtuous merit accumulated by them.

According to the Geluk presentation, when Svātantrikas have abandoned grasping at the true existence of phenomena, they believe their work is done. So what Yogācāra-Svātantrika-Mādhyamikas consider to be the end of the path, and therefore the attainment of Buddhahood, Tsong Khapa considers only to be the point of the elimination of all disturbing emotion obstacles, which occurs at the end of the seventh ground. Tsong Khapa[25] differentiates between the grasping at inherent existence, a disturbing emotion obstacle removed even by *śrāvakas* and *pratyekabuddhas*, and the subtle seeing of inherent existence without grasping at it, that is experienced by such advanced Mahāyānists as bodhisattvas on the eighth ground upon rising out of meditation. These bodhisattvas clearly understand the lack of inherent existence in objects and they do not "grasp" (*'dzin*) at them according to Tsong Khapa. Yet due to subtle karmic residues or propensities which are knowledge obstacles yet to be abandoned, they see phenomena appearing as real, thus as a mistaken appearance. Svātantrika-Mādhyamikas such as Śāntarakṣita do not make this subtle distinction between grasping at the true existence of phenomena and the more subtle mistaken appearance of inherent existence because they are not aware of it according to Tsong Khapa. They feel that the goal is accomplished after having abandoned grasping at the inherent existence of phenomena and thus do not abandon these subtle knowledge obstacles.[26] This flaw in their understanding results in a failure to remove the subtlest of knowledge obstacles, the mistaken appearance of true inherent existence and the latent propensities which cause it, and in an ultimate failure to attain Buddhahood until their understanding is more strictly aligned with that of the Prāsaṅgika-Mādhayamikas. Although Tsong Khapa does not explicitly relate the reason for this flaw to the Svātantrika-Mādhyamika's errors in his presentation of the two truths, one might speculate that he would if questioned.

Critical Analysis of the Geluk Presentation: What Śāntarakṣita Has to Say

In this section I will analyze the Geluk presentation of Śāntarakṣita's views on these path system issues by comparing their presentation with important relevant statements made by Śāntarakṣita in his own writings. Attention also will be paid to the commentaries of his disciple Kamalaśīla as they relate to the pertinent issues (see endnote 8 in the Introduction). As mentioned above, Śāntarakṣita makes very few explicit statements directly concerning the path system issues we are concerned with here in his writings, and they are usually made in contexts other than a direct discussion of the path system itself.[27] While a few vague statements by Śāntarakṣita lend credence to the Geluk presentation or at least do not contradict it, others lead one to question the value of the Geluk account as an accurate historical document of Śāntarakṣita's ideas. In fact, they tend to lead one to the conclusion that the Geluk account of the Yogācāra-Svātantrika-Madhyamaka view does not reflect Śāntarakṣita's own views on these important issues here; in the last analysis, his position may not actually be much different, if different at all, from Tsong Khapa's own positions asserted as a proponent of Prāsaṅgika-Madhyamaka views.

According to the Geluk system, although *śrāvakas* and *pratyekabuddhas* realize the same emptiness as Prāsaṅgikas, they are unable to abandon knowledge obstacles because they do not have the multiple reasonings demonstrating emptiness at their disposal as bodhisattvas do. Most importantly however, they lack the merit accumulated by the great compassion of the Prāsaṅgika-Madhayamaka bodhisattvas who have the Mahāyāna motivation, *bodhicitta* (*byang chub kyi sems*). The strength of the realization of emptiness alone for Hīnayāna arhats is metaphorically not strong enough by itself to cut and abandon the final knowledge obstacles which result from previous karmic stains. Gelukpas would claim that in contrast, because Śāntarakṣita sees the difference between Hīnayāna arhats and Mahāyānists who ultimately attain Buddhahood as a difference in the subtlety of their realizations, he does not specify compassion and the resultant accumulated merit (*puṇya*, *bsod nams*) as the key factor which empowers the purification of the latent propensities that cause the mistaken appearance of inherent existence to arise.[28] According to Tsong Khapa, these latent propensities and related mistaken appearances are the real knowledge obstacles. According to the Prāsaṅgika Mahāyānist, with wisdom one can attain liberation from cyclic existence but only with wisdom and *bodhicitta* and its ensuing merit can one attain Buddhahood. There is evidence in the following statement by Śāntarakṣita to back up this presentation of a supposed contrary position attributed to him, but I have not seen any Geluk authors specifically cite this passage. Śāntarakṣita writes in the *MAV*:

> When one realizes that in reality there is no inherent existence, then all disturbing emotions and knowledge obstacles will be abandoned.[29]

This passage does seem to support Tsong Khapa's presentation of Śāntarakṣita's so-called Yogācāra-Svātantrika-Madhyamaka position on the path system because it suggests that Buddhahood is attained simply by the realization of the lack of inherent existence, perhaps obliquely suggesting that Hīnayāna arhats have not yet achieved such a realization because they have only realized the selflessness of persons. In addition there is no mention of the necessity of merit to add strength to that realization of emptiness in order to abandon the final knowledge obstacles. Based on this statement alone, the Geluk presentation of the Yogācāra-Svātantrika-Madhyamaka view, with Śāntarakṣita being named as the chief proponent of that view, seems reasonable, or at least not contradicted, with regard to these path system issues concerning the status of *śrāvakas* and *pratyekabuddhas*.

However, one does have to extrapolate logical conclusions (which may or may not be implied) out of a vague statement to come to some sort of significant degree of agreement.

Towards the end of Kamalaśīla's commentary on the introductory stanzas of *TS,* he clarifies that Buddhas are superior to *śrāvaka* arhats and the like because they have not only eliminated all disturbing emotion obstacles which keep individuals bound in *saṃsāra*, but that they have also removed all the knowledge obstacles which obstruct omniscience. This sentiment is repeated in stanza 3337[30] of *TS,* in which Śāntarakṣita asserts that there is no room for either type of obstacle in a being realizing this selflessness which is directly known by Buddhas. When Kamalaśīla begins his commentary on this stanza in *TSP*, the first point that he makes is that omniscience is a result of the removal of disturbing emotion obstacles and knowledge obstacles. This position does concur with the Geluk presentation of Śāntarakṣita and the Yogācāra-Svātantrika-Madhyamaka School's view, but taken on its own, without accounting for what constitutes a disturbing emotion obstacle or knowledge obstacle, the position also does not differ from the Gelukpa School's own Prasaṅgika-Madhyamaka views. There is not enough detail in these passages to determine much of significance for our analysis. All Mādhyamikas claim *śrāvakas* eliminate disturbing emotion obstacles but not the knowledge obstacles that Buddha's eliminate.

The relevant questions are: How are these obstacles defined? And when are they removed? In terms of definition, the key point Gelukpas need to substantiate their criticism would be for Śāntarakṣita to claim that there is a distinction in subtlety between the realization of the selflessness of persons, which Gelukpas claim he presents as the realization of Hīnayāna arhats, and the selflessness of phenomena which Buddhas realize.

This necessity of finding such a distinction made by Śāntarakṣita is where it begins to get troublesome. When commenting further on stanza 3337 in his *TSP*, Kamalaśīla clarifies by stating that the disturbing emotion obstacles are removed via "the realization of selflessness." This perhaps would lend credence to the Gelukpa presentation of a distinction, but Kamalaśīla follows this by stating that knowledge obstacles are removed by continued and vigorous effort towards deepening this realization. No distinction is made between the selflessness of persons and the selflessness of phenomena or that deepening a realization of selflessness later entails selflessness of phenomena not previously known. He does not suggest that one selflessness is equated with the removal of disturbing emotion obstacles and one with knowledge obstacles as the Gelukpa doxographers would have us believe. Although not explicitly stated, Kamalaśīla seems to be suggesting (just as Gelukpas do in presenting their own Prasaṅgika view) that *śrāvakas* do realize emptiness. This he simply describes as "selflessness," and claims that a deepened understanding of this, or clarity, is what is needed for Buddhahood. This seems remarkably similar to the Prāsaṅgikas' own view.

In addition, Śāntarakṣita seems to suggest in stanza eighty-three of *MA* that something other than simply the realization of emptiness or selflessness of phenomena is required to abandon knowledge obstacles and attain Buddhahood. That which he states to be the result of realizing selflessness of phenomena is simply the abandonment of disturbing emotions:

> (83) Masters who know the selflessness of phenomena abandon disturbing emotions, which arise from perverted views, without effort since they have become accustomed to the lack of inherent existence.[31]

This suggests that since *śrāvakas* abandon disturbing emotions and attain liberation from *saṃsāra*, we can infer they must also realize the selflessness of phenomena. After all, Śāntarakṣita does not specify that "masters" must be bodhisattvas and we already know that he accepts the idea that *śrāvakas* abandon disturbing emotions. If this analysis is correct, then Śāntarakṣita's positions would accord with Tsong Khapa's own view but contradict the Geluk presentation of the Yogācāra-Svātantrika-Madhyamaka School's view for which Śāntarakṣita is considered the chief proponent. This would be the case because in the Geluk presentation of the Yogācāra-Svātantrika-Madhyamaka School's view, it is claimed that Hīnayāna arhats such as *śrāvakas* realize only a selflessness of persons and not of phenomena. In that presentation, the realization of the selflessness of phenomena is said to be the distinguishing factor between Hīnayāna arhats and Buddhas, but this stanza seems to suggest that something else distinguishes the two and that *śrāvakas* do realize the selflessness of phenomena. I realize that I am pulling conclusions out of cryptic passages, but I don't think I am presuming anything that would contradict other positions that Śāntarakṣita has claimed elsewhere or stretching very hard to arrive at these conclusions. I believe this to at least be a reasonable reading of Śāntarakṣita.

As mentioned before, Śāntarakṣita does not go into nearly the same amount of detail on path system issues as the later Gelukpas. On the basis of Kamalaśīla's comments above, and the conclusions I have drawn from them, we can surmise that a significant difference between Śāntarakṣita and the Gelukpas is that Gelukpas suggest the final knowledge obstacles are removed by the vast merit accumulated by bodhisattvas due to their great compassion. Śāntarakṣita and Kamalaśīla seem to suggest that one removes the knowledge obstacles through repeated meditation and a long-standing, determined practiced simply aimed at deepening the original realization of selflessness.

This conclusion seems to suggest that Śāntarakṣita was not as concerned with compassion as his Geluk critics, at least as an antidote to the subtle knowledge obstacles. But further examination reveals that this is probably not the case either. In stanza 3432 of *TS* and its commentary, Śāntarakṣita and Kamalaśīla stress the point of difference between bodhisattvas and *śrāvakas*. Bodhisattvas have great compassion and take as their sole purpose the freeing of all beings from *saṃsāra*. *Śrāvakas* who do not have this great compassion enter final *nirvāṇa* on death and do not remain for the sake of others. Since the bodhisattva path culminates in Buddhahood and the *śrāvaka* path, at least provisionally, terminates in arhatship and *nirvāṇa*, one could argue that compassion is the distinguishing characteristic in Śāntarakṣita's argument as well. Moreover, due to the bodhisattvas' decision to remain in *saṃsāra*, they could additionally deepen that original realization of selflessness through repeated and determined practice and meditation and thus eliminate the knowledge obstacles which *śrāvakas* do not eliminate due to their decision to simply enter final *nirvāṇa* at death. Thus, if my line of reasoning is correct, a possible further link between compassion and the removal of knowledge obstacles in Śāntarakṣita's thought is established.

Śāntarakṣita reinforces this interpretation of compassion playing a central role in the attainment of Buddhahood and, by implication, the removal of knowledge obstacles as well, in the ninety-fourth and ninety-fifth stanzas of *MA* and in the accompanying commentary in his own *MAV*:

> (94) The cause of abiding in the immeasurable is not experienced by the highest of worldly ones, much less experienced by Viṣṇu or Śiva.

(95) This ultimate, pure nectar is an attainment which belongs to none other than the *Tathāgata*, who is motivated by the causes and conditions of great compassion.

> Pure like the light of the moon, this [experience of] the nature of selflessness of persons and phenomena, this unconfined nectar, is [the experience of] the praiseworthy Protector (i.e, the Buddha).
>
> Therefore, the wisdom which knows the supreme [status of] all images (i.e., emptiness) [and is] the embodiment of gross and subtle compassion which has abandoned and is free from all disturbing emotions and knowledge obstacles will remain in *saṃsāra* for the supreme purpose of all.
>
> Likewise, since they have first realized selflessness, if even *śrāvakas* and *pratyekabuddhas* do not have completely pure minds [like Buddhas], then obviously that is also the case for the great gods Viṣṇu and Brahmā who cling to perverted views of the self.[32]

While this certainly does not explicitly make claims in precise concurrence with the Geluk stance on these issues, it does suggest commonalities and certainly no break from the way they understand them. While making a point about non-Buddhists as a part of a larger discussion about the role of compassion in the Mahāyāna path, Śāntarakṣita goes on here to make an interesting and revealing comparison between *śrāvakas* and *pratyekabuddhas* on the one hand and Buddhas on the other. Two points emerge which are of particular interest to our subject at hand. First, if we can take realizing selflessness to equate with realizing emptiness, which I think is reasonable given that he mentions both the selflessness of persons and phenomena, it seems as though Śāntarakṣita is claiming, just as Tsong Khapa would, that Hīnayāna arhats realize emptiness, or at least in Śantarakṣita's explicit language here, "the selflessness of persons and phenomena." This point runs utterly contrary to the standard Geluk presentation of the Yogācāra-Svātantrika-Madhyamaka view, commonly referred to as that of "Śāntarakṣita and the like" or "Śāntarakṣita and his son [Kamalaśīla]," which sees the distinguishing factor between Hīnayāna arhats and Buddhas as a distinction between realizing only the selflessness of persons and realizing both the selflessness of persons and phenomena. Secondly, this passage from *MA,* and the accompanying autocommentary in *MAV,* stresses the importance of compassion to the attainment of Buddhahood. Presuming that these Hīnayānists do cultivate the realization of selfless of persons and phenomena, Śāntarakṣita suggests that what distinguishes them from Buddhas, and thus what must be the cause of removing knowledge obstacles, is the vast compassion and accompanying merit which purifies the minds of great bodhisattvas who ultimately become Buddhas. Perhaps this continued deepening of understanding which Śāntarakṣita refers to in *TS* comes as a result of this purification of the mind experienced by bodhisattvas as they approach Buddhahood due to this great compassion and its merit accumulated while remaining in *saṃsāra* and continuing the meditation on emptiness. While Śāntarakṣita is certainly not as explicit about all of these path system issues as the Geluk scholars are, when examined closely his positions are seemingly identical, or at least not contradictory with those asserted by Tsong Khapa and his followers (described by themselves as Prasaṅgika-Mādhyamikas).

Autonomous Inferences (Svantantrānumāna)

The Geluk Critique

One of the seemingly most serious points of disagreement for Śāntarakṣita and his Geluk critics centers on the implications of methodological concerns about which form of logic is appropriate for use among holders of Madhyamaka tenets. Concerns about the proper form of logic to be utilized were so central to their understanding of Madhyamaka that Geluk scholars nominally designated sub-schools of Madhyamaka thought in part by the form of logical reasoning they utilized. This is a major topic of study in the Geluk curriculum on Madhyamaka and Śāntarakṣita devotes a significant section of his texts *MA* and *MAV* to issues related to this topic and issues concerning logic in general.[33] Śāntarakṣita, like several of his Mādhyamika predecessors such as Bhāvaviveka, and his own teacher Jñānagarbha, utilized autonomous inferences (*svatantrānumāna , rang rgyud kyi rjes dpag*) extensively in his writings. Bhāvaviveka considered their use to be a necessary component of the philosophical activities of a Mādhyamika, and his arguments in favor of such a position, against Buddhapalita's sole use of consequentialist arguments (*prasaṅga, thal 'gyur*), are well known.[34] He considered the autonomous inference necessary in the work of arguing with opponents for the purpose of demonstrating the correct view to them and for logically establishing emptiness. Gelukpas such as Tsong Khapa, who purport to follow Candrakīrti's criticism of Bhāvaviveka's arguments for the use of this tripartite autonomous inference, consider that by the very use of such inference there is an implied ontological commitment made to the existence of an inherent nature in entities and thus their use is incompatible with Madhyamaka tenets. While it is undeniable that Śāntarakṣita favors the use of autonomous inferences, at least in certain circumstances, and that the Geluk argument against the use of such inferential reasoning for proponents of Madhyamaka tenets is a powerful one, it is not clear that the specific way Śāntarakṣita utilizes such arguments was ever considered by Geluk authors or that his peculiar use of them is the actual target of their criticism. This section will present the Geluk critique of the use of autonomous inferences as well as Śāntarakṣita's own way of utilizing autonomous inferences and the explicit arguments he makes in their support. I will then briefly present Sara McClintock's reading of Śāntarakṣita's use of autonomous inferences in light of the Geluk critique as I think it will shed light on our discussion here. Finally, I will conclude with analysis of the strength of the Geluk critique as a refutation of Śāntarakṣita's unique way of using autonomous inferences.

Tṣong Khapa explains his positions[35] on the issue of appropriate forms of logic in four of his major texts: *LRCh*, *LSN*, *GRS*, and *RG*,[36] as well as in *dKa gnad brgyad gyi zin bris*.[37] Additionally, Kaydrub has taken up the issue in *TTC*.[38] Tsong Khapa outlines three basic logical methods, the first of which he finds unacceptable for Mādhyamikas and the second and third of which he finds acceptable. They are:

1. autonomous inference (*rang rgyud kyi rjes su dpag pa, svatantrānumāna*)
2. inference based on what is acknowledged by the opponent/ opponent acknowledged inference (*gzhan la grags pa'i rjes su dpag pa, parasiddhānumāna*)
3. consequentialist reasoning (*thal 'gyur, prasaṅga*)[39]

The tripartite autonomous inference was systematized by the great Buddhist logicians Dignāga and Dharmakīrti. The basic structure of the autonomous inference has three parts: a subject (*dharmin, chos can*), a predicate (*sādhyadharma, sgrub bya'i chos*) and a reason (*hetu, gtan *tshigs*) or evidence (*liṅga, rtags*). There is also an optional example (*dṛṣṭānta, dpe*) given at the end. The most common example of such an inference given in introductory text books on logic is, "Sound, the subject, is impermanent because it is a product, like a pot". The subject, "sound," is the basis about which something is to be proven. The predicate, that it "is impermanent," is that which is to be proved. And the reason, "because it is a product," is the justification of the predicate. For such an autonomous inference to be valid it must have three modes of criterion (*trirūpya, tshul gsum*). The first is that the subject has the property of the reason (*pakṣadharmatā, phyogs chos*). In this example, the first criterion is satisfied if all sounds actually *are* (i.e., "have the property of") products. The second modal criterion is what is known as the forward pervasion (*anvayavyāpti, rjes khyab*). This is the first of a two part examination of the relationship between the predicate and the reason. This criterion is satisfied if all instances of the predicate are pervaded by the reason, or in the given example, if all things impermanent are included among, or pervaded by, the category of things which are produced. The final criterion is the counter pervasion (*vyatirekavyāpti, ldog khyab*) and this is satisfied if there are no instances of the reason which are not instances of the predicate, or in the given example, if there are no products which are not impermanent. Proponents of this *svatantra* form of inference claim that this trimodal criterion creates an airtight form of logical inference.

Tsong Khapa and his Geluk followers find it problematic that a Mādhyamika would utilize an autonomous inference of this type in debate with their philosophical opponents. The reason is that this form of inference requires that there be a commonly appearing subject (*chos can mthun snang*) for both the proponent and opponent of the argument. In order for such a subject to exist, according to Gelukpas, the subject must be known in precisely the same way by the proponent and opponent. This requires that it have an ontological status wherein it may be established by way of its own characteristics or intrinsic identity (*rang gi mtshan nyid kyis grub pa*) or established from its own side (*rang ngos nas grub pa*). Such an objective ontological status on the side of the object is necessary if two different individuals know the object in precisely the same way. But, any entity which can be established in such a way, even conventionally, must, according to Gelukpas, have some sort of absolute or ultimate inherent nature. Thus, the use of this form of inference implies an ontological status for entities which ought to be unacceptable for a Mādhyamika. Gelukpas therefore claim that Svātantrika-Mādhyamikas must accept that entities exist by way of their own characteristics, or from their own side, or by way of their own inherent nature conventionally.[40] And for Gelukpas, this would imply that they accept such an ontological status for entities ultimately, that to claim an entity has some inherent nature conventionally is really just a masked way of claiming the same ultimately. If an entity has an absolute mode of existence conventionally, it must possess it ultimately as well. A proponent of the former claim could not avoid the latter according to Tsong Khapa. (Details of the way that these varying Mādhyamikas define ultimate and conventional truths will be discussed in the following section on the two truths, but this explanation of the problem should suffice for our purposes here.) Sara McClintock insightfully questions whether when Śāntarakṣita (and Kamalaśīla) use autonomous inference if the requirement of a commonly appearing subject refers to a subject which appears in *exactly* the same way, as their Geluk critics suggest, or if they simply mean a roughly commonly appearing subject.[41] If they simply mean the latter, then the strength of the Geluk criticism with regards to their particular usage of autonomous inference degenerates considerably.

Gelukpas, as proponents of the Prāsaṅgika-Madhyamaka system, rely on consequentialist arguments, which simply reveal the absurd consequences involved in maintaining the positions of their philosophical opponents but do not require that there be a commonly appearing subject to do so. In addition, as an alternative to autonomous inferences, they utilize a form of tripartite inference which is very similar but avoids the faults of using that form of inference by eliminating the requirement of a commonly appearing subject. The opponent acknowledged inference looks, by outward appearances, to be the same in structure and substance as the autonomous inference. However, there is one major distinction according to Gelukpas. The subject, predicate, reason, and example of the opponent acknowledged inferences are all established only by the opponent and usage of those in the reasoning is only in the way the opponent accepts them. This acceptance is merely feigned by the Mādhyamika proponent of the argument. Although the subject and other parts of the inference are apprehended by the Geluk proponent, they are not apprehended by the same sort of conventional or ultimate valid cognition as that of the opponent. This, according to Geluk authors, enables them to utilize the tripartite inference without making the problematic ontological commitments involved with using autonomous inference (*rang rgyud kyi rjes su dpag pa, svatantrānumāna*).

José Cabezón quotes Kaydrub's *sTong thun chen mo* in his discussion of this form of reasoning accepted by Gelukpas:

> . . . a syllogistic reason in which the subject, though not perceived by *pramāṇa* in a way that is compatible to both the proponent and the opponent, is nonetheless perceived by a *pramāṇa* in the system of the proponent and by a *pramāṇa* in the system of the opponent and is posited (by the proponent) while "feigning the acceptance" (*'khris nas*) of what the opponent believes in his/her system as regards the perception of the subject by a *pramāṇa*.[42]

Thus Gelukpas such as Kaydrub argue that one can use an inferential form of reasoning of the basic tripartite structure which is not an autonomous inference and thus does not require the problematic commonly known subject, but merely a subject known by the valid cognition of the proponent according to his/her views and by the opponent according to his/her views. The Prāsaṅgika proponent in this type of reasoning merely feigns the acceptance of the subject which his/her opponent accepts on the basis of valid cognition, while understanding that actually that subject does not exist in such a way as is presumed by the opponent.[43] But the structure and trimodal criterion of the inference can still be employed. Cabezón notes that it is yet to be conclusively determined if this is a Geluk innovation, or if this follows the precedent of Indian Prāsaṅgikas, whose heirs Gelukpas claim to be.[44]

Śāntarakṣita's Arguments on the Use of Autonomous Inferences

Śāntarakṣita utilizes autonomous inferences extensively in *MA* and *MAV* as he criticizes the views of his opponents. Although he states the importance of using inferential reasoning to establish emptiness early in *MAV*,[45] Śāntarakṣita begins his more formal discussion of the proper use of logic in the seventy-fifth stanza of his root text. There he writes that, "[Those who realize emptiness are] those who know it inferentially with reasons which make [the lack of a real nature] known and that cut superimpositions, as well as those powerful yogis who know it clearly by direct perception."[46] This alone does not explicitly claim autonomous inferences as necessary, and Tsong Khapa has made similar types of statements about the importance of defending philosophical points with both scripture and reason. It is due to Śāntarakṣita's larger following of the *pramāṇavāda* tradition and his extensive use of autonomous inferences in his writings that this position might at first be inferred.

Śāntarakṣita does not name Candrakīrti nor certainly a school named Prasaṅgika-Madhyamaka (a designation coined centuries later in Tibet), but his arguments which follow in the seventy-fifth through seventy-eighth stanzas in *MA* and commentary on them in *MAV* suggest that he may be aware of Mādhyamikas who maintain what later came to be known in Tibet as a Prāsaṅgika perspective and he addresses them specifically. Once again, the root of the Prāsaṅgikas' critique to which Śāntarakṣita seems to respond (or at least can be take to respond to, to some degree) is that proponents of autonomous inferences, such as Bhāvaviveka, maintain the need to have a compatibly established subject known in precisely the same way by both parties engaging in the debate in this form of logical argument. Svātantrika-Mādhyamikas would assert, according to their Prasaṅgika Geluk critics, that there is non-erroneous conventional valid cognition (*pramāṇa, tshad ma*) which establishes a common subject for both parties involved in the argument regardless of the particular tenets they maintain upon entrance into the argument. In further elaboration on the arguments discussed above, Gelukpas would disagree with this position, arguing that the valid cognition could only be non-erroneous for both parties if in fact its object was established by way of its own characteristics, an ontological impossibility, according to Gelukpas, for any Mādhyamika. Thus, according to Gelukpas, to accept a common subject on the basis of non-erroneous valid cognition is to accept that entities exist by way of their characteristics and are therefore not ultimately empty of an inherent nature. This is unacceptable for Mādhyamikas.

After claiming that emptiness must be established with both scriptural attestation and reason, Śāntarakṣita begins to give both sides of an argument that appears to be about the use of autonomous inferences by Mādhyamikas in establishing emptiness. He argues against an opponent who claims that the use of such inferences is problematic for Mādhyamikas because they presume that the components of the inference, such as the subject and the reason, inherently exist, thus undermining the argument that all phenomena lack inherent existence. Śāntarakṣita claims that one must utilize such validly established arguments precisely in order to establish the emptiness of an inherent nature in entities, the single most important Mādhyamika tenet. He writes:

> If no reason is asserted which establishes all phenomena as lacking any inherent nature, then since it is not established without a reason, the meaning of your assertions [concerning the lack of an inherent nature in phenomena] is not established.[47]

If one does not establish the emptiness of an inherent nature in entities, then simply making the claim carries no weight according to Śāntarakṣita's argument here. He follows this statement with what he feels would be his hypothetical opponent's critique of his use of autonomous inferences:

> [Qualm]: If [a reason] is asserted [which establishes all phenomena as lacking inherent existence], then there is an [inherently] existent reason. If that is the case, then the meaning of your assertions would not be established since the lack of inherent existence of all phenomena would not be established [since you must admit that the reason is inherently existent].[48]

Although the argument outlined by Śāntarakṣita here is that of a hypothetical opponent, it resembles the type of critique leveled by actual Prāsaṅgikas such as Candrakīrti and the later Geluk School in Tibet (though it also could be posed by a proponent of lower Buddhist tenets as well in a broad-based criticism of the notion of emptiness). Once again, the center of this argument rests on the notion that Svātantrika-Mādhyamikas argue that subjects and reasons can be established on the basis of non-erroneous conventional valid cognition as described above. If that is the case, it implies that they are established by way of their own characteristics and thus have some inherent nature. Thus, it would not make sense to argue for the lack of an inherent nature in entities on the basis of subjects and reasons which possess such a nature.

Śāntarakṣita sees that one of the keys to establishing a common subject is to deal properly with the argument that different people engage objects differently based on the tenets they hold. His attempt at establishing a common subject, which does not require that that subject have an inherent nature, is based on three primary criteria: that common subjects are known by all, that they are not generated by tenets, and that the sounds of the words used in the inference refer to objects which possess "the taste of appearances" they are intended to represent, and which therefore can serve as objects of a inference which is verifiable by use of the three criteria (*tshul gsum*) of a valid inference. He does *not* argue that the commonly known subject must be known in precisely the same way by both the proponent and opponent of the argument as his Geluk critics say that Svātantrika-Mādhyamikas would contend. Śāntarakṣita explains this in the following stanza from his root text and in his own commentary on it:

> (78) Because we have not rejected entities with regard to their possessing the taste (*rasa,*[49] *ngang*) of appearances, [this position is] unshaken with regard to the establishment of the subject and the thesis.
>
> [Some say] all inferences and the conventional objects [of knowledge] inferred (*rjes su dpag par bya ba'i tha snyad*) [by such reasoning] must be given up completely [since they depend on] different subjects generated by incompatible tenets. [However], the consciousnesses of eyes, and noses, etc. of everyone from masters to women to children [are a reference] for engaging [in such inferences] by relying on subjects which are the sound of the three criteria, etc. (*phyogs sgra la sogs pa*) which possess the taste of appearances.[50]

Although he does not explicitly say that he accepts that objects are established by non-erroneous valid cognition, perhaps it is not too much of a stretch on the part of his Prasaṅgika critics to claim that he must do so based upon the implications of his statement that he has "not rejected entities with regard to their possessing the taste of appearances," and the remarks quoted above commenting on the seventy-eighth stanza from *MAV*. Śāntarakṣita's acceptance of entities possessing the taste of appearances can be read to imply a tacit acceptance that entities do exist by way of their own characteristics (*rang gi tshan nyid kyis grub*) as Geluk authors and tenet system text writers maintain despite the fact that Śāntarakṣita never uses that precise language. If an object possesses the taste, or qualities by which it is known through its appearance to a variety of subjects, that seems to be synonymous with saying that it exists by way of its own characteristics or from its own side. While the centrality placed on the use of specific language and technical terms in tenet system texts by Geluk authors may overstate the primacy of their actual use, considering that Śāntarakṣita does not use that specific language, the meaning of the argument seems to correspond with his stated views here. However, it is also quite feasible that Śāntarakṣita is much looser in the way he understands autonomous inferences to be used and that possessing the taste of appearances does not equate with an object being known in precisely the same way by the proponent and opponent of an argument. I suppose the way one interprets this key phrase is an open question.

Śāntarakṣita goes on to argue for the importance of using logical inferences on the basis of common subjects by claiming that if we do not, then all logical reasoning which we can clearly know as valid must be discarded. He offers as an example of an inference which would have to be discarded the common inference which demonstrates how one can logically infer fire from the existence of smoke. Śāntarakṣita then proceeds to argue for the use of inferences based on common, conventionally established subjects. Given that the designations or conventionalities are not established on the basis of "polluted grasping," there is no problem with accepting subjects that have "the taste of appearances." He then argues that those who reject the possibility of such reasonable arguments tend towards nihilism in that what they describe as the lack of an inherent nature in entities is a rejection of the existence of those entities altogether:

> As it states [in the *Abhisamayālaṃkārāloka*],[51] "As long as we do not rely on polluted grasping, conventional designations will be thoroughly established. If one becomes a master in conventional designations, s/he will not be obscured in their understanding of the meaning of the *śāstras*."[52]

> In the view of those subjugators who have animosity toward the system of those postulating meaningful [arguments], the view that all phenomena lack any inherent existence is like the view of complete non-existence from the crown to the [lowest part of the] body.[53]

Clearly this was an issue of serious contention for Śāntarakṣita and one about which he was significantly concerned. While at this time in India we do not find evidence for distinct Madhyamaka schools designated on the basis of the forms of logic which they utilized, and Śāntarakṣita does not name his opponent, he does seem to have been aware of a very specific view rejecting the use of autonomous inferences for Mādhyamikas and felt the need to address this view in both his root text and auto-commentary.

But even after this rebuttal, Śāntarakṣita's view does not go without criticism by his later Geluk counterparts. While Śāntarakṣita says, "as long as we do not rely on polluted grasping," then the use of such inferences is not problematic, his Prasaṅgika critics would maintain that as long as one is using autonomous inferences they are relying on "polluted grasping."

Another interesting issue to consider here is one discussed briefly in the Introduction and raised by Sara McClintock in her article "The Role of the 'Given' in the Classification of Śāntarakṣita and Kamalaśīla as Svātantrika-Mādhyamikas."[54] In her article McClintock argues that Śāntarakṣita actually utilizes what she terms "sliding scales of analysis" in his arguments. When one looks at *MA* for example (although this would also apply to *TS*), one may notice, as I described in the Introduction to this study, that Śāntarakṣita shifts his framework of analysis as he proceeds through criticisms of the host of Buddhist and non-Buddhist views. When addressing non-Buddhists and Vaibhāṣikas, he does so from the perspective of the Sautrāntika system and feigns acceptance of the views of that system. When analyzing the Sautrāntika system, he does so from the perspective of the Yogācāra, feigning acceptance of the Yogācāra system in the process. Likewise, when analyzing the Yogācāra from a critical perspective, he shifts perspectives once more, this time to the system he considers to be the final philosophical view, the Madhyamaka, from which perspective there is nothing which is "unassailably real,"[55] contrary to the establishing of a common subject on the lower levels. Just as Sautrāntikas and Yogācāras use the tripartite autonomous inferences, so too does Śāntarakṣita when arguing from those perspectives against opponents of "lower" schools. However, McClintock argues that the form used actually resembles the opponent acknowledged inference accepted by Gelukpas such as Kaydrub. Since Śāntarakṣita and Kamalaśīla do not in the last analysis accept anything which is "given" to experience or which is unassailably real which could serve as the commonly appearing subject, it seems as though their provisional acceptance of such entities mirrors the feigned acceptance of the same in the Geluk opponent acknowledged inferences. And particularly given that Śāntarakṣita and Kamalaśīla shift the status they attribute to the given subjects of inferences as the scales of analysis shift, it draws one to question whether they could possibly accept an "objective mode of being" (*don gyi sdod lugs*) as a proponent of the sort of autonomous inference Gelukpas find problematic must accept.[56] McClintock argues that Śāntarakṣita's and Kamalaśīla's use of these inferences is informed by concerns about leading followers to the Madhyamaka view rather than with ontological commitments which may be questionable. Therefore it is an expression of skillful means in philosophical discourse.

Considering the claims Śāntarakṣita makes in *MA* and *MAV*, which seem to lead him directly into the sort of criticism of the use of autonomous inferences such as is found so prominently in Geluk literature, and contrasting that with the persuasive arguments McClintock makes in her article, one is drawn to think seriously about what is happening here in the work of Śāntarakṣita. I would argue that if McClintock is correct in her analysis, this would imply that Śāntarakṣita's position on autonomous inferences is not the target of refutation in the Geluk literature but rather, that their criticism may be more pointedly directed at other Mādhyamikas such as Bhāvaviveka. The arguments that target the positions of Bhāvaviveka, in his own criticism of Buddhapālita, could not accurately be applied to Śāntarakṣita. Those Geluk arguments target autonomous inference. Given the three forms of reasoning described above, it would be more accurate to characterize Śāntarakṣita's arguments as opponent acknowledged inferences than as autonomous inferences according to Geluk definitions. In fact, in his own discussion of the use of the tripartite inferences which he advocates, he never specifically labels them as autonomous inferences (*svatantrānumāna, rang rgyud kyi rjes dpag*). And that being the case, although Geluk authors do not employ "sliding scales" such as Śāntarakṣita and Kamalaśīla do, and thus their method differs in important ways, in the final analysis both appropriate forms of logic in the course of their Madhyamaka discourses in ways that do not seem to undermine the fundamental Madhyamaka ontology. In fact, one may look to Śāntarakṣita as an important influence on the famous confluence of the *pramāṇavāda* tradition and the Madhyamaka tradition in Tibet.

The Two Truths

Introduction

Since its earliest formulation in the works of Nāgārjuna, Madhyamaka thinkers have utilized a presentation of the two truths, ultimate truth and conventional truth, as a primary marker through which they have delineated their positions on central Buddhist philosophical topics in ontology and epistemology. Late Indian Mādhyamikas such as Śāntarakṣita, and the subsequent Tibetan inheritors of the Indian Madhyamaka tradition, were no exceptions. As Tibetans sorted through and tried to make sense of roughly a millennium of Madhyamaka discourse in India, they divided thinkers and views into a hierarchy of schools of thought with names such as "Prāsaṅgika-Madhyamaka" and "Svātantrika-Madhyamaka," etc. Gelukpas understood the primary distinctions between these schools to hinge on their positions on the two truths, as well as on the form of inferential reasoning proponents of each utilized, which in turn had implications for their positions on the two truths (discussed above).

A close analysis of the works of Śāntarakṣita and his Geluk commentators draws the careful reader to curious discrepancies between the way Śāntarakṣita presents his own views on the two truths and the way they are represented in works of his Gelukpa exegetes and doxographers,[57] who consider his particular presentation of Madhyamaka to be less subtle and profound than their own. It seems as though a very interesting hermeneutical task is at work in the writings of these Tibetan philosophers. As mentioned above, Geluk scholars tend to attribute to Śāntarakṣita views not stated by him which they feel are either implied in his writings or are stated by those Indian philosophers considered to be like-minded.[58] This section will begin with a brief look at Geluk treatments of the so-called Yogācāra-Svātantrika-Madhyamaka system's views on the two truths and proceed from there to contrast that with an examination of Śāntarakṣita's own presentation of his ideas pertaining to the two truths. From there we will briefly revisit issues concerning appropriate forms of logic. Investigating the discrepancies between the two presentations serves our purposes well by focusing our attention on the critical points on which the positions hinge, and in the end helping to clarify the views of both Śāntarakṣita and those of his Gelukpa interpreters.

Generally speaking, Mādhyamikas define an ultimate truth as an object's lack of having an independent, unchanging essence or nature (*svabhāva, rang bzhin*). The technical term *śūnyata,* or emptiness, refers specifically to this lack of an essence, to the fact that all phenomena are empty (*śūnya*) of having such a nature. A conventional truth is an object found by a discursive, discriminating mind in the throes of dualistic thinking, a mind distinguishing between the various objects it reifies and erroneously considers to have absolute reality. Specific descriptions about the way in which conventional truths exist are so central to Geluk distinctions between varying interpretations of Madhyamaka thought, as are the debates around issues concerning the proper form of logic to be utilized by Mādhyamikas in their philosophical arguments, that the names of Madhyamaka sub-schools are designated based on them. I will first present, in general, the basic orientation Gelukpa philosophers have toward Indian Madhyamaka thought concerning the two truths, and, in particular, the Yogācāra-Svātantrika-Madhyamaka attributed to Śāntarakṣita, and later come back to the implications the form of logic utilized may have for these issues. In this process, I will turn to Śāntarakṣita's own presentation of his views and critically analyze how the Geluk presentation of the same (or at least the Yogācāra-Svātantrika-Madhyamaka view) compares.

Geluk Presentation of the Two Truths According to the Yogācāra-Svātantrika-Madhyamaka System

Gelukpas use several technical terms to define ultimate and conventional truths, all of which they consider to be co-extensive or equivalent as descriptive terms for the ontological status of entities according to their own Prāsaṅgika-Madhyamaka system. According to the Prāsaṅgika-Madhyamaka system, these terms are all rejected as accurate descriptions of ultimate *or* conventional truths. It would be incorrect, according to Gelukpas, to describe either a ultimate or an conventional truth with any of these terms. If an object exists in one of these seven ways,[59] it would exist in all seven according to Gelukpas. These are:

1)	ultimately established existence	*don dam par grub pa*
2)	truly established existence	*den par grub pa*
3)	existence established in reality	*yang dag par grub pa*
4)	existence established by way of its own intrinsic identity/characteristics	*rang gi mtshan nyid kyis grub pa*
5)	existence established by way of its own inherent nature	*rang bzhin kyis grub pa*
6)	existence established from its own side	*rang ngos nas grub pa*
7)	existence established by its own entity	*rang gi ngo bo nyid kyis grub pa*

According to Gelukpas, Śāntarakṣita and his followers, representing the Yogācāra-Svātantrika-Madhyamaka view, describe an ultimate truth as an object's lack of having "ultimately established existence," "truly established existence," or "existence established in reality." True existence, real existence, or ultimate existence refers specifically to the established existence of any kind of absolute, unchanging, independent nature or essence. Gelukpas, as proponents of Prāsaṅgika-Madhyamaka, have no problem with this and would agree that ultimate truths do indeed lack any such nature.

The problem Gelukpas have with the Yogācāra-Svātantrika-Madhyamaka view, as they understand it, concerns their understanding of these competing Madhyamaka views on the ontological status of conventional truths. According to the Gelukpa presentation of the Yogācāra-Svātantrika-Madhyamaka view (once again, for whom Śāntarakṣita is considered to be the quintessential exponent), that view holds that conventional truths are accurately characterized as having "existence established by way of their own intrinsic identity/characteristics," "existence by way of their own inherent nature," "existence established from their own side," and "existence established by way of their own entity," conventionally. For example, Könchog Jigme Wangpo defines a Svātantrika-Mādhyamika as follows in his *Precious Garland of Tenets* (*Grub mtha' rin chen phreng ba*):

> The definition of a Svātantrika-[Mādhyamika] is : a Proponent of Non-Entityness[60] who asserts that phenomena have their existence established by way of their own intrinsic identity conventionally [although not ultimately].[61]

This, according to Gelukpas, is how Yogācāra-Svātantrika-Mādhyamikas hold that their view maintains a middle ground between absolute permanence on the one hand and absolute non-existence, or nihilism, on the other. If the existence of phenomena was not capable of being established by way of their own intrinsic identity or from their own side at least conventionally, that would indicate that they do not exist at all. According to the Gelukpa literature, Yogācāra-Svātantrika-Mādhyamikas, like Śāntarakṣita, would say, as mentioned above, that of course things exist by way of their own characteristics conventionally; that is how Mādhyamikas avoid falling into the extreme of nihilism. That is also incidentally how one can have commonly appearing objects such as tables and chairs, etc., which can, among other things, serve as the valid subjects of logical arguments, an issue taken up in the previous section. There is something, or some characteristics, on the side of the chair, for example, which causes an ignorant, unenlightened consciousness to recognize that object and correctly impute the conventional designation "chair" based on a non-defective conventional valid cognition. Such an imputation is not without a referent object to which it correctly points with the conventional designation.

Gelukpas are sharply critical of such a position. They argue against this competing Madhyamaka position, claiming that if one holds that objects are established by way of their own intrinsic identity, or are established by way of some sort of inherent nature of their own, or are established from their own side, even conventionally, that such an assertion implies that there *is* some sort of *ultimate* nature in things as well. They would criticize their Madhyamaka opponents by saying that although they claim that these entities only exist in this way conventionally, if one asserts that some nature of their own exists inherently in the objects in any way, even conventionally, then it is really just a masked way of continuing to cling to some independent essence or nature in things ultimately. There must be something true or absolute in the object if it causes a conventional consciousness to *correctly* recognize it, and label it and Gelugpas find this to be a problematic position for a Mādhyamika to hold. Thus, according to the Prāsaṅgika-Madhyamaka position of the Gelukpas, both ultimate and conventional truths are empty of all seven of the co-extensive terms used to define conventional and ultimate truths. The seven technical terms are rejected both for ultimate and conventional truths in contrast with their presentation of Yogācāra-Svātantrika-Madhyamaka, which is said to accept numbers four through seven (above) conventionally according to the Geluk presentation. Thus, while according to Gelukpas the Yogācāra-Svātantrika-Mādhyamikas accept that objects are established by way of their own inherent nature, established by way of their own intrinsic identity/characteristics, established by way of their own entities, and are established from their own side conventionally, Gelukpas, as proponents of the Prāsaṅgika-Madhyamaka position, reject the idea that even conventional truths are established in this way. Conventional truths for Prāsaṅgika-Mādhyamikas are actually falsities. There is nothing *true* about the way minds under the sway of ignorance conceptualize them. They are only true for a consciousness for whom the actual nature of reality is obscured. They do not exist as they appear to a conventional consciousness. Gelukpas such as Tsong Khapa feel they avoid the extreme of nihilism by -

accepting the functionality of conventional phenomena, despite the falsity of their appearances.

Śāntarakṣita's View

When we examine Śāntarakṣita's own writings on these issues, however, we find a different story. He does not use the technical terminology in the way Gelukpas claim that he does in describing ultimate and conventional truths. As a result, he himself paints a different picture than that presented about his views, or at least about the Yogācāra-Svātantrika-Madhyamaka view for which his views are said to be the quintessential example by his Gelukpa commentators.

As described above, Śāntarakṣita's clearest exposition of his position on the two truths comes in his treatise *MA* and its autocommentary, *MAV*. Therein he argues via the neither-one-nor-many reasoning that all phenomena lack any ultimately existing nature and follows that with the assertion that phenomena, nevertheless, do exist conventionally. The brief general verse presentation as it appears at the beginning of the text before its application to specific views reads as follows:

> (1) Those entities, as asserted by our own [Buddhist schools] and other [non-Buddhist] schools, have no inherent nature at all because in reality they have neither a singular nor a manifold nature —like a reflected image.

By examining those objects which Śāntarakṣita's philosophical rivals claim to have, or imply having, some sort of independent nature through the lens of the neither-one-nor- many argument, and concluding that they must not have such a nature since they have neither a singular nor a manifold nature, Śāntarakṣita considers that he has established the ultimate emptiness of phenomena through valid reasoning. In other words, he has demonstrated with rational argumentation that there is no independent, unchanging nature in entities since they have neither a unitary nor a manifold nature. He thereby establishes "emptiness" as the correct description of the ultimate status of objects. It is important to point out that throughout his neither-one-nor-many reasonings in the text, the object of negation is an object's own inherent nature (*svabhāva, rang bzhin*). A key feature of the Gelukpa presentation and critique of the Yogācāra-Svātantrika-Madhyamaka view is that Yogācāra-Svātantrika-Mādhyamikas accept that objects are established by way of their own inherent nature, at least conventionally, and this becomes a key point in the Geluk critique of that view. They claim that Yogācāra-Svātantrika-Mādhyamikas, like Śāntarakṣita, must accept that objects have some sort of ultimate inherent nature because they accept it conventionally, and thus their view is flawed. The problem is that Śāntarakṣita never says that he accepts objects as being established by way of their own inherent nature conventionally or ultimately. Whenever he mentions the technical term *svabhāva*, it is in the context of its ultimate rejection, as it is here in the application in the neither-one-nor-many argument.

After demonstrating in the first sixty stanzas that nothing has a truly single inherent nature, he concludes the argument by asserting that if there is nothing which is ultimately single, there also cannot be anything which is ultimately manifold since multiplicity depends on the aggregation of true singularities. Thus, as the opening stanza states, phenomena must "have no inherent nature at all." This is presented in stanzas sixty-one through sixty-three in *MA* where he states:

> (61) When analyzing any entity, [we find] that there are none which are truly single. For those for which there is nothing which is truly single, there must also be nothing which is [truly] manifold.
>
> (62) The existence of an entity belonging to a class other than that which has a single or a manifold [nature] does not make sense because the two are exhaustive of all possible alternatives.
>
> (63) Therefore, these entities are characterized only by conventionality. If [someone accepts] them as ultimate, what can I do for that person?

Śāntarakṣita follows this four stanzas later with a clear reiteration of his sense of having rejected the existence of an inherent nature in entities. He does *not* qualify his claim by stating that inherent nature is only rejected ultimately, but not conventionally, as Geluk doxographers argue:

> (67) Regarding the inherent nature of all entities, we have cleared away others' assertions by following the path of reasoning. Therefore there is nothing to be disputed [in our position].

Certainly Śāntarakṣita's rejection of an inherent nature is explicitly a rejection of the existence of such a nature in an ultimate truth or the ultimate existence of such a nature. His neither-one-nor-many reasoning is specifically concerned with the ultimate status of objects, not with conventional truths. However, thus far we find no evidence in his discussion of the two truths to indicate that he does accept an inherent nature conventionally. A possible explanation, or at a least partial explanation, for this Geluk account of the Yogācāra-Svātantrika-Madhyamaka view is that perhaps what is presented as the view of "Śāntarakṣita and his spiritual son [Kamalaśīla]" is actually a generic view of Yogācāra-Svātantrika-Madhyamaka constructed by piecing together the views of several like-minded thinkers. Perhaps the views of other Svātantrika-Madhyamaka thinkers, such as Bhāvaviveka, are utilized for a presentation of this aspect of conventional truths with the assumption that, due to the other commonalities in their views, they may also agree on this topic.[62] For example, when first discussing the issue of the two truths in the Yogācāra-Svātantrika-Madhyamaka section of his *Presentation of Tenets: Clear Exposition of the Presentations of Tenets, Beautiful Ornament for the Meru of the Subduer's Teachings* (*Grub pa'i mtha'i rnam par bzhag pa gsal bar bshad pa thub bstan lhun po'i mdzes rgyan*), Jang-gya Rolpay Dorje writes:

> The basis of division of the two truths, the divisions, the difference between real and unreal conventional truths, the sameness and difference of the two truths, and so forth are similar to what was explained in the context of the Sautrāntika-Svātantrika-Mādhyamikas.[63]

The implication of course is that, given that the issue of the two truths has already been discussed in the previous section on Sautrāntika-Svātantrika-Mādhyamikas, to go into it again here would only be repetitious since there are not significant differences. This assumption by Jang-gya *may* not be far off base and perhaps can be taken as implied by Śāntarakṣita based on his claims about logic, which we will consider again shortly. Thus far in our analysis, however, based solely on Śāntarakṣita's specific claims about the two truths, it seems as though Gelukpa authors are unfairly attributing unstated (i.e., unstated by Śāntarakṣita) views to Śāntarakṣita which may have merely been stated by those thought to have been like-minded.

When Śāntarakṣita himself defines a conventional truth, after spending two-thirds of his treatise rejecting the ultimate existence of some "own nature" or inherent nature in objects, he does not turn to the terms Gelukpas attribute to him. He does not define conventional truths as "established by way of their own nature," or "established by way of their own characteristics," or "established by way of their own entity," as Gelukpas claim is a fundamental tenet of Svātantrika-Mādhyamikas. Śāntarakṣita never uses such terminology. He clearly presents his definition of conventional truth in stanza sixty-four of *MA* as follows:

> (64) Those phenomena which are only agreeable when not put to the test of [ultimate] analysis, those phenomena which are generated and disintegrate, and those which have the ability to function are known to be of a conventional nature.

He elaborates further in his autocommentary by explaining that a conventional truth is that which is known by conceptual thought or designated with worldly conventions.[64] Śāntarakṣita's definition here not only does not support the Gelukpa presentation of the Yogācāra-Svātantrika-Madhyamaka view, but actually seems quite similar to the Gelukpa's own interpretation of Madhyamaka.

The issue one must inevitably turn to in order to get to the bottom of this problem is that of the use of autonomous inferences (*svatantrānumāna*, *rang rgyud kyi rjes dpag*). As mentioned in the previous section, Geluk scholars argue that the use of this sort of reasoning is incompatible with holding Madhyamaka tenets, specifically because their use implies that the proponent and opponent of the argument maintain that the subject of the argument has a certain ontological status.[65] This is the case because when utilizing an autonomous inference in one's formal argument, one must maintain that there is a commonly appearing subject (*chos can mthun snang*) for both the proponent and opponent of the argument. Thus, there must be a non-mistaken valid cognition (*pramāṇa*, *tshad ma*) of the subject by both parties in order for the argument to be valid. Otherwise, if the subject of the argument is not held in common, the two parties would not really be discussing the same subject. They would be talking past each other. Central to the Geluk argument here is that the subject must be established by the valid cognitions of both parties, in the same way, in order for the argument to be valid. If a Mādhyamika is arguing with a realist, someone who maintains the true existence of a nature in phenomena, by use of autonomous inferences, the Mādhyamika must have a valid cognition of the subject as something which truly exists as it appears and not as an object which lacks true existence. Otherwise, once again, the proponent and opponent would not have a common subject as the topic of the autonomous inference. This should not be possible for a Mādhyamika. For example, if the subject were a book, that conventional label (i.e., "book") would mean something entirely different for a Mādhyamika than it would for a holder of a realist tenet system that maintains that the appearing book which is the subject truly exists in the way it appears. In order for there to be a common non-mistaken valid cognition of a commonly appearing subject for both the proponent and opponent, the subject of the argument must have some sort of objective ontological status which is perceived in the same way by both parties to the argument. In other words, it must exist by way of it own intrinsic identity, by way of its own characteristics, from its own side. Thus, Gelukpas argue that to use autonomous inferences is to imply that objects exist by way of their own intrinsic identity, etc., even if it is not explicitly stated. It is a position that cannot be avoided by one who utilizes this form of reasoning. Thus, because in Geluk analysis Śāntarakṣita is a proponent of the use of autonomous inferences (see the discussion of this in the above section), he must accept that objects exist by way of their own intrinsic identity, by way of their own characteristics, from their own side, etc.

While Śāntarakṣita has not made many explicit statements on this subject, he has made some relevant claims in *MA* and *MAV* which warrant further investigation. This has been discussed to some extent above in the section on autonomous inferences, but it merits some expansion here. While these specific stanzas are not explicitly cited by Gelukpa authors in defense of their claims about the implications of using *svatantras* in general, they may have relevance here with regard to their treatment of Śāntarakṣita. Stanzas seventy-six and seventy-seven are supplied here primarily to give some context. The key statement is in the first half of stanza seventy-eight, where in the course of arguing for the use of reasoned inferences Śāntarakṣita claims that they can be effectively put to use because the commonly appearing subjects can be established by everybody from masters to children on the basis of their possessing the character or taste of their appearances.

> (76) Having discarded [views] concerning the way subjects exist based on particular discourses of scriptures, there are entities that are well known by everyone from masters to women to children.

(77) All these entities, including that thesis and the proof, are engaged as such. If that were not the case, we would have such problems as that of an unestablished base (*āśrayāsiddha, gzhi ma grub*), etc., as has been argued.

(78) Because I have not rejected entities with regard to their possessing the taste of appearances, [this position is] unshaken with regard to the establishment of the subject (*sgrub pa*) and the thesis (*bsgrub bya*).

It seems upon analysis of Śāntarakṣita's writings that the Geluk position that Śāntarakṣita, as a proponent of the use of autonomous inferences, must hold that entities are established to exist by way of their own intrinsic identity or own characteristics may not be too far of a stretch. Since the use of autonomous inference requires a subject commonly appearing to the proponent and opponent, that would seem to require the subject to have some specific intrinsic identity or characteristics from its own side which commonly appear to both parties. Śāntarakṣita's words can be read to suggest such a position when he says that he has not refuted the notion that entities do possess the character or taste (*ngang*) of appearances, known commonly both by "masters" and by those afflicted with ignorance. This seems to be suggesting that Śāntarakṣita does not reject a conventional intrinsic identity in objects, which can be commonly known by those with non-defective awareness. Gelukpas are quite sophisticated in the way in which they infer tenets regarding the two truths from issues concerning proper forms of logical analysis. Whether or not in the last analysis their understanding of Śāntarakṣita on these issues is completely in line with his own thinking is open for discussion. (See the above section on autonomous inferences.) If the type of analysis McClintock makes about Śāntarakṣita's use of autonomous inference is correct in claiming that he really does not maintain some sort of unassailably real common subject,[66] then a re-evaluation of the Geluk critique is in order. This is not to say that the Geluk critique would not be immensely useful for Geluk students in contrasting Yogācāra-Svātantrika-Madhyamaka views with Prāsaṅgika-Madhyamaka views in what Tillemans terms an "internal history" of Buddhist ideas.[67] Certainly they have drawn from inference tenets which he has not explicitly stated and attributed them to Śāntarakṣita, although it seems from this evidence that their presentation is not without some justification. It cannot be denied that Gelukpas have a strong case for the set of tenets they present as the

Yogācāra-Svātantrika-Madhyamaka view for their own purposes and for use within their own larger (ahistorical) philosophical project. However, if it were to be utilized as a critique of Śāntarakṣita's actual philosophical positions (which I would argue it is not in the standard Geluk curriculum), this would require further critical analysis.

Self-Cognizing Cognition[68]

The notion of self-cognizing cognition (*svasaṃvedana, rang rig*) operates as a critical issue in the thought of Śāntarakṣita, as well as a serious object of refutation in the thought of his Geluk critics, who include its refutation among the eight unique tenets of the Prasaṅgika-Madhyamaka.[69] The only issue about which Śāntarakṣita makes an affirming statement in the first two-thirds of the text, which applies the neither-one-nor-many argument to opponents' assertions, is that of self-cognizing cognition, albeit still in the context of refuting true singular existence. He begins the discussion of the topic in the sixteenth stanza of his root text when he writes:

> (16) Consciousness is produced in the opposite way from that which is of an inanimate nature. That which is not the nature of being inanimate is the self-knowledge[70] (*bdag nyid shes pa*) of this [consciousness].

The topic is brought up by Śāntarakṣita in the context of a refutation of the Vaibhāṣika position concerning the tenability of knowing objects which are external to the consciousness, a notion which Śāntarakṣita refutes. This of course is a primary bridge for Śāntarakṣita's brand of Madhyamaka to the Yogācāra view, which he conventionally accepts. In fact it is from his Yogācāra antecedents[71] that the notion is derived by Śāntarakṣita. One of the principal differences between the two understandings of self-cognizing cognition is that it is only accepted conventionally by Śāntarakṣita, while that limitation is not placed on its validity in the Yogācāra context. But it has been suggested that Śāntarakṣita's use of the concept is not a mere mirror of a Yogācāra concept, qualified by conventionality in his context. Paul Williams notes that while there may be some precedent to be found in Dharmakīrti's *Pramāṇaviniścaya*, "The idea of portraying self-awareness as the quality of consciousness understood as the reverse of insentience (*bems po*) may well have originated with Śāntarakṣita."[72] Williams also notes that it is Śāntarakṣita who is usually cited on this point in subsequent commentaries in which the topic arises. Thus for Śāntarakṣita it is the quality of being self-conscious that defines sentience. Unlike inanimate objects, which rely on sentient consciousnesses to be known, consciousness need not rely on anything for this purpose. Śāntarakṣita writes in *MAV*:

> Not relying on others to be illuminated, the nature which illuminates itself is called the self-cognizing cognition of consciousness.[73]

This line in the autocommentary is followed by the first two lines of the eighteenth stanza of the root text:

> (18) Therefore, this [consciousness] is capable of self-consciousness (*bdag shes*) since this is the nature of consciousness . . .

If consciousness were to rely on something else to be illuminated, it would be no different from insentient objects such as rocks, etc.[74] This definition of consciousness as being self-conscious seems to differ from more normative Yogācāra presentations of the idea. The mainline Yogācāra definition regards this self-cognizing aspect of consciousness as being a part of consciousness. While it is certainly inseparable from consciousness, it is seen as an aspect of consciousness which observes consciousness, almost as if from a removed perspective. For Śāntarakṣita, it is not a somewhat removed aspect of consciousness, but is the very nature of consciousness. In addition, for Śāntarakṣita its status is merely conventional, lacking any inherently existent nature, whereas for Yogācāras consciousness seems to have an ultimate status. While Gelukpas certainly would not accept self-cognizing cognition conventionally or ultimately, it seems as though they base their arguments against the notion generally on Yogācāra presentations and not specifically on the way Śāntarakṣita describes his position. There is a danger of conflating distinct interpretations of self-cognizing cognition with blanket refutations which do not distinguish subtle variances in interpretation and presentation. In texts such as Tsong Khapa's *GRS*, where we find an extensive refutation of the notion of self-cognizing cognition, he is clear that this is a part of his larger refutation of the Yogācāra system. He does not state that his refutation could broadly be applied to all notions of self-cognizing cognition, including that of Śāntarakṣita (and Kamalaśīla), but that seems to be the presumption among many Geluk adherents today. This is not to say that Gelukpas (including Tsong Khapa) would not find Śāntarakṣita's acceptance of self-cognizing cognition problematic. It is only to add the cautionary note that the arguments against self-cognizing cognition in the works of key writers such as Tsong Khapa are not aimed at the specific way Śāntarakṣita asserts it.

There are two common explanations for self-cognizing cognition. Perhaps the most common example given to illustrate the meaning of the term self-cognizing cognition is that of a lamp. It is explained that, much like a lamp illuminates itself at the same time as it illuminates a room, so too does consciousness illuminate or become conscious of itself as it is conscious of other objects. In other words it becomes conscious of itself being conscious of other objects. The second explanation for the existence of self-cognizing cognition, which is actually more of an argument than a simple explanation, is founded on the basis of memory. It is argued that because we can remember not only seeing an object, but also the consciousness which was cognizing (the object), this consciousness, whose object is consciousness, must be a function of self-cognizing consciousness as well. It is claimed in fact that memory and memory of being conscious is only possible because consciousness is self-conscious, that a part of consciousness is conscious of itself. Just as one can remember objects of consciousness like books and chairs, we can also remember being conscious of them because consciousness itself is an object of consciousness (i.e., of the self-cognizing nature of consciousness). The relationship between consciousness and self-cognizing consciousness is said to be a non-dual one in which there is no actual dichotomy of subject and object, but a relationship of simultaneous arising.

This notion has been the object of sharp criticism from numerous Indian Mādhyamikas including Bhāvaviveka, the quintessential exponent of the Sautrāntika-Svātantrika-Madhyamaka system according to Gelukpas. It has also been criticized by those most commonly associated with the Prāsaṅgika-Madhyamaka, such as Candrakīrti in *Madhyamakāvatāra* and Śāntideva in *Bodhicaryāvatāra*, not to mention the attack leveled against it by Tsong Khapa and his followers from the Geluk tradition.

In turn, the great nineteenth-century Nyingma scholar Mipham Gyatso (Mi-pham-rgya-tsho) (1846-1912) has defended Śāntarakṣita's position in his commentary *dbU ma rgyan gyi rnam bshad 'jam dbyangs bla ma dgyes pa'i zhal lung* with full knowledge of the arguments put forth by Prāsaṅgika scholars such as Candrakīrti and Śāntideva. He argues that even their rejections of the concept are only rejections of its ultimate existence and not that self-cognizing cognition is not a viable concept for conventional understanding.[75]

Gelukpas claim that the arguments made by both Candrakīrti and Śāntideva are concerned with rejecting this concept outright and not with the mere rejection of its ultimate existence. Mipham however finds support for the position that this is a mere rejection of the ultimate existence of self-cognizing cognition in Śāntideva's closing discussion of the topic, although it is a bit ambiguous whether his temperance is an affirmation of the conventional existence of self-cognizing cognition or not. Śāntideva writes:

> The manner in which something is seen, heard, or cognized is not what is refuted here, but the conceptualization of its true existence, which is the cause of suffering, is rejected here.[76]

There are several arguments on the basis of which self-cognizing cognition is rejected by Gelukpas. These stem primarily from the arguments originally made by Śāntideva in the ninth chapter of his *Bodhicryāvatāra* and by Candrakīrti in his *Madhyamakāvatāra.* These Geluk critiques can be found for example in Tsong Khapa's *LSN*, *GRS*, and *RG*, in Kaydrub's *TTC*, in Jang-gya's and Jamyang Shaypa's major tenet system texts, as well as in other sources.

Perhaps the most well known refutation is that based on the absurdity of an ensuing infinite regress. The basis of this argument is that if consciousness is self-conscious and that if the two (consciousness and self-consciousness) exist in a non-dual relationship with one another, then that which is consciousness must be self-conscious, and that self-consciousness must be a consciousness which is also self-conscious, and so on. Thus conscious and its self-consciousness would be caught up in an infinite regress where consciousness is endlessly reflexively conscious. One must pause to consider whether this argument is as strong when applied to Śāntarakṣita's particular way of defining self-cognizing cognition or if it is an argument specifically directed at a more normative Yoācāra presentation of self-cognizing cognition as understood by Gelukpas. It makes sense if self-cognizing cognition is a part of consciousness, which is aware of the conscious aspect of consciousness, as if from a removed perspective. But if, as Śāntarakṣita says, the very nature of consciousness, in contrast with insentient objects, is that it is reflexively aware, then the force of this infinite regress criticism seems less clear.

The Geluk School additionally argues against the notion of self-cognizing cognition based on the argument that its proponents assert that memories of consciousness necessitate self-cognizing consciousness. Memories are caused by previous cognitions. Thus, since we can remember being conscious, there must have been a previous cognitions of consciousness at the moment of the original consciousness which can now serve as the primary cause of the memory. In the inferential formats of Buddhist logic, there must exist a causal relationship between the subject and the reason. Gelukpas argue that to attempt to infer self-cognizing cognition from memory is absurd because there is in fact no necessary direct causal relationship between cognition and memory. They turn to Śāntideva who responds to the argument based on memory in the following manner:

> [Yogācāra]: If self-cognizing awareness does not exist, how is consciousness recalled?
> [Mādhyamika]: Recollection comes from its relation to something else that was experienced, like a rat's poison.[77]

Tsong Khapa clarifies this point and this passage when he argues that memory does not necessitate self-cognizing cognition as a bridge between earlier and later moment of consciousness because memory is nothing other than a return of a consciousness to its original object, albeit from a distance of time. In this respect, his response draws heavily on the arguments made by Candrakīrti in his refutation of self-cognizing cognition. Candrakīrti writes:

> The memory of a given event is simply "memory of an object" and not "memory of the experience of an object." Why is this so? If memory included "memory of an experience," then a second "experiential cognition" would be required to experience the memory itself, and a third to experience this second "experiential cognition"... This would involve the fallacy of eternal regression.[78]

Thus the argument favoring self-cognizing cognition based on memory falls into the absurdity of infinite regress according to Candrakīrti. This argument from memory which Candrakīrti and Tsong Khapa reject is not an argument explicitly put forth by Śāntarakṣita, but again, is one made by Yogācāra proponents of self-cognizing cognition.

Candrakīrti, additionally, seems quite clearly to reject self-cognizing cognition both ultimately and conventionally, as do his Geluk followers. This runs contrary to Mipham's claim that Candrakīrti only rejects self-cognizing cognition ultimately but not conventionally. Candrakīrti states:

> If this is supposed to be proven from the ultimate point of view, that is, by postulating the presence of intrinsically existent realities referred to as "cognition," "memory," and "object," then we suggest that our opponent consult our previous arguments concerning this issue. If, however, it is to be proven from the perspective of everyday experience, then there is a logical fallacy in such an argument which must be acknowledged. Reflexive awareness is taken as the proof of memory, while at the same time memory is used as the proof of reflexive awareness. The argument is circular and therefore invalid.... How could the unsubstantiated [concept of] reflexive awareness be proven by the unsubstantiated [concept of] memory?[79]

Here Candrakīrti clearly rejects self-cognizing cognition from the conventional perspective of everyday experience, thus undermining Mipham's claim of his conventional acceptance of the concept. Jang-gya (1717-1786) also refutes the defense of either ultimate or conventional self-cognizing cognition based on memory in his *Presentation of Tenets* (*Grub mtha'i rnam bzhag*). He writes:

> In our system that refutes it, it is not feasible to establish self-consciousness by the sign, memory. If later memory is set as the sign within the context of being established by its own nature, that sign is not a proof, just as when one [posits] "object of apprehension by an eye [consciousness" as the sign] in the proof of sound as an impermanent phenomenon. Even if [later memory is set as the sign] within the context of worldly conventions, it is not correct, because there is no memory that is a fruit of a self-consciousness. This is because when [it is established that] self-consciousness does not exist, a memory that is an effect of that is not established.

> Without a relation, no *probandum* is proved. It would be like inferring a water-crystal jewel from mere water and a fire-crystal jewel from mere fire.[80]

Gelukpas, additionally, find the notion of self-cognizing cognition, when coupled with the rejection of external objects, problematic because they argue it leads to the acceptance of inherent existence. If consciousness is merely self-conscious and there are no external objects, they argue, then consciousness must be self-produced since it would not depend on anything else to arise. And that which is self-produced must be inherently existent. After all, Śāntarakṣita does say in MAV:

> Not relying on others to be illuminated, that which is self-illuminating is called the self-cognizing cognition of consciousness.[81]

One might speculate that Śāntarakṣita could reply to such critics by claiming that if objects are truly external, then that sort of identity must be fixed and this would also presume inherent existence. Tsong Khapa would then probably counter that objects are not *truly* external, only conventionally external. And the debate could go on. Both sides could appeal to Nāgārjuna's *MMK* in their defence.

The entire subject of self-cognizing cognition is oftentimes an ambiguous one. The term has been variously defined by different writers. And subtle differences in definition by its proponents can have implications which greatly affect the tenability of arguments for and against it. Śāntarakṣita is considered to be one of its major proponents, but he dedicates relatively little space to the subject in his own writings. And while most of the critics of self-cognizing cognition come chronologically after him, Śāntarakṣita seems to be either unaware of or unconcerned with (perhaps due to thinking that they only reject it ultimately and not conventionally) Candrakīrti's or Bhāvaviveka's critiques. He simply does not address them. The Geluk School is vehemently opposed to the concept since it seems to imply a sort of inherently existing consciousness (at least according to the way that they understand its proponents' explanations). Geluk criticism of self-cognizing cognition seems for the most part to be aimed at the position as held by Yogācāras such as Dignāga. That view was the target for Candrakīrti's criticisms, which they follow. Almost no reference is found in Geluk writings relating to the manner in which Śāntarakṣita defines the term.

Gelukpas tend to define their opponent's view on self-cognizing cognition as it being one entity (*ngo bo gcig*) with consciousness, although a different phenomenon. The self-cognizing cognition of an eye consciousness and an eye consciousness are not identical. The self-cognizing dimension of it is "consciousness of another consciousness."[82] Yet Śāntarakṣita's definition tends to lead one to conclude that it is the very nature of consciousness to be self-conscious, not that it is one consciousness knowing another consciousness or another aspect of consciousness. In *MA*, Śāntarakṣita ties his acceptance of self-cognizing cognition to his rejection of external objects. Gelukpas could certainly find room to criticize Śāntarakṣita's position on epistemological grounds that would lead to the ontological problems discussed above. For example, they may argue that if consciousness is self-conscious and thus only depends on itself for its arising, then it must be permanent, as all self-produced phenomena must be. While the Nyingma scholar Mipham is strongly supportive of the basic tenet, his interest seems to come in relation to issues concerning Dzogchen, which probably did not exist when the notion was originally formulated in early first-millennium India, but perhaps needed to be redeemed in nineteenth-century Tibet. Regardless of these potentialities and the ambiguities in its various presentations, the topic is one which draws passionate arguments on both sides and thus is a subject which cannot be ignored.

Concluding Remarks

Many of the Geluk criticisms of the Yogācāra-Svātantrika-Madhyamaka, whose quintessential exponent was said to be Śāntarakṣita, were insightful, profound, and quite revealing. Yet often as we have seen in this part of the study, the question of specifically whom these criticisms are directed toward is a bit ambiguous as they often do not reflect the stated views of Śāntarakṣita. Claims made by others are often attributed to Śāntarakṣita under the assumption that he would agree based on other commonalities, and unstated views, which are thought to be implied by related claims, are drawn out and attributed to the school of thought which Śāntarakṣita is said to represent, the so-called Yogācāra-Svātantrika-Madhyamaka, and then criticized. So why did Gelukpas present Yogācāra-Svātantrika-Madhyamaka views and those of Śāntarakṣita the way they did? I will conclude this section by making some brief remarks which may begin to offer some explanation for the curious Geluk treatment of Śāntarakṣita and his views, again keeping in mind that he is seen in Geluk literature as the major figure representing the Yogācāra-Svātantrika-Madhyamaka system. There are three issues I wish to comment upon here: the pedagogical purposes of these Geluk writings, the historical and intellectual context in which they emerged, and the hermeneutical activities at work in the Geluk texts. I think all three of these interrelated components are important factors influencing the creation of Geluk philosophical commentaries and are important to consider when attempting to be an informed reader of this great literature.

Philologists, literary critics, and others interested in hermeneutics today agree that arriving at the precise authorial intent of any writer, much less one writing five centuries ago in a distinct cultural and historical context, is impossible. This is not to say that we cannot approach such an intent, as readers relying on evidence from historical data, that may aid in informing us about the context and the intended audience.[83] This evidence can come from the texts themselves as well as from other writings of the authors involved,[84] other textual evidence about the tradition in which the texts are situated and from which they emerge, and from additional historical data. All of this, although it cannot put us in the minds of the authors, can supply evidence to suggest reasonable, broad hypotheses about the intentions of the author.

The first issue to consider in attempting to understand the creation of these texts which are the subject of this aspect of the study, and to approach authorial intent, is to consider the probable purpose which Gelukpas such as the founder, Tsong Khapa, have for studying and writing about Śāntarakṣita and the Yogācāra-Svātantrika-Madhyamaka view. By considering the purpose behind the composition of these texts we can come to understand, to some extent, the intended audience and the pedagogical concerns of the Geluk authors better. If we were to set aside history just for the moment, *ideally* the ultimate purpose of virtually all Buddhist philosophical inquiry and writing is that it facilitates the ascent to Buddhahood, a state dependent on an accurate understanding of the nature of reality. For Gelukpas, that understanding is best exemplified in the Prāsaṅgika-Madhyamaka view whose key Indian systematizer was Candrakīrti.

In Geluk philosophical literature, an important pedagogical method for leading the student to a correct understanding of this view involves presenting a hierarchy of tenet systems based roughly on Indian Buddhist schools or on the writings of great Indian thinkers. In later Geluk literature, particularly in tenet system texts, these standardized schools were at times made up of contrived views based loosely on actual Indian thinkers or amalgamations of the views of several thinkers who may or may not have considered themselves like-minded.[85] The student begins by studying what are considered to be the lowest schools and slowly progresses up the hierarchical philosophical ladder. Each "higher" system is illuminated in part by contrasting it with the system just below it in a dialectical fashion. At times, this doxographical style does not represent a rigorous historical approach to Indian Buddhist philosophy and should not be considered as such. Instead, it describes general systems of Indian thought which were in part representative of actual positions held, although the details of which may be found to be at variance with the positions of individual thinkers to whom the ideas are generally attributed. As just mentioned, the schools of thought presented comprised an aggregation of tenets from like-minded thinkers and contrived tenets based on positions considered to be the inescapable logical outcomes of other stated positions, such as is the case with the issues concerning logic discussed above. Jeffrey Hopkins has commented that, "This pretended amalgamation of many schools into one is a technique used to avoid unnecessary complexity that might hinder the main purpose of this genre of exegesis."[86] The purpose is not to create a modern, historical account of Indian Buddhist philosophy, but rather a presentation of common philosophical ideas which can be utilized in discussion with one another by the Geluk students as a method for ultimately facilitating an ascent to the view which they consider necessary for the attainment of Buddhahood, namely the Prāsaṅgika-Madhyamaka. Being the views most closely related to their own, and considered to be only slightly less subtle, Svātantrika-Madhyamaka sub-schools of Madhyamaka thought are the ones most commonly utilized in this manner to contrast with and ultimately illuminate the Prāsaṅgika-Madhyamaka. The somewhat contrived creation of a school known as Yogācāra-Svātantrika-Madhyamaka out of this less than historical aggregation of views is accomplished in order to facilitate a larger soteriological goal. Thus the primary concern in presenting a school called Yogācāra-Svātantrika-Madhyamaka is not to give an historical account of Śāntarakṣita's views or that of any Indian Buddhist, but rather to present a system which best facilitates, by use in contrast, an understanding of the most important view for Tsong Khapa and his followers, the Prāsaṅgika-Madhyamaka. It is not an attempt to misrepresent history (nor an attempt to present history), but rather a pragmatic use of ideas intended to assist students in their ascent to the perfection of wisdom.[87] The hermeneutics behind this means of representation has the attainment of Buddhism's highest goals in mind on the one hand, and contextual and historical problems on the other (I will come to these shortly). Tom Tillemans makes a related point when discussing Tsong Khapa's treatment of the neither-one-nor-many argument in Śāntarakṣita's *MA* when he writes:

> Now, I think it is fair to say that Tsoṅ kha pa was less concerned with what Śāntarakṣita and others said, than with rationally reconstructing the logical situations they faced. We follow Imre Lakatos and make a distinction between internal and external history, the former being primarily logical deductions of what could have been said, given the key ideas of the philosopher in question, the latter being what was actually said, what actually took place. In this light, there is no doubt that Tsoṅ kha pa, the great debater, was a specialist at internal history; as such his stretching of terminology, his imposition of concepts which have no obvious textual justification, should not be judged by the severe criterion of the external historian. Bearing this distinction in mind, we deprive neither Tsoṅ kha pa, nor for that matter, ourselves, of the possibility of using fertile but foreign concepts.[88]

This is not to suggest that when proponents of these systems, such as Śāntarakṣita and Kamalaśīla, are named in Geluk literature, that they are chosen at random. Indeed, the Yogācāra-Svātantrika-Madhyamaka system presented in Geluk literature does largely represent their ideas accurately. But when claims are flatly made about the way Yogācāra-Svātantrika-Mādhyamikas describe conventional truths, claims using specific technical terms which have implications for the value of their entire system and which do not correspond to explicit statements by supposed key proponents of that system, there is a call for taking notice. Thus, while the Geluk assertions may well be justifiable sometimes, this is simply a cautionary note to highlight the fact that there is a complex of issues which need to be considered when reading these texts, and that these Geluk materials ought to be approached with this in mind if utilized for purposes which stretch outside those intended by their authors (which are mainly soteriological).

Of course one cannot romanticize the notion that Buddhist philosophical works are composed to facilitate ascent to Buddhahood to the point of ignoring historical circumstances which have undoubtedly impacted the time, manner, and content of the particular ideas which are discussed and presented. Thus the question about the purpose of composing these works may also be rephrased. Why did Tsong Khapa and his followers write about this system of thought in the particular way they did? That is to say, in the case of the Yogācāra-Svātantrika-Madhyamaka, why did they present tenets as if they were explicitly stated, when in fact they were not, even if such presentations can be rationally justified? What historical circumstances may have contributed to this?

Briefly, Tsong Khapa was writing and forming a new order of Tibetan Buddhism at one of the most fertile periods in Tibetan intellectual history. Madhyamaka was generally considered to be the correct philosophical viewpoint, but the precise manner of interpreting Madhyamaka thought was widely disputed. In the period of the early dissemination of Buddhism in Tibet (c. 800-1000), Śāntarakṣita's views were considered to be the pinnacle of philosophical presentations of the nature of reality. In the later period (c. 1100-1400), that assumption began to be questioned particularly after Patsab began to translate the works of Candrakīrti into Tibetan and teach the Prāsaṅgika view, and Dolpopa Sherab Gyeltsen (1292-1361) began to teach the Other-Emptiness (*gzhan stong*) view.[89] There were several competing perspectives on the correct understanding of emptiness at the time Tsong Khapa was writing. Perhaps in attempting to clearly distinguish and explain his own views, Tsong Khapa drew out the logical conclusions of competing Mādhyamikas and Madhyamaka tenet systems and presented them in this way for the sake of illuminating his own ideas in contrast. Thus, the tenets could be presented in a straightforward manner which would be easily engaged, and criticisms of those views could be standardized and made easy to follow. While his actual opponents may have argued that he merely set up straw men, one might suppose he felt that the thorough analysis of the type found in his major treatises would support his arguments and vindicate his efforts. And this was additionally a time when philosophical positions could be defended in public debate. Textually based arguments, while certainly polemic, were used to a large extent for educating disciples. Furthermore, the main point in describing systems of tenets for use in study was not to lay out the history of Indian Buddhist philosophy precisely, but to present sets of tenets which would contrast well with those of higher positions in order to help facilitate understanding. His purpose was more soteriological than historical. Tsong Khapa was likely most concerned with a presentation of Buddhist philosophical systems which would best facilitate, for his students, ascent to what he considered to be the highest view, that of the Prāsaṅgika-Madhyamaka, that which is seen as necessary for the attainment of Buddhahood. Thus the hermeneutical liberties he took in interpreting and presenting his Madhyamaka opponents' ideas seem to have a pedagogical purpose which is soteriological in nature—it concerns the ascent of his followers to Buddhahood, not a historical account of Indian Buddhist ideas.

Perhaps the ahistorical method of Tsong Khapa and the Geluk doxographers combined the two: purpose and context. Texts were composed with the idealistic goal of creating philosophical treatises that could assist followers on the path to enlightenment. And given that these, like all texts, are composed in a specific historical context, they required that the task be carried out in a manner which was informed by the pragmatic concerns of the time, ultimately resulting in the final form taken by the texts. With these considerations in mind, I think we can be more effective and informed readers of the philosophical commentaries of Tsong Khapa and the Geluk School in particular. And when applied and utilized more broadly, these types of considerations might help us become more informed readers of Buddhist philosophical commentaries in general.

When using these Tibetan texts as aids in constructing an external history of Indian Buddhist ideas, as many early scholars of Buddhism have done, caution is key. Tibetan commentaries can be quite useful as aids for penetrating difficult passages and ideas. After all, Tibetans were the first and have been by far the most thorough intellectual historians of Indian Buddhist philosophy. But in the last analysis, one ought to consider how the sorts of issues I have been discussing here might affect their presentation of these ideas. For reading the internal workings of the indigenous Tibetan philosopher Tsong Khapa, these thoughts I have mentioned here will hopefully serve as an aid to a more accurate reading of the writings of a figure whom I consider to be one of the great philosophical minds in human history.

Part III
Translations

The Ornament of the Middle Way

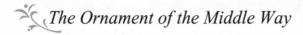

In Sanskrit [this text is called] *Madhyamakālaṃkāra*.
In Tibetan [this text is called] *The Ornament of the Middle Way*.
Homage to the youthful Mañjuśrī (Mañjuśrī Kumarabhuta).

(1) Those entities, as asserted by our own [Buddhist schools] and other [non-Buddhist] schools, have no inherent nature at all because in reality they have neither a singular nor a manifold nature – like a reflected image.

(2) Because they contribute to [the production of] successive effects, permanent [causal] entities are not themselves singular. If each successive effect is distinct, then [the argument in support of] permanent [causal] entities [that are truly singular] degenerates.

(3) Even those uncompounded objects of knowledge [known by] the knowledge which arises in meditation [for an *ārya*], according to the system [of the Vaibhāṣikas], are not unitary because they are related to successive moments of knowledge.

(4) If the nature of the object known by a previous consciousness continues to exist subsequently, then the previous cognition would still exist in the latter [and], similarly, the latter would exist in the former.

(5) Since the nature of the [latter] object does not arise in the earlier [time] and [the earlier object] does not arise at the latter time, uncompounded phenomena like consciousness must be objects known to arise momentarily.

(6) If the previous [uncompounded object] arises from the power of [the causes and conditions of the uncompounded object of] an earlier moment,

then this would not [actually] be uncompounded, like minds (*citta, sems*) and mental states *(caitta, sems las byung ba*).

(7) If you accept that these momentary [objects] arise independently because there is no dependence on others, then they must either exist permanently or not exist at all.

(8) What is the purpose of investigating objects which have no meaningful ability to act? What is the purpose of a lustful person inquiring as to whether a eunuch is attractive or not?

(9) It is clearly understood that a person [of the type asserted by Vātsīputrīyans] has neither a singular nor a manifold nature, since [such a person] cannot be explained as momentary or non-momentary.

(10) How can pervasive [entities such as space] be unitary given that they are related with a variety of directions? Gross [non-pervasive entities] are also not unitary since [some parts] of such entities can be visible [while other parts] are not visible.

(11) What is the nature of the central [partless] particle which faces singly towards [another] particle yet abides [with other partless particles in various directions] either [around and] joining with it, or around it [with space between them, or] around it without space between?

(12) If it is asserted that [the central particle] also faces entirely toward another such [unitary, partless] particle, then if that were so, wouldn't it be the case that [gross objects such as] land and water and the like would not be [spatially] expansive?

(13) If you accept [partless particles with sides] which face other such particles [in different directions], then if that is the case, how could [even] the most minute particles be singular and partless?

(14) Particles have thus been established to have no inherent nature. Therefore it is evident that eyes and [other gross] substantial [entities], etc., which are asserted [to be real] by many of our own [Buddhist] schools and other [non-Buddhist] schools, are directly known to have no inherent nature.

(15) The nature of these [entities] is [said to be] composed of those [particles]. The qualities of these [entities], their own actions, and even their universals (*spyi, sāmānya*) and particularities (*khyad pa, viśeṣa*) are said to be made up of those [particles and therefore must not inherently exist].

(16) Consciousness is produced in the opposite way from that which is of an inanimate nature. That which is not the nature of being inanimate is the self-knowledge of this [consciousness].

(17) Self-cognizing cognition is not an entity which [exists as] agent and action [with its object] because it would be incorrect for consciousness, which is of a single, partless nature, to be three (i.e., knower, knowing, and known).

(18) Therefore, this [consciousness] is capable of self-consciousness (*bdag shes*) since this is the nature of consciousness. How [though] could that cognize the nature of objects from which it is distinct?

(19) [Since] its nature does not exist in external objects (*gzhan*), given that you assert that objects of consciousness and consciousness are different, how could consciousness know objects other than consciousness?

(20) According to the position [of some], consciousness knows images in spite of the fact that in actuality the two (i.e., consciousness and images) are distinct. Since it is just like a mirror reflection, it can be suitably experienced by mere imputation.

(21) However, there cannot be externally cognized images for those who do not assert a consciousness which reflects images of objects.

(22) Since [images] are not different from the unitary consciousness, there cannot be a multiplicity of images. Therefore one would not be able to establish the knowledge of [external] objects with the force of that [image].

(23) Consciousness cannot be unitary since it is not separate from images. If that were not the case, then how would you explain the two (i.e., images and consciousness) as unitary?

(24) [Colors such as] white and the like arise in succession to the consciousness, yet because of arising quickly, foolish people think that they arise simultaneously.

(25) Why, when the mind which hears the sound of such words as *latā* [and *tāla*] arise very quickly, does it not hear [the two syllables] as if they were arising simultaneously [thus rendering the two words indistinguishable]?

(26) Even if we were to consider only conceptual minds, [the images] would still not be known in succession. Since they do not remain for a long time, all minds are similar [to images] in the rapidity with which they arise.[1]

(27) Therefore, all objects are not apprehended gradually. Rather, just as they appear, [they] are apprehended simultaneously as distinct images.

(28) Even with regard to [the example of] a burning torch, the arising of the mistaken instantaneous appearance of a wheel [of fire] is not [a result of] joining the boundaries between [memories of distinct] perceptions because it appears very clearly.

(29) This joining of boundaries is done by the memory [of the mental consciousness], not by the seeing [of an eye consciousness], because that [eye consciousness] cannot apprehend past objects.

(30) Since the object of that [memory] has passed, it is not clear. Therefore, the appearance of the wheel [of fire] is of a type which is not clear.

(31, 32) If one were to claim that when someone sees the base of the images of a painting, as many minds will arise simultaneously as there are images in that [painting], then if that were the case, even when cognition is of a single image type such as the color white, etc., since there is a distinct beginning, middle and end to that, there will be a variety of objects of observation [within that cognition of a single image].

(33) I honestly do not feel that [an image] such as the color white, etc., which is like the nature of a particle which is a partless singularity, has ever appeared to any consciousness.

(34) [According to our opponent,] the sources of the five [sense] consciousnesses are images of objects [made of] accumulated [partless particles]. Minds (*citta, sems*) and mental states (*caitta, sems byung*) are objects established in the sixth [source of perception].

(35) Even according to the scriptures of non-Buddhists (*phyi rol pa*) [such as the Vaiśeṣikas], the appearance [of gross objects] as singular would not occur because its objects are substances which have qualities (*guna, yon tan*), etc.

(36) [According to the views of the Jains and the Mīmāṁsakas], all entities are [manifold] like the nature of a gem [emitting colorful] rays. It would be irrational for the mind which apprehends those [entities] to appear in the nature of singularity.

(37) Even for proponents of the [Lokāyata] system, which accepts the establishment of all sense faculties and objects as compounds of [the four elements] such as earth and the like, [consciousness] is still incompatible with a singular [manner of] engaging entities.

(38) Even according to the position [of the Sāṃkhyas, which claims that the five mere existences] such as sound, etc. are [the nature of the three qualities such as] courage and the like, a consciousness of the appearance of a unitary object is illogical because objects appear in the nature of the three [qualities].

(39) Regarding the trifold nature of entities, if the appearance of that [type of entity] is incompatible with a consciousness, which is of a single nature, how could it (i.e., the consciousness) be asserted to apprehend that object?

(40) [Since] they do not even assert the existence of external objects, [Vedāntas ask] why the suitability of maintaining a permanent consciousness, which is said to arise either simultaneously or successively with various appearances, is so difficult [to accept].

(41) Even for the cognition of [the three non-compounded phenomena such as] space and the like, because of the appearance of many [conceptual

images of] letters for the appearance of the mere name, there are many clear appearances.

(42) Although there are some who assert consciousnesses to which manifold [images] do not appear, still it is not suitable to establish their existence from the perspective of the ultimate because it has already been shown that there is a logical fallacy [in asserting] the existence [of such] with these characteristics.

(43) Therefore it is established from all perspectives that consciousness occurs with the appearance of manifold images, and thus like the [many] distinct images [themselves], cannot logically be of a single nature.

(44) Images are manifest due to the ripening of latent potentialities of a beginningless [personal] continuum. Although they appear, since it is the result of a mistake, they are like the nature of an illusion.

(45) Although their view (i.e., the Yogācāra view) is virtuous, we should think about whether such things [as the images known by consciousness accepted by Yogācāras] actually exist or if they are something contentedly accepted only when left unanalyzed.

(46) Since contradictions would ensue for those unitary [images] *even if* the actual consciousness is manifold, [consciousness and images] are undoubtedly distinct entities.

(47) If images are not different from [the singular consciousness], then it will be very difficult to respond to the following consequence: that with regard to moving and rest and the like, due to the movement of one, all would move.

(48) Even according to the system of those maintaining external objects, if images are not separate [from each other], then they would all also certainly be engaged as a single phenomenon and not other than that.

(49) If you accept an equal number of consciousnesses and images, then it would be difficult to overcome the same type of analysis as is made regarding particles.

(50) If one [consciousness experiences] a variety [of images], wouldn't that be like the system of the [Jain] Sky Clad (*Digambara*)? A variety [of images] is not the nature of singularity just as manifold precious [gems] and the like [are not the nature of singularity].

(51) If the variety [of images] exists in a single nature, how could they appear in the nature of many, and how could parts such as those being obstructed and those which are unobstructed, etc. be distinguished?

(52) Some say that [consciousness] does not naturally possess images of these [objects]. In reality, images do not exist but appear to the consciousness by virtue of a mistake.

(53) If [images] do not exist, how can consciousness clearly experience those [objects]? That [clear, non-dual consciousness] is not like a consciousness which is distinct from the entities, [and those entities must possess images which appear to it].

(54) Likewise, that [image, such as yellow,] will not be known as that [yellow image] by anyone if entities are without [yellow images]. Likewise bliss is not experienced in suffering and non-white is not seen in white.

(55) With regard to images, "knowledge" (*shes pa*) is not actually the correct term because [the image] is distinct from consciousness itself (*shes pa'i bdag*), like flowers [growing] in the sky, etc.

(56) [Consciousness] is incapable of experiencing [images] even when they are examined because non-existent [images] have no [causal] ability, like the horn of a horse. [To assert that] a non-existent [image] has the ability to [cause the] generation of an appearing consciousness of itself is irrational.

(57) What reason is there which would account for a relationship between those [images] which are definitely experienced and consciousness? It is not the nature of that which does not exist and does not arise from it.

(58) If there were no cause [for images], how is it suitable that they arise only on occasion? If they have a cause, how could they not have an other-dependent nature (*paratantra-svabhāva, gzhan gi dbang gi ngo bo*)?

(59) If [images] do not exist, then consciousness [with images] also [would not exist] due to the non-existence of the images. Consciousness then, like a clear, round crystal, would not really experience [objects].

(60) If they say that this [eye consciousness which sees a mirage] is known as such as a result of a mistake, then why does it rely on mistakes? Even if it arises by the [power of delusion], still then that [consciousness of a mirage is] dependent on the power of others.

(61) When analyzing any entity, [we find] that there are none which are truly single. For those for which there is nothing which is truly single, there must also be nothing which is [truly] manifold.

(62) The existence of an entity belonging to a class other than that which has a single or a manifold [nature] does not make sense because the two are exhaustive of all possible alternatives.

(63) Therefore, these entities are characterized only by conventionality. If [someone accepts] them as ultimate, what can I do for that person?

(64) Those phenomena which are only agreeable when not put to the test of [ultimate] analysis, those phenomena which are generated and disintegrate, and those which have the ability to function are known to be of a conventional nature.

(65) Although they are agreeable only when not analyzed [by ultimate analysis], since it depends on the earlier cause, the subsequent fruit arises in correspondence with that.

(66) Therefore, if [one claims] that there is no conventional cause, that is said to be incorrect and is no good. If its substantial cause (*upādāna, nyer len*) is said to be real, then that must be explained.

(67) Regarding the inherent nature of all entities, we have cleared away others' assertions by following the path of reasoning. Therefore there is nothing to be disputed [in our position].

(68) If they are earnest, those [opponents] will not be able to find any fault in [the view of] those who assert neither existence nor non-existence, nor both existence and non-existence.

(69) Therefore, in reality there are not any established entities. Due to that, the *Tathāgatas* taught the non-production of all phenomena.

(70) Because they are harmonious with ultimate truths, some call this [non-production] ultimate truth, but in reality they (i.e., ultimate truths) are free from all accumulations of verbal fabrications (*prapañca, spros pa*).

(71) Due to the lack of [ultimate] production, there can be no non-production, etc. Because of the refutation of the nature of that [production], verbal expressions referring to that [non-production] do not exist.

(72) There is no point in applying [words] of negation to a non-existent object. Even if one relies on conceptual thought, it would be conventional, not ultimate.

(73) Well then, [what if someone were to say that] since by cognizing those [entities] the nature of them can be directly perceived, why don't non-masters also know [the ultimate nature of] entities in this way?

(74) They (i.e., non-masters) do not [know the ultimate nature of entities] because, due to the power of false imputations [of real existence] onto entities by the burdened, beginningless continuums of all sentient beings, [emptiness] is not known directly by living beings.

(75) [Those who realize emptiness are] those who know it inferentially with reasons which make [the lack of a real nature] known and that cut superimpositions, as well as those powerful yogis who know it clearly by direct perception.

(76) Having discarded [views] concerning the way subjects exist based on particular discourses of scriptures, there are entities which are well known by everyone from masters to women to children.

(77) All these entities, including that thesis and the proof, are engaged as such. If that were not the case, we would have such problems as that of an unestablished base (*āśrayāsiddha, gzhi ma grub*), etc., as has been argued.

(78) Because I have not rejected entities with regard to their possessing the taste (*rasa, ngang*) of appearances, [this position is] unshaken with regard to the establishment of the subject (*sgrub pa*) and the thesis (*bsgrub bya*).

(79) Therefore, the seeds of a similar type, which [stimulate] conception with entities or conception without [entities], etc. in the continuums [of beings] from beginningless existence, are objects of inferential [knowledge].

(80) Regarding this, they (i.e., the conceptions of entities) do not arise by the force of entities because these [entities ultimately] do not exist. The nature of entities has been thoroughly rejected in an extensive manner.

(81) Because they arise gradually, they are not sudden. Because they are not permanently arisen, they are not permanent. Because they themselves are similarly accustomed to those [previous habits of conceptualization], they first arise from their own kind.

(82) Therefore, the views of [the two extremes of] eternalism and absolute non-existence remain far away from the ideas put forth in this text. [Entities arise], change, and become like a seed, sprout, and plant.

(83) Masters who know the selflessness of phenomena abandon disturbing emotions, which arise from perverted views, without effort since they have become accustomed to a lack of inherent existence.

(84) Since entities which are causes and results are not negated conventionally, there is no confusion in establishing what is pure and what is an affliction.

(85) Since this teaching of causes and results is established, the positing of stainless accumulations [of wisdom and merit] is suitable according to this text.

(86) Pure results arise from pure causes just as the pure limb of ethics arises from the correct view.

(87) Likewise, impure [results] arise from impure causes just as sexual misconduct, etc. arise from the power of wrong views.

(88) Since it is harmed by the valid knowledge (*pramāṇa, tshad ma*) [established in this text that demonstrates that entities have no inherent nature], reification of entities is known as a mistaken awareness, like a consciousness of a mirage.

(89) Because of that [grasping at inherent existence], accomplishing the [six] perfections with the force arising from that [grasping will be of little power], just as [accomplishments] arising from wrong views [which cling to] "I" and "mine" are of little power.

(90) There is a great fruit arising from not seeing entities as [ultimately] existent because they arise from an extensive cause, like a sprout [arising from] a powerful seed, etc.

(91) That which is cause and result is mere consciousness only. Whatever is established by itself abides in consciousness.

(92) By relying on the Mind Only (*cittamatra, sems tsam pa*) [system], know that external entities do not exist. And by relying on this [Madhyamaka] system, know that no self at all exists, even in that [mind].

(93) Therefore, due to holding the reigns of logic as one rides the chariots of the two systems (i.e., Yogācāra and Madhyamaka), one attains [the path of] the actual Mahāyānist.

(94) The cause of abiding in the immeasurable is not experienced by the highest of worldly ones, much less experienced by Viṣṇu or Śiva.

(95) This ultimate, pure nectar is an attainment which belongs to none other than the *Tathāgata*, who is motivated by the causes and conditions of great compassion.

(96) Therefore, intelligent beings who follow the system of [the *Tathāgata*] should generate compassion for those believing in tenets which are based on mistaken [views].

(97) Therefore, due to possessing the wealth of intelligence, one sees that there is no essential [worth] to those other systems, and s/he generates great respect for the Protector (i.e., the Buddha).

(Colophon:)
The verses of *The Ornament of the Middle Way* were composed by the great master Śāntarakṣita, who has crossed to the other side of the ocean of the tenets of our own Buddhist schools and others' non-Buddhist schools and bowed down with the crown of his head to the nectar of the stainless lotus feet of the Lord of Speech (i.e., the Venerable Mañjuśrī).

This text was collected and translated by the Indian abbot Śīlendrabodhi and the great translator Yeshe De.

In the following translation of Gyel-tsab's *dbU ma rgyan gyi brjed byang* (*Remembering "The Ornament of the Middle Way"*), Gyel-tsab's text is indented. For the benefit of the reader, I have inserted and numbered the stanzas from Śāntarakṣita's *The Ornament of the Middle Way* (flush to the left) at the appropriate points where Gyel-tsab comments on them even though they do not appear embedded in Gyel-tsab's text in the Tibetan. The numbers in brackets correspond to the folio numbers in the version found in Gyel-stab's *Collected Works (gsuṅ 'bum)* 1981. See Bibliography for details.

Remembering "The Ornament of the Middle Way"

[578] Homage to [my] lama and to the venerable Mañjuśrī. There are three [topics taught] in the verses of *The Ornament of the Middle Way* composed by the great master Śāntarakṣita: the meaning of the title, the detailed explanation of the nature of the *śāstra*, and the concluding explanation. The first is easy to understand. As for the second, [there are three divisions]: [first], it is demonstrated that entities (*dngos bo*) do not ultimately exist; [second], it is demonstrated that they do exist conventionally; and [third], the refutation of opposing arguments [of other schools]. Regarding the first [of these, there are two subdivisions]: to put forth the reasoning and to establish the [three] modes.

As for the first [i.e., to put forth the reasoning], the four [lines in the root text beginning with] "Those," etc. pertain.

(1) Those entities, as asserted by our own [Buddhist schools] and other [non-Buddhist] schools, have no inherent nature at all because in reality they have neither a singular nor a manifold nature – like a reflected image.

The subject, all inner and outer entities, have no true existence as put forth by our schools and others because they lack being truly one or many – like a reflected image.

As for the second, [there are two things which need to be proven]: first, that the logical [579] mark or reason has the property of the subject (*phyogs chos*) and [second], the establishment of the pervasion (*khyab pa sgrub pa*). Regarding the first, [there are two divisions]: the establishment of the lack of true singular existence of entities and the establishment of the lack of true manifold [existence of entities]. Regarding the first [of those two], all-pervasive singularity is refuted and non-pervasive singularity is refuted. [Regarding the first, there are two divisions]: truly singular, permanent entities are refuted [and] truly singular, permanent persons are refuted. [Regarding the first among those two], the permanent entities as [asserted by] other schools are refuted and the permanent products [asserted] by our schools are refuted.

As for the first, [the permanent entities held by other schools], the two [lines in the root text beginning with] " Because," etc. pertain.

(2) Because they contribute to [the production of] successive effects, permanent [causal] entities are not themselves singular.

If [we] were to construct a consequentialist argument, [it would be as follows]: the subject, the *Prakṛti* (i.e., the Universal Principle of the Sāṃkhya system), would not be of a truly singular nature because it aids in the periodic [production of] many successive fruits [over time]. If one were to use an autonomous inference:[2] it follows that the subject, all mere fruits, [must] arise simultaneously because all arise from the one unobstructed, capable direct cause (i.e., *Prakṛti*]). If you accept this, then it is made clear by direct perception [that all effects do not in fact arise simultaneously]. Since such a fallacy occurs, therefore the mere cause, the subject [of the inference], is not truly singular because it aids in the production of many successive fruits. Therefore, having refuted the true, singular existence of the mere cause [by the reasoning set forth in the consequence and the autonomous inference above], the truly existent *Prakṛti* is refuted.

(2 cont.) If each successive effect is distinct, then [the argument in support of] permanent [causal] entities [that are truly singular] degenerates.

Regarding the two [lines in the root text pertaining to] the subsequent pervasion of this, if one says that [580] although *Prakṛti* is truly singular, it would not be contradictory to claim that it aids in the production of periodic fruits, then is it that the *Prakṛti* must have the ability to produce results successively [over time] or not? If not, then it must produce [all] fruits simultaneously, because that which produces fruits would not have the ability to gradually produce [them over time]. If so, then truly singular permanence is contradicted because [*Prakṛti*] has many different abilities to produce successive fruits.

As for the second (i.e., the actual permanence held by our schools), the collection of twenty [lines in the root text beginning with] "Even," etc. pertain.

(3) Even those uncompounded objects of knowledge [known by] the knowledge which arises in meditation [for an *ārya*], according to the system [of the Vaibhāṣikas], are not unitary because they are related to successive moments of knowledge.

The subjects, the three non-compounded phenomena, objects of knowledge established by the wisdom of the meditative equipoise of an *ārya*, which the Vaibhāṣika system asserts to be truly singular, are necessarily not truly singular because they are related as subject and object with the various successive [moments of] knowledge which arise in meditation. The pervasion is established since the wisdom which is known in such meditative equipoise would be [cognized] out of order, and the three uncompounded phenomena are necessarily momentary.

With regard to the first (i.e., the wisdom known in such meditative equipoise would be [cognized] out of order), in reference to [the lines in the root text which begin with] "If the nature," etc. pertain.

(4) If the nature of the object known by a previous consciousness continues to exist subsequently, then the previous cognition would still exist in the latter [and], similarly, the latter would exist in the former.

If it is said that even if they are related as subject and object with the various successive [moments of] wisdom obtained through meditation, they are truly singular, then do the three uncompounded phenomena which are the objects of the previous knowledge obtained from meditative equipoise still exist in the latter meditative knowledge (i.e., knowledge obtained from meditative equipoise) or not? In the first case, it would be that the wisdom of the previous meditative equipoise would exist at the time of the later because of that previous statement. And would it not be that the later meditative wisdom would exist at the time of the former because the later object would exist at the time of the earlier? If the pervasion is not established, then [your assertion that] consciousness and object occur simultaneously degenerates.

With regard to the second (i.e., the three uncompounded phenomena are necessarily impermanent), the four [lines in the root text beginning with] "Since the nature, " etc. pertain. [581]

(5) Since the nature of the [latter] object does not arise in the earlier [time] and [the earlier object] does not arise at the latter time, uncompounded phenomena like consciousness must be objects known to arise momentarily.

The subject, the three uncompounded phenomena would necessarily be momentary because the nature of the previous would not come to exist in the latter and the nature of the latter would not come to exist in the former, for example like the consciousness of meditative equipoise.

The subject, subsequent uncompounded phenomena, would not be uncompounded phenomena because they arise from the power of previous uncompounded phenomena like consciousness. If the reason is not considered to be established [by you Vaibhāṣikas], then the four [lines in the root text which begin with] "If," etc. pertain.

(6) If the previous [uncompounded object] arises from the power of [the causes and conditions of the uncompounded object of] an earlier moment, then this would not [actually] be uncompounded, like minds (*citta, sems*) and mental states (*caitta, sems las byung ba*).

The subject, those [three uncompounded phenomena], must arise from their own power because they [would otherwise have to] arise without dependence on other causes. If it is accepted, then they must permanently exist because this is an entity which does not cease after the cause ceases [since it would not depend on causes] or it never exists because it is a phenomenon which does not follow after a cause.

As for the refutation of the truly singular existence of persons, the four [lines in the root text which begin with] "If you accept," etc. pertain.

(7) If you accept that these momentary [objects] arise independently because there is no dependence on others, then they must either exist permanently or not exist at all.

(8) What is the purpose of investigating objects which have no meaningful ability to act? What is the purpose of a lustful person inquiring as to whether a eunuch is attractive or not?

(9) It is clearly understood that a person [of the type asserted by Vātsīputrīyans] has neither a singular nor a manifold nature, since [such a person] cannot be explained as momentary or non-momentary.

When Vātsīputrīyans say that there are truly singular persons which are inexpressibly [neither] permanent [nor] impermanent, [then the inference would be as follows]: The subject, persons, would not be truly singular because they are not expressed as permanent. [And] they would not be truly many because they arenot expressed as impermanent. There is a pervasion because if an entity does not have a manifold nature, it must be singular [and] if entities are of many natures, they must be manifold. In brief, they must not be truly singular because they are not expressible as impermanent or permanent.

As for the refutation of the truly singular space which is pervasive, [582] the two [lines in the root text beginning with] "How can" pertain.

(10) How can pervasive [entities such as space] be unitary given that they are related with a variety of directions?

The subject, [pervasive] time and space, etc., would not be truly singular because a tree, etc., which belong to different directions like east and the like, are simultaneously collected [in one place] and dispersed [over many]. Regarding the refutation of truly singular pervasiveness, there is the refutation of truly singular external [objects] and the refutation of inherently singular consciousness. Regarding the first [of these two], there is the refutation of truly singular gross [forms] and that of particles, and the meaning which is established by these [two] and their conclusion.

As for the first, the two [lines in the root text which begin with] "Gross"etc. pertain.

(10 cont.) Gross [non-pervasive entities] are also not unitary since [some parts] of such entities can be visible [while other parts] are not visible.

The subject, a jar, could not be truly singular because otherwise there would be three ensuing contradictions: there is a contradiction with being exposed and unexposed with regard to the substance, etc.; a contradiction with its dependence on mobility and immobility; and a contradiction of being colored and uncolored on the grounds of its qualities.As for the refutation of the true singularity of particles, the twelve [lines in the root text which begin with] "What is the nature," etc. pertain.

(11) What is the nature of the central [partless] particle which faces singly towards [another] particle yet abides [with other partless particles in various directions] either [around and] joining with it, or around it [with space between them, or] around it without space between?

(12) If it is asserted that [the central particle] also faces entirely toward another such [unitary, partless] particle, then if that were so, wouldn't it be the case that [gross objects such as] land and water and the like would not be [spatially] expansive?

(13) If you accept [partless particles with sides] which face other such particles [in different directions], then if that is the case, how could [even] the most minute particles be singular and partless?

> The subject, a particle which abides in the center of the ten directions, would not have a different place [of abiding from] the particle to the east and in the nine other directions because the part of the subject facing to the east and the parts of the subject facing the other nine directions are one. If you accept this, then it would not be possible to develop into gross forms like earth due to accepting that [previous inference]. If you accept each of the [ten] faces, then that subject (i.e., the particle in the center of the ten directions) must not be singular and without parts because the subject would have ten different faces facing the [surrounding] particles in the ten directions.
>
> Thirdly, therefore, [to put forth] the meaning established [583] by them, [there are two topics]: establishing the reasoning and establishing the pervasion as demonstrated in the four lines [in the root text beginning with] "Particles."[3]

(14) Particles have thus been established to have no inherent nature. Therefore it is evident that eyes and [other gross] substantial [entities,] etc., which are asserted [to be real] by many of our own [Buddhist] schools and other [non-Buddhist] schools, are directly known to have no inherent nature.

> It is made known and established that the subject, objects of knowledge, such as the [five] aggregates (*skandha*, *phung po*), the [eighteen] sources (*dhātu*, *khams*), and the [twelve] constituent elements (*āyatana*, *skye mched*) postulated by our schools, and the substance of that which possesses parts postulated by other [non-Buddhist] schools, do not have a true nature because particles have no true nature.

(15) The nature of these [entities] is [said to be] composed of those [particles]. The qualities of these [entities], their own actions, and even their

universals (*spyi, sāmānya*) and particularities (*khyad pa, viśeṣa*) are said to be made up of those [particles and therefore must not inherently exist].

[Regarding the four lines in the root text beginning with "The nature," etc.], there is a pervasion because our schools assert that the ten forms[4] are in the nature of combined particles and because other schools[5] hold that the substance of parts is constituted by particles. In addition, since they (i.e., proponents of partless particles such as Vaibhāṣikas) accept that there is a relationship to the substance of the gross parts with qualities such as form, smell, etc. and with [the qualification] of actions, such as lifting up and putting down, etc., and since they accept the existence [only] of a great universal and a partial universal of all these particularities such as blue, etc., the pervasion is established.

In order to refute truly singular consciousness [there are three topics]. There is the refutation of the two systems postulated by our own substantialist schools, the refutation of the systems of non-Buddhists, and the refutation of the system of Vijñaptivādins (*rnam rig pa*). Regarding the first [of those three], there are two subtopics: the refutation of the system postulated by the Vaibhāṣika Proponents of No Images (*rnam med bye brag smra ba*) and the refutation of the system of the Sautrāntikas. Regarding the first [of those two subtopics there are two further divisions]: to establish the difference between consciousness cognizing external objects (*don rig*) and self-cognizing consciousness (*rang rig*), and to establish the difference between the two substantialist [Buddhist schools]. Regarding the first [of those two divisions], that it is correct to postulate self-cognizing consciousness will be established and that it is incorrect to postulate consciousness cognizing external objects will also be established. Regarding the first of those subdivisions [the correctness of the view of self-cognizing cognition, there are three further subdivisions]: putting forth the reasoning, establishing the pervasion, and synopsizing the meaning. As for the first [of these three], the four [lines in the root text beginning with] "Consciousness," etc. pertain.

(16) Consciousness is produced in the opposite way from that which is of an inanimate nature. That which is not the nature of being inanimate is the self-knowledge of this [consciousness].

> [Regarding] the subject, consciousness has the quality of self-cognition because it is produced [584] in the opposite manner from the way inanimate objects are produced. There is a pervasion because an apprehending consciousness which is in the nature of being non-inanimate is the self-cognizing consciousness of that mind. In order to establish the pervasion, the four [lines in the root text beginning with] "Self-cognizing cognition" etc. pertain.

(17) Self-cognizing cognition is not an entity which [exists as] agent and action [with its object] because it would be incorrect for consciousness, which is of a single, partless nature, to be three (i.e., knower, knowing, and known).

> The self-cognizing cognition of that subject (i.e., consciousness) does not exist in a manner of substantive difference from the three (knower, knowing, and known) because the subject is one without any substantive parts. This pervasion is established because it would be incorrect to posit three different substances [such as] knower, knowing, [and known] for one which does not have substantial parts. To briefly synopsize the meaning, the two [lines in the root text beginning with] "Therefore" pertain.

(18) Therefore, this [consciousness] is capable of self-consciousness (*bdag shes*) since this is the nature of consciousness.

> That subject (i.e., consciousness) would be correctly posited as self-cognizing consciousness because the subject is the nature of the apprehending consciousness (*'dzin rnam*) [which is non-dual with its object].

> As for the incorrectness of [holding the view of] consciousness cognizing external objects (*don rig*), the six [lines in the root text beginning with] "How [though]" etc. pertain.[6]

(18 cont.) How [though] could that cognize the nature of objects from which it is distinct?

(19) [Since] its nature does not exist in external objects, given that you assert that objects of consciousness and consciousness are different, how could consciousness know objects other than consciousness?

> It would be incorrect [to posit] directly experienced external objects (*don dngos su myong*) because the object [and] the consciousness are different substances. That is the case because the nature of the object does not exist in the [perceiving] consciousness and the nature of the [perceiving] consciousness does not exist in the object. It would be incorrect [to posit] consciousness cognizing external objects in the same way as [the positing of] the correctness of self-cognizing consciousness because the object of consciousness [and the consciousness] are unrelated different substances.
>
> Regarding the dissimilarities in the two systems postulating objects, [we will first investigate what is considered as] the validity of the experience [of objects], having analyzed them with regard to the system of the Sautrāntikas, and [then secondly we will] demonstrate the incorrectness also of analyzing them according to the system of the Vaibhāṣikas. As for the first, the four [lines in the root text beginning with] "According to" pertain.

(20) According to the position [of some], consciousness knows images, in spite of the fact that in actuality the two (i.e., consciousness and images) are distinct. Since it is just like a mirror reflection, it can be suitably experienced by mere imputation.

> According to Sautrāntikas, when one analyzes objects, even though objects and consciousness are of different substances, s/he may hold the validity of the experience [of objects by the consciousness perceiving them] because s/he accepts [mirror-like reflections of] images of the object.
>
> As for the second, the four [lines in the root text beginning with] "However," etc. pertain.

(21) However, there cannot be externally cognized images for those who do not assert a consciousness which reflects images of objects.

> Having analyzed objects according to the system of the Vaibhāṣikas, even with this mode of experience, their system would be incorrect [585] because they do not accept the images of objects.
>
> Regarding the refutation of the system of the Sautrāntikas, there is the refutation of the systems of the Non-Pluralists (*sna tshogs gnyis med pa*), the Half-Eggists (*sgo nga phyed tshal ba*) and the Proponents of an Equal Number of Images and Consciousnesses (*rnam shes grangs mnyam pa*). As for the first [of these three divisions of Sautrāntika, the Non-Pluralists], the four [lines in the root text beginning with] "Since," etc. pertain.

(22) Since [images] are not different from the unitary consciousness, there cannot not be a multiplicity of images. Therefore one would not be able to establish the knowledge of [external] objects with the force of that [image].

> At the time that a multiplicity of images such as blue, yellow, white, and red are known to a single consciousness, these images could not be substantially distinct from one another because they are all indistinct from the one partless consciousness. If you accept this, then having appeared as images of the object, it would be incoherent to accept the establishment of the object as substantially different from the [consciousness which apprehends the images of the object] because those images are not of a different substance.

(23) Consciousness cannot be unitary since it is not separate from images. If that were not the case, then how would you explain the two (i.e., images and consciousness) as unitary?

> Regarding the four [lines in the root text beginning with] "Consciousness," etc., the subject (i.e., a consciousness apprehending an array of colors) would not be truly singular because it would be of one substance with [those] many images. If there is no pervasion [as Sautrāntikas would claim], then the subject, [a consciousness apprehending an array of colors], would not be truly

one substance with those images because the subject is a singular substance and those images are truly many substances.

Second, regarding the refutation of the system of the Half-Eggists, [there are two subtopics,] the statement of their assertions and the rejection [of those assertions].

(24) [Colors such as] white and the like arise in succession to the consciousness, yet because of arising quickly, foolish people think that they arise simultaneously.

First, regarding the four [lines in the root text beginning with] "[Colors such as]," etc., [the Half-Eggists] claim, "We do not have those faults because when numerous images such as blue and yellow, etc. appear to one consciousness (*shes pa*), even though the images such as white, etc. [actually] appear successively to the consciousness, because of the rapidity with which they are engaged, the foolish person mistakenly thinks that they have appeared simultaneously. For example, it is like thinking that the circle of light appears all at once even though [such a circle of light made by rapidly twirling] the burning end of a stick [forms] gradually.

Regarding the second [subtopic, there are two further divisions], the rejection of the assertion and the rejection of the examples. Regarding the first [of these two, there are again three further subtopics], the incorrectness of the consciousness focusing on the sound of the letter, [586] the incorrectness in terms of the approach of the bare conceptual thought toward the object, and the improperness in terms of all consciousnesses. As for the first [of these three further subtopics, the four lines in the root text beginning with] "Why," etc. pertain.

(25) Why, when the mind which hears the sound of such words as *latā* [and *tāla*] arise very quickly, does it not hear [the two syllables] as if they were arising simultaneously [thus rendering the two words indistinguishable]?

When *sara* and *rasa* are spoken, does a misconception arise as a result which hears *rasa* and *sara* simultaneously because they are heard so quickly? If you accept this, then it is clearly rejected by direct perception. As for the second, the two [lines in the root text beginning with] "Even for" etc. pertain.

(26) Even if we were to consider only conceptual minds, [the images] would still not be known in succession.

[The opponent claims] that when some conceptual cognitions engage the object, there arises a misconception that it apprehends the object instantaneously because it apprehends the object very quickly.

As for the third, the six lines [in the root text beginning with] "Since," etc. pertain.

(26 cont.) Since they do not remain for a long time, all minds are similar [to images] in the rapidity with which they arise.

(27) Therefore, all objects are not apprehended gradually. Rather, just as they appear, [they] are apprehended simultaneously as distinct images.

The opponent argues that] all minds mistakenly [think that they] apprehend objects simultaneously without knowledge that they are actually apprehended successively because the apprehension is very quick. An absurd consequence would entail [if that were the case] because it does not abide for long [as would be necessary to hold this series of images as appearing simultaneously] and yet it is not momentary, like for example the images which you assert.

Now regarding the second point, [the refutation of the example, there are two subdivisions]: positing the *absurdum* and establishing the pervasion. As for the first, the four [lines in the root text beginning with] "Even with regards," etc.pertain.

(28) Even with regard to [the example of] a burning torch, the arising of the mistaken instantaneous appearance of a wheel [of fire] is not [a result of] joining the boundaries between [memories of distinct] perceptions because it appears very clearly.

The subject, a mind which misapprehends the burning end of a stick as a circle [of fire], would be a perception of a non-conceptual mind rather than a mind which connects the boundaries of the earlier and the later moments of a consciousness because the object appears clearly. Regarding the second point, the eight [lines in the root text beginning with] "This joining," etc. pertain.

(29) This joining of boundaries is done by the memory [of the mental consciousness], not by the seeing [of an eye consciousness], because that [eye consciousness] cannot apprehend past objects.

(30) Since the object of that [memory] has passed, it is not clear. Therefore, the appearance of the wheel [of fire] is of a type which is not clear.

If one replies, "There is no pervasion," [they are wrong]; there would be a pervasion to that [inference] because if it is a mind which joins the boundaries of earlier and later [images], then there must be memory. The subject, a non-conceptual consciousness, could not join the boundaries of the former and later [images by means of memory] because it could not apprehend past objects. [For this position to be coherent] there would have to be [past] objects clearly appearing to the subject, and a mind which joins the boundaries of former and later [images] because it apprehends past objects, [yet it is impossible for there to be clearly appearing past objects]. [587] The subject, a mind which misapprehends the burning end of a stick as a circle, would not be a mind which joins the boundaries of former and later because if it is, the object would not clearly appear to it, but [you say] that the object does appear clearly.

Regarding the refutation of those who posit an equal number of images and consciousnesses, [there are two subtopics]: to put forth their assertions and to reject them. As for the first, the four [lines in the root text beginning with] "If were to claim," etc. pertain.

(31) If one were to claim that when someone sees the base of the images of a painting, as many minds will arise simultaneously as there are images in that [painting,] then

As with the [example] of a canvas in the four [root text lines], etc., they say that even when one sees a painting, when there appear many [different] images such as blue and yellow, since [we hold that as] many consciousnesses [as images] also arise simultaneously, we do not have the faults of those [other Sautrāntika schools like Non-Pluralists and Half Eggists]. If one says that, [then we come to] the second [subtopic, the rejection of what they put forth. There are two further subtopics], establishing that all minds exist with [the appearance of] multiple images, and demonstrating the impossibility of single partlessness. As for the first, the four [lines in the root text beginning with] "…If that", etc. pertain.

(32) . . . if that were the case, even when cognition is of a single image type such as the color white, etc., since there is a distinct beginning, middle and end to that, there will be a variety of objects of observation [within that cognition of a single image].

The subject, a consciousness perceiving a unitary image of [the color] white, must be perceiving many images because that white image would have many different [parts which are also individual images such as the one facing] north, south, etc. If you accept this, then there could be no consciousness apprehending only one image.

As for the second [subdivision], the four [lines in the root text beginning with] "I honestly do not feel," etc. pertain.

(33) I honestly do not feel that [an image] such as the color white, etc., which is like the nature of a particle which is a partless singularity, has ever appeared to any consciousness.

A truly singular partless [particle] would be impossible because [although] the existence of that should be perceptible, it cannot be perceived. If one says that the reason is not established, [then the four lines in the root text beginning with] "According to," etc. pertain.

(34) [According to our opponent,] the sources of the five [sense] consciousnesses are images of objects [made of] accumulated [partless parti-

cles]. Minds (*citta, sems*) and mental states (*caitta, sems byung*) are objects established in the sixth [source of perception].

> If that [reason] is not established, then with regard to the five [sense] consciousnesses such as the eye consciousness, etc., they direct [their attention] toward the accumulation of partless particles. And as for the mental consciousness which follows after that, it is similar to that [accumulation], but those mental consciousnesses which do not follow after that aim at the accumulation of mental factors and minds.

> Regarding the refutation of the systems of the non-Buddhists, there is the general refutation and the particular refutation. As for the first [of these two], the two [lines in the root text beginning with] "Even according to," etc. pertain. [588]

(35) Even according to the scriptures of non-Buddhists (*phyi rol pa*) [such as the Vaiśeṣikas], the appearance [of gross objects] as singular would not occur…

> Even according to the non-Buddhist system [of the Vaiśeṣikas], the existence of a consciousness apprehending only one object would not be possible because all minds have many images. As for the first among the five refutations directed toward the early classes [of non-Buddhists], the two [lines in the root text beginning with] "because," etc. pertain.

(35 cont.) ... because its objects are substances which have qualities (*guna, yon tan*), etc.

> According to the system of the Vaiśeṣikas and the Naiyāyikas, a mind which apprehends only one object could not exist because substances and the like which have parts must be apprehended with the qualification of qualities, actions, collections, and particularities, etc.

> As for the second, the four [lines in the root text beginning with] "According to,"etc. pertain.

(36) [According to the views of the Jains and the Mīmāṁsakas], all entities are [manifold] like the nature of a gem [emitting colorful] rays. It would be irrational for the mind which apprehends those [entities] to appear in the nature of singularity.

> According to the system of the Jains and the Mīmāmsakas, that [consciousness apprehending only one object] could not exist because all entities are truly many like the rays of a jewel.
>
> As for the third [class of non-Buddhists], the four [lines in the root text beginning with] "Even for those," etc. pertain.

(37) Even for proponents of the [Lokāyata] system, which accepts the establishment of all sense faculties and objects as compounds of [the four elements] such as earth and the like, [consciousness] is still incompatible with a singular [manner of] engaging entities.

> Even according to the system of the Lokāyatas (Hedonists), the previous thesis (i.e., "a consciousness apprehending only one object could not exist") [would hold true] because they accept that all forms, etc. such as objects, and organs such as the eye organ, etc. are in the nature of a collection of the four elements.
>
> As for the fourth, the eight [lines in the root text beginning with] "Even according to the position," etc. pertain.

(38) Even according to the position [of the Sāṃkhyas, which claims that the five mere existences] such as sound, etc. are [the nature of the three qualities such as] courage and the like, a consciousness of the appearance of a unitary object is illogical because objects appear in the nature of the three [qualities].

(39) Regarding the trifold nature of entities, if the appearance of that [type of entity] is incompatible with a consciousness, which is of a single nature, how could it (i.e., the consciousness) be asserted to apprehend that object?

> Even according to the Sāṃkhya system, that thesis (i.e., "a consciousness apprehending only one object could not exist") would

be correct because of accepting that the five mere existences (*pañca tanmātrāṇi, de tsam lnga*) – form, sound, and the like which are the nature of the three qualities (*guna, yon tan*): particles (*rajas, rdul*), darkness (*tamas, mun*), and courage (*sattva, snying stobs*) – are objects appearing to the mind. If one says, "There is no pervasion," [then in order to establish the pervasion, we argue that] the subject, a consciousness apprehending those five mere existences, would not apprehend the reality of the object because the five mere existences are in the true nature of the three [qualities]: happiness, suffering, and equanimity, and only one [of the three] objects would appear to it.

As for the fifth, the four [lines in the root text beginning with] "[Since] they," etc. pertain.

(40) [Since] they do not even assert the existence of external objects, [Vedāntas ask] why the suitability of maintaining a permanent consciousness, which is said to arise either simultaneously or successively with various appearances, is so difficult [to accept].

That [thesis, "a consciousness apprehending only one object could not exist,"] would hold true, even for the system put forth by the Vedāntas (*rigs byed gsang ba'i mthar smra ba*), because the consciousness to which an assortment of objects appears is gross (i.e., has parts related to the assortment of objects appearing to it).

As for the refutation of the system of the Sautrāntikas, [589] the four [lines in the root text beginning with] "Even for," etc. pertain.

(41) Even for the cognition of [the three non-compounded phenomena such as] space and the like, because of the appearance of many [conceptual images of] letters for the appearance of the mere name, there are many clear appearances.

The subject, an awareness apprehending non-compounded phenomena, would hold images of an assortment of objects because many generalities, [such as] sound generalities of letters, appear to it.

(42) Although there are some who assert consciousnesses to which manifold [images] do not appear, still it is not suitable to establish their existence from the perspective of the ultimate because it has already been shown that there is a logical fallacy [in asserting] the existence [of such] with these characteristics.

(43) Therefore it is established from all perspectives that consciousness occurs with the appearance of manifold images, and thus like the [many] distinct images [themselves], cannot logically be of a single nature.

Regarding the eight [lines in the root text beginning with] "Although," etc., even if there were some consciousnesses to which a variety of objects do not appear, still these would not be truly existent because true existence is refuted by reason. The subject, consciousness, cannot be of a truly singular nature because of the appearance of various images [to it] like, for example, the many images.

Regarding the refutation of the Proponents of Cognition (*Vijñavādins, rnam rig pa*), [there are three topics]: stating their assertions, examining the truth and mistakes [in their assertions], and refuting this [view]. As for the first [of these], the four [lines in the root text beginning with] "Images become," etc. pertain.

(44) Images are manifest due to the ripening of latent potentialities of a beginningless [personal] continuum. Although they appear, since it is the result of a mistake, they are like the nature of an illusion.

Although from beginningless time the appearances of objects which are produced by manifestations resulting from the ripening of latent potentialities (*vāsanā, bag chags*) appear as objects which have come forth, they are said to be like the nature of magical illusions appearing as objects while there are no objects.

As for the second [topic, examining the truth and mistakes in their assertions], the four [lines in the root text beginning with] "Although," etc. pertain.

(45) Although their view (i.e., the Yogācāra view) is virtuous, we should think about whether such things [as the images known by consciousness accepted by Yogācāras] actually exist or if they are something contentedly accepted only when left unanalyzed.

Although that view is good and virtuous in that it dispels many of the bad adherences of the Sautrāntika and [other] lower schools, however, is that non-dual consciousness, which it is comfortable to accept as singular when unexamined, true or is it false?

In the first case, [if it is true], then regarding the third point, [refuting this], there are two [further divisions]: refuting the Proponents of True Images and refuting the system of the Proponents of False Images. And regarding the first [of these two divisions, the refuting of the Proponents of True Images], there are three [further subdivisions]: the refutation of the system of the Half-Eggists, the refutation of the system of the Proponents of an Equal Number of Consciousnesses and Images, and the refutation of the system of the Non-Pluralists. Regarding the first of these three further subdivisions (i.e., the refutation of the system of the Half-Eggists), there are still three further subtopics: positing the *absurdum*, demonstrating the [arguments which] harm their assertions, and demonstrating the similar faults even for those who accept objects.

As for the first (i.e., the positing of the *absurdum* of the Half-Eggists), the four [lines in the root text beginning with] "Since", etc. pertain.

(46) Since contradictions would ensue for those unitary [images] *even if* the actual consciousness is manifold, [consciousness and images] are undoubtedly distinct entities.

[If there exists a truly existing consciousness which is non-dual with the images of the objects it perceives], that consciousness would have to be [the nature of] many, [590] because it is truly one with many images. Otherwise the images would be truly singular because they are truly substantially one with the [truly singular] consciousness. If you say, "There is no pervasion," then those two would be separate substances because the images are truly many and the consciousness is [truly] singular. If you accept this consequence, then as for the second point (i.e., demonstrating the arguments which harm the assertions of the Half-Eggists), the four [lines in the root text beginning with] "If images," etc. pertain.

(47) If images are not different from [the singular consciousness], then it will be very difficult to respond to the following consequence: that with regard to moving and rest and the like, due to the movement of one, all would move.

When we see the movement of one object, all would move, and when one is yellow, all would be yellow because all images are one. As for the third point (i.e., demonstrating the similarity of the faults even with those who accept objects), the four [lines in the root text beginning with] "Even according to," etc. pertain.

(48) Even according to the system of those maintaining external objects, if images are not separate [from each other], then they would all also certainly be engaged as a single phenomenon and not other than that.

Even according to the system of those who accept external objects, the images would not be truly singular because those faults cannot be avoided.

Regarding the second [topic], refuting the proponents of an equal number of consciousnesses and objects, the four [lines in the root text beginning with] "If you accept," etc. pertain.

(49) If you accept an equal number of consciousnesses and images, then it would be difficult to overcome the same type of analysis as is made regarding particles.

Could not many similar kinds of eye consciousnesses simultaneously be generated since the faults shown with regard to the accumulation of many simultaneous partless particles would be applicable?

As for the third topic (i.e., refuting the Yogācāra-Non-Pluralists), the eight [lines in the root text beginning with] "If one," etc. pertain.

(50) If one [consciousness experiences] a variety [of images], wouldn't that be like the system of the [Jain] Sky Clad (*Digambara*)? A variety [of images] is not the nature of singularity just as manifold precious [gems] and the like [are not the nature of singularity].

(51) If the variety [of images] exists in a single nature, how could they appear in the nature of many, and how could parts such as those being obstructed and those which are unobstructed, etc. be distinguished?

If one asserts that a variety of images would be truly in the nature of a singular consciousness [as the Non-Pluralists assert, it would be] like the system of the Vedāntas and the Nirgranthas. If that truly singular consciousness to which various objects appear is asserted, then there is a pervasion, because if various images appear [to it, it] would not be truly singular, like a heap of a variety of precious [gems]. There is also the appearance of various images to the consciousness. If you accept the singularity of images, then it would be impossible for many different images to appear, such as "visible" and "invisible," etc. and images of various sorts such as blue and yellow, etc., because the various images are truly singular.

As for refuting the Yogācāra Proponents of False Images (*Yogācāra-alīkākāravāda, nal 'byor spyod pa'i rnam brdzun pa*), [591] [there are two topics]: putting forth their assertions and refuting them.

(52) Some say that [consciousness] does not naturally possess images of these [objects]. In reality, images do not exist but appear to the consciousness by virtue of a mistake.

Regarding the four [lines in the root text beginning with] "Some say," etc., they (i.e., the Proponents of False Images) say, "We don't have the faults [of those Proponents of True Images] with regard to distinct and single substantial images since, [according to our view], the images appear even without existing in reality.

Regarding the second (i.e., refuting their assertions), and as for the first of the eight *absurdums* [used to refute the Proponents of False Images], such as [the *absurdum*] that experiencing images would be incorrect, and the [*absurdum* of] incorrectness of consciousness in general, etc., the four [lines in the root text beginning with] "If," etc. pertain.

(53) If [images] do not exist, how can consciousness clearly experience those [objects]? That [clear, non-dual consciousness] is not like a consciousness which is distinct from the entities, [and those entities must possess images which appear to it].

For images [of objects], the subject, the clear experience of them, would be incorrect because they do not exist in reality. There is a pervasion because there is no consciousness which is without images and [none which] is distinct from the entities of those images [which appear to it].

As for the second [*absurdum*], the four [lines in the root text beginning with] "Likewise," etc. pertain.

(54) Likewise, that [image, such as yellow,] will not be known as that [yellow image] by anyone if entities are without [yellow images]. Likewise bliss is not experienced in suffering and non-white is not seen in white.

The subject, consciousness, would incorrectly perceive the image, for example, because [in the same way] bliss cannot be known in suffering and blue cannot be seen in white.

As for [the *absurdum* showing] the incorrectness of direct experience, the four [lines in the root text beginning with] "With regards," etc. pertain.

(55) With regard to images, "knowledge" (*shes pa*) is not actually the correct term because [the image] is distinct from consciousness itself (*shes pa'i bdag*), like flowers [growing] in the sky, etc.

Images, the subject, would not be correctly experienced directly because they are not of the [same] substance as consciousness, like flowers [growing] in the sky.

As for [the fourth *absurdum* demonstrating] the incorrectness of experience having examined [the image], the four [lines in the root text beginning with]"[Consciousness]," etc. pertain.

(56) [Consciousness] is incapable of experiencing [images] even when they are examined because non-existent [images] have no [causal] ability, like the horn of a horse. [To assert that] a non-existent [image] has the ability to [cause the] generation of an appearing consciousness of itself is irrational.

The subject, consciousness, would be incorrect in its experience of the image, having examined it, because the image does not have the ability to produce itself as an image known to consciousness, for example, like an impotent horse. There is a pervasion, because if it does not exist in reality, it (i.e., the image), would not have the ability to produce the consciousness to which it appears.

[For] the subject, a consciousness to which the particle to the east appears nearer and the particle abiding to the west appears farther, wouldn't the particle to the east, appearing to be nearer, [592] be [the same as] the particle to the west which appears to be farther because particle to the east which appears nearer is partless? If you accept this, then the particle to the east would [also] appear farther. If you accept this, then it is contradicted by direct perception.

As for the [fifth] *absurdum*, that there would be no relationship betweenaspects and consciousness, the four [lines in the root text beginning with] "What," etc. pertain.

(57) What reason is there which would account for a relationship between those [images] which are definitely experienced and consciousness? It is not the nature of that which does not exist and does not arise from it.

When the consciousness is experienced, it would be incorrect to experience various images, because there is no relationship between consciousness and images. That is so because there is no causal relationship or relationship of identity.

As for the [sixth] *absurdum*, the incorrectness of being occasionally arisen, the four [lines in the root text beginning with] "If," etc. pertain.

(58) If there were no cause [for images], how is it suitable that they arise only on occasion? If they have a cause, how could they not have an other-dependent nature (*paratantra-svabhāva, gzhan gi dbang gi ngo bo*)?

Is there a cause of images or not? If not, then the subject, images, would be incorrect to have arisen occasionally since it has no cause. If [you respond] that the reason (*rtags, hetu*) is not established, then there is an *absurdum* because it would be a dependent entity due to being produced by an illusory cause (*'khrul pa'i rgyu pa*).

As for the *absurdum* of being a mere subjective image (*'dzin rnam, grāhaka-ākāra*), the four [lines in the root text beginning with] "If [images]," etc.pertain.

(59) If [images] do not exist, then consciousness [with images] also [would not exist] due to the non-existence of the images. Consciousness then, like a clear, round crystal, would not really experience [objects].

If someone claims that there are no images of apprehended objects, then the subject, consciousness, would merely consist of images of the apprehending subject (i.e., its own self-cognition) due to being a consciousness without images of objects (*gzung rnam*). If you accept this, then for apprehension which is like a clear, round crystal which is void of the images of the object, there would be no image for the apprehender because [images] are not perceived although they should be perceived.

As for the *absurdum* of being a dependent entity, the four [lines in the root text beginning with] "If they say," etc. pertain.

(60) If they say that this [eye consciousness which sees a mirage] is known as such as a result of a mistake, then why does it rely on mistakes? Even if it arises by the [power of delusion], still then that [consciousness of a mirage is] dependent on the power of others.

> If one says that, although in reality there are no [images of] objects, images appear due to a mistake, then the subject, images, would be other-dependent because they depend on a mistake. This is the case because they (i.e., the images) arise from the force of a mistake.
>
> As for the refutation, the establishment of being void of truly many, the four [lines in the root text beginning with] "When analyzing," etc. pertain.

(61) When analyzing any entity, [we find] that there are none which are truly single. For those for which there is nothing which is truly single, there must also be nothing which is [truly] manifold.

> The subject, entities, would not [593] be established as being truly many because there are no truly singular [entities]. As for establishing the pervasion [of the original statement of the neither-one-nor-many argument put forth in the first stanza of the text], the four [lines in the root text beginning with] "The existence," etc. pertain.

(62) The existence of an entity belonging to a class other than that which has a single or a manifold [nature] does not make sense because the two are exhaustive of all possible alternatives.

> If the true existence of one and the true existence of many are not established, then there must be no true existence because there are no entities[with a truly existent nature] that belong [neither] to the class of [entities with a] unitary [nature] nor with a manifold [nature]. That would be the case because it would be contradictory for there to be entities which rely on [a class other than] those of one and many, which are inclusive of all possibilities.
>
> Regarding the demonstration that entities do exist conventionally,

[there are three topics]: identifying the characteristics of entities, [identifying the characteristics] of conventional existence, and the refutation of the ultimate [existence of the] cause of the illusion. As for the first [of these three topics], the four [lines in the root text beginning with] "Therefore," etc. pertain.

(63) Therefore, these entities are characterized only by conventionality. If [someone accepts] them as ultimate, what can I do for that person?

The subject, these entities, must exist in a false manner because their basis is established and the establishment of true existence is [already] refuted. Regardingthe subsequent two [parts of the reason of the previous argument], for that subject (i.e., entities), it would be incorrect for me to refute that which I have truly established because that is truly established by valid cognition. Otherwise it would be incorrect to refute by valid cognition because it arises from previous causes. Therefore it is not established merely by one's wish,

As for the second [topic], the four [lines in the root text beginning with] "Those," etc. pertain.

(64) Those phenomena which are only agreeable when not put to the test of [ultimate] analysis, those phenomena which are generated and disintegrate, and those which have the ability to function are known to be of a conventional nature.

The subject, [entities which are characterized by] the three – [1] the inability to endure the examination of final (i.e., ultimate) analysis, [2] the character of being produced and ceasing, and [3] the ability to function – [these] are [described as] conventional truths because they are objects found by conventional valid cognition (*tha snyad pa'i tshad ma*).

As for the third [topic, the refutation of the true existence of the cause of the illusion], the eight [lines in the root text beginning with] "Although," etc. pertain.

(65) Although they are agreeable only when not analyzed [by ultimate

analysis], since it depends on the earlier cause, the subsequent fruit arises in correspondence with that.

(66) Therefore, if [one claims] that there is no conventional cause, that is said to be incorrect and is no good. If its substantial cause (*upādāna, nyer len*) is said to be real, then that must be explained.

> By saying that it is incorrect if [one holds the view that] there is no true cause of a pot, etc., this statement is not good because even though there is no true cause, subsequent fruits arise from previous similar types. Truly existent causes are impossible because true existence has already been refuted. [594]
>
> Regarding the refutation of [dissenting] arguments, there are seven subtopics: dispelling the contradictions with direct perception, dispelling the contradictions with scripture, expressing the ultimate truth, dispelling [dissenting] arguments regarding that [ultimate truth], putting forth the nature of conventional truth, showing the way that the nature of the Mahāyāna is more glorious than the others, and [showing how] if one knows this system, [s/he knows] the cause of the generation of compassion and faith.
>
> As for the first [of these seven], the eight[7] [lines in the root text beginning with] "Regarding," etc. pertain.

(67) Regarding the inherent nature of all entities, we have cleared away others' assertions by following the path of reasoning. Therefore there is nothing to be disputed [in our position].

(68) If they are earnest, those [opponents] will not be able to find any fault in [the view of] those who assert neither existence nor non-existence, nor both existence and non-existence.

> If one says, " If there are no entities which are established as truly existent, that contradicts direct perception," I respond that there are no faults of contradicting direct perception by virtue of refuting true existence because although entities bearing the investigation by the reasoning examining the final status (*mthar thug*

dpyod pa'i rigs pa) [of entities] are refuted, objects found by conventional valid cognition are not refuted. There would be no faults of contradicting direct perception, etc. with that explanation because we do not accept the true existence of the four extremes of existence, non-existence, both, or neither.

As for the second point, the four [lines in the root text beginning with] "Therefore," etc. pertain.

(69) Therefore, in reality there are not any established entities. Due to that, the *Tathāgatas* taught the non-production of all phenomena.

There is a reason for stating in the scriptures that all phenomena are not produced and do not cease. It is because there are no entities which are truly established.

As for the third, the twelve [lines in the root text beginning with] "Because," etc. pertain.

(70) Because they are harmonious with ultimate truths, some call this [non-production] ultimate truth, but in reality they (i.e., ultimate truths) are free from all accumulations of verbal fabrications (*prapañca, spros pa*).

(71) Due to the lack of [ultimate] production, there can be no non-production, etc. Because of the refutation of the nature of that [production], verbal expressions referring to that [non-production] do not exist.

(72) There is no point in applying [words] of negation to a non-existent object. Even if one relies on conceptual thought, it would be conventional, not ultimate.

The subject, the non-truly existent sprout, would be merely synonymous with the ultimate truth [of the object] because whatever object can be found by inferential knowledge can newly arise as [the object of] non-conceptual wisdom of the equipoise arising from meditation. Ultimately, it would be free from all elaborations, for just as true production is an object of negation, true non-production is [an object which is negated] as well because it does not ultimately exist. If one replies that the reason (*rtags*) is not established, then [in response to that objection we argue that] non-production is not ultimately established because [595] there would be no true production of the object of refutation. There is a pervasion because if there is no true production, then in meditative equipoise (*mnyam gzhag*), according to the view [of the wisdom realizing emptiness of a Noble One], there would not be application of the words which refute it. That is so because there would be no application of negating words (*dgag sgra*) without a base of negation. If they (i.e., Yogācāras) say that there is application of negating words to conceptually designated objects, then that subject would not be established as ultimately real but would be conventional because it would be a negation negating the object of refutation designated by conceptual thought.

Regarding [the fourth topic], dispelling arguments, [there are four sub-topics]: the *absurdum* that those of low intellect cognize emptiness through direct perception, the *absurdum* that there would be nobody who [directly] cognizes emptiness, the *absurdum* that there would be no establishing speech (*sgrub ngag*), and the *absurdum* that there would be no actions (*las, karma*) and effects, etc.

Regarding the first [subtopic, there are two further subdivisions]: [dispelling] arguments and responses [to objections]. As for the first [subdivision], the four [lines in the root text beginning with] "Well then," etc. pertain.

(73) Well then, [what if someone were to say that] since by cognizing those [entities] the nature of them can be directly perceived, why don't non-masters also know [the ultimate nature of] entities in this way?

If one says that even unintelligent people such as shepherds, etc. would cognize emptiness through direct perception because these people perceive entities directly, and all entities arise in the nature of being without true existence, then as for the second [subdivision, the response], the four [lines in the root text beginning with] "They do not.," etc. pertain.

(74) They (i.e., non-masters) do not [know the ultimate nature of entities] because, due to the power of false imputations [of real existence] onto entities by the burdened, beginningless continuums of all sentient beings, [emptiness] is not known directly by living beings.

> Even though it is so that there are no truly existent entities, there is a reason why shepherds, etc. do not cognize emptiness with direct perception. It is because from beginningless time [their] mental continuums are bound by the mistaken perception which exaggerates [the reality of] things [and imputes] true [existence].
>
> Well then, as for the second [subtopic], if one says that there would [then] not be anybody who cognizes emptiness, then the four [lines in the root text beginning with] "Those," etc. pertain.

(75) [Those who realize emptiness are] those who know it inferentially with reasons which make [the lack of a real nature] known and that cut superimpositions, as well as those powerful yogis who know it clearly by direct perception.

> Even though those of low intellect (*blun po*) do not cognize [emptiness], there are persons who cognize emptiness. Those bodhisattvas on the path of preparation (*sbyor lam*) and the path of accumulation (*tshog lam*) [cognize emptiness conceptually] by relying on reasoning (*gtan tshigs)* into [the nature of] reality. Bodhisattvas abiding on the [ten] grounds realize [emptiness] directly by [relying on] direct yogic [596] cognition.
>
> As for the third [subtopic, the *absurdum* that there would not be any meaningfully established speech], the twelve[8] [lines in the root text beginning with] "Having," etc. pertain.

(76) Having discarded [views] concerning the way subjects exist based on particular discourses of scriptures, there are entities which are well known by everyone from masters to women to children.

(77) All these entities, including that thesis and the proof,[9] are engaged as such. If that were not the case, we would have such problems as that of an

unestablished base (*āśrayāsiddha, gzhi ma grub*), etc., as has been argued.

(78) Because I have not rejected entities with regard to their possessing the taste (*rasa, ngang*) of appearances, [this position is] unshaken with regard to the establishment of the subject and the thesis.

> Although there are no truly existent entities, there would be no faults of lacking the establishing of speech, [and] reasoned inferences, etc. This is because by abandoning the subjects of the inference, etc., which are well known to those holders of uncommon tenets, the mere appearance of entities, subjects of the inference, etc. which are well known from the wise down to ordinary people are posited [correctly for the establishing of speech and reasoned inferences, etc.]. If it is not like this, then since the base is not established, there will be faults with regards to the subject not having the property of the reason (*phyogs chos*), etc. which [you] would not be able to answer because the subject, predicate and reason are given only to holders of incompatible tenets. We do not have the faults of the invalidity of positing the thesis and the proof according to us [Mādhyamikas] because [we assert] that the mere appearance of entities known to the non-conceptual consciousness, from the wise to the common people, is not negated.
>
> Regarding the *absurdum* of the invalidity of karma and results, [there are three further divisions]: the *absurdum* regarding the invalidity of previous and later lives, the *absurdum* regarding the invalidity of all afflicted emotions, and the *absurdum* regarding the invalidity of the accomplishment of accumulations. Regarding the first [of these three, there are still four further subdivisions]: positing the reasoning, establishing [the reason], [avoiding] the faults [of the two extremes] of permanence and nihilism, and demonstrating the possibility of liberation from cyclic existence.
>
> As for the first [division of the first subtopic of the fourth topic, positing the reason], the four [lines in the root text beginning with] "Therefore," etc. pertain.

(79) Therefore, the seeds of a similar type, which [stimulate] conception

with entities or conception without [entities], etc. in the continuums [of beings] from beginningless existence, are objects of inferential [knowledge].

> The subject, the conception without entities of a newborn baby, is preceded by its similar former type because it is consciousness, like a habituated desire. As for the second [division of the first subtopic of the fourth topic, establishing the pervasion], the eight[10] [lines in the root text beginning with] "Regarding," etc. pertain.

(80) Regarding this, they (i.e., the conceptions of entities) do not arise by the force of entities because these [entities ultimately] do not exist. The nature of entities has been thoroughly rejected in an extensive manner.

(81) Because they arise gradually, they are not sudden. Because they are not permanently arisen, they are not permanent. Because they themselves are similarly accustomed to those [previous habits of conceptualization], they first arise from their own kind.

> That subject (i.e., the conception of entities) would not be able to arise by the force of a partless object because there are no partless objects and because the true existence of entities has already been refuted. It would not be causeless because it occurs in [597] succession. [Its] nature would not be permanent because it is not permanently arising. Thus, a previous consciousness [precedes it] because it is consciousness.

> As for the third [division of the first subtopic of the fourth topic, avoiding the faults of the two extremes of permanence and nihilism], the four [lines in the root text beginning with] "Therefore," etc. pertain.

(82) Therefore, the views of [the two extremes of] eternalism and absolute non-existence remain far away from the ideas put forth in this text. [Entities arise], change, and become like a seed, sprout, and plant.

> The system of Madhyamaka does not have the faults of permanence or nihilism.[There is no fault of] permanence because after

the cause is eliminated (*ldog*), the subsequent effect ceases (*log*),[11] and there is no fault of nihilism because fruitsarise[12] from causes like sprouts arise from seeds.

As for the fourth [division of the first subtopic within the fourth topic, the possibility of liberation from cyclic existence], the four lines in the root text beginning with "Masters," etc. pertain.

(83) Masters who know the selflessness of phenomena abandon disturbing emotions, which arise from perverted views, without effort since they have become accustomed to a lack of inherent existence.

Ārya bodhisattvas, the subject, abandon afflictive emotions which arise from the cause of grasping at true existence without [much] effort because they are accustomed to emptiness that is already seen.

As for the second [division within the fourth subtopic of the fourth topic, the *absurdum* of positing the invalidity of all afflicted emotions], the four [lines in the root text beginning with] "Since," etc. pertain.

(84) Since entities which are causes and results are not negated conventionally, there is no confusion in establishing what is pure and what is an affliction.

There are not faults of distortion or deterioration in [the positions concerning] *saṃsāra* and liberation due to the refutation of the true existence of extremely afflictive emotions (*saṃkleśas, kun nyon*) because causes and results are accepted conventionally.

As for the third [division within the fourth subtopic of the fourth topic, the *absurdum* of positing the invalidity of accumulations of merit, the twenty-four lines in the root text beginning with] "Since this," etc. pertain.

(85) Since this teaching of causes and results is established, the positing of stainless accumulations [of wisdom and merit] is suitable according to this text.

(86) Pure results arise from pure causes just as the pure limb of ethics arises from the correct view.

(87) Likewise, impure [results] arise from impure causes just as sexual misconduct, etc. arise from the power of wrong views.

(88) Since it is harmed by the valid knowledge (*pramāṇa, tshad ma*) [established in this text that demonstrates that entities have no inherent nature], reification of entities is known as a mistaken awareness, like a consciousness of a mirage.

(89) Because of that [grasping at inherent existence], accomplishing the [six] perfections with the force arising from that [grasping will be of little power], just as [accomplishments] arising from wrong views [which cling to] "I" and "mine" are of little power.

(90) There is a great fruit arising from not seeing entities as [ultimately] existent because they arise from an extensive cause, like a sprout [arising from] a powerful seed, etc.

> According to this system, stainless accumulations also are suitable[13] because, having refuted true cause and effect, they are established conventionally. The subject, the merits which arise from the intention of the wisdom realizing emptiness, arise as pure results because the cause is pure, just as the morality which abandons taking life, etc. arises from the intention of the correct worldly view. The subject, the merits which arise from the intentions of grasping at true existence, would have the opposite predicate and reason like [for example] sexual desire arisen from the strength of the wrong view. The subject, the generosity which arises without the wisdom realizing emptiness, will generate fruits of little power because [598] the cause of giving arises from a perverted view, like the fruits which arise from grasping at "I" and "mine." That is the case because truly established phenomena are harmed by valid knowledge, like grasping at a mirage and considering it to be water [is harmed by valid knowledge].
>
> [In contrast with the relatively little worth to be found in the per-

formance of the six perfections and other acts of virtue when they are still grounded in erroneous views which cling to "I" and "mine"], the subject, generosity that arises on the basis of the [wisdom realizing] emptiness, produces pure effects because of arising from extensive, thoroughly pure causes of development, like the arising of a sprout of a fresh seed.

As for [the fifth topic], putting forth the nature of conventional [truth], the eight [lines in the root text beginning with] "That which," etc. pertain.

(91) That which is cause and result is mere consciousness only. Whatever is established by itself abides in consciousness.

(92) By relying on the Mind Only (*cittamatra, sems tsam pa*) [system], know that external entities do not exist. And by relying on this [Madhyamaka] system, know that no self at all exists, even in that [mind].

The subject, all phenomena which are included in cause and effect, are not other than the substance of consciousness because they are established by the mode of experience which knows them by direct valid cognition. There is a pervasion because if that is the reason, then they must abide in the substance of the consciousness. That subject (i.e., all phenomena which are included in cause and effect) should be known conventionally as merely in the nature of mind because it is void of external existence. Ultimately, the mere mind is not established because it ultimately does not have a singular or a manifold [nature].

As for [the sixth topic], the exalted nature of the Mahāyāna and the way it is superior as compared to other [systems], the twelve [lines in the root text beginning with] "Therefore, due to," etc. pertain.

(93) Therefore, due to holding the reigns of logic as one rides the chariots of the two systems (i.e., Yogācāra and Madhyamaka), one attains [the path of] the actual Mahāyānist.

(94) The cause of abiding in the immeasurable is not experienced by the highest of worldly ones, much less experienced by Viṣṇu or Śiva.

(95) This ultimate, pure nectar is an attainment which belongs to none other than the *Tathāgata*, who is motivated by the causes and conditions of great compassion.

> The subject, only bodhisattvas [on the path of] preparation [and on the path of] accumulation, will become Mahāyānists characterized as possessors of the [wisdom of] ultimate reality because only they hold the reins of the logic previously explained while riding on the chariot of the two systems holding the system of Mind Only as conventional (*tha snyad*) and the [Madhyamaka] system which asserts the non-existence of inherent nature (*rang gzhin*) ultimately. The subject, the wisdom realizing the empty nectar, the actual cause of abiding in the deathless stage for as long as *saṃsāra's* inestimable duration, [599] is not experienced by any non-Buddhists, including Viṣṇu and Śiva, etc., not by the crowns of worldly existence, and not even by *śrāvakas* and *pratyekabuddhas,* because this is directly, independently experienced only by the *Tathāgatas* who possess the cause of pure compassion.
>
> As regards the reason for generating faith and compassion when one cognizes this system, the eight [lines in the root text beginning with] "Therefore," etc. pertain.

(96) Therefore, intelligent beings who follow the system of [the *Tathāgata*] should generate compassion for those believing in tenets which are based on mistaken [views].

(97) Therefore, due to possessing the wealth of intelligence, one sees that there is no essential [worth] to those other systems, and s/he generates great respect for the Protector (i.e., the Buddha).

> The subject, bodhisattvas on [the path of] accumulation and [the path of] preparation, have reason for generating compassion for non-Buddhists because they see that [non-Buddhists] abide in the tenets which show mistaken paths to liberation. The subject,

bodhisattvas who abide on [the path of] accumulation and [the path of] preparation who possess the treasure of wisdom, have come to generate great respect for the Buddha because they see the triviality of the mistaken paths to liberation of all systems other than the Buddha's system.

This is the concluding explanation (i.e., the third and final major topic of this text) regarding the qualities of this *śāstra* composed by the great master Śāntarakṣita. As for these qualities, [the lines in the root text beginning with] "The verses," etc. [in the colophon] pertain.

(Colophon):
The verses of *The Ornament of the Middle Way* were composed by the great master Śāntarakṣita, who has crossed to the other side of the ocean of the tenets of our own Buddhist schools and others' non-Buddhist schools and bowed down with the crown of his head to the nectar of the stainless lotus feet of the Lord of Speech (i.e., the Venerable Mañjuśrī).
This text was collected and translated by the Indian abbot Śīlendrabodhi and the great translator Yeshe De.

He heard this dharma directly from the Venerable Mañjuśrī, the Lord of Speech, and it was like placing the pollen [of Mañjuśrī's lotus feet] on the crown of his head.

Having composed this [commentary] on *The Ornament of the Middle Way,* which was well taught by the the Lord of Scholars, Śāntarakṣita, and likewise [based] on the speech of [my] lama [Je Tsong Khapa], in order that it not be forgotten, I dedicate this to the mastery of the supreme system by all transmigratory beings.

May I also, having obtained the basis of good [human] endowments, having avoided the abyss of wrong views, and having relied with respect on supreme virtuous friends, [600] be like the powerful master, Śāntarakṣita.

May there be virtue [in this] remembrance [of these] teachings of the omniscient guru of the three realms, Losang Dragpa (bLo-bzang-grags-pa), by Gyel-tsab Chos Je [rGyal-tshab chos rjes].

And by this [merit] may there also abide vast and increasing, for a long time in all the doors of all the directions, the precious teachings of the Buddha.[14]

Manga Lam

Appendices

APPENDIX 1

Outline of Topics in *Madhyamakālaṃkāra* Based on Divisions Cited in Gyel-tsab's Commentary

1.0 The meaning of the title

2.0 The detailed explanation of the nature of the *śāstra*

2.1 Demonstration that entities do not ultimately exist

2.1.1 Putting forth the argument

2.1.2 Establishing the [three] modes (*tshul sgrub*) which validate the argument

2.1.2.1 Proving that the reason has the property of the subject (*phyogs chos*)

2.1.2.1.1 Establishing the lack of the true singular existence of entities

2.1.2.1.1.1 Refuting all-pervasive singularity

2.1.2.1.1.1.1 Refuting truly singular permanent entities

2.1.2.1.1.1.1.1 Refuting permanent entities asserted by other schools

2.1.2.1.1.1.1.2 Refuting permanent entities asserted by our schools

2.1.2.1.1.1.2 Refuting truly singular permanent persons

2.1.2.1.1.1.2.1 Refuting the two systems postulated by our own substantialist schools

2.1.2.1.1.1.2.1.1 Refuting Non-Aspectarian Vaibhāṣikas

2.1.2.1.1.1.2.1.1.1 Establishing the difference between self-cognizing cognition and consciousness cognizing external objects

2.1.2.1.1.1.2.1.1.1.1 Establishing the correctness of self-cognizing cognition

2.1.2.1.1.1.2.1.1.1.1.1 Putting forth the reasoning

2.1.2.1.1.1.2.1.1.1.1.2 Establishing the pervasion

2.1.2.1.1.1.2.1.1.1.1.3 Synopsizing the meaning

2.1.2.1.1.1.2.1.1.1.2 Establishing the incorrectness of consciousness cognizing external objects

2.1.2.1.1.1.2.1.2 Refuting Sautrāntikas

2.1.2.1.1.1.2.1.2.1 Sautrāntika Non-Pluralists

2.1.2.1.1.1.2.1.2.2 Sautrāntika Half-Eggists

2.1.2.1.1.1.2.1.2.3 Sautrāntika Proponents of an Equal Number of Consciousnesses and Images

2.1.2.1.1.1.2.1.2.4 Sautrāntika Proponents of False Images

2.1.2.1.1.1.2.1.2.4.1 Putting forth their assertions

2.1.2.1.1.1.2.1.2.4.2 Refuting them

2.1.2.1.1.1.2.1.3 Establishing the difference between the two substantialist Buddhist schools

2.1.2.1.1.1.2.2 Refuting Vijñaptivādin Proponents of True Images

2.1.2.1.1.1.2.2.1. Expressing their view

2.1.2.1.1.1.2.2.2. Examining the truth and mistakes in their view

2.1.2.1.1.1.2.2.3. Refuting their views

2.1.2.1.1.1.2.2.3.1 Proponents of True Images

2.1.2.1.1.1.2.2.3.1.1 Half-Eggists

2.1.2.1.1.1.2.2.3.1.1.1 Positing the *absurdum*

2.1.2.1.1.1.2.2.3.1.1.2 Pointing out the mistakes in their view

2.1.2.1.1.1.2.2.3.1.1.3 Expressing the mistakes in what they accept

2.1.2.1.1.1.2.2.3.1.2 Proponents of an Equal Number of Subjects and Objects

2.1.2.1.1.1.2.2.3.1.3 Non-Pluralists

2.1.2.1.1.1.2.3 Refuting Vijñaptivādin Proponents of False Images

2.1.2.1.1.1.2.3.1 Putting forth their assertions

2.1.2.1.1.1.2.3.2 Refuting them

2.1.2.1.1.1.2.3.2.1 The *absurdum* that the experience of images by consciousness is incorrect

2.1.2.1.1.1.2.3.2.2 The *absurdum* of the incorrectness of experiencing images at all

2.1.2.1.1.1.2.3.2.3 The *absurdum* showing the incorrectness of direct experience

2.1.2.1.1.1.2.3.2.4 The *absurdum* of the incorrectness of experience having examined the image

2.1.2.1.1.1.2.3.2.5 The *absurdum* of the incorrectness of the relationship between images and consciousness

2.1.2.1.1.1.2.3.2.6 The *absurdum* of the incorrectness of being occasionally arisen

2.1.2.1.1.1.2.3.2.7 The *absurdum* of being a mere subjective aspect

2.1.2.1.1.1.2.3.2.8 The *absurdum* of being a dependent entity

2.1.2.1.1.2 Refutation of non-pervasive singularity

2.1.2.1.2 Establishment of the lack of the true plural existence of entities

2.1.2.2 Establishment of the pervasion

2.2 Demonstration that entities do exist conventionally

2.2.1 Identifying the characteristics of entities

2.2.2 Identifying the characteristics of conventional existence

2.2.3 The refutation of the ultimate existence of the cause of the illusion

2.3 The refutation of dissenting arguments of other schools

2.3.1 Dispelling the contradictions with direct perception

2.3.2 Dispelling the contradictions with scripture

2.3.3 Expressing ultimate truth

2.3.4 Dispelling dissenting arguments regarding ultimate truth

2.3.4.1 The *absurdum* that those of low intellect know emptiness through direct perception

2.3.4.1.1 Dispelling the arguments.

2.3.4.1.2 Responding to objections

2.3.4.2 The *absurdum* that there would be nobody who directly cognizes emptiness

2.3.4.3 The *absurdum* that there would be no agreed upon, established speech

2.3.4.4 The *absurdum* that there would be no karma and effects

2.3.4.4.1 The *absurdum* regarding the invalidity of previous and later lives

2.3.4.4.1.1 Positing the reasoning

2.3.4.4.1.2 Establishing [the pervasion]

2.3.4.4.1.3 [Avoiding] the faults [of the two extremes] of permanence and nihilism

2.3.4.4.1.4 Demonstrating the possibility of liberation from cyclic existence

2.3.4.4.2 The *absurdum* regarding the invalidity of afflictive emotions

2.3.4.4.3 The *absurdum* regarding the invalidity of the accomplishment of accumulations

2.3.5 Putting forth the nature of conventional truth

2.3.6 Demonstrating the way in which the nature of the Mahāyāna is more glorious than others

2.3.7 Demonstrating how if one knows this system, s/he knows the cause of the generation of compassion and faith

3.0 The concluding explanation

The Tibetan texts of both *MA* and *JBy* provided here were copied from the 1976 Sarnath editions. The numbers in brackets in Gyel-tsab's text correspond to the folio numbers in the version found in Gyel-tsab's *Collected Works (gsuṅ 'bum)* 1981. See Bibliography for details.

Appendix 2

The Ornament of the Middle Way

by Śāntarakṣita

དབུ་མ་རྒྱན་གྱི་རྩ་བ།

དབུ་མ་རྒྱན་གྱི་ཚིག་ལེའུར་བྱས་པ་བཞུགས་སོ།།

རྒྱ་གར་སྐད་དུ། མ་དྷྱ་མ་ཀ་ཨ་ལཾ་ཀཱ་ར་ཀཱ་རི་ཀཱ
བོད་སྐད་དུ། དབུ་མ་རྒྱན་གྱི་ཚིག་ལེའུར་བྱས་པ།
འཇམ་དཔལ་གཞོན་ནུར་གྱུར་པ་ལ་ཕྱག་འཚལ་ལོ།

བདག་དང་གཞན་སྨྲའི་དངོས་འདི་དག།
ཡང་དག་ཏུ་ན་གཅིག་པ་དང་།།
དུ་མའི་རང་བཞིན་བྲལ་བའི་ཕྱིར།།
རང་བཞིན་མེད་དེ་གཟུགས་བརྙན་བཞིན། 1

འབྲས་བུ་རིམ་ཅན་ཉེར་སྦྱོར་བས།།
རྟག་རྣམས་གཅིག་པུའི་བདག་ཉིད་མིན།།

འབྲས་བུ་རེ་རེ་ཐ་དད་ན།།
དེ་དག་རྟག་ལས་ཉམས་པར་འགྱུར། 2

བསྒོམས་ལས་བྱུང་བའི་ཤེས་པ་ཡིས།།
ཤེས་བྱ་འདུས་མ་བྱས་སྨྲ་བའི།།
ལུགས་ལའང་གཅིག་མིན་དེ་དག་ནི།།
རིམ་ཅན་ཤེས་དང་འབྲེལ་ཕྱིར་རོ། 3

རྣམ་ཤེས་སྔ་མས་ཤེས་བྱ་བའི།།
རང་བཞིན་རྗེས་སུ་འབྲང་ན་ནི།།
ཤེས་པ་སྔ་མའང་ཕྱི་མར་འགྱུར།།
ཕྱི་མའང་དེ་བཞིན་སྔ་མར་འགྱུར། 4

སྔོན་དང་ཕྱི་མའི་གནས་རྣམས་སུ།།
དེ་ཡི་ངོ་བོ་མི་འབྱུང་ན།།
འདུས་མ་བྱས་དེ་ཤེས་པ་བཞིན།།
སྐད་ཅིག་འབྱུང་བར་ཤེས་པར་བྱ། 5

སྔ་མ་སྔ་མའི་སྐད་ཅིག་གི།
མཐུ་ཡིས་འབྱུང་བར་འགྱུར་བ་ན།།

འདུས་མ་བྱས་སུ་འདི་མི་འགྱུར།།
སེམས་དང་སེམས་ལས་བྱུང་བ་བཞིན།། 6

སྐད་ཅིག་མ་རྣམས་འདི་དག་ཏུ།།
རང་དབང་འབྱུང་བར་འདོད་ན་ནི།།
གཞན་ལ་ལྟོས་པ་མེད་པའི་ཕྱིར།།
རྟག་ཏུ་ཡོད་པའམ་མེད་པར་འགྱུར།། 7

དོན་བྱེད་ནུས་པ་མ་ཡིན་ལ།།
དེ་འདོད་བརྟགས་པས་ཅི་ཞིག་བྱ།།
མ་ཉིང་གཟུགས་བཟང་མི་བཟང་ཞེས།།
འདོད་ལྡན་རྣམས་ཀྱིས་བརྟགས་ཅི་ཕན།། 8

སྐད་ཅིག་སྐད་ཅིག་མ་ཡིན་པར།།
གང་ཟག་བསྟན་དུ་མི་རུང་བས།།
གཅིག་དང་དུ་མའི་རང་བཞིན་དང་།།
བྲལ་བར་གསལ་བར་རབ་ཏུ་ཤེས།། 9

ཐ་དད་ཕྱོགས་ཅན་དང་འབྲེལ་ཕྱིར།།
ཁྱབ་རྣམས་གཅིག་པུར་ག་ལ་འགྱུར།

བསྒྲིབས་དང་མ་བསྒྲིབས་དངོས་སོགས་ཕྱིར།།
རགས་པ་རྣམས་ཀྱང་གཅིག་པུ་མིན། 10

འཕྱུར་བ་དང་ནི་བསྒོར་བའམ།།
བར་མེད་རྣམ་པར་གནས་ཀྱང་རུང་།
དབུས་གནས་རྡུལ་ཕྲན་རྡུལ་གཅིག་ལ།།
བལྟས་པའི་རང་བཞིན་གང་ཡིན་པ།། 11

རྡུལ་ཕྲན་གཞན་ལ་ལྟ་བ་ཡང་།།
དེ་ཉིད་གལ་ཏེ་ཡིན་བརྗོད་ན།།
དེ་ལྟ་ཡིན་ན་ས་ཆུ་སོགས།།
ཇི་ལྟར་རྒྱས་འགྱུར་མ་ཡིན་ནམ།། 12

རྡུལ་ཕྲན་གཞན་ལ་ལྟ་བའི་ངོས།།
གལ་ཏེ་གཞན་དུ་འདོད་ན་ནི།།
རབ་ཏུ་ཕྲ་རྡུལ་ཇི་ལྟ་བུར།།
གཅིག་པུ་ཆ་ཤས་མེད་པར་འགྱུར།། 13

རྡུལ་ཕྲན་རང་བཞིན་མེད་གྲུབ་པ།།
དེ་ཕྱིར་མིག་དང་རྫས་ལ་སོགས།།

བདག་དང་གཞན་སྐྲུས་མང་པོ་དག།
རང་བཞིན་མེད་པར་མཐོང་པ་ཡིན། 14

དེ་ཡི་རང་བཞིན་ངེས་བརྩམས་དང་།།
དེ་ཡི་ཡོན་ཏན་དེ་ལས་བདག།
དེ་ཡི་སྐྱི་དང་ཁྱད་པར་ཡང་།།
དེ་དག་དེ་དང་འདྲ་བ་ཅན། 15

རྣམ་ཤེས་བེམ་པོའི་རང་བཞིན་ལས།།
བཟློག་པ་རབ་ཏུ་སྐྱེ་བ་སྟེ།།
བེམ་མིན་རང་བཞིན་གང་ཡིན་པ།།
དེ་འདི་བདག་ཉིད་ཤེས་པ་ཡིན།། 16

གཅིག་པུ་ཆ་མེད་རང་བཞིན་ལ།།
གསུམ་གྱི་རང་བཞིན་མི་འཐད་ཕྱིར།།
དེ་ཡི་རང་གི་རིག་པ་ནི།།
བྱ་དང་བྱེད་པའི་དངོས་པོར་མིན།། 17

དེའི་ཕྱིར་འདི་ནི་ཤེས་པ་ཡི།།
རང་བཞིན་ཡིན་པས་བདག་ཤེས་རུང་།།

དོན་གྱི་རང་བཞིན་གཞན་དག་ལ། །
དེ་ཡིས་ཇི་ལྟར་ཤེས་པར་འགྱུར། ། 18

དེ་ཡི་རང་བཞིན་གཞན་ལ་མེད། །
གང་གིས་དེ་ཤེས་གཞན་ཡང་ཤེས། །
ཤེས་དང་ཤེས་པར་བྱ་བའི་དོན། །
ཐ་དད་པར་ནི་འདོད་ཕྱིར་རོ། ། 19

ཤེས་པ་རྣམ་བཅས་ཕྱོགས་ལ་ནི། །
དངོས་སུ་དེ་གཉིས་ཐ་དད་ཀྱང་། །
དེ་དང་གཟུགས་བརྙན་འདྲ་བས་ན། །
བཏགས་པ་ཙམ་གྱིས་ཚོར་བར་རུང་། ། 20

དོན་གྱི་རྣམ་པས་བསྒྱུར་ལྡན་པའི། །
རྣམ་ཤེས་སུ་ཞིག་མི་འདོད་པ། །
དེ་ལ་ཕྱི་རོལ་རིག་པ་ཡི། །
རྣམ་པ་འདི་ཡང་ཡོད་མ་ཡིན། ། 21

ཤེས་གཅིག་ཐ་དད་མ་ཡིན་པས། །
རྣམ་པ་མང་པོར་མི་འགྱུར་ཏེ། །

དེ་ཕྱིར་དེ་ཡི་མཐུ་ཡིས་ནི།།
དོན་ཤེས་འགྱུར་བར་གཞག་པ་མེད།། 22

རྣམ་པ་རྣམས་དང་མ་བྲལ་བས།།
རྣམ་ཤེས་གཅིག་པར་མི་འགྱུར་རོ།།
དེ་ལྟ་མིན་ན་འདི་གཉིས་ལས།།
གཅིག་ཅེས་ཇི་སྐད་བརྗོད་པར་བྱ།། 23

དཀར་པོ་དག་ལ་སོགས་པ་ལ།།
ཤེས་པ་དེ་ནི་རིམ་འབྱུང་སྟེ།།
མགྱོགས་པར་འབྱུང་ཕྱིར་བླུན་པོ་དག།
ཅིག་ཅར་སྙམ་དུ་ཤེས་པ་ཡིན།། 24

ལྕུག་མའི་སྒྲ་ལ་སོགས་པའི་བློ།།
རབ་ཏུ་མགྱོགས་པར་འབྱུང་ཡིན་ན།།
དེ་ཕྱིར་ཅིག་ཅར་འབྱུང་བ་ཡིན།།
འདིར་ཡང་གཅིག་ཕྱིར་འབྱུང་མི་འགྱུར།། 25

ཡིད་ཀྱི་རྟོག་པ་འབའ་ཞིག་ལའང་།།
རིམ་དུ་ཤེས་པར་མི་འགྱུར་རོ།།

རིང་དུ་གནས་པ་མ་ཡིན་པས།།
བློ་རྣམས་ཀུན་ཀྱང་མགྱོགས་འབྱུང་འདྲ།། 26

དེ་ཕྱིར་ཡུལ་རྣམས་ཐམས་ཅད་ལ།།
རིམ་གྱིས་འཛིན་པར་མི་འགྱུར་གྱི།།
རྣམ་པ་དག་ནི་ཐ་དད་ལྟར།།
ཅིག་ཅར་འཛིན་པར་སྣང་བར་འགྱུར།། 27

མགལ་མེ་ལ་ཡང་ཅིག་ཅར་དུ།།
འཁོར་ལོར་སྣང་བའི་འཁྲུལ་པ་འབྱུང་།།
གསལ་བར་རབ་ཏུ་སྣང་བའི་ཕྱིར།།
མཐོང་བས་མཚམས་སྦྱོར་མ་ཡིན་ནོ།། 28

དེ་ལྟར་མཚམས་རྣམས་སྦྱོར་བ་ནི།།
དྲན་པས་བྱེད་པ་ཉིད་ཡིན་གྱི།།
མཐོང་བས་མ་ཡིན་འདས་པ་ཡི།།
ཡུལ་ལ་འཛིན་པ་མིན་ཕྱིར་རོ།། 29

དེ་ཡི་ཡུལ་དུ་གང་གྱུར་པ།།
དེ་ནི་ཞིག་པས་གསལ་མ་ཡིན།།

དེའི་ཕྱིར་འཁོར་ལོར་སྣང་བ་འདི།།
གསལ་བ་མ་ཡིན་འགྱུར་བའི་རིགས།། 30

རི་མོ་རྒྱུད་པ་མཐོང་བའི་ཚེ།།
དེ་ལ་དེ་བཞིན་སེམས་མང་པོ།།
ཇི་སྙེ་གཅིག་ཆའི་རྒྱུལ་གྱིས་སུ།།
འབྱུང་བར་འགྱུར་བ་འདོད་ན་ཀོ། 31

དེ་ལྟ་ཡིན་ན་དཀར་ལ་སོགས།།
རྣམ་པ་སྣ་གཅིག་ཤེས་པ་ཡང་།།
ཐོག་མ་དབུས་མཐའ་ཐ་དད་པས།།
དམིགས་པ་སྣ་ཚོགས་ཉིད་དུ་འགྱུར།། 32

རྡུལ་ཕྲན་བདག་ཉིད་དཀར་ལ་སོགས།།
གཅིག་པུའི་བདག་ཉིད་ཆ་མེད་པ།།
ཤེས་པ་གང་ལའང་སྣང་གྱུར་པར།།
བདག་གིས་རབ་ཏུ་ཚོར་བ་མེད།། 33

རྣམ་ཤེས་ལྔ་ཡི་ཁམས་རྣམས་ནི།
བསགས་ལ་དམིགས་པའི་རྣམ་པ་ཡིན།།

སེམས་དང་སེམས་བྱུང་དམིགས་པ་ནི།།
དྲུག་པར་བཞག་པ་བྱས་པ་ཡིན།། 34

ཕྱི་གཞུང་རྣམས་ལའང་རྣམ་ཤེས་ནི།།
གཅིག་ཏུ་སྣང་བར་མི་འགྱུར་ཏེ།།
ཡོན་ཏན་ལ་སོགས་ལྡན་པ་ཡི།།
རྫས་ལ་སོགས་པར་དམིགས་ཕྱིར་རོ།། 35

ནོར་བུ་གཟི་ཡི་བདག་ཉིད་ལྟར།།
དངོས་པོ་ཀུན་ཞེས་ལྟ་བ་ལ།།
དེ་ལ་འཛིན་པའི་སེམས་ཀྱང་ནི།།
གཅིག་པུའི་ངོ་བོར་སྣང་མི་རིགས།། 36

ས་ལ་སོགས་པ་འདུས་པ་ལ།།
ཡུལ་དང་དབང་པོར་ཀུན་འཛོག་པ།།
སུ་འདོད་དེ་ཡི་ལུགས་ལ་ཡང་།།
དངོས་པོ་གཅིག་དང་མཐུན་འཇུག་མེད།། 37

སྙིང་སྟོབས་ལ་སོགས་བདག་སྒྲ་སོགས།།
ཕྱོགས་ལའང་དོན་གཅིག་སྣང་བ་ཅན།།

ཤེས་པ་རིགས་པ་མ་ཡིན་ཏེ།།
གསུམ་གྱི་བདག་ཉིད་ཡུལ་སྣང་ཕྱིར།། 38

དངོས་པོའི་ངོ་བོ་རྣམ་གསུམ་ལ།།
དེ་ནི་གལ་ཏེ་རྣམ་གཅིག་སྟེ།།
དེ་དང་མི་མཐུན་སྣང་ན་ཀ།
དེ་ནི་དེར་འཛིན་ཇི་ལྟར་འདོད།། 39

ཕྱི་རོལ་ཡུལ་རྣམས་མེད་པར་ཡང་།།
སྔ་ཚོགས་སྣང་ལ་རྟག་པ་སྟེ།།
གཅིག་ཆའམ་ཇི་སྟེ་རིམ་འབྱུང་བའི།།
རྣམ་ཤེས་ཉུང་བར་ཤིན་ཏུ་དཀའ།། 40

ནམ་མཁའ་ལ་སོགས་ཤེས་པ་དག།
མིང་ཙམ་དུ་ནི་སྣང་བ་རྣམས།།
ཡི་གེ་དུ་མ་སྣང་བའི་ཕྱིར།།
སྣ་ཚོགས་སྣང་བར་གསལ་བ་ཡིན།། 41

རྣམ་ཤེས་སྣ་ཚོགས་མི་སྣང་བ།།
འགའ་ཞིག་ཡོད་པར་གཞུག་ན་ཡང་།།

འོན་ཀྱང་ཡང་དག་གཞན་མི་རུང་།།
མཚན་ཉིད་བཅས་ལ་གནོད་མཐོང་ཕྱིར། 42

དེ་ཕྱིར་སྣ་ཚོགས་སྣང་བ་ཡི།
རྣམ་ཤེས་རྣམ་པ་ཀུན་ཏུ་གནས།
ད་ནི་རྣམ་པ་ཐ་དད་ལྟར།
གཅིག་པུའི་རང་བཞིན་མི་རིགས་སོ། 43

ཅི་སྟེ་ཐོག་མ་མེད་རྒྱུད་ཉིད།
བག་ཆགས་སྨིན་པས་སྤྲུལ་པ་ཡི།
རྣམ་པ་དག་ནི་སྣང་བ་ཡང་།
ནོར་བས་སྒྱུ་མའི་རང་བཞིན་འདྲ། 44

དེ་དག་འོན་ཀྱང་དེ་དག་གི
།དངོས་དེ་ཡང་དག་ཉིད་དམ་ཅི།
འོན་ཏེ་མ་བརྟགས་གཅིག་པུ་ན།
དགའ་བར་ཁས་ལེན་འདི་བསམ་མོ། 45

གལ་ཏེ་ཡང་དག་རྣམ་པར་ཤེས།
དུ་མར་འགྱུར་རོ་ཡང་ན་ནི།

དེ་དག་གཅིག་འགྱུར་འགལ་ལྡན་པས།
གདོན་མི་ཟ་བར་སོ་སོར་འགྱུར། 46

རྣམ་པ་ཐ་དད་མ་ཡིན་ན།
གཡོ་དང་མི་གཡོ་ལ་སོགས་པ།
གཅིག་གིས་ཐམས་ཅད་གཡོ་ལ་སོགས།
ཐལ་བར་འགྱུར་ཏེ་ལན་གདབ་དཀའ། 47

ཕྱི་རོལ་དོན་གྱི་ཚུལ་ལ་ཡང་།
དེ་ལྟར་རྣམ་པ་མ་བྲལ་ན།
གཅིག་གི་ཆོས་སུ་ཐམས་ཅད་ཀྱང་།
འཇུག་པར་འགྱུར་ཏེ་བཟློག་པ་མེད། 48

ཇི་སྐད་རྣམ་པའི་གྲངས་བཞིན་དུ།
རྣམ་པར་ཤེས་པ་ཁས་ལེན་ན།
དེ་ཚེ་རྡུལ་ཕྲན་འདྲར་འགྱུར་བ།
དཔྱོད་པ་འདི་ལས་བཟློག་པར་དཀའ། 49

གལ་ཏེ་སྣ་ཚོགས་དེ་གཅིག་ན།
ནམ་མཁའི་གོས་ཅན་ལུགས་སམ་ཅི།

སྣ་ཚོགས་གཅིག་པའི་རང་བཞིན་མིན།
རིན་ཆེན་སྣ་ཚོགས་ལ་སོགས་འདྲ། 50

སྣ་ཚོགས་གཅིག་པུའི་རང་བཞིན་ན།
སྣ་ཚོགས་ངོ་བོར་སྣང་བ་དང་།
བསྒྲིབས་དང་མ་བསྒྲིབས་ལ་སོགས་པ།
ཐ་དད་འདི་ནི་ཇི་ལྟར་འགྱུར། 51

ཇི་སྟེ་ངོ་བོ་ཉིད་དུ་དེའི།
རྣམ་པ་འདི་དག་མེད་པ་སྟེ།
ཡང་དག་ཏུ་རྣམས་མེད་པ་ཡི།
རྣམ་པར་ཤེས་པ་ནོར་བས་སྣང་། 52

གལ་ཏེ་མེད་ན་ཇི་ལྟ་བུ།
དེ་དག་འདི་ལྟར་གསལ་བར་ཚོར།
དེ་ཡི་དངོས་ལས་ཐ་དད་པའི།
ཤེས་པ་དེ་འདྲ་མ་ཡིན་ནོ། 53

འདི་ལྟར་གང་ལ་དངོས་གང་མེད།
དེ་ལ་དེར་ཤེས་ཡོད་མ་ཡིན།

བདེ་བ་མིན་ལ་བདེ་སོགས་དང་།

དཀར་བ་རྣམས་ལའང་མི་དཀར་བཞིན། 54

རྣམ་པ་འདི་ལ་ཤེས་པའི་དོན།

དངོས་སུ་འཐད་པ་མ་ཡིན་ཏེ།

ཤེས་པའི་བདག་དང་བྲལ་བའི་ཕྱིར།

ནམ་མཁའི་མེ་ཏོག་ལ་སོགས་བཞིན། 55

མེད་པ་ནུས་པ་མེད་པས་ན།

གདགས་པའང་མི་རུང་རྟ་རུ་བཞིན།

མེད་པ་བདག་སྣང་ཤེས་སྐྱེད་པར།

ནུས་པ་རུང་བ་མ་ཡིན་ནོ། 56

གང་ཕྱིར་དེ་ཡོད་རེས་ཚོར་བ།

ཤེས་དང་འབྲེལ་བ་ཅི་ཞིག་ཡོད།

བདག་མེད་དེ་ཡི་བདག་ཉིད་དང་།

དེ་ལས་བྱུང་བ་མ་ཡིན་ནོ། 57

རྒྱུ་མེད་ན་ནི་གང་ཞིག་གིས།

རེས་འགའ་འབྱུང་བ་འདི་རུང་འགྱུར།

རྒྱུ་དང་ལྡན་ན་གང་ཞིག་གིས།
གཞན་གྱི་དབང་ལས་ལྡོག་པར་འགྱུར། 58

དེ་མེད་ན་ནི་ཤེས་དེ་ཡང་།
རྣམ་པ་མེད་པ་ཉིད་ཀྱིས་འགྱུར།
ཤེལ་སྒོང་དག་པ་འདྲ་བ་ཡིན།
ཤེས་པ་རབ་ཏུ་ཚོར་བ་མེད། 59

འདི་ནི་འཁྲུལ་པས་ཤེས་ཤེ་ན།
དེ་ཅི་འཁྲུལ་ལ་རག་ལས་སམ།
དེ་ཡི་མཐུ་ཡིས་བྱུང་ན་ནི།
དེ་ཡང་གཞན་གྱི་དབང་ཉིད་དོ། 60

དངོས་པོ་གང་གང་རྣམ་དཔྱད་པ།
དེ་དང་དེ་ལ་གཅིག་ཉིད་མེད།
གང་ལ་གཅིག་ཉིད་ཡོད་མིན་པ།
དེ་ལ་དུ་མ་ཉིད་ཀྱང་མེད། 61

གཅིག་དང་དུ་མ་མ་གཏོགས་པར།
རྣམ་པ་གཞན་དང་ལྡན་པ་ཡི།

དངོས་པོ་མི་རུང་འདི་གཉིས་ནི།
ཕན་ཚུན་སྤངས་ཏེ་གནས་ཕྱིར་རོ། 62

དེ་ཕྱིར་དངོས་པོ་འདི་དག་ནི།
ཀུན་རྫོབ་ཁོ་ནའི་མཚན་ཉིད་འཛིན།
གལ་ཏེ་འདི་བདག་དོན་འདོད་ན།
དེ་ལ་བདག་གིས་ཅི་ཞིག་བྱ། 63

མ་བརྟགས་གཅིག་པུ་ཉམས་དགའ་ཞིང་།
སྐྱེ་དང་འཇིག་པའི་ཆོས་ཅན་པ།
དོན་བྱེད་པ་དག་ནུས་རྣམས་ཀྱིས།
རང་བཞིན་ཀུན་རྫོབ་པ་ཡིན་རྟོགས། 64

བརྟག་པ་མ་བྱས་ཉམས་དགའ་བའང་།
བདག་རྒྱུ་སྔ་མ་སྔ་མ་ལ།
བརྟེན་ནས་ཕྱི་མ་ཕྱི་མ་ཡི།
འབྲས་བུ་དེ་འདྲ་འབྱུང་བ་ཡིན། 65

དེ་ཕྱིར་ཀུན་རྫོབ་རྒྱུ་མེད་ན།
རུང་མིན་ཞེས་པའང་ལེགས་པ་ཡིན།

གལ་ཏེ་འདི་ཡི་ཉེར་ལེན་པ།
ཡང་དག་ཡིན་ན་དེ་སྨྲོས་ཤིག 66

དངོས་པོ་ཀུན་གྱི་རང་བཞིན་ནི།
རིགས་པའི་ལམ་གྱི་རྗེས་འབྲང་བར།
གཞན་དག་འདོད་པ་སེལ་བར་བྱེད།
དེ་ཕྱིར་རྒོལ་བའི་གནས་མེད་དོ། 67

ཡོད་དང་མེད་དང་ཡོད་མེད་ཅེས།
ཁས་མི་ལེན་པ་གང་ཡིན་པ།
དེ་ལ་ནན་ཏན་ལྡན་པས་ཀྱང་།
ཅིར་ཡང་ཀླན་ཀ་བྱ་མི་ནུས། 68

དེ་ཕྱིར་ཡང་དག་ཉིད་དུ་ན།
དངོས་པོ་གང་ཡང་གྲུབ་པ་མེད།
དེ་ཕྱིར་དེ་བཞིན་གཤེགས་རྣམས་ཀྱིས།
ཆོས་རྣམས་ཐམས་ཅད་མ་སྐྱེས་གསུངས། 69

དམ་པའི་དོན་དང་མཐུན་པའི་ཕྱིར།
འདི་ནི་དམ་པའི་དོན་ཞེས་བྱ།

ཡང་དག་ཏུ་ན་སྤྲོས་པ་ཡི།
ཚོགས་རྣམས་ཀུན་ལས་དེ་གྲོལ་ཡིན། 70

སྐྱེ་ལ་སོགས་པ་མེད་པའི་ཕྱིར།
སྐྱེ་བ་མེད་ལ་སོགས་མི་སྲིད།
དེ་ཡི་ངོ་བོ་བཀག་པའི་ཕྱིར།
དེ་ཡི་ཚིག་གི་སྒྲ་མི་སྲིད། 71

ཡུལ་མེད་པ་ལ་དགག་པ་ཡི།
སྦྱོར་བ་ལེགས་པ་ཡོད་མ་ཡིན།
རྣམ་པར་རྟོག་ལ་རྟེན་ལ་ཡང་།
ཀུན་རྫོབ་པར་འགྱུར་ཡང་དག་མིན། 72

འོ་ན་དེ་ནི་རྟོགས་གྱུར་པས།
དེ་ཡི་རང་བཞིན་མངོན་སུམ་ཕྱིར།
མི་ཁས་རྣམས་ཀྱང་དངོས་རྣམས་ཀྱི།
དངོས་པོ་འདི་འདྲ་ཅེས་མི་རྟོགས། 73

མ་ཡིན་ཐོག་མེད་རྒྱུད་ལྡི་བར།
དངོས་པོར་སྒྲོ་བཏགས་དབང་བྱས་པས།

དེ་ཕྱིར་སྲོག་ཆགས་ཐམས་ཅད་ཀྱིས།
མངོན་སུམ་རྟོགས་པར་མི་འགྱུར་རོ། 74

དེ་ལ་སྒྲོ་བཏགས་གཅོད་བྱེད་པ།
ཤེས་པར་བྱེད་པའི་གཏན་ཚིགས་ཀྱིས།
རྗེས་སུ་དཔོག་རྣམས་ཤེས་པར་བྱེད།
རྣལ་འབྱོར་དབང་རྣམས་མངོན་སུམ་གསལ། 75

གཞུང་གིས་བསྐྱེད་པའི་བྱེ་བྲག་གི
ཆོས་ཅན་སྤྱངས་ནས་མཁས་པ་དང་།
བུད་མེད་བྱིས་པའི་བར་དག་ལ།
གྲགས་པར་གྱུར་པའི་དངོས་རྣམས་ལ། 76

བསྒྲུབ་དང་སྒྲུབ་པའི་དངོས་པོ་འདི།
མ་ལུས་ཡང་དག་འཇུག་པར་འགྱུར།
དེ་ལྟ་མིན་ན་གཞི་མ་གྲུབ།
ལ་སོགས་ལན་ནི་ཇི་སྐད་གདབ། 77

བདག་ནི་སྣང་བའི་ངང་ཅན་གྱིས།
དངོས་པོ་དགག་པར་མི་བྱེད་དེ།

དེ་ལྟ་བས་ན་བསྒྲུབ་པ་དང་།
བསྒྲུབ་བྱ་གཞག་པ་འཁྲུགས་པ་མེད། 78

དེ་ཕྱིར་ཐོག་མེད་སྲིད་པ་རྒྱུད་ནས།
དངོས་དང་དངོས་མེད་རྟོགས་སོགས་ཀྱི།
རིགས་དང་མཐུན་པའི་ས་བོན་ཉིད།
རྗེས་སུ་དཔག་པར་བྱ་བ་ཡིན། 79

འདི་ནི་དངོས་པོའི་མཐུ་སྟོབས་ཀྱིས།
འབྱུང་བ་མ་ཡིན་དེ་མེད་ཕྱིར།
དངོས་པོ་རྣམས་ཀྱི་བདག་ཉིད་དེ།
རྒྱ་ཆེན་རབ་ཏུ་བཀག་པ་ཡིན། 80

རིམ་གྱིས་འབྱུང་ཕྱིར་གློ་བུར་མིན།
རྟག་འབྱུང་མ་ཡིན་རྟག་མ་ཡིན།
དེ་བས་གོམས་འདྲ་དེ་ཉིད་ཕྱིར།
དང་པོ་རང་གི་རིགས་ལས་སྐྱེས། 81

དེ་ཕྱིར་རྟག་ཆད་ལྟ་བ་རྣམས།
གཞུང་འདི་ལ་ནི་རིང་དུ་གནས།

ལྡོག་དང་རྗེས་སུ་འཇུག་པ་ཡང་།
ས་བོན་མྱུ་གུ་ལྕུག་སོགས་བཞིན། 82

ཆོས་ལ་བདག་མེད་མཁས་པ་ནི།
རང་བཞིན་མེད་པ་གོམས་བྱས་པས།
ཕྱིན་ཅི་ལོག་ལས་བྱུང་བ་ཡི།
ཉོན་མོངས་བསྒྲིམ་པ་མེད་པར་སྤྱོད། 83

རྒྱུ་དང་འབྲས་བུའི་དངོས་པོ་ནི།
ཀུན་རྫོབ་ཏུ་ནི་མ་བཟློག་པས།
ཀུན་ནས་ཉོན་མོངས་རྣམ་བྱང་སོགས།
རྣམ་པར་གཞག་པ་འཁྲུགས་པ་མེད། 84

འདི་ལྟར་རྒྱུ་དང་འབྲས་བུ་ཡི།
ཆོས་འདི་རྣམ་པར་གཞག་པས་ན།
ཚོགས་རྣམས་དྲི་མ་མེད་པ་ཡང་།
གཞུང་འདི་ཉིད་ལ་རུང་བ་ཡིན། 85

རྣམ་པར་དག་པའི་རྒྱུ་ལས་ནི།
འབྲས་བུ་རྣམ་པར་དག་པ་འབྱུང་།

ཡང་དག་ལྟས་བྱུང་རྩུལ་ཁྲིམས་ཀྱི།
ཡན་ལག་ལ་སོགས་རྣམ་དག་བཞིན། 86

དེ་བཞིན་རྣམ་དག་མ་ཡིན་ལས།
འབྲས་བུ་རྣམ་དག་མ་ཡིན་འབྱུང་།
ལོག་ལྟའི་སྟོབས་ལས་བྱུང་བ་ཡི།
ལོག་པར་གཡེམ་ལ་སོགས་པ་བཞིན། 87

ཚད་མའི་གནོད་པ་ཡོད་པས་ན།
དངོས་པོ་དམིགས་པ་ཡོད་པ་ནི།
སྨིག་རྒྱུ་ལ་སོགས་ཞེས་པ་བཞིན།
ཕྱིན་ཅི་ལོག་པར་ཡོངས་སུ་རྟོག 88

དེ་ཕྱིར་དེ་མཐུས་བྱུང་བ་ཡི།
ཕ་རོལ་ཕྱིན་པ་བསྒྲུབ་པ་ཀུན།
བདག་དང་བདག་གིར་ལོག་པ་ལས།
བྱུང་བ་བཞིན་དུ་སྟོབས་ཆུང་ངོ་། 89

དངོས་པོར་དམིགས་པ་མེད་པ་ལས།
བྱུང་བ་འབྲས་བུ་ཆེན་པོ་སྟེ།

རྒྱུས་པའི་རྒྱུ་ལས་བྱུང་བའི་ཕྱིར།
ས་བོན་གྱུང་པོའི་སྨྱུག་སོགས་བཞིན། 90

རྒྱུ་དང་འབྲས་བུར་གྱུར་པ་ཡང་།
ཤེས་པ་འབའ་ཞིག་ཁོ་ན་སྟེ།
རང་གིས་གྲུབ་པ་གང་ཡིན་པ།
དེ་ནི་ཤེས་པར་གནས་པ་ཡིན། 91

སེམས་ཙམ་ལ་ནི་བརྟེན་ནས་སུ།
ཕྱི་རོལ་དངོས་མེད་ཤེས་པར་བྱ།
ཚུལ་འདིར་བརྟེན་ནས་དེ་ལ་ཡང་།
ཤིན་ཏུ་བདག་མེད་ཤེས་པར་བྱ། 92

ཚུལ་གཉིས་ཤིང་རྟ་ཞོན་ནས་སུ།
རིགས་པའི་སྲབ་སྐྱོགས་འཇུ་བྱེད་པ།
དེ་དག་དེ་ཕྱིར་ཇི་བཞིན་དོན།
ཐེག་པ་ཆེན་པོ་པ་ཉིད་འཐོབ། 93

ཁྱབ་དང་དབང་ལ་སོགས་མ་མྱོང་།
དཔག་ཏུ་མེད་པར་གནས་པའི་རྒྱུ།

འཇིག་རྟེན་སྤྱི་བོར་གྱུར་པས་ཀྱང་།
ཤིན་ཏུ་སྨྱོང་བ་མ་ཡིན་པ། 94

ཡང་དག་བདུད་རྩི་དག་པ་འདི།
ཐུགས་རྗེ་དག་པའི་རྒྱུ་ཅན་གྱི།
དེ་བཞིན་གཤེགས་པ་མ་གཏོགས་པར།
གཞན་གྱི་ལོངས་སྤྱོད་མ་ཡིན་ནོ། 95

དེ་ཕྱིར་ལོག་པར་བསྟན་པ་ཡི།
གྲུབ་མཐར་འཆེལ་བའི་བློ་ཅན་ལ།
དེ་ལུགས་རྗེས་འཇུག་བློ་ཅན་རྣམས།
སྙིང་རྗེ་ཉིད་ནི་རབ་ཏུ་སྐྱེ། 96

བློ་ནོར་ལྡན་པས་ལུགས་གཞན་ལ།
ཇི་ལྟར་སྙིང་པོ་མེད་མཐོང་བ།
དེ་ལྟར་དེ་དག་སྐྱོབ་པ་ལ།
གུས་པ་ཤིན་ཏུ་སྐྱེ་བར་འགྱུར། 97

དབུ་མའི་རྒྱན་གྱི་ཚིག་ལེའུར་བྱས་པ།

སློབ་དཔོན་ཞི་བ་འཚོ་བདག་དང་གཞན་གྱི་གྲུབ་པའི་མཐའ་རྒྱ་མཚོའི་ཕ་རོལ་ཏུ་སོན་པ་འཕགས་

པ་ངག་གི་དབང་ཕྱུག་གི་ཞབས་ཀྱི་པདྨོ་རྙོག་པ་མེད་པའི་ཟེའུ་འབྲུ་སྤྱི་བོས་ལེན་པས་མཛད་པ་རྫོགས་སོ།། རྒྱ་གར་གྱི་མཁན་པོ་སུ་རེན་དྲ་བོ་དྷི་དང་། ཞུ་ཆེན་གྱི་ལོ་ཙྪ་བ་བནྡེ་ཡེ་ཤེས་སྡེ་བསྒྱུར་ཅིང་ཞུས་ཏེ་གཏན་ལ་ཕབ་པའོ།། །།

APPENDIX 3

Remembering "The Ornament of the Middle Way"

by Gyel-tsab Chö-Je

[577] རྒྱལ་ཚབ་ཆོས་རྗེ་ལ་གནས་པའི་དབུ་མ་རྒྱན་
གྱི་བརྗེད་བྱང་བཞུགས།

[578] བླ་མ་དང་རྗེ་བཙུན་འཇམ་པའི་དབྱངས་ལ་ཕྱག་འཚལ་ལོ། བདག་ཉིད་ཆེན་པོ་སློབ་དཔོན་ཞི་བ་འཚོས་མཛད་པའི་དབུ་མའི་རྒྱན་གྱི་ཚིག་ལེའུར་བྱས་པ་གསུམ། མཚན་གྱི་དོན་དང་། བསྟན་བཅོས་ཀྱི་རང་བཞིན་རྒྱས་པ་བཤད་པ་དང་། བཤད་པ་ཡོངས་སུ་རྫོགས་པའི་བྱ་བའོ། དང་པོ་ནི། གོ་སླའོ། གཉིས་པ་ ལ། དོན་དམ་པར་དངོས་པོ་མེད་པར་བསྟན། ཀུན་རྫོབ་ཏུ་ཡོད་པར་བསྟན། དེ་ལ་ཀླན་ཀ་སྤང་བའོ། དང་པོ་ལ། རྟགས་དགོད། ཚུལ་སྒྲུབ་པའོ། དང་པོ་ནི། བདག་སོགས་བཞི་ལ། ཕྱི་ནང་གི་དངོས་པོ་དེ་དག་ཆོས་ཅན།

རང་སྡེ་དང་གཞན་སྡེས་སྨྲས་པ་ལྟར་བདེན་པར་མེད་དེ། བདེན་པའི་གཅིག་དང་དུ་མ་དང་བྲལ་བའི་ཕྱིར། མེ་ལོང་གི་གཟུགས་བརྙན་བཞིན། གཉིས་པ་ལ། ཕྱོགས་[579] ཆོས་དང་། ཁྱབ་པ་སྒྲུབ་པའོ། དང་པོ་ལ་ཁྱབ་པའི་གཅིག་དགག མ་ཁྱབ་པའི་གཅིག་དགག་པའོ། དང་པོ་ལ། རྟག་དངོས་གཅིག་བདེན་དགག གང་ཟག་གཅིག་བདེན་དགག་པའོ། དང་པོ་ལ། གཞན་སྡེས་བཏགས་པའི་རྟག་དངོས་དགག རང་སྡེས་བཏགས་པའི་རྟག་དངོས་དགག་པའོ།

དང་པོ་ནི། འབྲས་སོགས་བཞི་ལ། ཐལ་འགྱུར་དུ་བྱེད་ན། གཙོ་བོ་ཆོས་ཅན། གཅིག་པུའི་བདག་ཉིད་དུ་བདེན་པ་མ་ཡིན་པར་ཐལ། འབྲས་བུ་སྣ་ཕྱི་རིམ་ཅན་དུ་མ་ལ་ཕན་པ་སྣ་ཕྱི་རིམ་ཅན་དུ་མ་ཉེ་བར་སྦྱོར་བའི་ཕྱིར། རང་རྒྱུད་དུ་བྱེད་ན། འབྲས་བུ་ཙམ་ཆོས་ཅན།

ཅིག་ཆར་འབྱུང་བར་ཐལ། དངོས་རྒྱུ་ནུས་པ་ཐོགས་མེད་གཅིག་ལས་སྐྱེས་པའི་ཕྱིར། འདོད་ན། མངོན་སུམ་གྱིས་བསལ། དེ་ལྟར་ཐལ་བ་ལས། རྒྱུ་ཙམ་ཆོས་ཅན། གཅིག་ཏུ་བདེན་པ་མིན་ཏེ། འབྲས་བུ་སྣ་ཕྱི་དུ་མ་ལ་ཕན་པའི་ཉེ་བར་སྦྱོར་བའི་ཕྱིར། དེས་ན། རྒྱུ་ཙམ་གཅིག་བདེན་པ་ཁེགས་པས། གཙོ་བོའང་གཅིག་ཏུ་བདེན་པ་ཁེགས་པ་ཡིན་ནོ། དེའི་ཁྱབ་སྒྲུབ་ཕྱི་མ་གཉིས་ལ། གཙོ་བོ་གཅིག་ཏ [580] བདེན་ཡང་འབྲས་བུ་སྣ་ཕྱི་ལ་ཕན་པ་ཉེ་བར་སྦྱོར་བ་མི་འགལ་ལོ་ཞེ་ན། གཙོ་བོ་ལ་འབྲས་བུ་སྣ་ཕྱི་རིམ་གྱིས་བསྐྱེད་པའི་ནུས་པ་ཡོད་དམ་མེད། མེད་ན། འབྲས་བུ་ཅིག་ཅར་དུ་བསྐྱེད་པར་ཐལ། འབྲས་བུ་བསྐྱེད་པ་གང་ཞིག རིམ་གྱིས་བསྐྱེད་པའི་ནུས་པ་མེད་པའི་ཕྱིར། ཡོད་ན་རྟག་པ་གཅིག་བདེན་ལས་ཉམས་པར་ཐལ།

འབྲས་བུ་སྣ་ཕྱི་རེ་རེ་བསྐྱེད་པའི་ནུས་པ་མི་འདྲ་བ་དུ་མ་ཡོད་པའི་ཕྱིར། གཉིས་པ་ནི། སྒོམ་སོགས་རྐང་པ་ཉི་ཤུ་ལ། སྒོམ་བྱུང་འཕགས་པའི་མཉམ་གཞག་ཡེ་ཤེས་ཀྱིས་ཤེས་པར་བྱ་བའི་འདུས་མ་བྱས་གསུམ་གཅིག་ཏུ་བདེན་པར་འདོད་པ་བྱེ་བྲག་སྨྲ་བའི་ལུགས་ལའང་འདུས་མ་བྱས་གསུམ་པོ་ནི་ཆོས་ཅན། གཅིག་ཏུ་བདེན་པ་མིན་པར་ཐལ། སྒོམ་བྱུང་གི་ཤེས་པ་སྣ་ཕྱི་རིམ་ཅན་དུ་མ་དང་། ཡུལ་ཡུལ་ཅན་དུ་འབྲེལ་བའི་ཕྱིར། དེའི་ཁྱབ་སྒྲུབ་ལ། སྒོམ་བྱུང་གི་ཡེ་ཤེས་འཆོལ་བར་ཐལ་བ་དང་། འདུས་མ་བྱས་གསུམ་ག་སྐད་ཅིག་མར་ཐལ་བའོ། དང་པོ་ནི། རྣམ་ཤེས་སོགས་ལ། སྒོམ་བྱུང་གི་ཤེས་པ་སྣ་ཕྱི་རིམ་ཅན་དུ་མ་དང་ཡུལ་ཡུལ་ཅན་དུ་འབྲེལ་ཡང་གཅིག་ཏུ་བདེན་ནོ་ཞེ་ན། འོ་ན་སྒོམ་བྱུང་གི་ཤེས་པ་སྣ་མའི་ཡུལ་དུ་གྱུར་པའི་འདུས་མ་བྱས་གསུམ་སྒོམ་བྱུང་གི་ཤེས་པ་ཕྱི་མའི་དུས་ན་ཡོད་དམ་མེད། དང་པོ་ལྟར་ན།

སྒོམ་བྱུང་གི་ཤེས་པ་སྔ་མ་དེ་ཕྱི་མའི་དུས་ན་ཡོད་པར་ཐལ། ཕྱོགས་སྔ་དེའི་ཕྱིར། སྒོམ་བྱུང་ཤེས་པ་ཕྱི་མའང་སྔ་མའི་དུས་ན་ཡོད་པར་ཐལ། ཕྱི་མའི་ཡུལ་དེ་སྔ་མའི་དུས་ན་ཡོད་པའི་ཕྱིར་རོ། མ་ཁྱབ་ན། ཡུལ་ཤེས་དུས་མཉམ་ཉམས་སོ། གཉིས་པ་ལྟར་ན། སྔོ་སོགས [581] བཞི་ལ། འདུས་མ་བྱས་གསུམ་ཆོས་ཅན། སྐད་ཅིག་མར་ཐལ། སྔོན་གྱི་རང་བཞིན་དེ་ཕྱི་མའི་གནས་སྐབས་སུ་མི་འབྱུང་ཕྱི་མའི་རང་བཞིན་དེ་སྔོན་གྱི་གནས་སྐབས་སུ་མི་འབྱུང་བའི་དངོས་པོ་ཡིན་པའི་ཕྱིར། དཔེར་ན་སྒོམ་བྱུང་ཤེས་པ་བཞིན།

ཡང་འདུས་མ་བྱས་ཕྱི་མ་རྣམས་ཆོས་ཅན། འདུས་བྱས་སུ་མི་འགྱུར་བར་ཐལ། འདུས་མ་བྱས་སྔ་མ་སྔ་མའི་མཐུ་ལ་བརྟེན་ནས་བྱུང་བའི་ཕྱིར་རོ། དཔེར་ན་སྒོམ་བྱུང་གི་སེམས་སེམས་བྱུང་བཞིན། རྟགས་མ་གྲུབ་ན། སྐད་ཅིག་སོགས་བཞི་ལ། དེ་ཆོས་ཅན།

རང་དབང་དུ་འབྱུང་བར་ཐལ། རྒྱུ་གཞན་ལ་ལྟོས་མེད་དུ་འབྱུང་བའི་ཕྱིར། འདོད་ན། རྟག་ཏུ་འབྱུང་བར་ཐལ། རྒྱུ་ལོག་སྟོབས་ཀྱིས་མི་ལྡོག་པའི་དངོས་པོ་ཡིན་པའི་ཕྱིར། རྟག་ཏུ་མེད་པར་ཐལ། གཉིས་པ། གང་ཟག་གཅིག་བདེན་དགག་པ་ནི། སྐད་ཅིག་སོགས་བཞི་ལ།

གནས་མ་བུ་པའི་སྡེ་པ་ན་རེ། རྟག་མི་རྟག་གང་དུའང་བརྗོད་དུ་མེད་པའི་གང་ཟག་གཅིག་པུ་བདེན་ནོ་ཞེ་ན། གང་ཟག་ཆོས་ཅན། བདེན་པའི་གཅིག་བྲལ་དུ་ཐལ། རྟག་པར་བརྗོད་དུ་མེད་པའི་ཕྱིར། བདེན་པའི་དུ་བྲལ་དུ་ཐལ། མི་རྟག་པར་བརྗོད་དུ་མེད་པའི་ཕྱིར། ཁྱབ་པར་ཐལ། རང་བཞིན་དུ་མ་མེད་པའི་དངོས་པོ་ཡིན་ན་གཅིག་ཡིན་པས་སོ། རང་བཞིན་དུ་མའི་དངོས་པོ་ཡིན་ན་དུ་མ་ཡིན་དགོས་པའི་ཕྱིར། བསྡུ་ན། བདེན་པའི་གཅིག་ཏུ་བྲལ་དུ་ཐལ། རྟག་མི་རྟག་གང་དུའང་བརྗོད་དུ་མེད་པའི་ཕྱིར། ཁྱབ་པའི་ནམ་མཁའ་གཅིག་ [582] བདེན་དགག་པ་ནི། ཐ་དད་སོགས་གཉིས་ལ་ནམ་མཁའ་དང་དུས་ལ་སོགས་པ་རྣམས་ཆོས་ཅན། གཅིག་ཏུ་མི་བདེན་པར་ཐལ། ཤར་ལ་སོགས་པའི་ཕྱོགས་ཐ་དད་ན་ཡོད་པའི་ཕྱོགས་ཅན་ཞིང་ལ་སོགས་པ་

རྣམས་དང་དུས་ཅིག་ཅར་དུ་འཕྲོད་འདུས་འབྲེལ་བའི་ཕྱིར། མ་ཁྱབ་པའི་གཅིག་བདེན་དགག་པ་ལ། ཕྱི་རོལ་གཅིག་བདེན་དགག ཤེས་པ་གཅིག་བདེན་དགག་པའོ། དང་པོ་ཕྱི་རོལ་གཅིག་བདེན་དགག་ལ། རགས་པ་དང་། རྡུལ་ཕྲན་གཅིག་བདེན་དགག་པ་དང་།

དེ་དག་གིས་གྲུབ་པའི་དོན་ནོ། དང་པོ་ནི། སྒྲིབ་སོགས་གཉིས་ལ། བུམ་པ་ཆོས་ཅན། གཅིག་ཏུ་མི་བདེན་པར་ཐལ། བུམ་པ་ཆོས་ཅན། གཅིག་ཏུ་མི་བདེན་པར་ཐལ། བསྒྲིབས་མ་བསྒྲིབས་སོགས་རྫས་ལ་བརྟེན་པའི་འགལ་འདུ།

ལ་སོགས་པ་གཡོ་མི་གཡོ་སོགས་བྱ་བ་ལ་བརྟེན་པའི་འགལ་འདུ། མཚོན་གྱིས་བསྒྱུར་མ་བསྒྱུར་སོགས་ཡོན་ཏན་ལ་བརྟེན་པའི་འགལ་འདུ་སོགས་གསུམ་དང་ལྡན་པའི་ཕྱིར། རྡུལ་ཕྲན་གཅིག་བདེན་དགག་པ་ནི། དབྱུར་སོགས་བཅུ་གཉིས་ལ།

ཕྱོགས་བཅུའི་དབུས་ན་གནས་པའི་རྡུལ་ཕྲན་ཆོས་ཅན། ཤར་རྡུལ་དང་ཕྱོགས་གཞན་དགུའི་རྡུལ་གོ་ས་ཐ་དད་མེད་པར་ཐལ། ཁྱོད་ཀྱི་ཤར་ལ་བལྟ་བའི་ངོས་དེ་དང་ཁྱོད་ཕྱོགས་གཞན་དགུའི་རྡུལ་ལ་བལྟ་བའི་ངོས་གཅིག་ཡིན་པའི་ཕྱིར། འདོད་ན།

སའི་དཀྱིལ་འཁོར་ལ་སོགས་པའི་རགས་པ་རྒྱས་པ་མི་སྲིད་པར་ཐལ། འདོད་པ་དེའི་ཕྱིར། བལྟ་བའི་ངོས་སོ་སོར་འདོད་ན། དེ་ཆོས་ཅན། ཆ་མེད་ཀྱི་གཅིག་མིན་པར་ཐལ། ཕྱོགས་བཅུའི་རྡུལ་ལ་བལྟ་བའི་ཁྱོད་ཀྱི་ངོས་མི་འདྲ་བ་བཅུ་ཡོད་པའི་ཕྱིར། གསུམ་པ་དེས་གྲུབ་པའི་དོན་ལ། རྟགས་ [583] དགོད་པ་དང་། ཁྱབ་པ་སྒྲུབ་པ།

དེའི་ཕྱིར་ཞེས་པ་ཀྲང་པ་བཞེས་སྟོན་ཏོ། ཤེས་བྱ་ཆོས་ཅན། རང་སྡེས་སྨྲས་པའི་ཕུང་ཁམས་སྐྱེ་མཆེད་དང་། གཞན་སྡེས་སྨྲས་པའི་ཡན་ལག་ཅན་གྱི་རྫས་ལ་སོགས་པ་བདེན་པའི་རང་བཞིན་མེད་པར་མངོན་ཞིང་གྲུབ་པ་ཡིན་ཏེ། རྡུལ་ཕྲན་བདེན་པའི་རང་བཞིན་མེད་པ་དེའི་ཕྱིར།

ཁྱབ་པ་ཡོད་དེ། རང་སྡེས་གཟུགས་ཅན་བཅུ་རྡུལ་ཕྲ་རབ་བསགས་པའི་རང་བཞིན་དུ་ཁས་བླངས་

པའི་ཕྱིར། གཞན་གྱི་སྡེ་པས་ཡན་ལག་གིས་རྫས་རྡུལ་གྱིས་བརྩམས་ཤིང་། གཟུགས་དྲི་ལ་སོགས་པ་དེའི་ཡོན་ཏན་དང་། འདེགས་འཛོག་ལ་སོགས་པའི་ལས་དང་། ཡོད་པ་ཉིད་ལ་སོགས་པའི་སྤྱི་ཆེན་པོ་དང་། ཉེ་ཚེ་བ་དང་།

སྔོན་པོ་ལ་སོགས་པ་དེ་ལ་འདུ་བའི་ཁྱད་པར་རྣམས་རགས་པ་ཡན་ལག་གི་རྫས་ལ་འདུ་འབྲེལ་གྲུབ་པར་ཁས་བླངས་པའི་ཕྱིར། ཞེས་པ་གཅིག་བདེན་དགག་པ་ལ། རང་སྡེ་དོན་སྨྲ་གཉིས་ཀྱི་ལུགས་དགག ཕྱི་རོལ་པའི་ལུགས་དགག རྣམ་རིག་པའི་ལུགས་དགག་པའོ། དང་པོ་ལ། རྣམ་མེད་བྱེ་བྲག་སྨྲ་བའི་ལུགས་དགག མདོ་སྡེ་པའི་ལུགས་དགག་པའོ། དང་པོ་ལ་དོན་རིག་དང་། རང་རིག་མི་མཚུངས་པར་བསྒྲུབ། དོན་སྨྲ་གཉིས་ཀྱི་ལུགས་མི་མཚུངས་པར་བསྒྲུབ་པའོ། དང་པོ་ལ། རང་རིག་འཐད་པར་སྒྲུབ་པ་དང་། དོན་རིག་མི་འཐད་པར་སྒྲུབ་པའོ། དང་པོ་ལ། ཐལ་བ་འགོད། ཁྱབ་པ་སྒྲུབ། དོན་བསྡུ་བའོ། དང་པོ་ནི། རྣམ་ཤེས་སོགས་བཞི་ལ། རྣམ་ཤེས་ཆོས་ཅན། རང་རིག་འཐད་པར་ཐལ། ཁྱོད་མེམ་པོའི་རང་བཞིན་ [584] ལས་ལོག་པར་སྐྱེས་པའི་ཕྱིར། ཁྱབ་པར་ཐལ། བེམ་པོ་མ་ཡིན་པའི་རང་བཞིན་གང་ཡིན་པའི་འཛིན་རྣམ་དེ་ཤེས་པ་དེའི་རང་རིག་ཡིན་པའི་ཕྱིར། ཁྱབ་པ་སྒྲུབ་པ་ནི། གཅིག་སོགས་བཞི་ལ། དེ་ཆོས་ཅན། ཁྱོད་ཀྱི་རང་རིག་དེ་རིག་བྱ་རིག་བྱེད་རིག་པ་གསུམ་པོ་རྫས་ཐ་དད་པའི་ཚུལ་དུ་མེད་པར་ཐལ། ཁྱོད་རྫས་ཆ་ཤས་མེད་པའི་གཅིག་པའི་ཕྱིར། ཁྱབ་པར་ཐལ། རྫས་ཆ་ཤས་མེད་པའི་གཅིག་ལ་བྱ་བྱེད་རྫས་ཐ་དད་པ་གསུམ་མི་འཐད་པའི་ཕྱིར། དོན་བསྡུ་བ།

དེ་ཕྱིར་སོགས་གཉིས་ལ། དེ་ཆོས་ཅན། རང་རིག་འཐད་པར་ཐལ། ཁྱོད་འཛིན་རྣམ་གྱི་རང་བཞིན་ཡིན་པའི་ཕྱིར། དོན་རིག་མི་འཐད་པ་ནི། དོན་སོགས་དྲུག་ལ། དོན་དངོས་སུ་མྱོང་བ་མི་འཐད་པར་ཐལ། དོན་ཤེས་རྫས་ཐ་དད་ཡིན་པའི་ཕྱིར། དེར་ཐལ།

དོན་གྱི་རང་བཞིན་ཤེས་པ་ལ་མེད་ཤེས་པའི་རང་བཞིན་དོན་ལ་མེད་པའི་ཕྱིར། རང་རིག་འཐད་

པ་བཞིན་དོན་རིག་མི་འཐད་པར་ཐལ། དོན་ཤེས་འབྲེལ་མེད་རྫས་ཐ་དད་ཡིན་པའི་ཕྱིར། དོན་སྣ་གཉིས་ལུགས་མི་མཚུངས་པ་ལ། མདོ་སྡེ་པའི་ལུགས་ལ་དོན་བརྟགས་ནས་སྨྲོང་བ་འཐད། བྱེ་བྲག་སྨྲ་བའི་ལུགས་ལ་བརྟགས་ནས་སྨྲོང་བར་ཡང་མི་འཐད་པར་བསྟན་པའོ། དང་པོ་ནི། ཤེས་སོགས་བཞི་ལ། མདོ་སྡེ་པའི་ལུགས་ལ་དོན་ཤེས་རྫས་ཐ་དད་ཀྱང་དོན་བརྟགས་ནས་སྨྲོང་བ་འཐད་པར་ཐལ། དོན་གྱི་རྣམ་པ་ཁས་བླངས་པའི་ཕྱིར། གཉིས་པ་ནི་དོན་སོགས་བཞི་ལ། བྱེ་བྲག་སྨྲ་བའི་ལུགས་ལ་ཕྱི་རོལ་དོན་བརྟགས་ནས་སྨྲོང་བའི་རྣམ་པས་ཇི་ རྩལ་འདིའང་མི་འཐད་པར་ཐལ། དོན་གྱིས [585] རྣམ་པ་མི་འདོད་པའི་ཕྱིར། མདོ་སྡེ་པའི་ལུགས་དགག་པ་ལ། སྣ་ཚོགས་གཉིས་མེད་པ། སྒོ་ང་ཕྱེད་ཚལ་བ། རྣམ་ཤེས་གྲངས་མཉམ་པའི་ལུགས་དགག་པའོ། དང་པོ་ནི། ཤེས་སོགས་བཞི་ལ། ཤེས་པ་གཅིག་ལ་སྔོ་སེར་དཀར་དམར་སོགས་རྣམ་པ་དུ་མ་ཤར་བའི་ཚེ་རྣམ་པ་དེ་རྣམས་རྫས་ཐ་དད་མིན་པར་ཐལ། དེ་རྣམས་ཤེས་པ་ཆ་མེད་གཅིག་དང་ཐ་དད་མིན་པའི་ཕྱིར། འདོད་ན།

དོན་གྱི་རྣམ་པ་ཤར་བའི་སྒོ་ནས་དོན་རྫས་ཐ་དད་དུ་གྲུབ་པར་གཞག་ཏུ་མི་རུང་བར་ཐལ། རྣམ་པ་དེ་རྣམས་རྫས་ཐ་དད་མིན་པའི་ཕྱིར། རྣམ་པ་སོགས་བཞི་ལ། ཁྲ་འཛིན་དབང་ཤེས་ཆོས་ཅན། གཅིག་ཏུ་མི་བདེན་པར་ཐལ། རྣམ་པ་དུ་མ་དང་རྫས་གཅིག་ཡིན་པའི་ཕྱིར། མ་ཁྱབ་ན། ཆོས་ཅན། རྣམ་པ་དེ་རྣམས་དང་རྫས་གཅིག་ཏུ་མི་བདེན་པར་ཐལ། ཁྱོད་རྫས་གཅིག་ཡིན། རྣམ་པ་དེ་རྣམས་རྫས་དུ་མར་བདེན་པའི་ཕྱིར། གཉིས་པ་སྒོ་ང་ཕྱེད་ཚལ་བའི་ལུགས་དགག་པ་ལ། འདོད་པ་བརྗོད་པ་དང་། དེ་དགག་པའོ། དང་པོ་ནི། དཀར་སོགས་བཞི་ལ། ཁོ་ན་རེ། ཁོ་བོ་ཅག་ལ་སྐྱོན་དེ་དག་མེད་དེ། ཤེས་པ་གཅིག་ལ་སྔོ་སེར་སོགས་ཀྱི་རྣམ་པ་དུ་མ་ཤར་བའི་ཚེ་དཀར་པོ་ལ་སོགས་པའི་རྣམ་པ་རྣམས་ཤེས་པ་ལ་རིམ་གྱིས་སྣང་ཡང་འཇུག་པ་མགྱོགས་པའི་ཕྱིར། ཅིག་ཅར་དུ་སྣང་ངོ་སྙམ་དུ་འཁྲུལ་པ་ཡིན་ཏེ།

དཔེར་ན་མགལ་མེ་རིམ་གྱིས་འབྱུང་ཡང་ཅིག་ཅར་དུ་འཁྲུལ་བ་བཞིན་ནོ་ཞེས་ཟེར་རོ། གཉིས་
པ་ལ་དོན་དགག དཔེ་དགག་པའོ། དང་པོ་ལ། ཡི་གེ་ལ་དམིགས་པའི་བློས་མ་ [586]
ངེས། ཡིད་རྟོག་འབའ་ཞིག་ཡུལ་ལ་འཇུག་པས་མ་ངེས། བློ་ཀུན་གྱིས་མ་ངེས་པའོ། དང་པོ་
ནི། ལྕུག་སོགས་བཞི་ལ། སླ་ར་རླ་ས་ཞེས་བརྗོད་པའི་ཚེ། འབྲས་བུ་རོ་དང་མཚོ་གཉིས་གཅིག་
ཅར་དུ་ཐོས་པར་འཁྲུལ་པ་སྐྱེ་བར་ཐལ། དེ་གཉིས་ཐོས་པ་ཆེས་མྱུར་བའི་ཕྱིར། འདོད་ན།
མངོན་སུམ་གྱིས་བསལ། གཉིས་པ་ནི། ཡིད་སོགས་གཉིས་ལ། ཡིད་རྟོགས་འགའ་ཞིག་ཡུལ་
ལ་འཇུག་པའི་ཚེ། ཡུལ་ཅིག་ཅར་དུ་འཛིན་པའི་འཁྲུལ་པ་སྐྱེ་བར་ཐལ། ཡུལ་འཛིན་པ་ཆེས་
མྱུར་བའི་ཕྱིར། གསུམ་པ་བློ་ཀུན་གྱིས་མ་ངེས་པ་ནི། རིགས་སོགས་དྲུག་ལ།
བློ་ཀུན་ཆོས་ཅན། ཡུལ་རིམ་གྱིས་འཛིན་པ་མ་ངེས་པར་ཅིག་ཅར་འཛིན་པ་འཁྲུལ་བར་ཐལ།
ཡུལ་འཛིན་པ་ཆེས་མྱུར་བའི་ཕྱིར། དེར་ཐལ། སྐད་ཅིག་མ་ཡིན་པའི་རིང་དུ་མི་གནས་པའི་
ཕྱིར། དཔེར་ན་ཁྱོད་རང་འདོད་པའི་རྣམ་པ་རྣམས་བཞིན། གཉིས་པ་ལ། ཐལ་བ་དགོད།
ཁྱབ་པ་སྒྲུབ་པའོ། དང་པོ་ནི། མགལ་སོགས་བཞི་ལ། མགལ་མེ་ལ་འཁོར་ལོར་འཁྲུལ་པའི་
བློ་འདི་ཆོས་ཅན། མཐོང་བ་རྟོག་མེད་ཤེས་པ་ཡིན་གྱི་སྔ་ཕྱི་མཚམས་སྦྱོར་བའི་བློ་མ་ཡིན་པར་
ཐལ། ཡུལ་གསལ་བར་སྣང་བའི་ཕྱིར། གཉིས་པ་ནི། འདི་སོགས་བརྒྱད་ལ། མ་ཁྱབ་བོ་ཞེ་ན།
དེ་ལ་ཁྱབ་པ་ཡོད་པར་ཐལ། སྔ་ཕྱི་མཚམས་སྦྱོར་བའི་བློ་ཡིན་ན་དྲན་པ་ཡིན་དགོས་པའི་ཕྱིར།
རྟོག་མེད་ཤེས་པ་ཆོས་ཅན། སྔ་ཕྱི་མཚམས་སྦྱོར་བ་མིན་པར་ཐལ། ཡུལ་འདས་པ་མི་འཛིན་
པའི་ཕྱིར། སྔ་ཕྱི་མཚམས་སྦྱོར་བའི་བློ་ཆོས་ཅན། ཡུལ་གསལ་བར་སྣང་བ་ཡིན་པར་ཐལ།
ཡུལ་འདས་པ་འཛིན་པའི་ཕྱིར། [587] མགལ་མེ་ལ་འཁོར་ལོར་འཁྲུལ་པའི་བློ་འདི་ཆོས་ཅན།
སྔ་ཕྱི་མཚམས་སྦྱོར་བའི་བློ་མིན་པར་ཐལ། དེ་ཡིན་ན་ཡུལ་གསལ་བར་སྣང་མི་རིགས་པ་ལས།
དེ་ཡིན་ན་ཡུལ་གསལ་བར་སྣང་མི་རིགས་པ་ལས་ཡུལ་གསལ་བར་སྣང་བའི་ཕྱིར། རྣམ་ཤེས་

གྲངས་མཉམ་པ་དགག་པ་ལ། འདོད་པ་བརྗོད་པ་དང་། དེ་དགག་པའོ། དང་པོ་འདོད་པ་བརྗོད་པ་ནི། རི་སོགས་བཞི་ལ། ཁོ་ན་རེ། རས་གཞི་ལ་སོགས་པའི་རི་མོ་རྒྱུད་པ་མཐོང་བ་བཞིན། སྤོ་སེར་གྱི་རྣམ་པ་དུ་མ་སྣང་བའི་ཚེ།

རྣམ་ཤེས་ཀྱང་དུ་མ་ཅིག་ཅར་དུ་འབྱུང་བས་ཁོ་བོ་ལ་སྐྱོན་དེ་དག་མེད་དོ་ཞེ་ན། གཉིས་པ་ལ། བློ་ཐམས་ཅད་དུ་མའི་རྣམ་པ་དུ་བསྒྲུབ། ཆ་མེད་གཅིག་མི་སྲིད་པར་བསྟན་པའོ། དང་པོ་ནི། དེ་སོགས་བཞི་ལ། དཀར་པོའི་རྣམ་པ་གཅིག་པུ་ལ་དམིགས་པའི་ཤེས་པ་ཆོས། དུ་མའི་རྣམ་པ་ཅན་དུ་ཐལ། དཀར་པོ་དེ་ལ་ལྷོ་ཤར་སོགས་ཐ་དད་དུ་མ་ཡོད་པའི་ཕྱིར། འདོད་ན། རྣམ་པ་གཅིག་ཁོ་ན་འཛིན་པའི་ཤེས་པ་མི་སྲིད་པར་འགྱུར་རོ། གཉིས་པ་ནི། རྡུལ་སོགས་བརྒྱད་ལ། ཆ་མེད་གཅིག་ཏུ་བདེན་པ་མི་སྲིད་པར་ཐལ། དེར་དམིགས་རུང་མ་དམིགས་པའི་ཕྱིར། རྟགས་མ་གྲུབ་ན། དེར་ཐལ། མིག་གི་རྣམ་ཤེས་སོགས་རྣམ་ཤེས་ལྔ་ནི་རྡུལ་ཕྲ་རབ་བསགས་པ་ལ་དམིགས་ཤིང་།

དེའི་རྗེས་སུ་འབྲང་བའི་ཡིད་ཤེས་ནི་དེ་དང་འདྲ་ལ་མི་འབྲང་བའི་ཡིད་རྣམས་སེམས་སེམས་བྱུང་ཚོགས་པ་ལ་དམིགས་པའི་ཕྱིར། ཕྱི་རོལ་པའི་ལུགས་དགག་པ་ལ། སྤྱིར་དགག སོ་སོར་དགག་པའོ། དང་པོ་ནི། ཕྱི་སོགས་གཉིས་ལ། ཕྱི་རོལ་པའི་ [588] ལུགས་ལའང་ཡུལ་གཅིག་ཁོ་ན་འཛིན་པའི་བློ་མི་སྲིད་པར་ཐལ། བློ་ཐམས་ཅད་དུ་མའི་རྣམ་པ་ཅན་ཡིན་པའི་ཕྱིར། གཉིས་པ་ལ། ཕྱོགས་སྔ་དགག་པ་ལྔ་པའི་དང་པོ་ནི། ཡོན་ཏན་སོགས་གཉིས་ལ།

བྱེ་བྲག་པ་དང་རིག་པ་ཅན་པའི་ལུགས་ལ་ཡུལ་གཅིག་ཁོ་ན་འཛིན་པའི་བློ་མི་སྲིད་པར་ཐལ། ཡན་ལག་ཅན་གྱི་རྫས་ལ་སོགས་པ་ཡོན་ཏན་དང་། ལས་དང་། འདུ་བས་ཁྱད་པར་དུ་བྱས་ནས་འཛིན་དགོས་པའི་ཕྱིར། གཉིས་པ་ནི། ནོར་སོགས་བཞི་ལ། རྒྱལ་བ་བའམ་ཟད་བྱེད་པའི་

ལུགས་ལ་དེ་མི་སྲིད་པར་ཐལ། དངོས་པོ་ཐམས་ཅད་ནོར་བུའི་གཟི་ལྟར་དུ་མར་བདེན་པའི་ཕྱིར། གསུམ་པ་ནི། ས་སོགས་བཞི་ལ། རྒྱང་ཕན་གྱི་ལུགས་ལའང་བསལ་བ་སྨྲ་མ། གཟུགས་སོགས་ཡུལ་དང་མིག་སོགས་དབང་པོ་ཀུན་འབྱུང་བཞི་འདུས་པའི་རང་བཞིན་དུ་ཁས་བླངས་པའི་ཕྱིར་དང་། བཞི་པ་ནི། སྙིང་སོགས་བརྒྱད་ལ། གྲངས་ཅན་གྱི་ལུགས་ལའང་དེ་འཐད་པར་ཐལ།

གཟུགས་སྒྲ་སོགས་དེ་ཙམ་ལྔ་པོ་རྡུལ་མུན་སྙིང་སྟོབས་གསུམ་གྱི་བདག་ཉིད་དུ་གྱུར་པའི་ཡུལ་བློ་ལ་སྣང་བར་འདོད་པའི་ཕྱིར། མ་ཁྱབ་ཅེ་ན། དེ་ཙམ་ལྔ་འཛིན་པའི་ཤེས་པ་ཆོས་ཅན། ཡུལ་གྱི་གནས་ལུགས་ཇི་ལྟ་བ་བཞིན་འཛིན་པ་མིན་པར་ཐལ།

དེ་ཙམ་ལྔ་པོ་བདེ་སྡུག་བཏང་སྙོམས་གསུམ་གྱི་རང་བཞིན་དུ་བདེན། ཁྱོད་ལ་ཡུལ་གཅིག་ཁོ་ནའི་རྣམ་པ་སྣང་བའི་ཕྱིར། ལྔ་པ་ནི། ཕྱི་སོགས་བཞི་ལ། རིག་བྱེད་གསང་བའི་མཐར་སྨྲ་བའི་ལུགས་ལའང་དེར་ཐལ། ཡུལ་སྣ་ཚོགས་སྣང་བའི་ཤེས་པ་རགས་པ་ཡིན་པའི་ཕྱིར།

མདོ་སྡེ་པའི་ལུགས་དགག་པ་ནི། རྣམ་སོགས [589] བཞི་ལ། འདུས་མ་བྱས་འཛིན་པའི་བློ་ཆོས་ཅན། ཡུལ་སྣ་སོགས་པའི་རྣམ་པ་ཅན་དུ་ཐལ། ཡི་གེའི་སྤྱི་སྟེ་སྒྲ་སྤྱི་དུ་མ་སྣང་བའི་ཕྱིར། རྣམ་སོགས་བརྒྱད་ལ། རྣམ་པ་སྣ་ཚོགས་མི་སྣང་བའི་ཤེས་པ་འགའ་ཞིག་ཡོད་ནའང་བདེན་པར་མ་གྲུབ་པར་ཐལ། བདེན་པར་གྲུབ་པ་ལ་རིགས་པས་གནོད་པའི་ཕྱིར། རྣམ་ཤེས་ཆོས་ཅན། གཅིག་པུའི་རང་བཞིན་དུ་མི་བདེན་པར་ཐལ། རྣམ་པ་སྣ་ཚོགས་སྣང་བའི་ཕྱིར། དཔེར་ན་རྣམ་པ་དུ་མ་བཞིན། རྣམ་རིག་པ་དགག་པ་ལ། འདོད་པ་བརྗོད། བདེན་རྫུན་བརྟགས། དེ་དགག་པའོ། དང་པོ་འདོད་པ་བརྗོད་པ་ནི། ཅི་སོགས་བཞི་ལ།

ཇི་སྟེ་ཐོག་མ་མེད་པ་ནས་བརྒྱུད་ཏེ་འོངས་པའི་དོན་སྣང་གི་བག་ཆགས་སྨིན་པས་སྤྲུལ་པས་ཏེ་བསྐྱེད་པའི་དོན་དུ་སྣང་བའང་དོན་མེད་བཞིན་དུ་དོན་དུ་སྣང་བ་སྒྱུ་མའི་རང་བཞིན་དང་འདྲའོ་

ཞེས་ཟེར་རོ། གཉིས་པ་བདེན་རྫུན་བརྟགས་པ་ནི། དེ་སོགས་བཞི་ལ། ལྟ་བ་དེ་མདོ་སྡེ་པ་མན་ཆད་ཀྱི་མངོན་ཞེན་ངན་པ་མང་པོའི་གཉེན་པོ་བྱེད་པས་དེ་དག་བས་དེ་བཟང་པོ་ཡིན་ཡང་། གཉིས་མེད་ཀྱི་ཤེས་པ་བདེན་ནམ་བརྫུན་པ་མ་བརྟགས་གཅིག་པུ་ཉམས་དགའ་བ་ཡིན། དང་པོ་ལྟར་ན། གསུམ་པ་དེ་དགག་པ་ལ་གཉིས། རྣམ་བདེན་པ་དང་། རྣམ་རྫུན་པའི་ལུགས་དགག་པའོ། དང་པོ་རྣམ་བདེན་པ་ལ་གསུམ། སྒོང་ཕྱེད་ཚལ་བ། རྣམ་ཤེས་གྲངས་མཉམ་པ། སྣ་ཚོགས་གཉིས་མེད་པའི་ལུགས་དགག་པའོ། དང་པོ་ལ་ཐལ་བ་དགོད། འདོད་པ་ལ་གནོད་པ་བསྟན་པ། དོན་ཁས་བླངས་པ་ལའང་སྐྱོན་མཚུངས་པ་བསྟན་པའོ། དང་པོ་ནི། གལ་སོགས་བཞི་ལ། རྣམ་ཤེས་དུ་མར་ཐལ། རྣམ་པ་དུ་མ་དང་ [590] གཅིག་ཏུ་བདེན་པའི་ཕྱིར་དང་། རྣམ་པ་རྣམས་གཅིག་ཏུ་ཐལ། རྣམ་ཤེས་དང་རྫས་གཅིག་ཏུ་བདེན་པའི་ཕྱིར། ཁྱབ་པ་མེད་ན། དེ་གཉིས་རྫས་སོ་སོར་ཐལ། རྣམ་ཤེས་གཅིག་དང་རྣམས་དུ་མར་བདེན་པའི་ཕྱིར། ཐལ་བར་འདོད་ན། གཉིས་པ་ནི། རྣམ་སོགས་བཞི་ལ་རྣམ་པ་གཅིག་གཡོ་བར་མཐོང་བའི་ཚེ་ཐམས་ཅད་གཡོ་བ་དང་། གཅིག་སེར་བའི་ཚེ་ཐམས་ཅད་སེར་པོར་ཐལ།

རྣམ་པ་རྣམས་གཅིག་ཡིན་པའི་ཕྱིར། གསུམ་པ་ནི། ཕྱི་སོགས་བཞི་ལ། དོན་ཁས་བླངས་པའི་ལུགས་ལའང་རྣམ་པ་རྣམས་གཅིག་ཏུ་མི་བདེན་པར་ཐལ། སྐྱོན་དེ་དག་བཟློག་ཏུ་མེད་པའི་ཕྱིར། གཉིས་པ་ནི། ཅི་སྟེ་སོགས་བཞི་ལ། མིག་གི་རྣམ་ཤེས་རིགས་མཐུན་དུ་མ་ཅིག་ཅར་དུ་མི་སྐྱེ་བར་ཐལ། རྡུལ་ཆ་མེད་དུ་མ་ཅིག་ཅར་ཚོགས་པ་ལ་བཀོད་པའི་སྐྱོན་དེ་མཚུངས་པའི་ཕྱིར། གསུམ་པ་ནི། གལ་སོགས་བརྒྱད་ལ། རྣམ་པ་སྣ་ཚོགས་པ་དེ་ཤེས་པ་གཅིག་གི་རང་བཞིན་དུ་བདེན་ནོ་ཞེ་ན། གཅེར་བུ་བ་རིག་བྱེད་གསང་བའི་མཐར་སྨྲ་བའི་ལུགས་ལྟར་ཡུལ་སྣ་ཚོགས་སྣང་བའི་ཤེས་པ་གཅིག་བདེན་འདོད་ན་རྣམ་པ་སྣ་ཚོགས་སྣང་ན་གཅིག་ཏུ་མི་བདེན་པས་ཁྱབ། རིན་པོ་ཆེ་སྣ་ཚོགས་པའི་ཕུང་པོ་བཞིན། ཞེས་པའང་རྣམ་པ་སྣ་ཚོགས་པ་སྣང་བ་ཡིན་ནོ། རྣམ་

པ་རྣམས་གཅིག་ཏུ་འདོད་ན། སྔོ་སེར་སོགས་རྣམ་པ་སྣ་ཚོགས་པའི་རྣམ་པ་སྣང་བ་དང་། སྒྲིབས་མ་སྒྲིབས་ལ་སོགས་པའི་རྣམ་པ་ཐ་དད་པ་དུ་མ་སྣང་བ་འདི་མི་འཐད་པར་ཐལ། རྣམ་པ་སྣ་ཚོགས་པ་རྣམས་གཅིག་ཏུ་བདེན་པའི་ཕྱིར། རྣམ་རྫུན་པ་དགག་པ་ལ། [591] འདོད་པ་བརྗོད་པ་དང་། དེ་དགག་པའོ། ཅི་སོགས་བཞི་ལ། ལོ་ན་རེ།

རྣམ་པ་རྫས་གཅིག་དང་ཐ་དད་ལ་བཀོད་པའི་སྐྱོན་དེ་ཁོ་བོ་ལ་མེད། རྣམ་པ་འདི་རྣམ་པ་དངོས་པོར་མེད་བཞིན་དུ་སྣང་བ་ཡིན་ནོ་ཞེས་ཟེར་རོ། གཉིས་པ་ལ། རྣམ་པ་མྱོང་བ་མི་འཐད་པར་ཐལ་བ། ཕྱིར་ཤེས་པ་མི་འཐད་པར་ཐལ་བ་སོགས་བརྒྱད་ཡོད་པའི་དང་པོ་ནི།

གལ་སོགས་བཞི་ལ། རྣམ་པ་ཆོས་ཅན། གསལ་བར་ཚོར་ཞིང་མྱོང་བ་མི་འཐད་པར་ཐལ། དངོས་པོར་མེད་པའི་ཕྱིར། ཁྱབ་པར་ཐལ། རྣམ་པའི་དངོས་པོ་ལས་ཐ་དད་པས་ཏེ་རྣམ་པས་དབེན་པའི་ཤེས་པ་མ་དམིགས་པའི་ཕྱིར། གཉིས་པ་ནི། འདི་སོགས་བཞི་ལ། ཤེས་པ་ཆོས་ཅན། རྣམ་པ་ཤེས་པ་མི་འཐད་པར་ཐལ། ཁྱོད་ལ་རྣམ་པ་མེད་པའི་ཕྱིར། དཔེར་ན། སྡུག་བསྔལ་ལ་བདེ་བ་དང་། དཀར་པོ་ལ་སྔོན་པོ་མེད་པས་མི་ཤེས་པ་བཞིན་ནོ། དངོས་སུ་མྱོང་བ་མི་འཐད་པ་ནི། རྣམ་སོགས་བཞི་ལ། རྣམ་པ་ཆོས་ཅན། དངོས་སུ་མྱོང་བ་མི་འཐད་པར་ཐལ། ཤེས་པའི་རྫས་མིན་པའི་ཕྱིར། ནམ་མཁའི་མེ་ཏོག་བཞིན།

བརྟགས་མྱོང་མི་འཐད་པ་ནི། མེད་སོགས་བཞི་ལ། ཤེས་པ་ཆོས་ཅན། རྣམ་པ་བརྟགས་ནས་མྱོང་བ་མི་འཐད་པར་ཐལ། རྣམ་པ་ལ་ཁྱོད་རྣམ་ལྡན་དུ་བསྐྱེད་པའི་ནུས་པ་མེད་པའི་ཕྱིར། དཔེར་ན། རྟ་རྒྱུ་བཞིན། ཁྱབ་པར་ཐལ། དངོས་པོར་མེད་ན་རང་སྣང་མཁན་གྱི་ཤེས་པ་བསྐྱེད་པའི་ནུས་པ་མེད་དགོས་པའི་ཕྱིར། ཤར་རྟུལ་ཉེ་བར་སྣང་། ནུབ་རྟུལ་རིང་བར་གནས་པའི་ཤེས་པ་ཆོས་ཅན། ཤར་རྟུལ་ཉེ་བར་སྣང་བའི་ཆ་ [592]

དེ་ནུབ་རྟུལ་རིང་བར་སྣང་བའི་ཆ་ཡིན་པར་ཐལ། ཤར་རྟུལ་ཉེ་བར་སྣང་བ་གང་ཞིག ཁྱོད་ཆ་

མེད་ཡིན་པའི་ཕྱིར། འདོད་ན། ཤར་རྒྱལ་རིང་བར་སྣང་བར་ཐལ། དེའི་ཕྱིར། འདོད་ན། མངོན་སུམ་གྱིས་བསལ་ལོ། རྣམ་ཤེས་འབྲེལ་མེད་དུ་ཐལ་བ་ནི། གང་སོགས་བཞི་ལ། ཤེས་པ་སྐྱོང་བའི་ཚེ་རྣམ་པ་སྣ་ཚོགས་སྐྱོང་བར་མི་འཐད་པར་ཐལ། རྣམ་པ་དང་ཤེས་པ་འབྲེལ་བ་མེད་པའི་ཕྱིར། དེར་ཐལ། བདག་གཅིག་དེ་བྱུང་གི་འབྲེལ་པ་མེད་པའི་ཕྱིར།

རེས་འགའ་འབྱུང་བར་མི་འཐད་པར་ཐལ་བ་ནི། རྒྱུ་སོགས་བཞི་ལ། རྣམ་པ་རྣམས་ལ་རྒྱུ་ཡོད་དམ་མེད། མེད་ན། རྣམ་པ་ཆོས་ཅན། རེས་འགའ་འབྱུང་བ་མི་འཐད་པར་ཐལ། རྒྱུ་མེད་པའི་ཕྱིར། རྟགས་མ་གྲུབ་ན། གཞན་དབང་དུ་ཐལ། འཁྲུལ་པའི་རྒྱུ་ལས་སྐྱེས་པའི་ཕྱིར། འཛིན་རྣམ་འབའ་ཞིག་པར་ཐལ་བ་ནི། དེ་སོགས་བཞི་ལ། གཟུང་རྣམ་གྱིས་བདེན་པའོ་ཞེ་ན། ཤེས་པ་ཆོས་ཅན། གཟུང་རྣམ་མེད་པར་འཛིན་རྣམ་འབའ་ཞིག་པར་ཐལ། གཟུང་རྣམ་གྱིས་དབེན་པའི་ཤེས་པ་ཡིན་པའི་ཕྱིར། འདོད་ན། གཟུང་རྣམ་གྱིས་དབེན་པའི་ཤེལ་སྒོང་ལྟ་བུའི་འཛིན་རྣམ་མེད་པར་ཐལ། དམིགས་རུང་མ་དམིགས་པའི་ཕྱིར།

གཞན་དབང་དུ་ཐལ་བ་ནི་འདི་སོགས་བཞི་ལ། ཁོ་ན་རེ། དོན་ལ་མེད་ཀྱང་འཁྲུལ་པའི་དབང་གིས་རྣམ་པ་སྣང་བ་ཡིན་ཞེ་ན། རྣམ་པ་ཆོས་ཅན། གཞན་དབང་དུ་ཐལ། འཁྲུལ་པ་ལ་རག་ལས་པ་སྟེ་འཁྲུལ་པའི་མཐུ་ལས་བྱུང་བའི་ཕྱིར། བདེན་པའི་དུ་བྲལ་སྒྲུབ་པ་ནི།

དངོས་སོགས་བཞི་ལ། དངོས་པོ་ཆོས་ཅན། བདེན་པའི་ [593] དུ་མར་མ་གྲུབ་པར་ཐལ། བདེན་པའི་གཅིག་མེད་པའི་ཕྱིར། ཁྱབ་པ་སྒྲུབ་པ་ནི། གཅིག་སོགས་བཞི་ལ། བདེན་པའི་གཅིག་དང་དུ་མར་མ་གྲུབ་ན་བདེན་པར་མེད་དགོས་པར་ཐལ། གཅིག་དང་དུ་མ་ལས་མ་གཏོགས་པའི་དངོས་པོ་མེད་པའི་ཕྱིར། དེར་ཐལ།

གཅིག་དང་དུ་མ་གཉིས་ཕན་ཚུན་སྤངས་འགལ་ལ་བརྟེན་པའི་དངོས་འགལ་ཡིན་པའི་ཕྱིར། ཀུན་རྫོབ་ཏུ་དངོས་པོ་ཡོད་པར་བསྟན་པ་ལ། དངོས་པོ་དང་། ཀུན་རྫོབ་ཀྱི་ངོ་བོ་ངོས་བཟུང་།

འཁྲུལ་རྒྱུ་བདེན་པ་བཀག་པའོ། དང་པོ་ནི། དེ་སོགས་བཞི་ལ། དངོས་པོ་འདི་དག་ཆོས་ཅན། རྫུན་པར་ཐལ། གཞི་གྲུབ་བདེན་པར་གྲུབ་པ་བཀག་ཟིན་པ་དེའི་ཕྱིར། ཕྱི་མ་གཉིས་ལ། དེ་ཆོས་ཅན། བདེན་པར་གྲུབ་པ་བདག་གིས་དགག་མི་རིགས་པར་ཐལ། བདེན་པར་ཚད་མས་གྲུབ་པའི་ཕྱིར། ཡང་ན་ཚད་མས་དགག་མི་རིགས་པར་ཐལ།

འདོད་པ་ཙམ་གྱིས་བཞག་པ་མ་ཡིན་པར་བདག་རྒྱུ་སྔ་མ་ལས་འབྱུང་བའི་ཕྱིར། གཉིས་པ་ནི། མ་སོགས་བཞི་ལ། མཐར་ཐུག་དཔྱོད་པའི་རིགས་པས་དཔྱད་མི་བཟོད་པ་དང་། སྐྱེ་འཇིག་བྱེད་པ་དང་། དོན་བྱེད་ནུས་པ་གསུམ་ཆོས་ཅན། ཀུན་རྫོབ་བདེན་པ་ཡིན་ཏེ། ཐ་སྙད་པའི་ཚད་མས་རྙེད་དོན་ཡིན་པའི་ཕྱིར། གསུམ་པ་ནི། བརྟགས་སོགས་བརྒྱད་ལ།

བུམ་པ་སོགས་ལ་རྒྱུ་བདེན་པ་མེད་ན་མི་རུང་། ཞེས་པ་དེས་ལེགས་པ་བསླུས་པ་མིན་པར་ཐལ། རྒྱུ་བདེན་པ་མེད་ཀྱང་རིགས་འདྲ་སྔ་མ་ལས་འབྲས་བུ་ཕྱི་མ་འབྱུང་བའི་ཕྱིར། རྒྱུ་བདེན་པ་མི་སྲིད་པར་ཐལ་བ་དང་། བདེན་པ་བཀག་ཟིན་ [594] པའི་ཕྱིར། དེ་ལ་ཀླན་ཀ་སྤང་བ་ལ། མངོན་སུམ་དང་འགལ་བ་སྤང་བ་དང་། ལུང་འགལ་སྤང་བ། དོན་དམ་པའི་བདེན་པ་བསྟན། དེ་ལ་རྩོད་པ་སྤང་བ། ཀུན་རྫོབ་ཀྱི་ངོ་བོ་ངོས་བཟུང་བ། ཐེག་པ་ཆེན་པོའི་ངོ་བོ་དེ་དང་གཞན་ལས་ཁྱད་འཕགས་ཚུལ། ལུགས་འདི་རྟོགས་ན་སྙིང་རྗེ་དང་དད་པ་སྐྱེ་བའི་རྒྱུ་མཚན་ནོ། དང་པོ་ནི། དངོས་སོགས་བཞི་ལ། བདེན་པར་གྲུབ་པའི་དངོས་པོ་མེད་ན།

མངོན་སུམ་དང་འགལ་ལོ་ཞེ་ན། བདེན་པ་བཀག་པས་མངོན་སུམ་དང་འགལ་བའི་སྐྱོན་མེད་པར་ཐལ། མཐར་ཐུག་དཔྱོད་པའི་རིགས་པས་དཔྱད་བཟོད་ཀྱི་དངོས་པོ་བཀག་གི་ཐ་སྙད་པའི་ཚད་མས་རྙེད་དོན་མ་བཀག་པའི་ཕྱིར།

ཇི་སྐད་བཤད་པའི་མངོན་སུམ་དང་འགལ་བ་ལ་སོགས་པའི་སྐྱོན་མེད་པར་ཐལ། ཡོད་པ་དང་མེད་པ་གཉིས་ཀ་གཉིས་མིན་སོགས་མཐའ་བཞི་པོ་བདེན་པར་ཁས་མ་བླངས་པའི་ཕྱིར། གཉིས་

པ་ནི། དེ་ཕྱིར་སོགས་བཞི་ལ། ལུང་ལས་ཆོས་ཐམས་ཅད་མ་སྐྱེས་པ་མ་འགགས་པར་གསུངས་པ་ལ་རྒྱུ་མཚན་ཡོད་དེ། ཡང་དག་པར་གྲུབ་པའི་དངོས་པོ་མེད་པའི་ཕྱིར། གསུམ་པ་ནི། དམ་སོགས་བཅུ་གཉིས་ལ། སྨྱུ་གུ་བདེན་མེད་ཆོས་ཅན།

རྣམ་གྲངས་པའི་དོན་དམ་བདེན་པར་ཐལ། རིགས་ཤེས་རྗེས་དཔག་གིས་རྙེད་དོན་གང་ཞིག ཁྱོད་གོམས་པ་ལས་མཉམ་གཞག་མི་རྟོག་ཡེ་ཤེས་གསར་དུ་འབྱུང་བའི་ཕྱིར། དོན་དམ་པར་སྤྲོས་པ་ཀུན་ལས་གྲོལ་བར་ཐལ། དགག་བྱ་བདེན་སྐྱེ་མེད་པ་བཞིན་བདེན་པའི་སྐྱེ་མེད་ཀྱང་དོན་དམ་པར་མེད་པའི་ཕྱིར། རྟགས་མ་གྲུབ་ན། སྐྱེ་མེད་དོན་དམ་པར་མ་གྲུབ་པར་ཐལ། དགག་བྱ་ [595] བདེན་སྐྱེ་མེད་པའི་ཕྱིར། ཁྱབ་པར་ཐལ། བདེན་སྐྱེ་གཞི་མེད་ན་མཉམ་གཞག་གི་གཟིགས་ངོར་དེ་བཀག་པའི་ཚིག་གི་སྒྲ་མི་སྦྱོར་བའི་ཕྱིར། དེར་ཐལ་དགག་གཞི་མེད་པ་ལ་དགག་སྒྲ་སྦྱོར་བ་མེད་པའི་ཕྱིར། རྟོག་བཏགས་ལ་དགག་སྒྲ་སྦྱོར་ཞེ་ན། དེ་ཆོས་ཅན། ཀུན་རྫོབ་པར་འགྱུར་གྱི་བདེན་པར་མ་གྲུབ་པར་ཐལ། དགག་བྱ་རྟོག་བཏགས་བཀག་པའི་བཀག་པ་ཡིན་པའི་ཕྱིར། རྩོད་སྤང་ལ། བླུན་པོས་སྟོང་ཉིད་མངོན་སུམ་དུ་རྟོགས་པར་ཐལ་བ་སྟོང་ཉིད་རྟོགས་པའི་གང་ཟག་མེད་པར་ཐལ་བ། སྒྲུབ་ངག་མེད་པར་ཐལ་བ།

ལས་འབྲས་སོགས་མེད་པར་ཐལ་བའོ། དང་པོ་ལ་རྩོད་པ་དང་། ལན་ནོ། དང་པོ་ནི། འོན་སོགས་བཞི་ལ། མི་མཁས་པ་གནག་རྫི་སོགས་ཀྱིས་ཀྱང་སྟོང་ཉིད་མངོན་སུམ་དུ་རྟོགས་པར་ཐལ། དངོས་པོ་མངོན་སུམ་དུ་རྟོགས་པ་གང་ཞིག

དངོས་པོ་ཐམས་ཅད་བདེན་མེད་ཀྱི་ངོར་སྐྱེས་པའི་ཕྱིར་ཞེ་ན། གཉིས་པ་ནི། མ་ཡིན་སོགས་བཞི་ལ། དངོས་པོ་བདེན་མེད་ཡིན་ཀྱང་གནག་རྫི་ལ་སོགས་པས་སྟོང་ཉིད་མངོན་སུམ་དུ་མི་རྟོགས་པའི་རྒྱུ་མཚན་ཡོད་དེ།

ཐོག་མ་མེད་པ་ནས་དངོས་པོ་བདེན་པར་སྒྲོ་བཏགས་པའི་འཁྲུལ་པས་རྒྱུད་བསླད་པ་ཡིན་པའི་

ཕྱིར། གཉིས་པ་ནི། འོ་ན། སྟོང་ཉིད་རྟོགས་པའི་གང་ཟག་མེད་པར་འགྱུར་རོ་ཞེ་ན། དེ་སོགས་བཞི་ལ། ཉན་ཐོས་མི་རྟོགས་ཀྱང་སྟོང་ཉིད་རྟོགས་པའི་གང་ཟག་ཡོད་པར་ཐལ། ཚོགས་སྦྱོར་ལ་གནས་པའི་བྱང་ཆུབ་སེམས་དཔའ་རྣམས་ཀྱིས་གཏན་ཚིགས་ཡང་དག་ལ་བརྟེན་ནས་རྟོགས། ས་ལ་གནས་པའི་སེམས་དཔའ་རྣམས་ཀྱིས་རྣལ་ [596] འབྱོར་མངོན་སུམ་གྱིས་གཟིགས་པའི་ཕྱིར། གསུམ་པ་ནི། གཞུང་སོགས་བཞི་ལ།

དངོས་པོ་བདེན་པར་མེད་ཀྱང་རྟགས་སྦྱོར་སྒྲུབ་ངག་སོགས་མེད་པའི་སྐྱོན་མེད་པར་ཐལ། ཐུན་མོང་མ་ཡིན་པའི་གྲུབ་མཐའ་ལ་གྲགས་པའི་ཆོས་ཅན་སོགས་སྤངས་ནས་མཁས་པ་ནས་བྱིས་པའི་བར་ལ་གྲགས་པའི་དངོས་པོར་སྣང་ཙམ་འདི་ཆོས་ཅན་སོགས་སུ་འཛིན་པའི་ཕྱིར། དེ་མིན་ན་ཆོས་ཅན་གཞི་མ་གྲུབ་པས་ཕྱོགས་ཀྱི་སྐྱོན་དུ་འགྱུར་བ་སོགས་ལ་ལན་གདབ་མི་ནུས་པར་ཐལ། ཐུན་མོང་མིན་པའི་གྲུབ་མཐས་བརྟགས་པ་ཁོ་ན་ལ་བརྟགས་སྦྱོར་དོན་གསུམ་འཛིན་པའི་ཕྱིར། ཁོ་བོ་ལ་བསྒྲུབ་བྱ་སྒྲུབ་བྱེད་བཞག་ཏུ་མི་རུང་བའི་སྐྱོན་མེད་པར་ཐལ། མཁས་པ་ནས་བྱིས་པའི་བར་གྱི་རྟོག་མེད་ཤེས་པ་ལ་སྣང་བའི་དངོས་པོ་སྣང་ཙམ་འདི་མི་འགོག་པའི་ཕྱིར། ལས་འབྲས་མི་འཐད་པར་ཐལ་བ་ལ། སྐྱེ་བ་སྔ་ཕྱི་མི་འཐད་པར་ཐལ་བ། ཀུན་ཉོན་མི་འཐད་པར་ཐལ་བ། ཚོགས་རྫོགས་པ་མི་འཐད་པར་ཐལ་བའོ། དང་པོ་ལ། རྟགས་དགོད། དེ་སྒྲུབ་པ། རྟག་ཆད་ཀྱི་སྐྱོན་མེད་པ། སྲིད་པ་ལས་ཐར་པ་སྲིད་པར་བསྟན་པའོ། དང་པོ་ནི། དེ་སོགས་བཞི་ལ། སྐྱེས་མ་ཐག་གི་དངོས་པོ་མེད་པའི་རྟོག་པ་འདི་ཆོས་ཅན། རིགས་འདྲ་སྔ་མ་སྔོན་དུ་སོང་སྟེ། རིག་པ་ཡིན་པའི་ཕྱིར། འདོད་ཆགས་གོམས་པ་བཞིན། གཉིས་པ་ནི། འདི་སོགས་དགུ་ལ། དེ་ཆོས་ཅན་དོན་ཆ་མེད་ཀྱི་སྟོབས་ལས་མ་བྱུང་བར་ཐལ། དེ་མེད་པའི་ཕྱིར་དང་། དངོས་པོ་བདེན་པ་བཀག་པའི་ཕྱིར་དང་། རྒྱུ་མེད་མིན་པར་ཐལ། རིམ་གྱིས་འབྱུང་ [597] བའི་ཕྱིར། ངོ་བོ་རྟག་པ་མིན་པར་ཐལ། རྟག་ཏུ་འབྱུང་བ་མ་ཡིན་པའི་ཕྱིར། དེས་ན་

རིག་པ་སྔོན་དུ་སོང་སྟེ། རིག་པ་ཡིན་པའི་ཕྱིར། གསུམ་པ་ནི། དེ་སོགས་བཞི་ལ། དབུ་མའི་ལུགས་ལ་རྟག་ཆད་ཀྱི་སྐྱོན་མེད་པར་ཐལ། རྒྱུ་ལོག་རྗེས་སུ་འབྲས་བུ་ལྡོག་པས་རྟག་པ་དང་། རྒྱུ་ལས་འབྲས་བུ་མི་འབྱུང་པས་ཆད་པའི་སྐྱོན་མེད་པའི་ཕྱིར། ས་བོན་ལས་མྱུ་གུ་འབྱུང་བ་བཞིན། བཞི་པ་ནི། ཆོས་སོགས་བཞི་ལ། བྱང་སེམས་འཕགས་པ་ཆོས་ཅན། བདེན་འཛིན་གྱི་རྒྱུ་ལས་བྱུང་བའི་ཉོན་མོངས་སྒྲིམ་མི་དགོས་པར་སྤོང་བར་འགྱུར་ཏེ།

སྟོང་ཉིད་མཐོང་ཟིན་གོམས་པར་བྱེད་པའི་ཕྱིར། གཉིས་པ་ནི། རྒྱུ་སོགས་བཞི་ལ། ཀུན་ཉོན་བདེན་པ་བཀག་པས་འཁོར་འདས་ཀྱི་རྣམ་གཞག་འཁྲུགས་ཤིང་ཉམས་པའི་སྐྱོན་མེད་པར་ཐལ། རྒྱུ་འབྲས་ཀུན་རྫོབ་ཏུ་ཁས་བླངས་པའི་ཕྱིར། གསུམ་པ་ནི། འདི་སོགས་རྣམས་ལ། ཚོགས་དྲི་མེད་སོགས་པའང་ལུགས་འདི་ལ་མི་རུང་བར་ཐལ། རྒྱུ་འབྲས་བདེན་པ་བཀག་ནས་རྫུན་པ་འཇོག་པའི་ཕྱིར། སྟོང་ཉིད་ཀྱི་ལྟ་བས་ཀུན་ནས་བསླངས་པའི་བསོད་ནམས་ཆོས་ཅན། འབྲས་བུ་རྣམ་དག་ཏུ་འབྱུང་སྟེ། རྒྱུ་རྣམ་དག་ཡིན་པའི་ཕྱིར། འཇིག་རྟེན་པའི་ཡང་དག་པའི་ལྟ་བས་ཀུན་ནས་བསླངས་པའི་སྲོག་གཅོད་སྤོང་པའི་ཚུལ་ཁྲིམས་སོགས་བཞིན། བདེན་འཛིན་གྱི་ཀུན་ནས་བསླངས་པའི་བསོད་ནམས་ཆོས་ཅན། ཆོས་རྟགས་གོ་ལྡོག

ལོག་ལྟའི་སྟོབས་ལས་བྱུང་བའི་འདོད་ལོག་བཞིན། སྟོང་ཉིད་ཀྱི་ལྟ་བས་ཀུན་ནས་མ་བསླངས་པའི་སྦྱིན་པ་ཆོས་ཅན། ཁྱོད་ཀྱི་འབྲས་བུ་སྟོབས་ཆུང་སྟེ། ཁྱོད་རྒྱུ་ཕྱིན་ཅི་ལོག [598] ལས་བྱུང་བའི་ཕྱིར། བདག་དང་བདག་གིར་འཛིན་པ་ལས་འབྱུང་བའི་འབྲས་བུ་བཞིན། དེར་ཐལ། དངོས་པོར་བདེན་པར་གྲུབ་པ་ལ་ཚད་མས་གནོད་པའི་ཕྱིར། སྨིག་རྒྱུ་ལ་ཆུར་འཛིན་པ་བཞིན། སྟོང་ཉིད་ཀྱིས་ཀུན་ནས་བསངས་པའི་སྦྱིན་པ་ཆོས་ཅན། འབྲས་བུ་རྣམ་དག་འབྱུང་སྟེ། རྒྱུས་པའི་རྒྱུ་རྣམ་དག་ལས་འབྱུང་བའི་ཕྱིར། ས་བོན་གྲུང་པོའི་མྱུ་གུ་འབྱུང་བ་བཞིན། ཀུན་རྫོབ་པའི་ངོ་བོ་ངོས་བཟུང་བ་ནི། རྒྱུ་སོགས་བརྒྱད་ལ།

རྒྱུ་འབྲས་ཀྱིས་བསྡུས་པའི་ཆོས་འདི་རྣམས་ཆོས་ཅན། ཤེས་པའི་རྫས་ལས་གཞན་མིན་པར་ཐལ། མངོན་སུམ་ཚད་མས་ཉམས་སུ་མྱོང་བའི་ཚུལ་གྱིས་གྲུབ་པའི་ཕྱིར། ཁྱབ་པར་ཐལ། རྟགས་དེ་ཡིན་ན་ཤེས་པའི་རྫས་སུ་གནས་དགོས་པའི་ཕྱིར། དེ་ཆོས་ཅན། ཐ་སྙད་དུ་སེམས་ཙམ་གྱིས་བདག་ཉིད་དུ་ཤེས་པར་བྱ་སྟེ། ཕྱི་དོན་གྱིས་དབེན་པའི་ཕྱིར། དོན་དམ་པར་སེམས་ཙམ་དུ་མ་གྲུབ་སྟེ། དོན་དམ་པར་གཅིག་དང་དུ་མ་དང་བྲལ་བའི་ཕྱིར།

ཐེག་ཆེན་གྱི་སའི་ངོ་བོ་དང་གཞན་ལས་འཕགས་ཚུལ་ནི། ཚུལ་སོགས་བཅུ་གཉིས་ལས།

ཚོགས་སྦྱོར་བའི་སེམས་དཔའ་ཆོས་ཅན། དེ་ཁོ་ན་ཉིད་ཀྱི་དོན་ཅན་གྱི་ཐེག་པ་ཆེན་པོ་པ་ཐོབ་པར་འགྱུར་ཏེ། ཐ་སྙད་ཙམ་དུ་སེམས་ཙམ་གྱི་ཚུལ་དང་། དོན་དམ་པར་རང་བཞིན་མེད་པའི་ཚུལ་གཉིས་ཀྱི་ཤིང་རྟ་ལ་ཞོན།

སྔར་བཤད་པའི་རིགས་པའི་སྒྲུབ་བསྐྱོགས་འཇུག་པར་བྱེད་པ་ཡིན་པའི་ཕྱིར། དུས་དཔག་མེད་འཁོར་བ་ཇི་སྲིད་དུ་འཆི་བ་མེད་པའི་གོ་འཕང་ལ་གནས་པའི་རྒྱུ་ཡང་དག་པའི་བདུད་རྩི་རང་བཞིན་མེད་རྟོགས་ཀྱི་ཤེས་རབ་ཆོས་ཅན། [599]

ཁྱབ་འཇུག་དང་དབང་ཕྱུག་སོགས་ཀྱི་ཕྱི་རོལ་པ་ཐམས་ཅད་དང་། འཇིག་རྟེན་གྱི་སྐྱེ་བོ་ཉན་རང་དགྲ་བཅོམ་པ་རྣམས་ཀྱིས་ཀྱང་ཉམས་སུ་མི་མྱོང་བར་ཐལ། ཐུགས་རྗེ་དག་པའི་རྒྱུ་ཅན་གྱི་དེ་བཞིན་གཤེགས་པ་ཉག་གཅིག་གིས་རང་དབང་དུ་མངོན་སུམ་དུ་མྱོང་བའི་ཕྱིར།

ལུགས་འདི་རྟོགས་ན་སྙིང་རྗེ་དང་དད་པ་སྐྱེ་བའི་རྒྱུ་མཚན་ནི། དེ་སོགས་བརྒྱད་ལ། ཚོགས་སྦྱོར་བའི་སེམས་དཔའ་དག་ཆོས་ཅན། ཕྱི་རོལ་པ་རྣམས་ལ་སྙིང་རྗེ་སྐྱེ་བའི་རྒྱུ་མཚན་ཡོད་དེ། དེ་དག་ཐར་ལམ་ཕྱིན་ཅི་ལོག་ཏུ་སྟོན་པའི་གྲུབ་མཐའ་ལ་འཆེལ་ཞིང་གཞོལ་བར་མཐོང་བའི་ཕྱིར། བློ་གྲོས་ཀྱི་ནོར་དང་ལྡན་པའི་ཚོགས་སྦྱོར་ལ་གནས་པའི་བྱང་སེམས་ཆོས་ཅན། ཐུབ་པ་ལ་གུས་པ་ཆེན་པོ་སྐྱེ་བར་འགྱུར་ཏེ། ཐུབ་པའི་ལུགས་ལས་ལུགས་གཞན་ཐམས་ཅད་ཐར་ལམ་ལས་

ཕྱིན་ཅི་ལོག་ཏུ་གྱུར་པས་སྙིང་པོ་མེད་པར་གཟིགས་པའི་ཕྱིར། བཤད་པ་ཡོངས་སུ་རྫོགས་པའི་བྱ་བ་ནི། བསྟན་བཅོས་འདི་སློབ་དཔོན་ཞི་བ་འཚོས་མཛད་ལ། དེའི་ཡོན་ཏན་ནི་བདག་དང་སོགས་སོ། ངག་གི་དབང་ཕྱུག་ནི་རྗེས་བཙུན་འཇམ་པའི་དབྱངས་སོ།

ཟེ་འབྲུ་སྐྱི་བོས་ལེན་པ་ནི་དེ་ལ་དངོས་སུ་ཆོས་ཉན་པའོ། མཁས་པའི་དབང་པོ་དཔལ་ལྡན་ཞི་བ་འཚོས། ལེགས་པར་བཤད་པའི་དབུ་མ་རྒྱན་འདི་ལ། བླ་མའི་གསུང་བཞིན་བརྗེད་བྱང་འདི་བྱས་པས། འགྲོ་ཀུན་ཐེག་མཆོག་ལུགས་ལ་མཁས་པར་ཤོག

བདག་ཀྱང་དལ་བའི་རྟེན་བཟང་ཐོབ་གྱུར་ནས། བཤེས་གཉེན་མཆོག་རྣམས་གུས་པས་བསྟེན་བྱེད་ཅིང་། ལྟ་ངན་ལོག་པའི་གཡང་ས་རབ་སྤངས་ནས། མཁས་པའི་ [600] དབང་པོ་ཞི་འཚོ་འདྲ་བར་ཤོག

ཁམས་གསུམ་གྱི་བླ་མ་ཐམས་ཅད་མཁྱེན་པ་བློ་བཟང་གྲགས་པའི་གསུང་རྒྱལ་ཚབ་ཆོས་རྗེས་བརྗེད་བྱང་དུ་བྱས་པ་དགེ་བར་གྱུར་ཅིག

༄ རྣམ་གྲོལ་ཞི་བའི་རྒྱ་མཚོར་རོ་གཅིག་ཏུ། གཞོལ་བའི་མཐའ་ཡས་ཆོས་ཚུལ་དལ་འབབ་ཀླུང་། ཚིག་གི་གཟེགས་མ་རེས་ཀྱང་དུག་གསུམ་གྱི། དྲི་མ་ཡོངས་འཁྲུད་ལེགས་བཤད་བདུད་རྩི་འདི། དཔར་དུ་བསྒྲུབ་པའི་རྣམ་དཀར་ཕུང་པོའི་མཐུས།

ཡང་དག་ཆོས་ཀྱི་སྒོ་མོ་སྟོང་ཕྲག་བརྒྱ། གདངས་ཏེ་རྒྱུད་ལྡན་འགྲོ་བ་མ་ལུས་པ། ངེས་ལེགས་ནོར་བུའི་མཛོད་ལ་དབང་འབྱོར་ཤོག ཅེས་པ་འདི་ཉིད་ནང་བསྟན་གྲུབ་མཐའ་རིས་མེད་ཀྱི་གསུང་རབ་དག་དཔར་དུ་བསྒྲུབ་དང་བསྒྲུབ་འགྱུར་གང་ལའང་སྦྱར་ཚོག་པའི་དགེ་བསྔོའི་སྨོན་ཚིག་ཏུ། ཤཱཀྱའི་དགེ་སློང་ཆོས་སྨྲ་བ་ངག་དབང་བློ་བཟང་བསྟན་འཛིན་རྒྱ་མཚོས་སྦྱར་བའོ།།

Notes

Notes to the Introduction

1 This follows dating by the Theravāda tradition.

2 There has been some degree of variance among Tibetan schools regarding the breadth and depth of use of Indian commentaries. In his comparison of the monastic education systems of the Geluk monastic colleges at Sera and the Nyingma (rNying-ma) monastic college at Namdroling, Georges Dreyfus (1997b) notes that Namdroling traditionally counts thirteen major Indian treatises in its primary curriculum as opposed to only five in the Geluk tradition. Yet twice the amount of time is spent on the five in the Geluk tradition when compared with the amount of time spent on the thirteen in the Nyingma tradition. When examined closely, the two traditions study the same fundamental subjects but the approach is different. Gelukpas spend more time in debate as a pedagogical tool whereas Nyingmapas place more focus on the Indian treatises themselves. Dreyfus writes, "The Geluk tradition is often praised by outsiders for its dialectical depth but criticized for its limitations in knowing the fundamental Indian treatises. Thus Geluk scholars are sometimes characterized as having a 'limited [textual] vision' (*mthong bya chung ba*)." Dreyfus 1997b, 46. See also Dreyfus 2003 for an extensive study of the Tibetan monastic educational systems.

3 Frauwallner 1961, 141-143. For additional discussion of issues concerning the dating of Śāntarakṣita, see Ruegg 1982, 514-515.

4 There has been some debate in recent years over the name of the school of Tibetan Buddhism which is commonly known today both within the school and to the wider community as *Geluk*. Some have argued that it should be referred to as the Gandenpa (*dGa'-ldan-pa*), as the first followers of Tsong Khapa were called after the founding of his first monastery at *dGa'-ldan* in 1409. This argument is strengthened by the fact that the first appearance of the name *Geluk* did not occur until the late sixteenth century. See van der Kuijp 1985. Others have argued that as a reopening of Atīśa's lineage it should be called the New Kadampa (*bKa'-gdams gSar-ma*) as it was once and sometimes is still referred to today. Gelukpas often refer to themselves as the New Kadam Tradition, tracing their lineage back to Atīśa, Dromtonpa (*'Brom-ston-pa*), and the Kadam

School of the tenth and eleventh centuries. Tsong Khapa is said to have retrieved and reunified the three primary Kadam lineages which had previously been dispersed through three distinct lines traced back to Dromtonpa, Atīśa's disciple and founder of the school. This is made more controversial today due to the use of this name by a splinter faction which has broken off from the mainline Geluk tradition. While historical knowledge of the evolution of the name of the school is important, I will refer to the school in this study as Geluk given that this is the way the school which traces its lineage primarily back to Tsong Khapa most commonly refers to itself today.

5 By use of the broad appellation "Geluk School" or "Geluk scholars," I do not intend to give the impression that scholars from the tradition following primarily from the writings and teachings of Tsong Khapa are by any means univocal. There are numerous issues in the philosophical literature in which prominent scholars from the tradition disagree on important points. The various monastic textbooks from the colleges at monastic centers such as Sera, Drepung, and Ganden, for example, have important points of divergence and these discrepancies will be highlighted at appropriate points in this study. This said however, there is much more in common among Geluk scholars than there are differences and there is much that can be accurately described as pan-Geluk. For instances in which there is no disagreement among Geluk scholars, I will use the term "Geluk" to refer to what can be considered to be a pan-Geluk stance.

6 *Pramāṇavāda* is a Sanskrit neologism commonly used by modern scholars to refer to those indigenous philosophers writing about the logico-epistemological traditions of India and about *pramāṇas.*

7 I am currently working on complete translations of *Madhyamakālaṃkāravṛtti* and *Madhyamakālaṃkāravpañjikā* for future publication in a second volume.

8 While one cannot blindly presume that Kamalaśīla in *MAP* merely mirrors the thought of Śāntarakṣita, a close examination reveals that he does seem to remain very close. There are not glaring instances where he seems to have gone astray. Given that Kamalaśīla was Śāntarakṣita's direct disciple and that his commentary was likely composed within close proximity to Śāntarakṣita himself, I feel that it can largely be relied upon as further illumination of Śāntarakṣita's thought, as long as it is used with a critical eye which acknowledges what appear to be liberal divergences or additions for what they are or may be.

9 Eckel (2003) takes a similar approach in analyzing Tsong Khapa's presentation of Bhāvaviveka's views on conventional truths.

10 Although Gelukpas generally consider Śāntarakṣita to be the quintessential source for the Yogācāra-Svātantrika-Madhymaka School, he does not appear to be the first Indian Mādhyamika to put forth a Yogācāra-Madhyamaka synthesis. Ārya Vimuktisena (ca. late fifth - early sixth C.E..) [Ruegg 1982, 514; Makransky 1997, 4] is acknowledged by Thubkan (*Thu'u-bkwan-blo-bzang-chos-kyi-nyi-ma*) in his *Grub mtha' thams cad kyi khungs dang 'dod tshul ston pa legs bshad shel gyi me long* (25-26) to be an adherent to the same Yogācāra-Svātantrika-Madhyamaka system. Thubkan also considers Śrigupta, the teacher of

Śāntarakṣita's teacher (Jñānagarbha), to be a proponent of the same system. Bhāvaviveka (500-570 C.E.) criticized Mādhyamikas who accepted Mind Only as a provisional step towards an ultimate Madhyamaka view by accepting that objects are not external to the mind and then arguing that the mind also does not exist ultimately. Bhāvaviveka likened this to first dirtying oneself with mud before cleaning off. Regardless of what he thought of such a view, Bhāvaviveka's criticism does indicate that such a position was current in his time and thus well before Śāntarakṣita. See also Ruegg 1981, 87-99 for a history of the Yogācāra-Mahyamaka synthesis.

11 Although the term Yogācāra-Svātantrika-Madhyamaka (*rnal 'byor spyod pa'i dbu ma rang rgyud pa*) is not found as the name of a sub-school of Madhyamaka thought in Sanskrit literature and is not used by any of the Indian authors considered by Tibetans to be exponents of its doctrine, it has become common parlance among Tibetan doxographers in general and specifically among those from the Geluk tradition. For further discussion of this issue, see Ruegg 2000, 3-4. While its historical utility in the Indian context is questionable at best, I will use the term in this study with the above words of caution since this book aims in part to get at the Geluk context of understanding Śāntarakṣita's Madhyamaka ideas and this term is the key taxonomic device utilized by Gelukpas in designating the school of which Śāntarakṣita is said to be the primary representative.

12 The verses of Śāntarakṣita's root text, *MA*, are additionally embedded in the prose of his autocommentary, *MAV*. There has been some debate as to whether or not they should simply be considered to be one text. In this study I will consider the verses to be *MA*, since they exist on their own in the text *MA*, and the prose commentary on those verses to be *MAV*.

13 As mentioned in n. 10 above, although Śāntarakṣita had predecessors in fusing Yogācāra and Madhyamaka thought, he was the first to fuse those two with the *pramāṇavāda* tradition of Dignāga and Dharmakīrti and their followers. As such, he was also influential upon Tibetan Mādhyamikas who likewise wedded the Madhyamaka tradition with the *pramāṇavāda* tradition, although often in different ways than Śāntarakṣita.

14 Śāntarakṣita, *MA*. All instances of cited translations where the stanza number is indicated in parentheses at the beginning refer to Śāntarakṣita's *MA*. The numbered Tibetan stanzas can be found in Appendix 2. All translations in this study from Indian and Tibetan primary sources are my own unless otherwise noted. Complete Tibetan texts of *MA* and *JBy* are provided in the Appendices; therefore, the Tibetan for these passages is not provided in the notes in the body of this study.

15 According to Gelukpas, there are five great logical reasonings utilized by all four major Buddhist philosophical schools, albeit in different ways. For example, they would claim that Sautrāntikas will utilize the neither-one-nor-many argument, but only for refuting a self of persons. They would not use it to refute inherent existence in phenomena as Mādhyamikas such as Śāntarakṣita do. Gelukpas claim that while the diamond sliver argument is favored by Prāsaṅgika-

Mādhyamikas, the neither-one-nor-many argument tends to be favored by Svātanrika-Mādhyamikas, citing its quintessential expression in Śāntarakṣita's *MA* and also various renditions of the argument (discussed in Part I of this study) in the works of other Svātantrika-Mādhyamikas such as Jñānagarbha, Ārya Vimuktisena, and Haribhadra.

16 This was a commonly held tenet among Yogācāras, Sautrāntikas, and Pramāṇavādas.

17 Paul Williams 1998 treats Śāntarakṣita's views on self-cognizing cognition rather extensively.

18 Ruegg 1981, 88.

19 We know for example that Jains took his criticisms of their views as found in his other major philosophical treatise, the encyclopedic *Tattvasaṃgraha*, seriously enough to compose rebuttals to his arguments. Interestingly, the only two extant Sanskrit manuscripts of *Tattvasaṃgraha* were found in Jain temples in Jaiselmer and Patna.

20 Authorship of *The Testament of Ba* (*sBa bzhed*), one of the earliest Tibetan histories of the establishment of Buddhism in Tibet is commonly attributed to Ba Salnang. It largely chronicles the reign of Trisong Detsen. See Kapstein 2000a, 23-35.

21 Roerich 1949, 38-43.

22 Frauwallner 1961 141-143; Ruegg 1981, 89; and *Deb ther sngon po,* vol. Ka, fol. 21b.

23 Roerich, trans. 1949, 43.

24 Ibid.

25 Lang 1990, 128.

26 Certainly there were Chinese figures promoting a gradual approach in China as witnessed in the divide between Northern and Southern Ch'an traditions, but it appears from Tibetan records that only proponents of a "Sudden" tradition were teaching in Tibet at this time.

27 It is also referred to as the Council of Lhasa. See Demiéville 1952.

28 For example, see Ye-shes-sDe, *lTa ba khyad par*.

29 Lang 1990, 130.

30 Ibid., 127. See this article for an extensive discussion of the introduction of Prāsaṅgika-Madhyamaka into Tibet.

31 David S. Ruegg (1981, 89) comments on the importance of Śāntarakṣita to Tibetan Buddhism when he writes, "It was due to him and his illustrious disciple Kamalaśīla that the Yogācāra-Madhyamaka became the leading school of the Madhyamaka at that time [in Tibet], and so influenced very deeply much Buddhist thought in Tibet not only during his lifetime, but for centuries afterwards."

32 Bu-ston 1966, 908. Cited and translated in Lang 1990, 133. "Pa-tshab Nyi-ma-grags studied in Kashmir for twenty-three years, invited the scholar Kanakavarman [to Tibet], and translated and explained Madhyamaka texts."

33 Lang 1990, 137.

34 This treatise is also mentioned by Śāntarakṣita in *TS,* 2083. See Ichigō 1985, 330.

35 See McClintock 2002 for a discussion of omniscience and reasoning in *TS* and Kamalaśīla's *TSP*.

36 Ruegg 1981, 93.

37 Tsong Khapa *LSN*, 141-142.

38 Eckel (1987, 27-31) is not convinced by either of Tsong Khapa's arguments.

39 Of course, if we could verify Śāntarakṣita's authorship, it would be informative in terms of what it would tell us about the way he understood the views of his own teacher, Jñānagarbha.

40 See for example Ruegg 1967, 15; Conze 1973, 238-239; and Lopez 1987, 20-21.

41 See Lopez 1995.

42 For a more extensive examination of Śāntarakṣita's *pramāṇavāda* thought, see McClintock 2002 and 2003, and Dreyfus 1997a.

43 See Doctor 2004a for a translation of Mipham's commentary on *MA*.

44 See Part II of this study, and particularly the conclusion of Part II, for a discussion of various ways to read and utilize Geluk commentaries on Śāntarakṣita.

45 Although "Geluk" was not the name of the tradition following Tsong Khapa during Gyel-tsab's time, he is considered by virtually all Gelukpas today to be a key figure in the tradition's early history. I doubt that anybody in the Geluk School today would not consider Gyel-tsab to have been a key figure in early Geluk history.

46 *JBy* is found both in the *Collected Works* of Tsong Khapa and in the *Collected Works* of Gyel-tsab. It is considered to be a transcription of Gyel-tsab's lecture notes written down as he listened to Tsong Khapa give commentary on *MA*.

47 See n. 8 for discussion on the use of Kamalaśīla's commentaries.

48 See the colophon to *JBy*.

49 Other primary texts considered to be key source material for this view include the treatises of his two disciples, including most prominently Kamalaśīla's *Madhyamakāloka* and Haribhadra's two commentaries on the *Abhisamayālaṃkāra: Abhisamayālaṃkārālokā* and *Sphuṭārthā*.

50 This is not to suggest that the various colleges don't have their preferences.

51 For discussions on the use of oral commentary in Tibetan traditions, see Klein

1994 and Dreyfus 2003.

52 The great Nyingma scholar/adept Mipham (*Mi-pham-'jam dbyangs rnam rgyal rgya mtsho*) (1846-1912), who authored the most extensive Tibetan commentary on *MA,* considered the integration of the two Mahāyāna philosophical systems into one in a single treatise to be a mark of that work's superiority. See Mipham's *dbU ma rgyan gyi rnam bshad 'jam dbyangs bla ma dgyes pa'i zhal lung*, translated in Doctor 2004a.

53 For example see Hopkins 1983, 362, where he writes, "Shāntarakṣhita founded the Yogāchāra-Svātantrika-Mādhyamika system. He is similar to a Yogāchārin, or Cittamāttrin, in that he shows that external objects do not exist either conventionally or ultimately and that objects conventionally are the same entity as the perceiving consciousness. He is a Svātantrika because he holds that phenomena only conventionally exist inherently and a Mādhyamika because he accepts that all phenomena do not exist ultimately." He follows an ahistorical Geluk reading without mentioning that even the label "Yogācāra-Svātantrika-Madhyamaka" was probably unknown in India in general or to Śāntarakṣita and was probably not coined until centuries after his death in Tibet.

54 The notion of self-cognizing cognition is also a commonly accepted tenet in the Buddhist epistemological (*pramāṇavāda*) tradition, many of whose most well known proponents are also considered to be Yogācāras.

55 This has also been the mainline view of Śāntarakṣita among many Tibetan scholars, particularly from the Geluk school. Mipham's commentary is an exception to this. See Doctor 2002. Kajiyama 1978 and McClintock 2002 are also exceptions to this overly simplified understanding of Śāntarakṣita's thought in modern scholarship.

56 Regarding issues concerning his integration of Madhyamaka and the logic traditions prevalent in Indian Buddhism at the time, see McClintock 2003.

57 Śāntarakṣita *MA* 91.

58 Kajiyama (1978, 140) poignantly demonstrates that a similar process is taking place in Kamalaśīla's *Bhāvanākramas*. In describing Kamalaśīla's *Bhāvanākramas,* Kajiyama argues that, "[There are] four stages [which] are plainly distinguishable: (1) the preliminary stage in which external realities admitted in the systems of the Sarvāstivāda and Sautrāntika are presented as the object of criticism; (2) the stage in which only the mind with manifested images is admitted — the system of the Satyākāravāda-yogācāra school forms the object of meditation; (3) the meditation stage in which the images of cognition as well as the duality of subject and object are condemned to be unreal and in which the knowledge without duality is proclaimed to be real - this being the standpoint of the Alīkākāravāda-yogācārin; (4) the stage in which even the non-dual knowledge (*advayajñāna*) or the pure illumination of cognition (*prakāśamātra*) is declared to be empty of an intrinsic nature. This latter stage is the highest one proclaimed by the Mādhyamika. Kamalaśīla's description of the method of gradual transcendence of the Buddhist philosophies for the attainment of the final

truth of emptiness perfectly corresponds to that of his master, Śāntarakṣita."

59 The inferential presentation of the argument appears in the first stanza of *MA* as follows: "Those entities, as asserted by our own [Buddhist schools] and other [non-Buddhist schools] have no inherent nature at all because in reality they have neither singular nor manifold nature – like a reflected image."

60 Many of the ideas discussed here were first conceived after reading, in the summer of 2000, a draft copy of Sara McClintock's article "The Role of the 'Given' in the Classification of Śāntarakṣita and Kamalaśīla as Yogācāra-Svātantrika-Mādhyamikas" (since published as McClintock 2003) which inspired me to reflect further on my previous reading of Śāntarakṣita's works. Therein she describes what she calls the "sliding scales of analysis" at work in the philosophical writings of Śāntarakṣita and Kamalaśīla, where the two frameworks of analysis and perspective shift depending on the ideas of their philosophical opponent, ostensibly as an act of skillful means. Her article is primarily concerned with the form of inferential reasoning the two are utilizing and the ontological implications of such vis-à-vis the Geluk critique of the use of autonomous inferences (*svatantrānumāna, rang rgyud kyi rjes dpag*) by proponents of Madhyamaka tenets. My argument draws from these insights and applies them to other dimensions of Śāntarakṣita's thought, specifically his philosophical syncretism. See also Kajiyama 1978 and Dreyfus 1997a.

61 Although Śāntarakṣita's approach is not perfectly mirrored in the various doxographical projects of the four schools of Tibetan Buddhism, I think that the general Tibetan approach to the study of Indian philosophy takes its cue from Śāntarakṣita's approach. Like Śāntarakaṣita, Tibetans study tenet systems in a graded hierarchy where each progressive school is illuminated in part by contrasting it with the one just below it. The broader picture of the system is geared towards leading the student/reader to the highest and ultimate view. Śāntarakṣita was the first major figure teaching Buddhist philosophy in Tibet and he set the tone for how philosophical analysis ought to be approached. Thus, I would argue that the fact that the Tibetan style so closely resembles Śāntarakṣita's own is no accident. He himself wrote a massive doxographical-style text in *TS* and inspired some of the first indigenous Tibetan tenet system texts. such as Yeshe De's *lTa ba khyad par*. For more on *lTa ba khyad par*, see Ruegg 1981b.

62 He actually critiques several types of Sautrāntika positions, with each considered to be progressively more subtle than the previous position. He then does the same with several types of Yogācāra positions. For the sake of simplicity in conveying the main point here, I have confined myself to discussing the major shifts from Sautrāntika to Yogācāra and from Yogācāra to Madhyamaka.

63 Śāntarakṣita, *MAV*, 60-61 (This and all subsequent page number citations to *MAV* refer to the 1986 Sarnath edition. See Bibliography for details.): *de dge 'on kyang de dag ge dngos de yang dag nyid dam ci// 'on te ma brtags gcig pu na// dga' bar khas len 'di bsam mo// lugs 'di ni tshad ma dang lung shin tu gsal bas shes par bya ba dang//dmigs pa can mtha' yas pa dag gi mngon par zhen pa ngan pa'i gnyen po yang yin pas shin tu dkar ba ste 'di ltar rdul phra ram la sogs*

pa yod pa dag dgag par byed pa dang tshor bar bya ba dang tshor ba po'i mthsan nyid dang 'gal ba yang ston pa sngar bshad pa'i tshad ma ni tshul 'di rab tu gsal bar byed pa'o// tshul 'di ni lung dang ldan pa yang yin te/

64 Ibid., 61-62: *mkhas pa dag tshul 'di la brten nas bdag dang bdag gi dang gzung ba dang 'dzin pa rab tu dbye ba dang bcas pa rnams la phyin ci logs tu gyur pa rnams sel to// 'on kyang 'di la dpyad par bya ba cung zad tsam 'di yod de/ci rnam de dag de kho na nyid yin nam 'on te ci gzugs brnyan la sogs pa ltar ma brgags pa gcig pu na dga' ba zhig yin/ 'dis cir 'gyur//*

65 Kajiyama (1978, 141) remarked in a similar vein on *MA* that, "lower doctrines were not simply rejected, but admitted as steps leading to understanding of the highest one."

Notes to Part I

1 See n. 8 in the Introduction for a discussion of the use of Kamalaśīla's commentary.

2 For a discussion of the issue of *āśrayāsiddha* in *ZBr*, see Tillemans and Lopez 1998.

3 It is interesting to note for example that when Tsong Khapa discusses the issue of the viability of autonomous inferences in investigating unestablished subjects according to the system of Śāntarakṣita, he does so in reliance on the assertions of Kamalaśīla. Tsong Khapa is quick to turn to the *Madhyamakāloka* over the *MAV* or even *MAP,* which, one might assume would be closer to Śāntarakṣita's position. Tsong Khapa correctly points out that Kamalaśīla offers conflicting opinions on the issue in his two texts, *MAP* and *Madhyamakāloka,* and remarks that the thought of Kamalaśīla must have been immature at the time of composing the *MAP* and that Kamalaśīla's mature position is found in the *Madhyamakāloka*. Tsong Khapa writes in *ZBr*:

> This commentary (*Madhyamakālaṃkārapañjikā*) says that in the case of entities which are not well known and are imputed by non-Buddhists, only *prasaṅgas* are established, but for renowned entities which have their own nature, both [*prasaṅgas* and *svatantrahetus*] are appropriate. In addition, Tibetan scholars such as Chaba [Chökyi Sengay] and the like said that [unrenowned] subjects [such as those] imputed by non-Buddhists are inappropriate for autonomous inferences. The *Madhyamakāloka* [on the other hand] says that if one holds as the subject [an unacknowledged entity] such as previously described, as long as the subject and the reason are mere negations, an autonomous inference is quite appropriate. This is said many times…
>
> *'di dka' 'grel las gzhan sdes btags pa'i ma grags pa la ni/ thal bar sgrub pa kho na yin la grags pa'i rang gi ngo bo rnams la ni/ gnyis ka ltar na yang nyes pa med ces 'chad cing/ cha pa la sogs pa bod kyi mkhas pa*

rnams kyis kyang/ gzhan gyis btags pa'i chos can la rang rgyud mi rung bar 'chad do// dbu a snang ba las ni sngar bshad ba lta bu'i chos can du bzung ba la yang/ rtags chos rnam bcad tsam yin na rang rgyud shin tu yang rung bar lan mang du bshad de// ZBr, 41. This and all further citations from *ZBr* refer to pages in the 1976 Sarnath edition. See Bibliography for details.

Tsong Khapa continues a few lines down.

Regarding [the fact that] that which was just explained from the *Madhyamakālaṃkārapañjikā* differs from this explanation in the *Madhyamakāloka*, since Dharmamitra said that the *Madhyamakālaṃkārapañjikā* is Kamalaśīla's, it ought to be investigated as to whether it was composed at a time when this Master's thought was not fully developed.

des na dka' 'grel las sngar ltar bshad pa 'di dbu ma snang ba dand mi mthun no// dka' 'grel 'di kam la shi' la'i yin par chos kyi bshes gnyen yang bzhed pas/ 'di ni slob dpon thugs mrdzogs pa'i skabs su gcig tu mdzad dam brtag go// ZBr, 42.

4 I am referring again to *grub mtha'* texts by scholars such as Jamyang Shayba, Jang-gya, Thubkan Lobsang Chökyi Nyima, Könchog Jigme Wangpo, Jetsun Chökyi Gyelten, etc. See Bibliography for details.

5 To my knowledge there are no major Geluk commentaries on Kamalaśīla's *Madhyamakāloka* or on the other major treatises of Indian representatives of what Gelukpas refer to as Yogācāra-Svātantrika-Madhyamaka. This is not to say that major treatises such as *Madhyamakāloka* and the three-part *Bhāvanākrama,* as well as Haribhadra's commentaries on the *Abhisamayālaṃkāra,* are ignored. They are widely cited in Geluk treatises. They are simply not themselves the subject of individual Geluk commentaries. The exception to this would be the recent publication of His Holiness Tenzin Gyatso, Dalai Lama XIV's *The Stages of Meditation,* which is a transcribed oral commentary on Kamalaśīla's *Bhāvanākrama* based on public teachings His Holiness gave in 1997 and 1998.

6 Śāntarakṣita, *MAV*, 19: *gang dag su rnams dag brten blo mang' sa la bzhuds// chos tshul zab mo rgya mtsho lta bu'i pha rol gzigs// lhag par mos pa yongs bsgoms thugs [la] mnga' che rnams kyi// bla bzhugs de dag rnams la rtag tu phyag 'tshal lo//* All page numbers in citations to *MAV* refer to the 1986 Sarnath edition. See the Bibliography for details. In all future references, it will simply be referred to as *MAV*.

7 *MAV*, 19: *yang dag par na rang bzhin med par rtogs na nyon mongs pa dang// shes bya'i sgrib pa mtha' dag spong bar 'gyur te/*

8 Śāntarakṣita's primary canonical source for issues concerning the Mahāyāna path system is *The Ornament of Clear Realization* (*Abhisamayālaṃkāra*), which is cited 87 times in *MAV* and *MAP*. Kamalaśīla's *Stages of Meditation* (*Bhāvanākrama*) also elaborates on this point and these issues extensively.

9 *MAV*, 19-20*: de bas na rigs pa cang lung gi[s]/ chos thams cad rang bzhin med*

par khong du chud par bya ba'i phyir rab tu 'bad do//

10 Ibid., 20: *de la lung dngos po'i stobs kyis zhugs pa'i rjes su dpag pa dang bral ba ni dad pas yongs su 'brang ba rnams kyang shin tu yongs su tshim par mi 'gyur bas rigs pa je brjod par bya'o//* Tsong Khapa elaborates on this point rather extensively in *ZBr*, stressing the fact that faith alone or faith with scriptures is not enough, but rather that sound inference is a necessity in establishing the correct understanding of emptiness. See *ZBr*, 27-33.

11 Śāntarakṣita was profoundly influenced by the thought of Dignāga and particularly Dharmakīrti, who established the logico-epistemological tradition in earnest among Buddhists in India during the second half of the first millennium.

12 While the most famous and comprehensive application of this argument is presented by Śāntarakṣita in the *MA*, he applies the neither-one-nor-many reasoning at various points in other works, such as *TS*.

13 *Ngos po* is a complex term with different nuanced meanings in different contexts. For instance, it often refers specifically to functional things which produce effects. I will use the terms "phenomena" and "entities" interchangeably for the Tibetan term *dngos po* in the context of its application in this argument.

14 These arguments are found throughout Indian *sūtra* and *śāstra* literature as well as in Tibetan commentarial literature. For example, Atiśa alludes to the five and mentions the "diamond sliver" argument and the neither-one-nor-many argument specifically in stanzas 48-51 of *Bodhipathapradīpa* (*Byang chub lam gyi sgron ma*). Specifically regarding the neither-one-nor-many argument he says in stanza 50:

> Moreover, when all phenomena are examined with the neither-one-nor-many argument, since no actual entity is found, there is certainly no actual inherent nature.
>
> *yang na chos rnams thams cad dag/ gcig dang du mas rnam dpyad na/ ngo bo nyid ni mi dmigs pas/ rang bzhin med pa nyid du nges//*

Jetsun Chökyi Gyeltsen's monastic textbook on the Perfection of Wisdom, *Phar phyin skabs dang po'i spyi don skal bzang klu dbang gi rol mtsho,* lists the five arguments demonstrating selflessness as follows: "In general there are many reasonings which set forth selflessness since there is the proof which investigates the nature of phenomena [and determines them to be] neither of a single nor manifold [nature], the diamond sliver proof which investigates causes, the proof which investigates results and rejects the production of existence and non-existence, the proof which investigates both causes and results and rejects the four extremes, and the king of all proofs, the proof from dependent arising."

spyir bdag med gtan la 'bebs pa'i rigs pa la du ma yod de/ chos rnams kyi ngo bo la dphod pa gcig du bral kyi gtan tshigs/ rgyu la dphod pa rdo rje gzigs ma'i gtan tshigs/ 'bras bu la dpyod pa yod med skye 'gog gi gtan tshigs/ rgyu 'bras gnyis ka la dpyod pa mu bzhi skye 'gog gi gtan tshigs/ rigs pa'i rgyal po rten 'brel gyi gtan tshigs rnams su yod pa'i phyir//

See Jetsun Chökyi *Gyeltsen, Phar phyin skabs dang po'i spyi don skal bzang klu dbang gi rol mtsho,* 49. Jetsunpa proceeds from here to briefly outline the arguments. He cites *MA* for the first, Nāgārjuna's *Mūlamadhyamakakārikā* for the second, Kamalaśīla's *Madhyamalāloka* for the third, and Jñānagarbha's *Satyadvayavibhaṅga* for the fourth. After explaining the fifth briefly, he goes into some detail in his explanation of the mechanics of the neither-one-nor-many argument. In his analysis of the neither-one-nor-many inference, Jetsunpa looks at and analyzes the three criteria (*tshul gsum*) for determining its validity. See Tillemans 1984 for a detailed look at this section.

15 For documentation of the teacher-student relationship between Śrigupta and Jñānagarbha, see Tāranātha 1970, 252-253, and Ruegg 1981, 69. Śrigupta is categorized by the Geluk-pa doxographer Thubkan in *Grub mtha' thams cad kyi khungs dang 'dod tshul ston pa legs bshad shel gyi me long* (1995-96, 25-26) as a proponent of the Yogācāra-Svātantrika-Madhyamaka view, whereas Jñānagarbha is generally considered to be a Sautrāntika-Svātantrika-Mādhyamika.

16 Translated from *Satyadvayavibhaṅgakārikā* in Eckel 1987, 22.

17 See Ruegg 1981, 99-100 for a discussion of Jetāri and these texts.

18 McClintock 2002, 75.

19 See Cabezón 1992, 147-152.

20 The Sanskrit of this stanza exists as found in *Bodhicaryāvatārapañjikā* by Prajñākaramati (cited in Ichigō 1985, 22): *niḥsvabhāvā amī bhāvās tattvataḥ/ ekānekasvabhāvena viyogāt pratibimbavat//*

21 The neither-one-nor-many argument, as it is extensively applied here by Śāntarakṣita in *MA,* is not only of interest for revealing his own interpretation of Madhayamaka thought. It is also of interest to this study because therein he presents refutations of rival positions, refutations which went on to become standard arguments among Tibetan Mādhyamikas in general and Gelukpas in particular throughout their philosophical literature.

22 Although Śāntarakṣita does not specifically name his opponent in the *MA* verse, he does in *MAV,* as does Gyel-tsab in *JBy.* The argument can be applied however to any asserted permanent and singular cause of periodic or impermanent effects.

23 *MAV,* 21: *'bras bu rnams ni rgyu ma tshang na shol gyi/ gang gi tshe rgyu'i nus pa thogs pa med par gyur ba de'i tshe/ de dag la shol ba srid par ga la 'gyur//*

24 Ibid., 22: *de'i tshe shan gcig byed pa'i rkyen rnams kyang mgul nas btags pa bzhin du stobs kyis drangs nas gnas te/ 'bras bu rgyun mi 'chad pa bzlog pa med pa nyid du 'gyur ro//*

25 Ibid., 22-23: *'dis ni gang dag lhan cig byed pa'i rgyur de nyid nus pa'i sgrar brjod de/ de'i rim gyis 'bras bu'i rim byes so zhes smra ba de dag la lan btab par gyur to// 'bras bu rim can rnams la de dag gi rang bzhin gzhan dang gzhan du rim can nyid do zhe na ni de dag la rtag par 'dod pa dor bar bya ste/ 'bras bu*

so so bas snga ma dang phyi ma'i rang bzhin 'jig pa dang 'byung bar 'gyur ba'i phyir ro//

26 Gyel-tsab, *JBy*, fol. 579. See *JBy* text in full in Appendix 3. Henceforth, all folio numbers correspond to the version of the text in the *Collected Works (gsuṅ 'bum) of Gyel-tsab rje Dar-ma-rin-chen*. Numbers in brackets in the Tibetan text in the Appendix refer to folio numbers in this edition.

27 Ibid.

28 *ZBr*, 68: *don byed pa la mi rtag pas khyab pas rtag pa la don byed pa gnyis ka mi 'thad par bstan/*

29 Kamalaśīla, *MAP* (critical edition in Ichigō 1985, 33). Hereafter, all page citations for *MAP* refer to Ichigō's critical edition.

30 These three uncompounded phenomena (*'dus ma byas gsum*) according to the *Abhidharmakośa* are analytic cessation (*so sor brtags 'gog*), non-analytic cessation (*so sor brtags min gyi 'gog pa*), and space (*nam mkha'*). See Rigzin 1993, 144.

31 *MAV*, 23: *yul dang yul can yin pa'i phyir/ rnam par shes pa rim can dang 'brel ba can dag kyang gcig pu'i rang bzhin du mi 'gyur ram zhe na/ mi 'gyur te/*

32 *JBy*, fol. 580.

33 Geshe Jigme Dawa, personal correspondence.

34 *MAV*, 23-24: *rnam shes snga mas shes bya ba'i// rang bzhin rjes su 'brang na ni// shes pa snga ma'ng phyir mar 'gyur// phyi ma'ng de bzhin sngar mar 'gyur// de lta ma yin na rnam par shes pa snga mas shes par bya ba 'dus ma byas kyi rang bzhin ni phyi ma'i dus na'ng yod la/ rnam par shes pa snga ma ni med pa dang/ de bzhin du shes pa phyi mas shes par bya ba ni snga na yod la/ shes pa phyi ma ni med do// zhes bya ba nyams par 'gyur ro// ji ste shes pa phyi ma dang snga mas shes par bya ba de'i ngo bo sngon dand phyi ma'i gnas dag med na/ gal te de ltar na ni/ sngon dang phyi ma'i gnas rnams su// de'i ngo bo mi 'byung na//'dus ma byas te shes pa bzhin//skad cig 'byung bar shes par bya//*

35 Ibid., 25: *snga ma snga ma'i skad cig gi// mthu yis 'byung bar 'gyur bas na// 'dus ma byas su 'di mi 'gyur// sems dang sems las byung bzhin// ci ste skad cig phyi ma rnams su rang dbang du 'byung ngo zhe na dltar 'gyur ba ni ni nus te/ skad cig ma rnams 'di dag tu// rang dbang 'byung bar 'dod na ni//gzhan la ltos pa med pa'i phyir// rtag tu yod pa'm med par 'gyur// res 'da' 'byung ba'i phyir de dag kyang sems dang sems las byung ba de bzhin du rten cing 'brel bar 'byung ba nyid du gsal bar shes par bya'o//*

36 *JBy*, fol. 581.

37 *ZBr*, 56-57: *rang sde'i 'dus ma byas kyi dngos po snga phyi gcig yin pa mi khegs na gzhan sdes gtso bo la sogs pa 'bras bu rim can la sbyor par khas blangs pas/ rtag dngos kyi gcig yin pa 'gog mi nus pa rnam pa thams cad du mtshungs te/ rigs pa gnyis don gcig tu snang ba'i phyir ro//*

38 Ibid., 58: *'dus ma byas gzhan gnyis kyang shes pa gzhan gyi rim can du shes par 'dod pas de 'gog pa'i yang sngar bzhin du bya'o//*

39 *MAV*, 25-26.

40 This verse from *Pramanāvārttika* is also cited by Kamalaśīla in *TSP*, 191: 12-13.

41 This stanza was not composed by Śāntarakṣita. It is drawn from Dharmakīrti's *Pramāṇavārttika,* 1: 211 to support the argument being made. It is unclear whether Śāntarakṣita inserted this quote himself or if perhaps his disciple Kamalaśīla inserted it.

42 See Tillemans and Lopez 1998 for an extensive discussion of this section of Tsong Khapa's *ZBr*.

43 There is some controversy as to whether Vātsīputrīyans were a Buddhist school or not. See Dunne 2000 for a discussion of this issue in Geluk doxographical literature. Śāntarakṣita considers this position to be non-Buddhist, labeling them as "outsiders" and therefore evoking a strong tone of condescension.

44 *JBy*, fol. 581.

45 *MAV*, 27-28: *skad cig skad cig ma yin par//gang zag bstan du mi rung bas// gcig dang du ma'i rang bzhin dang//bral bar gsal bar rab tu shes// pha rol gyis khas blangs pa'i gang zag chos can la/ gtan tshigs kyi rtsa ba gcig dang du ma'i rang bzhin dang bral ba nyid tshegs med pa nyid du 'grub bo// skad cig par gyur na ni du ma'i rang bzhin du 'gyur te/ sdad cig re re la yang rang bzhin gzhan 'byung ba'i phyir ro// skad cig ma yin na ni rtag tu brtan pa gcig pu'i ngo bo yin pa'i phyir gcig pu'i rang bzhin du 'gyur ro//*

46 *JBy*, fol. 581.

47 The first two lines are translated together in the first interrogative sentence of stanza 10. The third and fourth lines are translated together in the second sentence. It is often difficult, if not impossible, to translate verses from Sanskrit or Tibetan into English in a way that maintains the structural integrity while simultaneously offering a meaningful translation. Thus, I have sacrificed the integrity of the four line stanza format for more accurate and meaningful translations of the content.

48 *MAV*, 28-29: *nam mka' la sogs pa phyogs tha dad pa'i shing la sogs pa dang 'brel ba de dag gi gcig dang 'brel ba'i rang bzhin gang yin pa de nyid gzhan dang 'brel pa can yang yin na ni des na de dang 'brel ba'i phyir de gcig pu'i bdag nyid yin pa bzhin du gzhan yang de dang tha dad ma yin par 'gyur ro//*

49 *JBy*, fol. 582.

50 Kamalaśīla *MAP*, 51. Śāntarakṣita again does not name his opponent, but Kamalaśīla does in *MAP*. Most arguments made in this portion of the text are made from a Sautrāntika perspective. In this refutation of a tenet common to both Vaibhāṣikas and Sautrāntikas, the position of the proponent of the argument is not clearly delineated.

51 *JBy,* fol. 582.

52 *MAV*, 31-34.

53 Certainly Vaibhāṣika and Sautrāntika positions could be targeted by the type of reasoning Śāntarakṣita applies here as they hold similar positions regarding partless particles. While Gelukpas are aware that in India there were numerous philosophical systems and schools of thought including the eighteen divisions of Vaibhāṣika, the so-called "Hīnayāna" schools in India are essentialized traditionally into two major representative schools, Vaibhāṣika and Sautrāntika (with minor subdivisions), in their doxographical literature. Thus, in my reading of this text with several Geluk Geshes, they all simplify the situation by remarking that there are two specific opponents here, Vaibhāṣika and Sautrāntika, whereas Śāntarakṣita is not so specific. Both Śāntarakṣita and his Geluk commentators would apply a similar reasoning and critique to any system asserting partless particles.

54 *JBy*, fol. 582.

55 Kamalaśīla, *Sarvadharmaniḥsvabhāvasiddhi* (*Chos thams cad rang bzhin med par grub pa*), critical edition: Moriyama 1984a, 78: *ji ltar rdul phra rab rnams lus can yin pa'i gdon mi za bar phyogs cha tha dad par khas blang dgos so// de lta ma yin na shar dang byang la sogs pa'i phyogs cha tha dad par ngas med pa'i phyir ri la sogs pa bsags par mi 'gyur ro//*

56 For a discussion of the religious use of reason in the thought of Śāntarakṣita, see McClintock 2002.

57 For a discussion of the five *skandha*s, twelve *āyatana*s, and eighteen *dhātu*s in *abhidharma* literature, see Patt 1993.

58 *MAV*, 34: *rdul phran rang bzhin med grub pa// de phyir dmigs dang rdzas la sogs// bdag dan gzhan smras mang po dag// rang bzhin med par mngon pa yin// rdul phr rab rnams med pa nyid du nges na rang gi sde pa dag mif dang gzugs dang de'i rnam par shes pa la sogs pa de kho na nyid du 'dod pa dang/ gzegs zan pa la sogs pas smras pa'i rdzas dang yon tan la sogs pa bsgrim mi dgos par rang bzhin gyis stong par nges so/ ci 'di rgyal po'i bka' 'm zhes na/ ma yin te/*

59 *JBy*, fol. 583.

60 In the Geluk doxographical literature such as Jetsun Chökyi *Gyeltsen*'s *Grub mtha'i rnam gzhag* and Könchok Jigme Wangpo's *Grub pa'i mtha'i rnam par bzhag pa rin po che'i phreng ba* among others, the Sautrāntika position is said to hold that impermanent, functional, gross objects are ultimate truths.

61 *MAV*, 34-35: *rang gi sde pa dag ni gzugs can gyi khams bcu po de dag rdul phra rab la sogs pa yin par brjod de/ de dag de med na mi rung ngo/ 'di ltar mig dang gzugs rnams la brten nas mig gi rnam par shes pa 'byung ngo zhes bya ba la sogs pa de la brten pa/ dang dmigs pa rnams par shes pa'i khams lnga yang de med na ci la brten te skye bar 'gyur/ rnam par shes pa'i khams lnga med na de ma thag pa'i rkyen des mngon par bsgrubs pa'i yid kyi rnam par shes pa yang mi 'thad pa'i rang bzhin nyid do/ d ltar rnam par shes pa drug gi tshogs*

ma grub na/ rnam par shes pa de 'das ma thag pa'i yid kyang yang dag par rnam par gzhag par mi rigs so// de ltar sems rang bzhin med par gyur na de dang grub pa dnag bde ba gcig pa dang tshor ba dang 'du shes dang sems pa la sogs sems las byung ba rnams kyang rang bzhin med par bde blag tu shes so// ldan pa ma yin pa'i 'du byed rnams kyang rnam par rtog pa la dpa' ba mkhas pa rnams kyis lan brgyar dum bu dum bur bshig zin pas shi zin pa de dag la bsnan mi dgos so//

62 Ibid., 37: *de bas na 'brel pa can med pa'i phyir 'du ba yang rang bzhin med pa kho na'o// rtag pa'i dngos po nam mkha' kang/ dus dang/ phyogs dang/ bdag dang/ phra rab dag kyang bsal te/ rang bzhin med par sngar bstan zin to// gzugs kyi phung po dphad pa'i zhar la rnampar shes pa'i phung po mtshungs par ldan pa dang bcas yang rang bzhin med par bstan to//*

63 The Sanskrit term *svasaṃvedana,* or *rang rig* in the Tibetan, has been translated in a number of different ways including "self-knowledge," "self-awareness," "reflexive awareness," "the self-cognition of knowledge," etc. I have chosen to follow the suggestion of Geshe Ngawang Samten, which is probably closest with the final example offered here, and translate the term as "self-cognizing cognition" in order to convey the full meaning of a term which indicates a consciousness which is conscious of itself and its knowledge. I also find that "reflexive awareness" or "reflexive consciousness" is effective in conveying the sense of there being no subject-object dichotomy between consciousness and its self-consciousness, which is the sense in which it is used by Śāntarakṣita. Paul Williams has suggested that the term may be used with slightly nuanced meanings by various authors and can be effectively translated in different ways depending on the context. See Williams 1998.

64 William explains that, "Śāntarakṣita wants to argue that since consciousness is by its very nature the exact opposite of insentience, it is not possible in reality for consciousness to contact insentient objects. Thus in knowing an object, consciousness must really be apprehending itself in the form of an object. Therefore, from the reflexive nature of consciousness as its uniquely defining quality one moves to an epistemology where consciousness apprehends itself in the form of the object." Williams 1998, 33-34.

65 Ibid., 28.

66 Ibid., 24.

67 For the purposes of this study we will define "dualist" as one who accepts the existence of external objects, as opposed to the common usage in Western philosophical traditions of "dualist" specifically referring to a duality of mind and body. The usage here is not unrelated but is also not identical. Duality refers here to a duality between consciousness and its objects.

68 One example of such a school of thought, which Śāntarakṣita may have had in mind, that maintained the existence of external objects and rejected self-cognizing cognition was the Vaibhāṣika School. Śāntarakṣita does not name a specific opponent, nor does Gyel-tsab in his *JBy*. Kamalaśīla suggests in his comments on this verse in *TSP* that this could be addressed at any dualist.

69 *TS,* 1998. The number following the abbreviation refers to the stanza number, as it will in all future references to *TS*.

70 *MAV*, 38

71 Ibid.

72 Although not explicitly stated, it seems reasonable to presume the opponents he has in mind here are Sautrāntikas who accept self-cognizing cognition while asserting a real separation of consciousness and its objects. They claim that a non-deceptive, directly perceiving consciousness knows its objects clearly. Śāntarakṣita finds this notion absurd.

73 *PV,* 1: 38. Translation adapted from Ichigō 1985, LXXI-LXXII. See also Kajiyama 1966, 147; Katsura 1969, 25; and Tosaki 1979, 38.

74 *JBy*, fols. 583-584.

75 *TS,* 2000: *kriyākārakabhāvena na svasaṁvittir asya tu/ ekasyānaṁśarūpasya trairūpyānupapattitaḥ//*

76 *JBy*, fol. 584.

77 *MAV*, 39-40: *gsal bar byed pa gzhan la mi ltos par rang gsal ba'i bdag nyid ni rnam par shes pa'i rang rig pa zhes bya'o//*

78 *TS,* 2001: *tad saya bodharūpatvād yuktaṁ tāvat svavedanam/ parasya tva artharūpasya tena saṁvedanaṁ katham//*

79 *JBy*, fol. 584.

80 The Tibetan translated here is *rang rig 'thad par thal.*

81 *TS*, 2078; translation adapted from Ichigō 1985, LXXI-LXXIII.

82 *JBy*, fol. 584.

83 *MAP*, 85.

84 On this point, Kamalaśīla adds in *Sarvadharmaniḥsvabhāvasiddhi*that consciousness must have images (*ākāra, rnam pa*): "One must accept that consciousness naturally possesses images." Critical edition of the Tibetan in Moriyama 1984, 79: *rnam par shes pa yang gdon mi za bar rnam pa dang bcas pa nyid du khas blang dgos te/*

85 *MAV*, 42: *gzhan yang shes pa rnam pa med pa'i phyogs 'di ni shes pa rnam pa dang bcas pa'i phyogs shin tu 'brel ba med pas kyang ches dman par bstan pa/*

86 *TS,* 2004: *nirbhāsijñānapakṣe tu tayor bhede 'pi tattvataḥ/ pratibimbasya tādrūpydād bhāktaṁ syād api vedanam//*

87 *MAV*, 42: *des gzhag pa shes pa'i bdag nyid du gyur pa'i gzugs brnyan rigs pa gang yin pa de nyid don shes ba'o//de'i phyir na don gyi 'bras bu gzugs brnyan myong ba la don kyang myong ngo zhes gdags so//*

88 This discrepancy between Śāntarakṣita's autocommentary and Gyel-tsab's commentary seems to suggest that Śāntarakṣita may have had a broader category of

opponent in mind or a different agenda than Gyel-tsab. Perhaps Gyel-tsab finds the particular utility of the forthcoming arguments to be in their application to the rejection of various potential Sautrāntika positions, whereas Śāntarakṣita is more concerned with the advocacy and presentation of a specific epistemological standpoint.

89 *JBy*, fol. 584.

90 Ibid.

91 Thubkan, *Grub mtha' thams cad kyi khungs dang 'dod tshul ston pa legs bshad shel gyi me long*, 25-26: *rang rgyud pa la dbye na/ gzhi'i rnam gzhag sems tsam pa dang mthus par khas len pa'i rnal 'byor spyod pa dang mdo sde pa ltar rdul phra rab bsags pa'i phyi rol gyi don khas len pa'i mdo sde spyod pa'i dbu ma rang rgyud pa gnyis dang/ snga ma la yang rnam bden pa dang mthun pa dang/ rnam rdzun pa dang mthun pa'i dbu ma ba gnyis yod pa'i zhi ba 'tsho dang ka ma la shi'la dang' 'phags pa grol sde lta bu snga ma dang/ slob dpon seng ge bzang po/ dze ta/ri/ lva ba pa lta bu phyi ma yin la phyi ma la yang rnam dzun dri bcas pa dang mthun pa dang dri med pa dang mthun pa gnyis yod do//*

92 *TS*, 2005: *yena tviṣṭaṁ na vijñānam arthākāroparāgavat/ tasyāyam api naivāsti prakāro bāhyavedane//*

93 *MAV*, 43: *rig pa med pa'i rang bzhin yin pas rig pa'i don gyi dngos po ni don las ring du gyur nyid do/ 'brel ba'i rgyu gzugs brnyan yang khas mi len pas gdags pa yang mi srid do//fal te de lta na shes pa rnam pa dang bcas pa nyid du ni rung ngo// de yang de lta ma yin te//*

94 *TS*, 2036: *jñānād avyatiriktatvān nākārabahutā bhavet/ tataś ca tadbalenāsti nārthasaṁvedanasthitiḥ//*

95 *JBy*, fol. 585.

96 *TS*, 2037: *ākārāvyatiriktatvāt jñāne vā nekatā bhavet/ anyathā katham ekatvam anayoḥ parikalpyate//*

97 *MAV*, 44-45: *rnam par shes de rnam pa du ma dang tha dad pa ma yin pa'i lus yin na ni/ rnam pa de dag gi bye brag bzhin du du mar 'gyur ro//rnam par shes pa ni gcig pu kho na'i rang bzhin yin la/ rnam pa ni du ma yin na de'i tshe 'gal ba'i chos su gnas pas rnam par shes pa gnyis tha dad pa ma yin par ni 'gal lo//*

98 See Moriyama 1984b for further discussion of Kamalaśīla and Haribhadra's treatments of these issues.

99 Stanzas 24-30 in *MA* are all borrowed by Śāntarakṣita from the *Pratyakṣalakṣaṇaparīkṣā* chapter of *TS*, which deals extensively with question of direct perception. Both Śāntarakṣita's *TS* and the *TSP* of Kamalaśīla draw extensive influence from Dignāga and Dharmakīrti on these issues. See Funayama 1992 for a detailed study of this chapter of *TS*.

100 *JBy*, fol. 586.

101 *MAV*, 45: *me tog utpa la'i 'dab ma brgya ' bigs pa bzhin du/ shin tu myur ba'i phyir rim gyis dngos po la yang gcig ca'o snyam du shes so zhes 'dzer te/ dper*

na mgal me'i 'khor lo mthong ba bzhin te/ mthong ba de ni byur du bskor ba'i phyir ro zhes zer ro//

102 The Sanskrit word *latā* is translated into Tibetan as *lcug ma* and into English as "vine."

103 *TS,* 1250: *latātālādibuddhīnām atyarthaṁ laghuvarttanam/ sakṛd bhāvābhimāno' taḥ kim atrāpi na varttate//*

104 *MAV*, 45-46: *lcug ma dang/ ta la dang/ mtsho dang/ ro bro ba dang zhes bya ba la sogs pa yi ge'i 'bru'i yul rnams kyi blo dag kyang rab tu mgyogs par 'byung du 'dra ste/ de bas na mgyogs par 'byung ba'i phyir ri mo rkang pa la sogs pa bzhin du cig car du ci'i phyir mi shes/*

105 *TS,* 1251. This stanza was borrowed from Dharmakīrti's *Pramāṇavārttika*, 3.138: *śuddhe ca mānase kalpe vyavasīyeta na kramaḥ/ tulyā ca sarvabuddhīnām āśuvṛttiś cirāsthiteḥ//*

106 *TS,* 1252: *ataḥ sarvatra viṣaye na kramagrahaṇaṁ bhavet/ sakṛdgrahaṇabhāsas tu bhavec chabdādibodhavat//*

107 *JBy*, fol. 586.

108 *TS,* 1253: *pi sakṛd bhrāntiś cakrābhāsā pravarttate/ na dṛśāṁ pratisandhānād vispaṣṭaṁ pratibhāsanāt//*

109 *MAV*, 47: *ci gsal bar snang ba dang mtshams sbyor ba 'gal lam/ 'gal te/*

110 *TS,* 1255: *yaś cāsyā viṣayo nāsau vinaśṭatvāt parisphuṭaḥ/ tataḥ parisphuṭo nāyaṁ cakrābhāsaḥ prasajyate//*

111 *MAV*, 48: *dran pa ni mdun na 'dub pa'i dngos po la yang shin tu gsal bar rtogs pa ma yin no//*

112 *JBy*, fols. 586-587.

113 While Gyel-tsab names this opponent as Sautrāntika Proponents of an Equal Number of Images and Consciousnesses, the critique can equally be applied to Yogācāra Proponents of an Equal Number of Images and Consciousnesses as well. Both Kamalaśīla and Haribhadra use similar reasonings in their refutations of Yogācāra Satyākāra-vādins. See Moriyama 1984c for a detailed study of their critiques.

114 *MAV*, 49-50: *ji ltar sngon po dang dkar po la sogs pa rnam pa mang po de bzhin du gcig pur 'dod pa dkar po la sogs pa la yang tshu rol dang/ pha rol dang dpung gi cha'i ngo bo'i rnam pa mang po nyid de/ de la yang de'i bdag nyid kyi shes pa du ma nyid du 'gyur ro// du mar 'dod do zhes na/ 'o na gcig pur gyur pa gang yin/ gang yan lag med pa'i rdul gyi yul 'dzin pa ste/ yul de'i yan lag rnam par dbye bar nges par byed pa ni/ shin tu zhib pa'i shes rab can rnambs kyis kyang mi nus so// lta ba de yang myong bar byed pa ma yin par brjod pa/*

115 *JBy*, fol. 587.

116 *MAV,* 50-51: *rdul phran bdag nyid kdar la sogs// gcig pu'i bdag nyid cha med*

pa// la'ng snang gyur par// bdag gis rab tu tshor ba med// bdag gis rab tu sems btud kyang// cha shas thams cad kyis stong pa'i rdul ma mthong ste/ ma mthong bzhin du de khas blangs shing bdag la ji ltar bslu/ rtog pa dang ldan pa rnams kyis yod par khas len pa'i rgyu ni dmigs pa yin na/ de ni de med pas rung ba ma yin no//

117 It seems reasonable to presume that Śāntarakṣita has Sautrāntikas in mind.

118 *MAV,* 52.

119 *MAP*, 103-107.

120 Translated in Sopa and Hopkins 1989, 155-156.

121 *JBy*, fols. 587-588.

122 Ichigō 1985, 106. In his critical edition of *MA,* Ichigō identifies *lHa'i bla ma* as Suraguru, or Surācārya, who is associated with the Lokāyata School.

123 *MAV,* 54: *'dus par rnam par gzhag pa'i rgyu ni 'dus pa can du ma yin pas 'dus pa la 'dzin pa'i shes pa ni gcig dang mthun par 'jug par mi rigs so/*

124 *JBy*, fol. 588.

125 *MAV,* 54.

126 *MAP*, 107.

127 Courage is the first of the three qualities which comprise all five mere existences. The other two qualities are atoms or particles (*paramāṇu, rdul phran*) and darkness (*tamas, mun pa*).

128 *TS,* 39: *tryākāraṁ vastuno rūpam ekākārāś ca tadvidaḥ/ tāḥ kathaṁ tatra yujyante bhāvinyas tadvilakṣaṇāḥ//*

129 *JBy*, fol. 588.

130 Precise dating of Śaṅkara is contested. His birth has been dated as early as 686 and as late as 788. The later date would place him as being born in the year of Śāntarakṣita's death. Considering that Śāntarakṣita spent the last years of his life in Tibet, if these dates are correct, then he never could have heard of Śaṅkara and thus Śāntarakṣita must be addressing one of his predecessors.

131 *MAV,* 56-57: *phyi rol yul rnams med par yang// sna tshogs snang la rtag pa ste// cig ca'm ji ste rim 'byung ba'i// rnam shes rung ba shin tu dka'// ci skad brjod pa de dag gi phyogs la yang sna tshogs su sla ba nyid de/ 'di ltar sngon po dang ser po'i rnam pa du ma dag dang tha dad pa ma yin pa'i phyir rnam pa de'i rang gi ngo bo bzhin du du mar 'gyur ro// .....rim gyi phyogs la nyes pa 'di yang yod de/*

132 *JBy*, fol. 588.

133 Shankara (Śaṅkara) 1947m 12-24.

134 When I questioned one eminent Geluk scholar, Geshe Jigme Dawa, on certain aspects of the Vedānta position with regard to Gyel-tsab's comments, I was told

that in general Tibetans do not study the non-Buddhist schools in much detail because there is no real need to do so. They are only studied roughly in order to illuminate fallacies to be avoided and to highlight certain philosophical points and good qualities in Buddhist views. Since these opponents never really posed the threat in Tibet that they did in India as a rival school of thought, they have not been taken as seriously by Tibetans as they were by their Indian Buddhist predecessors. These views are used as examples to illustrate how to refute certain ideas and to illuminate specific points. But there is no soteriological purpose in extensively studying these systems as there is with the lower Buddhist systems and thus they receive minimal attention. Śāntarakṣita on the other hand may have engaged Vedāntins in India, an thus his portrayal of their view here is a bit curious, though he does treat them more extensively in *TS*.

135 *JBy*, fol. 589.

136 Śāntarakṣita refrains again from naming his opponent in either *MA* or *MAV,* although Kamalaśīla does indicate that he is referring to Sautrāntikas in the *MAP* (crit. ed. in Ichigō, 1985, 115) as does Gyel-tsab in *JBy*, fol. 589.

137 *MA,* 58-59.

138 *MAV,* 58-59: *skabs kyi mjub sdud do// yang 'dir gsungs pa/ sor mo tshogs rnams las gzhan min//gzhan ma yin pa yod ma yin// de ltar ma grub tshigs sogs med// de phyir tshogs pa tsam yang med// tshogs pa dang ni bcas pa yi// sor mo la sogs rnams kyis ni// dngos po thams cad med par bstan// tshogs ma gtogs pa'i ngos phra med// de ltar don gcig shes byed// blo ni gang du brtag par bya// sems byung tshogs dang bcas sems kyi// dmigs pa gcig 'dir ji ltar 'gyur//*

139 See Appendix 1 for a topical outline of *MA* based on Gyel-tsab's delineation of topics. The outline should prove useful to the reader in general as a layout of the main points of the entire text as seen by Gyel-tsab. It will be particularly relevant here in light of the multilayered critique Śāntarakṣita levels against several subschools of Yogācāra thought.

140 We witness the sliding scales, discussed in the Introduction, at work in this text as Śāntarakṣita criticizes non-Buddhist and Vaibhāṣika views from a Sautrāntika perspective, or as if he were a Sautrāntika. He then refutes Sautrāntika views from a Yogācāra perspective, as if he were a Yogācāra, and ultimately will critique Yogācāra positions from a Madhyamaka perspective. If Śāntarakṣita is feigning acceptance of these views in some sense as he proceeds up the sliding scale, then it could be argued that his use of tri-modal inference in the case of feigning Yogācāra and Svātantrika positions may be somewhat akin to that of his Geluk critics who also feign acceptance of a commonly appearing subject when they utilize the tri-modal forms of inference which they insist are not *svatantras*, but rather are opponent-acknowledged inferences. See Part II of this book. Also see McClintock 2002 for a discussion of the "sliding scales" and other related issues.

141 *MAV,* 59-60: *ji ste thog ma med rgyud kyi// bag chags smin pas sprul pa yi// rnam pa dag ni snang ba yang// nor bas sgyu ma'i rang bzhin 'dra// dmigs pa*

bden par 'dod pa'i shes pa la snang ba'i rnam pa 'di dag kyang thog ma med pa'i srid par 'byung ba can dngos po la mngon par zhen pa'i bag chags yongs su smin pa'i mthus snang ngo//

142 *JBy*, fol. 589.

143 *MAV*, 60-62: *de dge 'on kyang de dag ge dngos de yang dag nyid dam ci// 'on te ma brtags gcig pu na// dga' bar khas len 'di bsam mo// lugs 'di ni tshad ma dang lung shin tu gsal bas shes par bya ba dang//dmigs pa can mtha' yas pa dag gi mngon par zhen pa ngan pa'i gnyen po yang yin pas shin tu dkar ba ste 'di ltar rdul phra ram la sogs pa yod pa dag dgag par byed pa dang tshor bar bya ba dang tshor ba po'i mthsan nyid dang 'gal ba yang ston pa sngar bshad pa'i tshad ma ni tshul 'di rab tu gsal bar byed pa'o// tshul 'di ni lung dang ldan pa yang yin te/ lang kar gshegs pa'i mdo las/ thog ma med pa'i blos bsgos pas// sems ni gzugs brnyan lta bu ste// don gyi rnam par snang yang ni// yang dag ji bzhin don mthong med/ gang zag rgyu dang phung po dang// rkyen dang de bzhin rdul rnams dang// gtso bo dbang phyug byed pa dag// sems tsam po las rnam par brtags.. don yod ma yin sems nyid de//phyi rol don mthong log pa yin// rigs pas rnam par bltas na ni// gzung dang 'dzin pa 'gag par 'gyur// zhes gsungs so// mkhas pa dag tshul 'di la brten nas bdag dang bdag gi dang gzung ba dang 'dzin pa rab tu dbye ba dang bcas pa rnams la phyin ci logs tu gyur pa rnams sel to// 'on kyang 'di la dpyad par bya ba cung zad tsam 'di yod de/ci rnam de dag de kho na nyid yin nam 'on te ci gzugs brnyan la sogs pa ltar ma brgags pa gcig pu na dga' ba zhig yin/ 'dis cir 'gyur//*

144 *JBy*, fol. 589.

145 Both Haribhadra and Kamalaśīla use the neither-one-nor-many reasoning to refute Yogācāra-Satyākā-vādins in their *Abhisamayālaṁkārāloka Prajñāpāramitāvyākhyā* and *Madhyamakāloka* respectively. For a detailed treatment of their arguments, see Moriyama 1984b and 1984c.

146 *MAV*, 62: *gal te yang dag rnam par shes// du mar 'gyur ro yang na ni// de dag gcig 'gyur 'gal ldan pas// gdon mi za bar so sor 'gyur// yang dag pa'i rnam pa dang tha dad pa ma yin pas rnam pa rang gi ngo bo bzhin du rnam par shes pa du mar 'gyur ba'm yang na rnam par shes pa gcig pu dang tha mi dad pas rnam pa rnams kyang rnam shes pa'i rang gi ngo bo bzhin du gcig pu nyid du 'gyur ba bzlog par dka'o//*

147 *JBy,* fol. 590.

148 *MAV*, 63: *tha dad pa ma yin zhes bya ba ni de nyid yin no zhes bstan par 'gyur ro// de bas na gal te rnam pa gcig gyo ba la sogs pa'i byed pa zin tam/ ser po la sogs pa'i bdag nyid du gyur na shag ma rnams kyang rnam pa de lta bur 'gyur ro// de lta ma yin na gdon mi za bar sna tshogs nyid du 'gyur ro//*

149 *JBy*, fols. 589-590.

150 When Ichigō (1985, CXL) translates the related section of the root text verse as, "If (knowledge and its image) are inseparable," I think he misses the point of the argument Śāntarakṣita makes. The emphasis of this argument is different. It fo-

cuses on the nature of the object since the object of a singular consciousness must be single. Thus, the images that make up the object, if they are inseparable, must all be the same. Moving and non-moving parts of an object of a truly singular nature would therefore be absurd. Thus the verse should read, "images are not separate from each other."

151 *MAV*, 65-66: *gal te bar med par gnas pa'i rdul phra rab kyi ngo bo rnams ltar rigs mthun pa'i rnam par shes pa mang po 'di dag kyang 'byung na/ de'i tshe rdul phra rab la dpyad pa ci 'dra ba sngar byas pa de 'dra ba nyid rnam par shes pa rnams la yang bzlog par dka' bo 'gyur te/ 'di ltar dbus su 'dod pa'i rnam par shes pa rdul gyis bskor ba lta bur 'dod pa gang yin pa de'i rang bzhin gang gis gcig la mngon du phyogs pa de nyid kyis ci gzhan la yang phyogs sam/*

152 Nirgrantha (*gcer bu pa*) was a common term utilized by Buddhists in India to refer to Jains, particularly Digambaras.

153 Kamalaśīla also only mentions the Jain Digambaras in the *MAP*.

154 *JBy*, fols. 590-591.

155 *MAV*, 68: *rnam par shes pa de ni don dam par na shel sgong dag pa lta bu ste/*

156 Ibid.: *de la yang thog ma med pa'i dus kyi phyin ci logs gi bag chags smin pa'i mthus rnam pa rnams snang ste/*

157 *JBy*, fol. 591.

158 Ibid.

159 Ibid.

160 The root text says *rta ru* ("horse horn") whereas Gyel-tsab's commentary uses the traditional example of an "impotent horse" as an example of something without causal efficacy. This would make more sense in this instance. Ichigō's critical edition of *MA* also has *rta ru*. Ichigō 1985, 150.

161 *JBy* fol. 591.

162 Ibid., fol. 592.

163 *MAV*, 70-71: *de ni shes pa'i bdag nyid ma yin te/ shes pa bzhin du yod pa'i skyon du 'gyur ba'm rnam pa bzhin du rnam par shes pa yang med pa'i skyon du 'gyur ba'i phyir ro// med pa'i ngo bo de shes pa las byung ba yang ma yin te/ bskyed par bya ba'i ngo bo nyid med pa'i phyir ro// med pa'I ngo bo de shes pa las byung ba yang ma yin te/*

164 *JBy*, fol. 592.

165 Ibid.

166 *MAV*, 71-72: *rnam pa ni med pa nyid kyi phyir rgyu med pa nyid do// rgyu med na res 'g' 'byung bar mi srid de/ ltos pa med pa'i phyir ro// ci lte nyes pa 'di 'byung du 'ong zhes rgyu dang ldan par khas len na gal te de lta na yod par khas blangs ma thag pa med na mi 'byung ba'i gzhan gi dbang nyid du de 'gyur ba la ji ltar lan gdab par nus/ rten cing 'brel bar 'byung ba las gzhan gyi dbang du*

ni gud na med do// rkyen las byung ba'i rang bzhin las kyang yod pa gzhan ma yin no//

167 *JBy,* fol. 592.

168 Ibid.

169 *TS,* 1995. *tad evaṁ sarvapakṣeṣu naivaikātmā sa yujyate/ ekāniṣpattito'nekasvabhāvo'pi na sambhavī//*

170 Āryadeva,. *Catuḥśataka*, 14:19 in Bhattacharya 1931, 214, cited in Ichigō 1985: *tasya tasyaikatā nāsti yo yo bhāvaḥ parīkṣyate/ na santi tenāneke'pi yenaiko'pi na vidyante//*

171 *MAV,* 75-76: *pha rol dang bdag gi lta ba'i rjes su 'brang ba dag gis khas blangs pa rtag pa dang/ mi rtag pa dang/ mi rtag pa dang/ khyab pa dang/ cig shos dang/ rdul dang/ rags pa dang/ shes bya dang/ shes pa la sogs pa so sor tha dad pa'i dngos po gang la gcig pur brtags na de la de ltar brtags pa de'i tshe/ brtag pa'i khur lci ba bzod pa phra rab tsam yang med do// gang gcig pa'i rang zhin du mi 'thad pa de du ma'i bdag nyid du khas blangs pa na rigs pa ma yin pa nyid de/ 'di ltar du ma ni gcig bsags pa'i mtshan nyid do// gcig med na de yang med de// shing la sogs pa med na nags tshal la sogs pa med pa bzhin no// de'i phyir/ dngos po gang dang gang brtags pa// de dang de la gcig pa med// gang la gcig nyid yod min pa// de la du ma'ng med pa yin// zhes gsungs so//*

172 See for example, *MAV* 19-20: "Therefore always exert great effort toward realizing the lack of inherent nature in all phenomena by use of reasoning and scriptures." *de bas na rigs pa cang lung gi[s]/ chos thams cad rang bzhin med par khong du chud par bya ba'i phyir rab tu 'bad do//*

And *MAV* 20: "With regard to that point, scriptures without inference derived from the power of cogent evidence will not completely satisfy even those disciples following entirely by faith. Thus [I] will explain [the lack of inherent nature] with inferential reasoning." *de la lung dngos po'I stobs kyis zhugs pa'I rjes su dpag pa dang bral ba ni dad pas yongs su 'brang ba rnams kyang shin tu yongs su tshim par mi 'gyur bas rigs pa je brjod par bya'o//*

173 See Tillemans 1984.

174 *MAV,* 81: *smig rgyu chu yi rnam shes la// dgon dang 'od zer gdungs de bzhin// zhes bya ba de gnas med do// de dag rgyu nyid du yod kyang dmigs pa nyid du mi rigs te/ rgyu'i don kyang gzhan dmigs pa'i don kyang gzhan te/*

175 *MAV,* 78: *gal te de lta na yang de ma lus pa dpyad zin pas yang dbyung ba ma rigs so//*

176 *MAV,* 81-82: *gcig pu'i bdag nyid dang/ du ma'i bdag nyid ni phan tshun spangs te gnas pa'i mtshan nyid yin pas phung po gzhan bsal po//*

177 *JBy*, fol. 593.

178 *MAV,* 87-88: *glang po che'i rtsal gyi mdo las gyang/ sha ri'i bu 'di ji snyam du sems// gang chos rnams kyi ngo bo nyid shes pa de yod pa yin nam/ 'on te med pa yin/gsol ba/ bcom ldan 'das gang chos thams cad kyi ngo bo nyid 'tshal ba*

de ni sgyu ma'i ngo bo nyid 'tshal ba ste/ bcom ldan 'das de ni ma mchis shing/ mchis pa ma lags so// de ci'i slad du zhe na/ bcom ldan 'das kyis chos thams cad ni sgyu ma'i ngo bo nyid do zhes bstan pa'i slad du ste/ sgyu ma lta bu gang lags pa ni ma mchis pa'o// 'di lta ste/ chos thams cad kyi ngo bo nyid 'tshal ba de ni 'tshal ba ma mchis pa'o// de ci'i slad du zhe na/ 'di la gang yang yang dag par chos gang yang mi dmigs pa'i slad du'o// zhes bya ba la sogs pa gsungs so//

179 *JBy*, fol. 593.

180 *MAV*, 87-88: *'o na ci ste kun rdzob kyi ngo bo 'di gal te ci dngos po med pa yin nam/ 'di dngos po med pa yin na ni mthong ba dang 'dod pa'i don byed pa dang 'gal lo zhes na/ de ni de lta ma yin par bstan pa//*

181 *MAV*, 88-93.

182 Ichigō 1985, LXI-LXIII.

183 Translated in Ichigō 1985, LXIII.

184 *MAV*, 88-89: *kun rdzob ni sgra'i tha snyad tsam gyis bdag nyid ma yin gyi/ mthong ba dang 'dod pa'i dngos po rten cing 'brel bar 'byung ba rnams ni brtag mi bzod pas yang dag pa'i kun rdzob ste/*

185 Ibid., 91: *brtags mi bzod la don byed nus pa'i dngos po nyid ni yang dag pa'i dun rdzob ces bya ste/*

186 While neither Gyel-tsab in *JBy* nor Tsong Khapa in *ZBr* raises the issue of the distinction between real and unreal conventional truths, in Geluk doxographical literature a standard critique of Svātantrika-Mādhyamikas in general, including Śāntarakṣita, centers on the supposed distinction they draw between real and unreal conventional truths. For Gelukpas, all conventional truths are falsities in that they do not exist in the way they appear. Thus a distinction between real and unreal conventional truths does not make sense and seems to imply some sort of real nature in real conventional truths. Kamalaśīla does make this distinction in *MAP*, as does Śāntarakṣita's teacher, Jñānagarbha, in *Satyadvayavibhaṅgavṛtti* (*bDen pa gnyis rnam par 'byed pa'i 'grel pa*). One might infer that the key issues which would inform Śāntarakṣita's definition of unreal conventionalities, if he were to postulate and define them, would be whether or not they were actual dependent arisings and whether they could function in the way they appear.

187 *MAV*, 90-91: *skyob pas kyang/ dper na yan lag tshogs rnams la shing rta zhes ni bya par 'dod// de bzhin phung po rgyur byas nas// kun rdzob tu ni sems can brjod// ces gsungs so//*

188 *JBy*, fol. 593.

189 *MAV*, 91: *brtag mi bzod la don byed nus pa'i dngos po nyid ni yang dag pa'i kun rdzob cas bya ste/ gang zag la sogs pa ltar sgra tsam ni ma yin no zhes bya ba'o// de lta bu de la yang brjod pa'i tshul gyis brtags pas dpyad mi bzod pa'i rang gi rgyu la brten nas 'byung na rgyu med par ji ltar 'gyur/ shes rab dang ye shes kyis dpyad na gang gi rgyu'i rang bzhin yod pa de blo gros dang ldan pas smros shig/*

190 *JBy*, fol. 593.

191 Ibid., fol. 594.

192 Cited in Candrakīrti, *Prasannapadā*, 16:4-5; Āraydeva, *Catuḥśataka*, 16:25; Bodhibhadra, *Jñānasārasamuccayanibandhana* 155: 5: *sad asat sadasac ceti yasya pakṣo na vidyate/upālambhaś cireṇāpa tasya vaktuṁ na śakyate//*

193 It is of significant interest to note here, as in many other instances in both Śāntarakṣita's root text and autocommentary, that he uses language Geluk doxographers claim Yogācāra-Svātantrika-Mādhyamikas would not use to describe emptiness or ultimate truth. Gelukpas, beginning with Tsong Khapa in his major writings on Madhyamaka such as the Special Insight (*lhag mthong*) chapter of *LRCh*, *LSN*, and *GRS*, down through all the major Geluk tenet system texts and the oral commentators today, all clearly explain, while stressing the point's importance, that Yogācāra-Svātantrika-Mādhyamikas will say entities do not truly exist (*den par med*) or do not ultimately exist (*don dam par med*), but that they will not say that they do not inherently exist (*rang bzhin med)* or have inherent existence (*rang bzhin yod*). It is a key point in Geluk critiques that Svātantrika-Mādhyamikas accept inherent existence (*rang bzhin yod*), at least conventionally. And, according to Gelukpas, if they accept it conventionally, they must accept it ultimately. Here is just one example, from the sixty-seventh stanza of *MA,* in which Śāntarakṣita discusses emptiness or ultimate truth in terms of a lack of inherent existence. Similarly there are numerous occasions when he simply says that entities do not exist, instead of qualifying such a statement with "ultimately" or "truly" as Geluk scholars claim Svātantrika-Mādhyamikas feel is necessary for delineating a definitive position. When I questioned modern scholars from within the Geluk tradition about this point, it was suggested that the purpose of those Geluk commentaries, particularly in tenet system texts, was not necessarily a word-for-word commentary, but a commentary on the "meaning of the views" (*lta ba'i don*). These are presented is such a way as to best facilitate ascent to the highest view, the Prasaṅgika-Madhyamaka, by facilitating clear contrasts between the views of the so-called "higher" and "lower" Mādhyamikas. I discuss these points in the sections on the two truths and Geluk hermeneutics in the following chapter, and only raise them here to point out an example and draw attention to the issue as it arises in the text.

194 *JBy*, fol. 594.

195 Translated in Eckel 1987, 22.

196 *MAV,* 94-98: *de phyir yang dag nyid du na// dngos po gang yang grub pa med// de phyir de bzhin gshegs rnams kyis// chos rnams thams cad ma skyes gsungs// yang dag par na dngos po phra rab kyang yongs su grub par mi 'thad de/ ji ltar bstan pa'i tshul gyis gcig dand du ma'i rang bzhin dang bral ba'i phyir ro// de'i phyir yang dag par na gang gis skye ba dang sngon du 'gro ba'i gnas pa dang/ mi rtag pa dand de la brten pa'i dngos po'i chos bzhan yang yod par 'gyur ram/ de lta bas na blo gros rgya mtshos bstan pa las 'di skad gsungs te/ gang dag rten cang 'brel 'byung ba// de dag dngos nyid ci yang min// gang dag ngo bo nyid med pas// de dag gang du 'byung ba med//ce'o// glang po'i rtsal gyi mdo las*

kyang// gang zhig skye bar 'gyur ba yi// chos de gang yang mi dmigs na// 'byung ba med pa'i chos rnams la// byis pa dag ni 'byung bar 'dod// ces gsungs so// dkon mchog 'byung gnas kyi mdo las kyang// gang la rang bzhin yod pa ma yin te// rang bzhin med pas gzhan rkyen ji ltar 'gyur// rang bzhin med pas gzhan gyis ji ltar bskyed// rgyu 'di bde bar gshegs pas bstan pa yin// zhes gsungs so// de'i phyir yab dang sras mjal ba'i mdo las kyang/ rten cing 'brel bar 'byung ba la 'jug pas chos kyi dbyings la 'jug pa stib oa bstab te. bcom ldan 'das de la ma rig pa ni ma rig pa nyid kyis ma mchis so// de ci'i slad du zhes na sdi ltar ma rig pa ni rang bzhin dang bral ba ste/ chos gang la yang rang bzhin ma mchis pa de ni dngos po ma mchis pa'o// gang yongs su ma grub pa de ni mi skye ba'o/ gang mi skye ba de ni mi 'gag pa'o// gang ma skyes pa ma 'gags pa de ni 'das pa zhes gdags par bgyi ba ma lags/ m'ongs pa dang/ da ltar byungs ba zhes gdags par bgyi ba ma lags so// gang dus gsum du mi dmigs pa de ni mings ma mchis pa/ mtshan nyid ma mchis pa// mtshan ma ma mchis pa/ gdags su ma mchis pa ste/ gzhan du ma lags kyi ming tsam dang/ brda tsam dang/ tha snyad tsam/ kun rdzob tsam dang/ brjod pa tsam dang/ gdags pa tsam du sems can rnams gzud pa'i don du bgyi ba ma gtogs par ma rig pa de ni don dam par dmigs su ma mchis so/ chos gang don dam par dmigs su ma mchis pa de ni gdags su ma mchis ma tha snyad du bgyir ma mchis pa brjod du ma mchis pa ste bchom ldan 'das gang ming tsam zhes bgyi ba nas gdags pa tsam gyi bar de dag kyang yang dag par ma lags pa zhes rgya cher'byung ngo// de ltar byas na chos kyi 'khor lo bskor ba na// gzod nas zhi zhing ma skyes dang// rang bzhin mya ngan 'das pa zhes// chos rnams mgon po khyod kyis bstan// ces bya ba'i tshigs su bcad pa 'di legs par bshad par 'gyur te/ 'dis ni chos thams cad dus gsum du mnyam pa nyid du yongs su bstan to//

197 *MAV*, 98-99: *yab dang sras mjal ba'i mdo las/ ji sdad du/ chos 'di dag thams can ni dus gsum du mnyam pa nyid kyis mnyam pa ste/ 'das pa'i dus na yang chos thams cad rang bzhin dang bral ba'o// m 'ongs pa dang/ da ltar byung ba'i dus na yang chos thams cad rang bzhin dang bral ba'o zhes gsungs pa lta bu'o// yang de nyid las gsal bar mdzad de/ chos thams cad ni rang bzhin gyis stong pa'o// chos gang la rang bzhin ma mchis pa de ni 'das pa ma lags/ ma 'ongs pa ma lags/ da ltar byung ba ma lags so// de ci'i slad da zhe na/ rang bzhin ma mchis pa ni 'das pa zhes gdags par bgyi ba ma lags/ ma 'ongs pa dang da ltar byung ba zhes gdags par bgyi ba ma lags so zhes 'byung ngo// skye ba med pa la sogs pa yang/ yang dag pa'i kun rdzob tu gtogs pa yin du zin kyang/*

198 *JBy*, fol.594.

199 *MAV*, 99-100: *dam pa'i don dang mthun pa'i phyir// 'di ni dam pa'i don zhes bya// yang dag tu na spros/ pa yi// tshogs rnams kun las de grol yin// don dam pa ni dngos po dang dngos po med pa dang / skye ba dang mi skye badang/ stong pa dang mi stong pa la sogs pa spros pa'i dra ba mtha' dag spangs pa'o// skye ba med pa la sogs pa ni de la 'jugs pa dang mthun pa'i phyir don dam pa zhes nye bar 'dogs so// yang dag kun rdzob rnams kyi skas// med par yang dag khang pa yi// steng du 'gro bar bya ba ni// mkhas la rung ba ma yin no// ci'iphyir dngos su don dam pa ma yin pa bstan pa//*

200 Personal correspondence, Sarnath, India, 1997-1998.

201 *JBy*, fols. 594-595.

202 *MAV*, 105: *de rtogs na de'i rang gi ngo bo mi rtags pa ni mi rigs te/ bum pas dben pa'i sa gzhi dmigs na de'i bdag nyid du gyur pa bum pas dben pa rtogs pa bzhin no//*

203 Ibid., 105-106: *ma yin thog med rgyud lci bar/ ngos por sgro btags dbang byas pas// de phyir srog chags thams cad kyis//mngon sum rtogs par mi 'gyur ro// thog ma med pa'i srid par skyes pa dngos po la mngon par zhen pa'i dug gis dkrugs pa'i blo can dag gis mngon sum tsam du rtogs pas rnams pa kong du chud par mi nus te/*

204 *JBy*, fols. 594-595.

205 *JBy*, fols. 595-596.

206 This refers to the three criteria (*trairūpya, tshul gsum*) for a valid autonomous inference. The three are 1) that the mark is of the property of the subject (*pakṣadharmatā, phyogs chos*), (2) that the forward pervasion (*anvayavyāpti, rjes khyab*) entails, and (3) that the counter pervasion (*vyatirekavyāpti, ldog khyab*) entails.

207 *MAV*, 107-108: *chos thams cad rang bzhin med par khas blangs na/ phogs kyi chos la sogs pa rang las ma grub ba'i phyir rjes su dpag pa dang/ rjes su dpag par bya ba'i tha snyad mi 'grub pa ma yin nam/ de'i phyir rjes su dpog pos ji ltar gtan la dbab/ gal te yang chos thams cad rang bzhin med par sgrub pa'i gtan tshigs ma brjod na/ de'i tshe gtan tshigs med par mi 'grub pa'i phyir 'dod pa'i don mi 'grub bo//*

208 Ibid., 108: *ci ste brjod na ni gtan tshigs yod de/ de lta na yang chos thams cad rang bzhin med par mi 'grub pas 'dod pa'i don mi 'grub bo/*

209 Tsong Khapa discusses the issue of unestablished bases quite extensively in *ZBr*. Interestingly, he draws more heavily on Kamalaśīla's *Madhyamakāloka* than on Śāntarakṣita's *MA*, despite the title of his text. See Tillemans and Lopez 1998 for an extensive discussion of this topic and translation of the relevant section of *ZBr*.

210 *MAV, 109: rjes su dpag pa dang rjes su dpag par bya ba'i tha snyad thams cad ni phan tshun mi mthun pas grub pa'i mthas bskyed pa chos can tha dad pa yang su btang ste/ mkhas pa dang bud med dang byis pa'i par gyi mig dang rna ba la sogs pa'i shes pa la snang ba'i ngang can gyi phyogs sgra la sogs pa'i chos can la brten nas 'jug go/*

211 As mentioned briefly above, Sara McClintock (2003) has argued that Śāntarkṣita is using "sliding scales of analysis" in which he utilizes autonomous inferences (*svatantrānumāna*) when analyzing lower views from a Sautrāntika perspective, and when analyzing the Sautrāntika position from a Yogācāra perspective, yet in his final shift (when finally analyzing Yogācāra views from a Madhyamaka perspective) he no longer uses autonomous inferences. If this is the case, and Śāntarakṣita is only using such a form of reasoning when it is acceptable from the perspective of the tenets whose acceptance he in a sense is feigning, then use in such a circumstance should not be problematic. McClintock argues that it is

questionable whether Śāntarakṣita accepts anything as unassailably real, even conventionally, since by arguing from both Sautrāntika and Yogācāra perspectives at different points in his texts he offers two alternative versions of what is conventionally unassailably real. And when he moves to a Madhyamaka perspective, he rejects the prospect altogether, implying that the conventional use of autonomous inference is merely an instance of skillful means. I would agree with her on this point and add that what Śāntarakṣita is doing is not that dissimilar in theory from the way Gelukpas use opponent-acknowledged inference while feigning acceptance of the commonly appearing subject when arguing with realist opponents. See Cabezón 1988.

212 *MAV,* 109: *de lta min na du ba dang/ yod pa la sogs pa'i me dang mi rtag pa nyid la sogs pa bsgrub par 'dod pa thams cad kyi gtan tshigs kyi gzhi la grub par mi 'gyur te/ sgrub pa'i chos can yan lag can dang//nam mkha'i yon tan la sogs pa'i ngo bo rnams ma grub pa'i phyir ro//de lta na chos gnyi ga dang ldan pa'i dpe'i chos can yang mi 'grub panyid do/*

213 Ibid., 110: *ji skad du 'dzin pa stug la mi brten na// tha snyad rab tu 'grub 'gyur la/ tha snyad rnams la khas gyur na// bstan bcos don la rmongs pa med// ces gsungs pa lta bu'o//*

214 Ibid., 110-111: *don ma pa'i tshul la sdang bas dbang sgyur ba gang dag 'di lta ste/ chos thams cad rang bzhin med par lat ba nyid ni med pa nyid du lta bar spy bo nas dbang bskur bnyid yin no zhes smra ba dang// de ltas rgyu dang 'bras bu skur 'debs pa/ log ltas dkar phyogs drungs 'byin dam chos kyi// lo tog ser ba nam mkha'i me tog 'di//legs 'dod rnams kyis rgyang ring spang bar bya//*

215 Ibid., 113: *dngos po la sogs par rnam par rtog pa'i phyir tshe 'di la dang po byung ba dag kyang 'drang ba la goms pa'i bag chags las skye bar rjes su dpag ste/*

216 *JBy*, fol. 596.

217 *JBy*, fols. 596-597.

218 Geshe Ngawang Samten suggested in personal correspondence that the commentary erroneously reversed *ldog* and *log* in this sentence. His assertion is based on the way this argument is presented in other Madhyamaka commentaries such as Tsong Khapa's *GRS,* etc.

219 The text actually has *mi 'byung* ("do not arise"); this is probably a mistake in printing, given the context. If it were not a mistake, the text would have to say that,"true effects do not arise from true causes," but this does not really make sense in the context of the argument.

220 *JBy*, fol. 597.

221 *MAV,* 115: *dkon mchog sprin las kyang/ ji ltar byang chub sems dpa' theg pa chen po la mkhas pa yin zhe na/ 'di la byang chub sems dpa' bslab pa thams cad la yang slob la/ slob pa yang mi dmigs / bslab pa'i lam la yang mi dmigs/ gang slob pa de yang mi dmigs te/ rgyu de dang rkyen de dang gzhi des chad par lta bar mi 'gyur zhes gsungs so//*

222 See Roger Jackson 1993 for a translation of Gyel-tsab's commentary on this chapter and a discussion of these issues in Geluk analysis of Dharmakīrti.

223 *MAV*, 116.

224 This issue will be taken up in detail in Part II.

225 *JBy*, fol. 597.

226 Offshoots of this argument can be found in Japanese Buddhism in the writings of the thirteenth-century Zen master Dōgen, who, like Śāntarakṣita, was quite critical of this popular notion (in Dōgen's case, among corrupt Tendai monks at Mt. Hiei who utilized it to justify their laziness). They claimed that one need not practice Buddhism nor worry about being virtuous as opposed to non-virtuous because it was all an aspect of the original Buddha nature (*tathāgatagarbha*). For a discussion of Dōgen's sophisticated response to this, see Abe 1992 and Grosnick 1979. In the Indian context, according to Śāntarakṣita, it stems from a misunderstanding of Madhyamaka and the functioning of the two truths in that system.

227 *MAV,* 118: *dge ba dang mi dge ba'i las kyi rnam par smin pa sdug pa dang mi sdug pa 'byung ba dang/ dngos gang yang dag ji bzhin pa//de ni de 'dra'i rtags sems kyi/ rgyu yin*

228 *JBy*, fol. 597.

229 *MAV,* 122: *'bras bu thams cad ni rgyu'i rjes su 'gro ba dang/ ldog pa dang mthun par byed pas de rnam par dag pa dang/ rnam par ma dag pa gnyis kyis rnam par dag pa dang rnam par ma dag par 'gyur te/*

230 The text in the *gsung bum* and Sarnath versions erroneously reads *mi rung* ("unsuitable") instead of *rung* ("suitable"). Based on the context of this argument, this is clearly a typographical error.

231 *JBy*, fol. 597.

232 *MAV,* 123: *yang dag par na dngos po thams cad ni gcig dang du ma'i rang bzhin du mi 'thad pas yod pa la gnod pa'i tshad ma ni sngar bshad zin to// rig par byas ba dang rig par byed pa'i mtshan nyid dang/ yul de nyid la gnod pa'i tshad ma yang sngar bshad zin to// de lta bas na 'di yang dag par yod do zhes mngon par zhen te/ sbyin par bya ba la sogs pa dngos po thams cad la dmigs pa ni thsad ma'i gnod pa yod pa'i phyir phyin ci log yin te/ smig rgyu'i tshogs la chur shes pa bzhin no//*

233 Śāntarakṣita's argument here is reiterated on numerous occasions throughout Candrakīrti's *Madhyamakāvatāra.*

234 *MAV,* 123-124: *ji ltar phyi dang nang gi mu stegs can rnams kyis sbyin pa dang/ tshul khrims la sogs pa la nan tan byed pa/ 'jig tshogs la lta ba las byung ba ni de ma thag tu bla na med pa yang dag par rdogs pa'i byang chub kyi yan lag tu mi 'gyur te/*

235 This same point is central to Candrakīrti's message in *Madhyamakāvatāra-*

bhāṣya, where he argues that the full import of the perfections is not realized by a being who does not have a direct realization of emptiness.

236 *JBy*, fols. 597-598.

237 I don't think that this necessarily undermines the utility found in the way Geluk doxographers who rely primarily on the standard definitions present Śāntarakṣita's ideas. For them, the ideas are used primarily in a dialectical process aimed towards a clear exposition of their own tenets.

238 *MAV,* 127: *rang gi rig pa yang kun rdzob kyi bden par gtogs pa nyid de gcig dang du ma'i rang bzhin du brtag mi bzod pa'i phyir ro zhes bya bas gtan la phab zin to//*

239 *JB*y, fol. 598.

240 *MAV,* 129: *Lang kar gshegs pa las/ phyi rol gzugs ni yod ma yin// rang gi sems ni phyi rol snang//zhes bstan pa 'di yang legs par bshad pa yin no snyam du sems so// blo'i mthu mi chung ba dang lhag par mngon du brtson pa dag gis kyang sems de la gcig dang du ma'i rnag bzhin du brtags na/ don dam par snying po mi mthosng bas/ yang dag par 'dod pa ma yin no// de'i phyir*

241 *MAV,* 129-130*: sems tsam gyi sthul la brten nas/ mtshungs par ldan pa dang bcas pa'i sems las phyi rol du 'dod pa bdag dang bdag gi dpe/ gzung ba dang 'dzin pa la sogs pa rang bzhin med par tsegs med pa kho nar rtogs so// tshul 'di ni rang 'byung ba med pas sems de rang bzhin med par rtogs su zin kyang/ mtha' thams cad spangs pa dbu ma'i lam las 'di rtogs na/ gcig dang du ma'i rang bzhin dang bral bas rang bzhin med par shin tu rtogs so//*

242 *JBy*, fol. 598.

243 For an in-depth discussion of the implications of this stanza with regard to the path system, see Part II of this study.

244 *MAV,* 143-144: *zla ba'i 'od zer ltar dag pa gang zag dang chos la bdag med pa'i rang zhin nyi tshe ba ma yin pa'i bdud rtsi 'di ni skyob pa shin tu gsol te/ des na rnam pa thams cad kyi mchog dang ldan pa'i shes rab dang/ thugs rje'i rdul phra rab 'dus pa'i sku/ nyon mongs pa dang/ shes bya'i sgrib pa phung po ma lus pa dang bral ba/ thams cad kyi mchog 'khor ba ji srid bar bzhugs so// 'di ltar de ni bdag med pa dang po rtogs pas blo rnam par dag pa nyan thos dang/ rang sangs rgyas rnams kyis yang ma yin na/ log pa bdag tu lta ba la zhen pa lha chen po khyab 'jug dang/ tsangs pa la sogs pa'i sa ma yin par lta ci smos//*

245 *JBy*, fols. 598-599.

246 *MAV,* 144-145: *log par bstan pa'i chos 'dul byed pa rnams dang de'i rjes su 'gro ba rnams la de kho na shes pa 'di lta bu tshol bas de kho na mchog gtan la phebs nas bde bar gshegs pa'i bstan pa snying rje'i rigs kyi kyim khas len pa' skyes bu lcid kyer ba/ rtogs pa dang ldan pa rnams kyi snying rje chen po/ mi mthun pa'i phyogs chung ngu dang yang ma 'dres pa skye ste/ gzhan sdug bsngal dang bral bar 'dod pa ni snying rje chen po yin no// de dag gi sdug bsngal dang/ de'i rgyu rab tu 'phel na skye bar 'gyur te/ bud shing bsnan na me lce 'bar ba bzhin no./*

Notes to Part II

1 I am referring here to the major philosophical treatises of Tsong Khapa, such as the *lhag mthong* chapter of *Byang chub lam rim chen mo*, *Drang nges legs bshad snying po*, *dGongs pa rab gsal*, and Kaydrub's *sTong thun chen mo,* as well as the numerous tenet system texts (*grub mtha'*) and monastic text books (*yig cha*) which discuss Śāntarakṣita's views. I do not mean however, to give the impression that scholars from the Geluk School are by any means univocal. In fact, there are important issues on which Geluk scholars disagree and I will highlight these when they are relevant to this study. Nevertheless, with such variances noted, I think it is fair to say that there is a fairly standard Geluk presentation and understanding of Śāntarakṣita and the Yogācāra-Svātantrika-Madhyamaka School.

2 The exceptions to the portrayal in Geluk tenet system literature of a univocal Yogācāra-Svātantrika-Madhyamaka view are in the tenet system texts of Thubkan (commonly referred to as Thu'u bkwan grub mtha') and Jamyang Shayba. Both distinguish two divisions of followers of the Yogācāra-Svātantrika-Madhyamaka, "Proponents of False Images" (*rnam rdzunpa dang mthun pa*) and "Proponents of True Images" (*rnam bden pa dang mthun pa*), in correspondence with normative Geluk divisions of Yogācāras in other tenet system texts. Here Thubkan categorizes Śāntarakṣita, Kamalaśīla, and Ārya Vimuktisena as "Proponents of True Images" and Haribhadra, Jetāri, and Lavapa as "Proponents of False Images"; he does not mention Śrigupta. *Thu'u bkwan grub mtha'*, 25-26. Jamyang Shayba categorizes them in the same way except that he does not mention Lavapa and adds Kambala as a Proponent of False Images.

3 An additional issue which I will not discuss here in detail beyond the treatment of this issue in Part I is the question of external objects. Certainly Gelukpas would have a problem with the fact that Śāntarakṣita rejects the existence of external objects conventionally. I am not addressing this problem extensively in this section of the book because the Geluk criticism of the rejection of external objects is aimed at the stance as it has been put forth by Yogācāra tenet holders, whose view seems to differ in significant ways from Śāntarakṣita's way of rejecting external objects. For Yogācāras, it is explicitly a rejection of the ultimate existence of external objects. For Śāntarakṣita, it is a rejection of external objects conventionally (and ultimately). Additionally, Gelukpas target the Yogācāra Followers of Scripture such as Asaṅga and Vasubandhu who assert a "mind-basis-of-all" (*ālayavijñāna, kun gzhi rnam shes*) which is the cause of all perceptions of objects, and that those perceptions occur simultaneously with the arising of the objects. Śāntarakṣita does not accept the mind-basis-of-all. There are a number of additional issues regarding external objects which are elaborated upon in detail by Yogācāras which are not taken up by Śāntarakṣita, and thus the worth of examining the Geluk critiques of the Yogācāra rejections of external objects in the context of their understanding of Śāntarakṣita is highly questionable.

4 Cabezón 1990, 8.

5 This is not to suggest that the authors of the major treatises, such as Tsong Khapa

and Kaydrub, did not rely on the primary Indian sources. This is only to suggest that later Geluk readers tend not to follow that example but rely instead primarily on tenet system texts and monastic textbooks for their understanding of Śāntarakṣita's views, secondarily on the great treatises of Tsong Khapa, etc., and thirdly on the actual Indian texts themselves, if at all. In discussing doxography in general in the Geluk tradition of *grub-mtha'* and its fourfold classification model of Indian Buddhist "schools" of philosophy, Jeffrey Hopkins writes, "In Tibet, students are taught this fourfold classification first, without mention of the diversity of opinion that it conceals. Then, over decades of study, students gradually recognize the structure of such presentations of schools of thought as a technique for gaining access to a vast store of opinion, as a way to focus on topics crucial to authors within Indian Buddhism. The task of then distinguishing between what is clearly said in the Indian texts and what is interpretation and interpolation over centuries of commentary becomes a fascinating enterprise for the more hardy among Tibetan scholars." Hopkins 1996, 176.

6 Thurman 1978, 20.

7 We see this in China in the various Pan-C'iao systems which emerged to help contextualize variances in Indian Buddhist doctrines.

8 Tsong Khapa, *LRCh* (Sarnath, 1993: 568). All further citations for *LRCh* refer to the Sarnath edition. Translated in Napper 1989, 159: *de kho na nyid rtogs par 'dod pa rnams kyis ni rgyal ba'i gsung rab la brten dgos la/ gsung rab kyang gdul bya sna tshogs kyi bsam pa'i dbang gis sna tshogs pa yin pas na ji 'dra ba zhig la brten nas zab mo'i don btsal bar bya snyam na/ nges pa'i don gyi gsungs rab la brten nas de kho na nyid rtogs par bya dgos so// 'o na ji 'dra ba zhig nges don dang ji 'dra ba zhig drang don yin snyam na/ 'di ni brjod bya'i sgo nas gzhag ste/ don dam pa ston pa ni nges pa'i don dang kun rdzob ston pa ni drang ba'i don kyi gsung rab tu gzung ngo//*

9 Ibid., 161: *dbU ma snang ba las kyang/ de lta bas na don dam pa brjod pa kho na nges pa'i don yin la/ ldog pa ni drang ba'i don yin no zhes bya bar khong du chud par bya'o//*

10 Jang-gya makes a similar claim about their position on interpretable and definitive scriptures when he says in *Grub pa'i mtha'i rnam par bshag pa gsal bar bshad pa thub bstan lhun po'i mdzes rgya,* "Also, with respect to the middle wheel [sutras], those passages that explicitly or implicitly affix the qualification 'ultimately' to the object of negation are asserted to be literal and definitive. In those [middle wheel] sutras, those which teach with [statements] such as 'Form does not exist,' without clearly affixing the qualification 'ultimately' or 'truly' are asserted to be interpretable and not suitable to be taken literally. These should be known in detail from Tsong-kha-pa's *Essence of the Good Explanations.*" Lopez 1987, 382.

11 *LRCh*, 570: *dbU ma snang ba las/ nges pa'i don yang gang la bya zhe na/ tshad ma dang bcas pa dang don dam pa'i dbang du mdzad nas bshad pa gang yin pa ste/ de ni de las logs shig tu gzhan gis gang du'ng drang bar mi nus pa'i phyir ro// zhes so// de ltar gsungs pa'i shugs kyis ni drang ba'i don shes par nus te/ 'di'i don ji ltar bstan pa ltar gzung du mi rung bar dgongs pa bshad nas don*

gshan la drang dgos pa'm/ sgra ji zhin par bzung bas chog kyang de tsam zhig ni mthar thug pa'i de kho na nyid ma yin gyi/ de las gzhan du da dung de'i de kho na nyid btsal dgos bas na drang ba'i don nam don drang dgos pa'o//

12 A detailed study of Kamalaśīla's *Madhyamakāloka*, which has yet to be undertaken, would be an important contribution to the modern study of the history of Buddhist thought.

13 Without any pejorative connotation intended, I will use the term "Hīnayāna arhats" as a taxonomic device interchangeably with *śrāvakas* and *pratyekabuddhas*. I think that the term "Hīnayāna" is used more in the abstract in Mahāyāna discourse to help illuminate their own positions by contrast. It would be difficult to find actual Buddhists in history for whom all the nuanced meanings of the term would aptly apply.

14 As mentioned above, it is not appropriate to simply assume that because Kamalaśīla was Śāntarakṣita's disciple they share all views. However, careful examination of *MAP* and *TSP* indicates that at least in those texts commenting directly on Śāntarakṣita's own writings, Kamalaśīla demonstrates a real faithfulness to Śāntarakṣita's positions. Students however do diverge from their teachers, as Śāntarakṣita did from his teacher Jñānagarbha, and it would not be wise in an historical analysis of Indian ideas to uncritically accept all of Kamalaśīla's writings and positions to be those of Śāntarakṣita as well, as we saw in our discussion of hermeneutics above. However, since it is likely that Kamalaśīla's commentaries were composed in close proximity to Śāntarakṣita, and given the apparent faithfulness of the commentaries to the primary texts, it can critically be assumed that Kamalaśīla's commentaries *MAP* and *TSP* represent further clarification of the positions of Śāntarakṣita. We will not however consider the independent treatises of Kamalaśīla such as the three *Bhāvanākramas* and the *Madhyamakāloka.* We will also not consider Haribhadra's commentaries on *ASA,* which may have more of a bearing on the Geluk presentation of the standard Yogācāra-Svātantrika-Madhyamaka positions on the path system. We are concerned here specifically with the views of Śāntarakṣita.

15 Ichigō 1985, 341-342.

16 Nakamura 1980, 283.

17 Kaydrub has argued that *ASA* was written from a Prāsaṅgika-Madhyamaka perspective, but his view is an exception to the mainstream Geluk position on the subject.

18 I use this term in the most general and broad senses as William James (1901) and Abraham Maslow (1970) have applied the term.

19 According to the Geluk presentation of the Yogācāra-Svātantrika-Madhyamaka position, there is a distinction between the grosser grasping at a self-sufficient substantially existent person, which is a disturbing emotion obstacle abandoned before the attainment of arhatship, and the more subtle grasping at the true establishment of persons (*gang zag gyi bden par grub pa'i 'dzin pa*) which is a knowledge obstacle abandoned at a later stage. Thus, in the Geluk presentation,

the Yogācāra-Svātantrika-Mādhyamikas describe a more subtle selflessness of persons than their Hīnayāna counterparts. This more subtle selflessness of persons is described in the context of the lack of true existence of phenomena, which is a key ontological distinguishing factor between Mādhyamikas and their Hīnayāna counterparts. On this level, the emptiness of a truly existent person is the same as the emptiness of truly existent phenomena. See also n. 21 below for further definitions.

20 The term "grasping" (*'dzin*) is key and will be important to the Geluk critique.

21 The grasping at true establishment of persons (*gang zag gyi bden par grub pa'i 'dzin pa*), which is considered to be a knowledge obstacle in this system, relates more precisely to the grasping at the true establishment of the aggregates as opposed to the more gross grasping at the self-sufficient substantially existent person which is categorized as a mere disturbing emotion obstacle.

22 *LRCh*, 766: *dbu ma ba gzhan gyis chos kyi bdag 'dzin du bzhed pa slob dpon 'dis nyon mongs can gri ma rig par bzhed pa.*

23 Tsong-kha-pa-blo-bzang-grags-pa, *Drang ba dang nges pa'i don rnam par phye ba'i bstan bcos legs bshad snying po.* Bylakuppee: Sera-Mey Computer Project Center Books, 176-179.

24 As mentioned above, there are differing opinions among Geluk monastic college textbook authors on the exact status of these mistaken appearances. For example, Jetsun Chökyi Gyeltsen argues that these mistaken appearances are subtle, latent karmic propensities (*bag chags, vāsanā*) from previous *kleśas* resulting from earlier karmic acts. He says that the bodhisattva at this stage knows that the objects appearing in this way are not real in the same way that one knows that the illusions a magician produces are not real although they appear as real. Thus they do not grasp at these. Jamyang Shayba argues that they are moments of consciousnesses, not latent karmic propensities from previous *kleśas*. Jetsun Chökyi Gyeltsen adds for clarification's sake that this appearance is not established by way of its own characteristics (*rang gi tshan nyid kyis grub, svalakṣaṇasiddhi*) because it only appears from the side of the latent propensity and not from the side of the object. For Jetsun Chökyi Gyeltsen, both the propensity, which is the cause, and the appearance, which is the result, are knowledge obstacles which need to be abandoned. These subtle stains or propensities, which are knowledge obstacles, are contrasted with the grosser seeds (*sa bon, bīja*), which are disturbing emotion obstacles.

25 This subject is also treated extensively by Kaydrub in his *sTong thun chen mo*. See José Cabezón's translation of this section of Kaydrub's text in Cabezón 1992, 201-256.

26 *LRCh*, 766-768.

27 Since Śāntarakṣita does not clearly present his stance on many path system issues comprehensively or in any one place in an orderly presentation, we have to find statements throughout his works and piece them together to draw out his positions. The issue of omniscience is addressed in detail in *TS* and *TSP* and we can

derive useful information there, but detailed information about the particular issues of concern to us here are a bit more oblique.

28 One might also ask Tsong Khapa why they do not purify these knowledge obstacles and attain Buddhahood regardless since they are Mahāyānists with the great compassion of bodhisattvas and would presumably accrue the ensuing merit.

29 *MAV*, 19: *yang dag par na rang bzhin med par rtogs na nyon mongs pa dang// shes bya'i sgrib pa mtha' dag spong bar 'gyur te//*

30 *TS*, 3337: *ātmātmīyagrahakṛtaḥ snehaḥ saṃskāragocaraḥ/ hetur virodhi nairātymadarsanaṃ tasya bādhakam//*

31 It is interesting to note that when Gyel-tsab comments on this verse in *JBy*, we see perhaps the early roots of the Geluk presentation of some of Śāntarakṣita's views. He seems at first to simply restate the stanzas in the form of autonomous inferences for the purpose of clarifying and/or illuminating Śāntarakṣita's positions. This, however, does not seem to be all that is going on upon further analysis. For example, he comments on the above stanza as follows: *byang sems 'phags pa chos can/ bden 'dzin gyi rgyu las byung ba'i nyon mongs sgrim mi dgos par spong bar 'gyur te/ stong nyid mthong zin goms par byed pa'i phyir//* "*Ārya* bodhisattvas, the subject, abandon afflictive emotions which arise from the cause of grasping at true existence without [much] effort because they are accustomed to emptiness that is already seen." Two subtle, yet significant changes occur here in Gyel-tsab's restatement of the position. "Masters who know the selflessness of phenomena" has been changed to "*ārya* bodhisattvas." This is significant because Gyel-tsab seems to want to make clear that for Yogācāra-Svātantrika-Mādhyamikas like Śāntarakṣita only *ārya* bodhisattvas could have realized the selflessness of phenomena and not *ārya śrāvakas* or *pratyekabuddhas*. It is not so clear that Śāntarakṣita is concerned about this, but it is one of the key points for Gyel-tsab in distinguishing the Yogācāra-Svātantrika-Madhyamaka view from the Prāsaṅgika-Madhyamaka view. The other change made is that "lack of inherent existence" is changed to "emptiness". This again seems like a slight change but has great significance regarding the way Gelukpas explain the Yogācāra-Svātantrika-Madhyamaka views concerning the two truths. Gelukpas argue that Yogācāra-Svātantrika-Mādhyamikas accept inherent existence, at least conventionally, although its main proponents such as Śāntarakṣita never explicitly make such a claim.

32 *MAV*, 143-144: *zla ba'i 'od zer ltar dag pa gang zag dang chos la bdag med pa'i rang zhin nyi tshe ba ma yin pa'i bdud rtsi 'di ni skyob pa shin tu gsol te/ des na rnam pa thams cad kyi mchog dang ldan pa'i shes rab dang/ thugs rje'i rdul phra rab 'dus pa'i sku/ nyong mongs pa dang/ shes bya'i sgrib pa phung po ma lus pa dang bral ba/ thams cad kyi mchog 'khor ba ji srid bar bzhugs so// 'di ltar de ni bdag med pa dang po rtogs pas blo rnam par dag pa nyan thos dang/ rang sangs rgyas rnams kyis yang ma yin na/ log pa bdag tu lta ba la zhen pa lha chen po khyab 'jug dang/ tsangs pa la sogs pa'i sa ma yin par lta ci smos//*

33 Tsong Khapa dedicates a significant portion of his commentary on *MA*, *ZBr*, to

a discussion of proper forms of inference and debate. This portion is structured as a simple presentation of Śāntarakṣita's positions on issues concerning inferences, particularly the issue of non-existent subjects or unestablished bases (*gzhi ma grub, āśrayāsiddha*). In his presentation, Tsong Khapa relies primarily on the positions put forth by Kamalaśīla in his *Madhyamakāloka* rather that on positions actually put forth by Śāntarakṣita in *MA*, the text upon which he is ostensibly commenting. In fact Tsong Khapa points out a difference in the positions put forth by Kamalaśīla in the *MAP* and those in the *Madhyamakāloka* and ponders as to whether the positions stated in the *MAP,* which ostensibly would be closest to Śāntarakṣita's own views, were not in fact a reflection of Kamalaśīla during an immature stage of his thinking. The specific issue concerns when consequentialist arguments (*thal 'gyur, prasaṅga*) or autonomous inferences (*rang rgyud kyi rjes dpag, svatantrānumāna*) ought to be utilized in refuting opponents from Buddhist and non-Buddhist schools. In the *MAP*, Kamalaśīla says that for unestablished bases such as the *ātman* or *Prakṛti,* consequentialist arguments ought to be utilized. However, in the context of the neither-one-nor-many argument and the refutation of positions of lower Buddhist schools, one can use autonomous inferences. In the *Madhyamakāloka* he says that it is suitable to use autonomous inferences for both, and this is the position which is considered to be aligned with that of Śāntarakṣita. This is curious since it is the *MAP* which is a commentary on Śāntarakṣita's own text and thus the one which one would assume would present those ideas which are closest to Śāntarakṣṇta's own ideas.

34 See for example Hopkins 1983, 431-538.

35 Jeffrey Hopkins (1989) points out that Tsong Khapa shifts his interpretation of the critique of using autonomous inferences slightly between *LRCh* and *LSN.*

36 See Yotsuya 1999.

37 Tsong Khapa outlines what are referred to as the eight unique tenets of the Prasaṅgika-Madhyamaka view in this short text.

38 See Cabezón 1988 and 1992 and McClintock 2003 for a treatment of Kaydrub's presentation of the issue. The Geluk criticism of the use of autonomous inferences is found throughout their philosophical literature, but those mentioned above are the primary sources for the later Geluk secondary sources such as monastic text books.

39 Yotsuya 1999, 27.

40 When I questioned several eminent Geluk scholars about the fact that Śāntarakṣita never says that entities inherently exist or exist from their own side, even conventionally, they all replied that Śāntarakṣita must accept this if he wants to use autonomous inferences.

41 McClintock, 2003.

42 Kaydrub, *TTC*. Translated in Cabezón 1988, 221.

43 Cabezón 1988, 222.

44 Ibid.

45 Śāntarakṣita writes in *MAV*, 19-20, "Therefore always exert great effort toward realizing the lack of inherent nature in all phenomena by use of reasoning and scriptures. With regard to that point, scriptures without inference derived from the power of cogent evidence will not completely satisfy even those disciples following entirely by faith. Thus [I] will explain [the lack of inherent nature] with inferential reasoning." *de bas na rigs pa cang lung gi[s]/ chos thams cad rang bzhin med par khong du chud par bya ba'i phyir rab tu 'bad do// de la lung dngos po'i stobs kyis zhugs pa'i rjes su dpag pa dand bral ba ni dad pas yongs su 'brang ba rnams kyang shin tu yongs su tshim par mi 'gyur bas rigs pa je brjod par bya'o//*

46 *MAV*, 108: *gal te yang chos thams cad rang bzhin med par sgrub pa'i gtan tshigs ma brjod na/ de'i tshe gtan tshigs med par mi 'grub pa'i phyir 'dod pa'i don mi 'grub bo//*

47 Ibid.

48 Negi 1993-2000, 930.

49 *MAV*, 108: *rjes su dpag pa dang rjes su dpag par bya ba'i tha snyad thams cad ni phan tshun mi mthun pas grub pa'i mthas bskyed pa chos can tha dad pa yongs su btang ste/ mkhas pa dang bud med dang byis pa'i par gyi mig dang rna ba la sogs pa'i shes pa la snang ba'i ngang can gyi phogs sgra la sogs pa'i chos can la brten nas 'jug go/*

50 Ichigō 1985. It is interesting to note that Śāntarakṣita cites his own disciple Haribhadra here.

51 Śāntarakṣita here refers to the conceptual doctrinal categories employed to generate an inferential understanding of Buddhist views as represented in the *śāstras*.

52 *MAV*, 110-111: *ji skad du/ 'dzin pa stug la mi brten na// tha snyad rab tu 'grub 'gyur la// tha snyad rnams la mkhas gyur na// bstan bcos don la rmongs pa med// ces gsungs pa lta bu'o// don dam pa'i tshul la sdang bas dbang sgyur ba gang dag 'di lta ste/ chos thams cad rang bzhin med par lta ba nyid ni med pa nyid du lta bar spyi bo nas dbang bskur ba nyid yin no zhes smra ba/*

53 McClintock 2003.

54 Ibid.

55 Ibid.

56 Several scholars, including Tillemans 1983, Lopez 1987, Cabezón 1990, Hopkins 1996, Blumenthal 2002, 2004a, and Eckel 2003, have made note of the discrepancies between Indian authors and their portrayal in Geluk doxographical literature. None however (other than myself in Blumenthal 2004a) have closely examined the philosophical workings taking place with specific regard to the issue of the two truths in the thought of Śāntarakṣita and the Geluk analysis of the so-called Yogācāra-Svātantrika-Madhyamaka.

57 An example of this can be found in Tsong Khapa's text *dbU ma dgongs pa rab gsal.* Discussions of the Svātantrika system generally rely heavily on Bhāvaviveka and Jñānagarbha for the Sautrāntika-Svātantrika-Madhyamaka and on Śāntarakṣita, Kamalaśīla, and Haribhadra for the Yogācāra-Svātantrika-Madhyamaka. In his general discussions on the topic of the object of negation (*dgag bya*) for Svātantrika-Mādhyamikas of all stripes, Tsong Khapa notes that there is not a reliable or extensive discussion of this topic in any of the Svātantrika literature other than in Kamalaśīla's *Madhayamakāloka* (*dbU ma snang ba*). Thus, he implies that the position found there could be considered representative of all so-called Svātantrika-Mādhyamikas. Tsong Khapa, *GRS* (1999:102-103). He goes on to quote Kamalaśīla extensively and explain that position. The point here is that Tsong Khapa's interpretation of Kamalaśīla's position on the object of negation is taken to be that of all Svātantrika-Mādhyamikas. And in fact others, including Śāntarakṣita, do discuss the object of negation, although perhaps not in the same depth or in a precise way which will ultimately fit as needed within the Geluk doxographical project.

58 Jeffrey Hopkins lists sixteen such terms in *Meditation on Emptiness* (Hopkins 1983, 39 and 631-632).

59 Könchog Jigme Wangpo defines a Proponent of Non-Entityness a few lines above in the same chapter as one who claims phenomena have no truly established existence. (1995: 35-36).

60 Translation adapted from Sopa and Hopkins 1989, 282. See Könchog Jigme Wangpo (1995: 36): *rang gi mtshan nyid kyis grub pa snyad du khas len pa'i ngo bo nyid med par smra ba de/ rang rgyud pa'i mtshan nyid.*

61 Tsong Khapa certainly traces the origin of this Svātantrika-Madhyamaka stance to Bhāvaviveka in *LSN*. But even his attribution of this stance to Bhāvaviveka stands on shaky ground and relies on extracting tenets Bhāvaviveka did not explicitly state, but rather are thought to have been implied by the way he criticizes Yogācāra in his *Madhyamakahṛdayakārikā*. See Eckel 2003 for a discussion of this issue in Bhāvaviveka's thought.

62 Translated in Lopez 1987, 380.

63 *MAV*, 88-93.

64 For an extensive discussion of the Geluk stance on the question of *svatantras*, see Cabezón 1988.

65 McClintock 2003.

66 Tillemans 1983, 312.

67 The term has been translated in a number of ways by various scholars and there seems to be little consensus. It has been translated variously as "self-awareness," "self-knowledge," "self-consciousness," "auto-cognition," "reflexive-consciousness," and "reflexive awareness." Among those I did not choose to use, I think that the latter two probably come closest to the actual meaning of the terms in the original languages. I chose to use the term "self-cognizing cognition" on

the recommendation of Geshe Ngawang Samten. Through personal correspondence, he pointed out that the connotation of the term is not merely that of the relatively vague term "self-awareness," but rather of a substantial consciousness which actually cognizes itself. Thus either "self-cognizing consciousness" or "self-cognizing cognition" would be appropriate translations in this context. Perhaps as Paul Williams (1998) has suggested, the term is variously used by different authors in different contexts and a variety of translations are appropriate for different situations. For the purposes of our study in the context of its use by Śāntarakṣita, I feel that "self-cognizing cognition" is the most appropriate translation equivalent.

68 See, for example, Tsong Khapa's *KNG* and *GRS*, and Jang-gya's *Grub-mtha'i rnam bzhag*. For an extensive discussion of the "unique tenets," see Cozort 1998. Therein are included relevant translations from Jang-gya, Jamyang Shayba, and Ngawang Belden.

69 "Self-knowledge" (*bdag nyid shes pa*) here is a synonym for "self-cognizing cognition" (*rang rig*).

70 See Matilal 1986b for a discussion of *svasaṃvedana* in the context of Dignāga. Dignāga and his follower Dharmakīti, both of whom are generally associated with the Yogācāra School, were very influential on the thought of Śāntarakṣita on this issue among others, although it is not clear that Dignāga and Śāntarakṣita accept self-cognizing cognition precisely in the same way.

71 Williams 1998, 25.

72 *MAV*, 39-40: *gsal bar byed pa gzhan la mi ltos par rang gsal ba'i bdag nyid ni rnam par shes pa'i rang rig pa zhes bya'o//*

73 Matilal 1986b notes that Nyāya scholars who opposed Dignāga, Dharmakīrti, and their followers on this issue of self-cognizing cognition counter this point by simply defining cognition as the ability to illuminate other objects, adding however that this does not require a quality of self-illumination.

74 Mipham has a great deal at stake here in his attempts at defending the notion of self-cognizing cognition because it is an important part of a philosophical standpoint which can serve as the basis of Dzogchen. For a detailed treatment of this subject see Williams 1998, xi-xix.

75 Śāntideva 1997, 119.

76 Ibid., 118. It is additionally noted by the Wallaces that, "According to the *sPyod 'jug rnam bshad rgyal sras 'jug ngog*s, the analogy here refers to an animal, such as a bear, which while sleeping is bitten and infected by a rat. Although the bear is not conscious of being poisoned at the time it is bitten, it 'recalls' this upon waking up and sensing the inflammation of the bite."

77 Huntington and Wangchen 1989, 244 n. 101.

78 Ibid., 244.

79 Translation in Cozort 1998, 439-440.

80 *MAV*, 39-40: *gsal bar byed pa gzhan la mi ltos par rang gsal ba'i bdag nyid ni rnam par shes pa'irang rig zhes bya'o//*

81 Ibid., 155-156.

82 For a detailed discussion of Śāntarakṣita and Kamalaśīla's audience, with particular reference to *TS* and *TSP*, see McClintock 2002, 27-41.

83 These would include *MA*, *MAV*, *MAP* for Śāntarakṣita and writings from the extensive Geluk catalog, including the works discussed in this study by Tsong Khapa, Kaydrub, Gyel-tsab, and the other important tenet system authors and monastic textbook authors.

84 Cabezón (1990, 8) argues that, "in the scholastic tradition of Tibetan Buddhism, especially in the literature of the dGe lugs pa sect, the *siddhānta* schematization served as a de facto canonization of Buddhist philosophy that came to define what was philosophically normative."

85 Hopkins 1996, 175.

86 See also the discussion of Kenneth Pike's distinction between emic and etic viewpoints in Lopez 1987, 27-28, in relation to the Geluk doxographical project.

87 Tillemans 1983, 312.

88 See Stearns 1999 for an extensive discussion of Dolpopa and the intellectual climate of Tibet during his time.

Notes to Part III

1 This stanza corresponds to Dharmakīrti's *Pramāṇavārttika*: 3.138.

2 It seems as though the consequentialist argument and the autonomous inference were mistakenly switched since the first argument appears to be an autonomous inference and the second a consequence.

3 An error seems to have been made in the commitment of the text to print here. Instead of referring to the line beginning with *rdul phrin,* which is the first word of the four-line, fourteenth stanza, the text erroneously refers to the four lines beginning with *pyir.* This is actually the first word of the second line of the stanza.

4 The ten forms refer here to the five sense organs and the five sense objects within the schemata of the twelve *āyatanas* elaborated upon specifically within the Vaibhāṣika system and most notably in Vasubandhu's *Abhidharmakośa.*

5 Refers to the non-Buddhist schools, particularly the Vaiśeṣika system

6 The *JBy* most likely incorrectly states that the next "six" lines pertain instead of the next "four" lines since the next reference to the *MA* in the *JBy* begins with a reference to the four lines in the root text beginning with the first line of the twentieth stanza.

7 The commentary erroneously states that "four" lines in the root text pertain to this topic, meaning just stanza 67, but actually there are two stanzas pertaining to this topic upon which Gyel-tsab comments, namely stanzas 67 and 68.

8 The edition of Gyel-tsab's text from his *Collected Works* as well as the Sarnath edition read "four," but I think that this is an error and that it should say "twelve" for several reasons. First of all, Śāntarakṣita discusses all twelve root text lines (stanzas 76-78 as opposed to just stanza 76) collectively and comments on them together in his autocommentary. Secondly, Gyel-tsab also comments on the meaning of all twelve lines together (much like Śāntarakṣita). And finally, if we are not to assume that Gyel-tsab intended to say that his following section of commentary was on the three root text stanzas consisting of twelve lines, then we would have to assume that he skipped stanzas 77 and 78 because the next stanza he identifies in his work is 79. Since he passes over no other stanzas in his commentary, it only makes sense that this "four" is a mistake and that it should read "twelve."

9 The Tibetan words are abbreviated as *bsgrub dang sgrub*, rather than *bsgrub bya dang sgrub par byed*.

10 Gyel-tsab's commentary actually says "nine," but this is probably an error because he comments specifically on the eight lines of the two stanzas which are clearly demarcated in the root text. This error is found in both the *Collected Works* and the 1976 Sarnath version, but in all likelihood the Sarnath version was simply copied uncritically from the *Collected Works*.

11 In personal correspondence, Geshe Ngawang Samten suggested that the commentary erroneously reversed *ldog* and *log* in this sentence. His view is based on the way that this argument is presented in other Mādhyamika commentaries such as *dbU ma dgongs pa rab gsal*, etc.

12 The text actually has *mi 'byung* ("do not arise"), but in personal correspondence Geshe Jigme Dawa has suggested that this is probably a mistake in printing given the context. If it were not a mistake, the text would have to say that, "true effects do not arise from true causes," but this does not really make sense in the context of the argument.

13 The text in the *Collected Works* and Sarnath editions erroneously says *mi rung* (unsuitable) instead of *rung* ("suitable"). This is clearly a typographical error, based on the context of the argument.

14 This is the printer's dedication.

Bibliography

Modern Scholarship

Abe, Masao. 1992. *A Study of Dōgen: His Philosophy and Religion*. Edited by Steven Heine. Albany: SUNY Press.

Ames, William L. 1988. "The Soteriological Purpose of Nāgārjuna's Philosophy: A Study of Chapter Twenty-three of the 'Mūla-Mādhyamikakārikās'." JIABS 11 (2): 7-20.

Blumenthal, James. 2002. "Remarks on the dGe-lugs-pa Analysis of Śāntarakṣita's Views on the Status of Hīnayāna Arhats." IIJBS 3: 33-56.

_______. 2004a. "Remarks on the dGe-lugs-pa Analysis of Śāntarakṣita's Views on the Two Truths. " In Friquegnon and Blumenthal 2004

_______. 2004b. "Multiple Provisionalities: Dynamic Aspects of Yogācāra-Madhyamaka Synthesis in the *Madhyamakālaṃkāra* of Śāntarakṣita." In Friquegnon and Blumenthal 2004.

Cabezón, José Ignacio. 1988. "The Prāsaṅgikas' Views on Logic: Tibetan dGe-lugs pa Exegesis on the Question of Svatantras." JIP 16: 217-224.

_______. 1990. "The Canonization of Philosophy and the Rhetoric of Siddhānta in Tibetan Buddhism." In *Buddha Nature: A Festschrift in Honor of Minoru Kiyota*. San Francisco: Buddhist Books International.

_______. 1992. *A Dose of Emptiness: An Annotated Translation of the sTong thun chen mo of mKhas grub dGe legs dpal bzang*. Albany: SUNY Press.

_______. 1995. " Buddhist Studies as a Discipline and the Role of Theory." JIABS 18 (2): 124-144.

Chandra, Lokesh. 1963. *Materials for a History of Tibetan Literature*. Satapitaka Series,vols. 28-30. New Delhi: International Academy of Indian Culture.

Chogdup, Thubtan. 1996. "The Development of Mādhyamika Philosophy in Tibet." In Doboom 1996.

Chimpa, Lama. 1995. " The Methodology of Translations from Classical Tibetan." In Doboom 1995.

Conze, Edward. 1973. *Buddhist Thought in India.* Ann Arbor: University of Michigan Press.

_______. 1975. *The Large Sutra on Perfect Wisdom.* Berkeley: University of California Press.

Cozort, Daniel. 1998. *The Unique Tenets of the Middle Way Consequence School.* Ithaca: Snow Lion Publications.

Dargyay, Lobsang. 1987. "Tsong-Kha-pa's Understanding of Prāsaṅgika Thought." JIABS 10 (1): 55-65.

Das, Sarat Chandra. [1902] 1993. *A Tibetan-English Dictionary.* Calcutta. Reprint, Kyoto: Rinsen Book Co.

Demiéville, Paul. 1952. *Le concile de Lhasa: une controverse sur le quiétisme entre bouddhistes de l'Inde et de la Chine au VIIIe siècle de l'ère chrétienne.* Bibliothèque de l'Institut des Hautes Études Chinoises, vol. 7. Paris: Imprimerie Nationale de France.

Doboom, Tulku, ed. 1995. *Buddhist Translations: Problems and Perspectives.* New Delhi: Manohar Publications.

_______. 1996. *Indo-Tibetan Mādhyamika Studies.* Delhi: Tibet House.

Doctor, Thomas, trans. 2004a. *Speech of Delight: Mipham's Commentary on Śāntarakṣita's* Ornament of the Middle Way. Ithaca: Snow Lion Publications.

________2004b. "Five Extraordinary Assertions: Mi pham's commentary on the Madhyamakālaṃkāra." In Friquegnon and Blumenthal 2004.

Donnelly, Paul. 1997. "A Tibetan Formulation of Mādhyamika Philosophy: A Study and Translation of Tsong-kha-pa's *Ocean of Reasoning.*" Ph.D. dissertation, University of Wisconsin.

Dreyfus, Georges B. J. 1995. "Upon Translating Philosophical Terminology." In Doboom 1995.

_______. 1997a. *Recognizing Reality: Dharmakīrti's Philosophy and Its Tibetan Interpretations.* Albany: SUNY Press.

_______. 1997b. "Tibetan Scholastic Education and the Role of Soteriology." JIABS 20 (1): 31-62.

_______. 2003. *The Sound of Two Hands Clapping: The Education of a Tibetan Buddhist Monk.* Berkeley: University of California Press.

Dreyfus, Georges and Sara McClintock, eds. 2003. *The Svātantrika-Prāsaṅgika Distinction: What Difference Does a Difference Make?* Boston: Wisdom Publications.

Dudjom Rinpoche. 1991. *The Nyingma School of Tibetan Buddhism.* Vol. 1, *The Translations*. Trans. Gyurme Dorje and Matthew Kapstein. Boston: Wisdom Publications.

Dunne, John D. 1999. "Foundations of Dharmakīrti's Philosophy: A Study of the Central Issues in His Ontology, Logic and Epistemology with Special Attention to the *Svopajñavṛtti*." Ph.D. dissertation, Harvard University.

_______. 2000. "On Essences, Goals, and Social Justice: An Exercise in Buddhist Theology." In *Buddhist Theology: Critical Reflections by Contemporary Buddhist Scholars*, edited by Roger Jackson and John Makransky. Surrey: Curzon Press.

Eckel, M.D. 1980. "A Question of Nihilism: Bhāvaviveka's Response to the Fundamental Problems of Mādhyamika Philosophy." Ph.D. dissertation, Harvard University.

_______. 1986a. "The Concept of Reason in Jñānagarbha's Svātantrika Madhyamaka." In *Studies In Indian Logic and Epistemology*, edited by B.K. Matilal and R.D. Evans. Dordrecht: D Reidel Publishing Company.

_______. 1986b."Bhāvaviveka's Critique of the Yogācāra Philosophy in Chapter XXV of the Prajñāpradīpa." In *Miscellanea Buddhica,* Indiske Studier 5. Copenhagen: Akademisk Forlag.

_______. 1987. *Jñānagarbha's Commentary on the Distinction between the Two Truths*. Albany: SUNY Press.

_______. 1992. *To See the Buddha: A Philosopher's Quest for the Meaning of Emptiness*. San Francisco: Harper.

_______. 2003. "The Satisfaction of No Analysis: On Tsong-kha-pa's Approach to Svātantrika-Madhyamaka." In Dreyfus and McClintock 2003.

Frauwallner, Erich. 1961. "Landmarks in the History of Indian Logic." WZKSO 5: 125-148.

Friquegnon, Marie-Louise. 2001. *On Shantarakshita*. Belmont: Wadsworth.

Friquegnon, Marie-Louise and James Blumenthal, eds. 2004. *Contributions to the Study of the Thought of Śāntarakṣita.* Binghamton, N.Y.: Global Scholarly Publications.

Funayama, Toru. 1992. *A Study of* kapanāpoḍha*: A Translation of "Tattvasaṃgraha" vv. 1212-1263 by Śāntarakṣita and the "Tattvasaṃgrahapañjikā" by Kamalaśīla on the Definition of Direct Perception*. Kyoto: Ainbun: Annals of the Institute for Research In Humanities, Kyoto University.

_______. 1995. "Arcaṭa, Śāntarakṣita, Jinendrabuddhi, and Kamalaśīla on the Aim of a Treatise (*prayojana*)." *WZKS* 39: 181-201.

Garfield, Jay. 1995. *The Fundamental Wisdom of the Middle Way: Nāgārjuna's Mūlamadhyamakakārikā.* New York: Oxford University Press.

_______. 2002. *Empty Words: Buddhist Philosophy and Cross-Cultural Interpretation.* New York: Oxford University Press.

Griffiths, Paul J. 1981. "Buddhist Hybrid English: Some Notes on Philology and Hermeneutics for Buddhologists." JIABS 4 (2): 9-25.

Grosnick, William Henry. 1979. "The Zen Master Dōgen's Understanding of the Buddha-Nature in Light of the Historical Development of the Buddha-Nature Concept in India, China, and Japan." Ph.D. dissertation, University of Wisconsin.

Gyamtso Rinpoche, Khenpo Tsultrim. 2001. *Progressive Stages of Meditation on Emptiness*. Auckland: Zhyisil Chokyi Ghatsal Publications.

Gyatso, Tenzin, Dalai Lama XIV. 1988. *The Dalai Lama at Harvard*. Trans. Jeffrey Hopkins. Ithaca: Snow Lion Publications.

_______. 2001. *Stages of Meditation*. Trans. by Ven. Geshe Lobsang Jordhen, Losang Choephel Ganchenpa, and Jeremy Russell. Ithaca: Snow Lion Publications.

Hopkins, Jeffrey. 1983. *Meditation on Emptiness*. London: Wisdom Publications.

_______. 1989. "A Tibetan Delineation of a Different View of Emptiness in the Indian Middle Way School." TJ 14 (1): 10-43.

_______. 1992. "A Tibetan Perspective on the Nature of Spiritual Experience." In *Paths To Liberation: The Mārga and Its Transformations in Buddhist Thought,* edited by Robert E. Buswell, Jr. and Robert M. Gimello. Honolulu: University of Hawaii Press.

_______. 1996. "The Tibetan Genre of Doxography: Structuring a Worldview." In *Tibetan Literature: Studies in Genre,* edited by José Ignacio Cabezón and Roger R. Jackson. Ithaca: Snow Lion Publications.

_______. 1999. *Emptiness in the Mind-Only School of Buddhism. Dynamic Responses to Dzong-ka-ba's* The Essence of Eloquence, vol. 1. Berkeley: University of California Press.

_______. 2002. *Reflections on Reality: The Three Natures and Non-Natures in the Mind-Only School. Dynamic Responses to Dzong-ka-ba's* The Essence of Eloquence, vol. 2. Berkeley: University of California Press.

Huntington, C.W., Jr. 1983. "The System of the Two Truths in the *Prasannapadā* and the *Mādhyamikāvatāra*: A Synopsis of Mādhyamika Soteriology." JIP 11: 77-106.

Huntington, C.W., Jr. with Geshe Namgyal Wangchen. 1989. *The Emptiness of Emptiness: An Introduction to Early Indian Madhyamika*. Honolulu: University of Hawaii Press.

Ichigō, Masamichi. 1972. "A Synopsis of the *Madhyamakālaṃkāra* of Śāntarakṣita." JIBS 20: 989-995.

_______. 1985. *Madhyamakālaṃkāra of Śāntarakṣita with His Own Commentary or Vṛtti and with the Subcommentary or Pañjikā of Kamalaśīla*. Kyoto: Buneido.

_______. 1989. "Śāntarakṣita's Madhyamakālaṃkāra." In *Studies in the Literature of the Great Vehicle*, edited by Luis O. Gómez and Jonathan A. Silk. Ann Arbor: Collegiate Institue for the Study of Buddhist Literature and Center for South and Southeast Asian Studies, The University of Michigan.

Iida, Shotaro. 1973. "The Nature of Saṁvṛti and the Relationship of Paramārtha to It in Svātantrika-Mādhyamika." In *The Problem of Two Truths in Buddhism and Vedānta*, edited by Mervyn Sprung. Dordrecht, Holland: D. Reidel Publishing Company, Inc..

Iida, Shotaro and Jay Hirabayashi. 1977. " Another Look at the Mādhyamika vs. Yogācāra Controversy Concerning Existence and Non-existence." In *Prajnaparamita and Related Systems: Studies in Honor of Edward Conze*, edited by Lewis Lancaster. Berkeley: Berkeley Buddhist Studies Series.

Jackson, David. 1986. "A Recent Study of Śāntarakṣita's Madhyamakālaṃkāra." *Berliner Indologische Studien*, Band 2.

_______. 1990. "The Earliest Printings of Tsong-kha-pa's Works: The Old dGa'ldan Editions." In *Reflections on Tibetan Culture: Essays in Memory of Turrell V. Wylie*. Lewiston, NY: The Edwin Mellen Press.

Jackson, Roger R. 1993. *Is Enlightenment Possible?: Dharmakīrti and rGyal tshab rje on Knowledge, Rebirth, No-Self and Liberation.* Ithaca: Snow Lion Publications.

Jaini, Padmanabh S. 1979. *The Jaina Path of Purification.* Berkeley: University of California Press.

_______. 1992. "On the Ignorance of the Arhat" In *Paths To Liberation: The Mārga and Its Transformations in Buddhist Thought,* edited by Robert E. Buswell, Jr. and Robert M. Gimello. Honolulu: University of Hawaii Press.

James, William. [1901] 1961. *The Varieties of Religious Experience*. London: Collier Macmillan Publishers.

Jha, Ganganatha. 1986. *The Tattvasaṅgraha of Shāntarakṣita with the Commentary of Kamalashīla.* 2 vols. Reprint, Delhi: Motilal Banarsidass.

Jinpa, Thupten. 1998. "Delineating Reason's Scope for Negation: Tsongkhapa's Contribution to Madhyamaka's Dialectical Method." JIP 26: 275-308.

_______. 2002. *Self, Reality, and Reason in Tibetan Philosophy: Tsongkhapa's Quest for the Middle Way.* London: RoutledgeCurzon.

Kajiyama, Yuichi. 1957. "Introduction to the Logic of Svātantrika-Mādhyamika." *Nava-Nalanda Mahavihara Research Publication*, 1: 291-331.

_______. 1978. "Later Mādhyamikas on Epistemology and Meditation." In *Mahāyāna Buddhist Meditation: Theory and Practice*, edited by Minoru Kiyota. Honolulu: University of Hawaii Press.

Kalupahana, David J. 1986. *Nāgārjuna: The Philosophy of the Middle Way*. Albany: SUNY Press.

Kapstein, Matthew. 1988. " Mi-pham's Theory of Interpretation." In Lopez 1988a.

_______.2000a. *The Tibetan Assimilation of Buddhism: Conversion, Contestation, and Memory*. New York: Oxford University Press.

_______. 2000b. "We are all Gzhan stong pas – Reflections on *The Reflexive Nature of Awareness: A Tibetan Madhyamaka Defence*." JBE 7: 102-125.

_______. 2001. "Śāntarakṣita on the Fallacies of Personalistic Vitalism." In Matthew Kapstein, *Reason's Traces: Identity and Interpretation in Indian and Tibetan Buddhist Thought*. Boston: Wisdom Publications.

Keenan, John. 1989. "Asaṅga's Understanding of Mādhyamika: Notes on the Shung-chung-lun." JIABS 12 (1): 93-107.

Klein, Anne. 1994. *The Path to the Middle: Oral Mādhyamika Philosophy in Tibet: The Spoken Scholarship of Kensur Yeshey Tupden*. Albany: SUNY Press.

_______. 1998. *Knowledge and Liberation: Tibetan Buddhist Epistemology in Support of Transformative Religious Experience*. Ithaca: Snow Lion Publications.

Krasser, Helmut. 1992. "On the Relationship between Dharmottara, Śāntarakṣita, and Kamalaśīla." In *Tibetan Studies. Proceedings of the 5th Seminar of the International Association of Tibetan Studies*, edited by S. Ihara and Z. Yamaguchi. Narita: Naritasan Shinshoji.

La Vallée Poussin, Louis de. 1971. *L'Abhidharmakośa de Vasubandhu*. 6 vols. Bruxelles: Institut Belge des Hautes Études Chinoises.

Lamotte, E. 1988a. *History of Indian Buddhism: From the Origins to the Śaka Era*. Paris: Peeters Press.

_______. 1988b. "Assessment of Textual Interpretation in Buddhism." In Lopez 1988a.

Lang, Karen Christina. 1990. "sPa-tshab nyi-ma grags and the Introduction of Prāsaṅgika- Madhyamaka into Tibet." In *Reflections on Tibetan Culture: Essays in Memory of Turrell V. Wylie*. Lewiston, NY: The Edwin Mellen Press.

Lindtner, C. 1981. "Atiśa's Introduction to the Two Truths, and Its Sources." JIP 9: 161-214.

_______. 1987. *Nagarjuniana: Studies in the Writings and Philosophy of Nāgārjuna*. Delhi: Motilal Banarasidass.

Lipman, K. 1979. "A Study of Śāntarakṣita's *Mādhyamikalaṃkāra*." Ph.D. dissertation, University of Saskatchewan.

Lopez, Donald S. 1987. *A Study of Svātantrika*. Ithaca: Snow Lion Publications.

_______. 1988b. "Do *Śrāvakas* Understand Emptiness?" JIP 16: 65-105.

_______. 1995. "Foreigner at the Lama's Feet." In *Curators of the Buddha: The Study of Buddhism under Colonialism,* edited by Donald Lopez. Chicago: University of Chicago Press.

_______. 1996. "Polemic Literature (*dGag lan*)." In *Tibetan Literature: Studies in Genre*, edited by José Ignacio Cabezón and Roger R. Jackson. Ithaca: Snow Lion Publications.

_______, ed. 1988a. *Buddhist Hermeneutics*. Honolulu: University of Hawaii Press.

MacDonald, Anne Elizabeth. 1988. "bLo gsal grub mtha." M.A. thesis, University of British Columbia.

Magee, William. 2000. *The Nature of Things*. Ithaca: Snow Lion Publications.

Makransky, John. 1997. *Buddhahood Embodied: Sources of Controversy in India and Tibet.* Albany: SUNY Press.

Maslow, Abraham H. 1970. *Religions, Values, and Peak Experiences*. Dallas, PA: Penguin Books.

Matilal, Bimal K. 1986a. "Buddhist Logic and Epistemology." In *Buddhist Logic and Epistemology,* edited by B.K. Matilal and Robert Evans. Dordrecht: D. Reidel.

_______. 1986b. "Sva-samvedana: Self Awareness." In *A Net Cast Wide: Investigations into Indian Thought in Memory of David Friedman*, edited by Julius J. Lipner and Dermott Killingly. Newcastle upon Tyne: Grevatt and Grevatt, 1986.

_______. 1986c. *Perception: An Essay on Classical Indian Theories of Knowledge.* Oxford: Oxford University Press.

McClintock, Sara Louise. 2000. "Knowing All through Knowing One: Mystical Communion or Logical Trick in the *Tattvasaṃgraha* and *Tattvasaṃgrahapañjikā.*" JIABS 23 (2): 225-244.

_______. 2002. "Omniscience and the Rhetoric of Reason in the *Tattvasaṃgraha* and *Tattvasaṃgrahapañjikā.*" Ph.D. dissertation, Harvard University.

_______. 2003. "The Role of the 'Given' in the Classification of Śāntarakṣita and Kamalaśīla as Svātantrika-Mādhyamikas." In Dreyfus and McClintock 2003.

Mimaki, Katsumi. 1977. "Le Grub mtha'rnam bźag rin chen phreṅ ba de dKon mchog 'jigs med dbaṅ po (1728-1791)." Kyoto: *Zinbun (Memoirs of the Research Institute for Humanistic Studies, Kyoto University)* 14: 55-112.

_______. 1982. *bLo gsal grub mtha': Chapitres IX (Vaibhāṣika) et XI (Yogācāra) edites, Chapitre XII (Mādhyamika)edite et traduit*. Kyoto: Zinbun Kagaku Kenkyūsyo (Institute for Research in the Humanities, Kyoto University).

_______. 1983. "The *bLo gsal grub mtha'* and the Mādhyamika Classification in Tibetan *grub mtha'* Literature." In Steinkellner and Tauscher 1983.

Monier-Williams, Monier. [1889] 1986. *A Sanskrit-English Dictionary*. Oxford: Clarendon Press. Reprint, Tokyo: Meicho Fukyukai Co., Ltd.

Moriyama, Seitetsu. 1984a. *An Annotated Translation of Kamalaśīla's "Sarvadharmaniḥsvabhāvasiddhi."* Part IV. Berkeley: Department of Oriental Languages, University of California, Berkeley.

_______. 1984b. "Kamalaśīla's and Haribhadra's Refutation of the Satyākāra and Alīkākāra-vādins of the Yogācāra School, Part I: A Translation of a Portion of Haribhadra's *Abhisamayālaṁkārālokā Prajñāpāramitāvyākhyā*." In *Memoirs of the Postgraduate Research Institute Bukkyo University*, No. 12.

_______. 1984c. "Kamalaśīla's and Haribhadra's Refutation of the Satyākāra and Alīkākāra-vādins of the Yogācāra School, Part II." In Tsuboi Shunei hakase koki-kinen-ronshū *Bukkyō bunka ronkō*.

_______. 1984d. "Kamalaśīla's and Haribhadra's Refutation of the Satyākāra and Alīkākāra-vādins of the Yogācāra School, Part III." In *Journal of Humanistic Studies* (Jimbungaku-Ronshū) 18.

_______. 1991. "The Later Mādhyamika and Dharmakīrti." In *Studies in the Buddhist Epistemological Tradition*, edited by E. Steinkellner. Proceedings of the Second International Dharmakīrti Conference. Vienna: Verlag der Österreichischen Akademie der Wissenschaften.

Nagao, Gadjin. 1986. *The Foundational Standpoint of Mādhyamika*. Delhi: Motilal Banarsidass.

_______. 1991. *Mādhyamika and Yogācāra*. Albany: SUNY Press.

Nakamura, Hajime. 1987. *Indian Buddhism: A Survey with Bibliographical Notes*. Delhi: Motilal Banarsidass.

Napper, Elizabeth. 1989. *Dependent Arising and Emptiness: A Tibetan Buddhist Interpretation of Mādhyamika Philosophy Emphasizing the Compatibility of Emptiness and Conventional Phenomena*. Boston: Wisdom Publications.

_______. 1995. "Styles and Principles of Translation." In Doboom 1995.

Naughton, Alex T. 1991. *Classic Mahāyāna Soteriology: An Annotated Translation of Chapters 1-7 of Haribhadra's Short Commentary on the Abhisamayālaṃkāra Sūtra, Known As Sphutārā*. Otani: Otani University Shin Buddhist Comprehensive Research Institute.

Negi, J.S., ed. 1993-2000. *Tibetan-Sanskrit Dictionary* (*Bod skad dang legs sbyar gyi tshig mdzod chen mo*). 6 vols. Sarnath, Varanasi: Central Institute of Higher Tibetan Studies.

Newland, Guy. 1983. *The Two Truths*. Ithaca: Snow Lion Publications.

_______. 1996. "Debate Manuals (*Yig cha*) in dGe-lugs Monastic Colleges." In *Tibetan Literature: Studies in Genre,* edited by José Cabezón and Roger R. Jackson. Ithaca: Snow Lion Publications.

Patt, David. 1993. "Elucidating the Path to Liberation: A Study of the Commentary on the Abhidharmakośa by the First Dalai Lama." Ph.D. dissertation, University of Wisconsin. 1993.

Pike, Kenneth. 1967. *Language in Relation to a Unified Theory of the Structure of Human Behavior.* The Hague: Mouton and Co.

Pollack, Sheldon. 1985. "The Theory of Practice and the Practice of Theory in Indian Intellectual History." JAOS 105: 499-515.

_______. 1989a. "The Idea of *Śāstra* in Traditional India." In *Shastric Traditions in Indian Arts*, edited by A.L. Dallapiccola. Stuttgart: Franz Steiner Verlag.

_______. 1989b. "Playing by the Rules: *Śāstra* and Sanskrit Literature." In *Shastric Traditions in Indian Arts*, edited by A.L. Dallapiccola. Stuttgart: Franz Steiner Verlag.

Potter, Karl. 1963. *Presuppositions of India's Philosophies*. Englewood Cliffs: Prentice Hall.

Rigzin, Tsepak. 1993. *Tibetan-English Dictionary of Buddhist Terminology.* Revised and Enlarged Edition. Dharamsala: Library of Tibetan Works and Archives.

Roerich, George N., trans. 1978. *The Blue Annals*. Delhi: Motilal Banarsidass.

Ruegg, David Seyfort. 1967. *The Study of Indian and Tibetan Thought: Some Problems and Perspectives.* Leiden: E.J. Brill.

_______. 1980. "On the Reception and Early History of the dBu-ma (Madhyamaka) in Tibet." In *Tibetan Studies in Honour of Hugh Richardson*, edited by Michael Aris and Aung San Suu Kyi. Warminster, England: Aris and Phillips Ltd.

_______. 1981a. *The Literature of the Madhyamaka School of Philosophy in India*. Wiesbaden: Otto Harrassowitz.

_______. 1981b. "Autour du *lTa ba'i khyad par* de Ye śes sde (version de Touen-houang, Pelliot Tibétain 814)." *Journal Asiatique* : 208-229.

_______. 1982. "Towards a Chronology of the Madhyamaka School." In *Indological and Buddhist Studies*, edited by L.A. Hercus et al. Canberra: Faculty of Asian Studies.

_______. 1983. " On Thesis and Assertion in the Madhyamaka/dBu ma." In Steinkellner and Tauscher 1983.

_______. 1985a. "Some Reflections on the Place of Philosophy in the Study of Buddhism." JIABS 18 (2): 145-181.

_______. 1985b. "Purport, Implicature and Presupposition: Sanskrit Abhiprāya and Tibetan dgoṅs pa/dgoṅs gzi as Hermeneutical Concepts." JIP 13: 309-325.

_______. 1991. "On Pramāṇa Theory in Tsong kha pa's Madhyamaka Philosophy." In *Studies in the Buddhist Epistemological Tradition*, edited by E. Steinkellner. Proceedings of the Second International Dharmakīrti Conference. Vienna: Verlag der Österreichischen Akademie der Wissenschaften.

_______. 1995. "On Translating Tibetan Philosophical Texts." In Doboom 1995.

_______. 2000. *Three Studies in the History of Indian and Tibetan Madhyamaka Philosophy*. Studies in Indian and Tibetan Madhayamaka Thought: Part I. WSTB 50. Vienna: Arbeitskreis für Tibetische und Buddhistische Studien Universität Wien..

Ruegg, D.S. and L. Schmithausen, eds. 1990. *Earliest Buddhism and Madhyamaka*. Leiden: E.J. Brill.

Shankara (Śaṅkara). 1947. *Shankara's "Crest Jewel of Discrimination": Timeless Teachings on Nonduality*. Trans. by Swami Prabhavanda and Christopher Isherwood. Hollywood: Vedanta Press.

Shantideva. 1997. *A Guide to the Bodhisattva's Way of Life*. Translated by Vesna A. Wallace and B. Alan Wallace. Ithaca: Snow Lion Publications.

Siderits, Mark. 1985. "Was Śāntarakṣita a 'Positivist'?" In *Buddhist Logic and Epistemology*, edited by B.K. Matilal and R.D. Evans. Dordrecht: D.Reidel.

Snellgrove, David. 1987. *Indo-Tibetan Buddhism: Indian Buddhists and Their Tibetan Successors*. 2 vols. Boston: Shambhala Publications.

Sopa, Geshe Lhundup. 1983. *Lectures on Tibetan Religious Culture*. Dharamsala: Library of Tibetan Works and Archives.

Sopa, Geshe Lhundup and J. Hopkins. 1989. *Cutting through Appearances: Theory and Practice in Tibetan Buddhism*. Ithaca: Snow Lion Publications.

Steinkellner, E.. 1990. "Is Dharmakīrti a Mādhyamika?" In Ruegg and Schmithausen 1990.

Steinkellner, E. and H. Tauscher, eds. 1983. *Contributions on Tibetan and Buddhist Religion and Philosophy*. WSTB 11. Vienna: Arbeitskreis für Tibetische und Buddhistische Studien, Universität Wien.

Sutton, Florin Giripescu. 1991. *Existence and Enlightenment in the Laṇkāvatāra-sūtra: A Study in the Ontology and Epistemology of the Yogācāra School of Mahāyāna Buddhism*. Albany: SUNY Press.

Suzuki, D.T. 1932. *The Laṇkāvatāra Sūtra*. London: Routledge and Kegan Paul.

Tāranātha. 1970. *Tāranātha's History of Buddhism in India*. Trans. by Lama Chimpa and Alaka Chattopadhyaya. Simla: Indian Institute of Advanced Study.

Thakur, Anantalal. 1972. "Śāntarakṣita and Kamalaśīla." *Journal of the Ganganatha Jha Kendriya Sanskrit Vidyapeetha* (Ganganatha Jha Research Institute, Allahabad) 28 (1-2): 663-674.

Tharchin, Geshe. 1986. *Buddhist Logic in India, Tibet, and Mongolia*. Howell, New Jersey: Mahāyāna Sūtra and Tantra Press.

Thurman, Robert A.F. 1978. "Buddhist Hermeneutics." *Journal of the American Academy of Religions* 46 (1): 19-39.

_______. 1984. *Tsong Khapa's Speech of Gold in the* Essence of True Eloquence: *Reason and Enlightenment in the Central Philosophy of Tibet.* Princeton: Princeton University Press.

_______, ed. and trans. 1982. *The Life and Teachings of Tsong kha pa*. Dharamsala: Library of Tibetan Works and Archives.

Tillemans, Tom J.F. 1982. "The 'Neither One Nor Many' Argument for *Śūnyatā* and Its Tibetan Interpretations: Background Information and Source Materials." *Études de Lettres*. Lausanne: University of Lausanne.

_______. 1983. "The 'Neither One Nor Many' Argument for *Śūnyatā* and Its Tibetan Interpretations." In Steinkellner and Tauscher 1983.

_______. 1984. "Two Tibetan Texts on the 'Neither One Nor Many' Argument for *Śūnyatā*." JIP 12: 134-169.

_______. 1988. "Appendix: Supplementary Notes on Tsong kha pa's Position on Opponent-Acknowledged Reason (*gzhan grags kyi gtan tshigs*) and Similarly Appearing Topics (*chos can mthun snang ba*)." Unpublished manuscript.

_______. 1990. *Materials for the Study of Āryadeva, Dharmapāla, and Candrakīrti: The Catuḥśataka of Āryadeva, Chapters XII and XIII, with the Commentaries of Dharmapāla and Candrakīrti: Introduction, Translation, Sanskrit, Tibetan, and Chinese Texts, Notes*. 2 vols. WSTB 24.1 and 24.2. Vienna: Arbeitskreis für Tibetische und Buddhistische Studien Universität Wien.

_______. 1992. "Tsong kha pa et al. on the Bhāvaviveka-Candrakīrti Debate." In *Tibetan Studies. Proceedings of the 5th Seminar of International Association of Tibetan Studies*, edited by S. Ihara and Z. Yamaguchi. Narita, Naritasan Shinshoji.

_______. 1995. "Remarks on Philology." JIABS 18 (2): 269-277.

_______. 1999. *Scripture, Logic, Language: Essays on Dharmakīrti and His Tibetan Successors*. Boston: Wisdom Publications.

_______. 2002. "What are Mādhyamikas Refuting? Śāntarakṣita, Kamalaśīla *et alii* on Superimpositions (*samāropa*)." Unpublished paper delivered at the American Philosophical Association-Central Division Annual Meeting in Chicago, April 26, 2002.

Tillemans, Tom J.F. and Donald Lopez. 1998. "What Can One Reasonably Say about Nonexistence? A Tibetan Work on the Problem of *Āśrayāsiddha*." JIP 26: 23-51.

van der Kuijp, L. 1983. *Contributions to the Development of Tibetan Buddhist Epistemology*. Wiesbaden: Franz Steiner Verlag.

_______. 1985. "Miscellanea Apropos of the Philosophy of Mind in Tibet: Mind in Tibetan Buddhism." TJ 10 (1): 32-43.

Watanabe, Shoko, compiler. 1985. *Glossary of the Tattvasaṅgrahapañjikā: Tibetan-Sanskrit-Japanese, Part I.* Acta Indologica 5. Narita, Japan:Naritasan Shinjoshi.

Warder, A. K. 1980. *Indian Buddhism.* 2nd revised edition. Delhi: Motilal Banarsidass.

Williams, Paul. 1979. "Tsong-kha-pa on kun-rdzob-bden-pa." In *Tibetan Studies in Honour of Hugh Richardson.* Warminster, England: Aris and Phillips Ltd.

_______. 1983a. "A Note on Mi skyod rdo rje's Critique of dGe-lugs pa Mādhyamika." JIP 11: 125-145.

_______. 1983b. "On Rang Rig." In Steinkellner and Tauscher 1983.

_______. 1986. *Mahāyāna Buddhism: The Doctrinal Foundations.* London: Routledge.

_______. 1989. "Introduction: Some Random Reflections on the Study of Tibetan Mādhyamika." TJ 14 (1): 1-9.

_______.1998. *The Reflexive Nature of Awareness: A Tibetan Madhyamaka Defence.* Richmond, Surrey: Curzon Press.

Wilson, Joe Bransford. 1995. "Problems and Methods in Translation of Buddhist Texts from Tibetan." In Doboom 1995.

Woo, Jeson. 2000. "Oneness and Manyness: Vācaspatimiśra and Ratnakīrti on an Aspect of Causality." JIP 28: 225-231.

Wylie, Turrell. 1959. "A Standard System of Tibetan Transcription." *Harvard Journal of Asian Studies* 22: 261-267.

Yotsuya, Kodo. 1999. *The Critique of Svatantra Reasoning by Candrakīrti and Tsong-kha-pa: A Study of Philosophical Proof According to Two Prāsaṅgika Madhyamaka Traditions of India and Tibet.* Stuttgart: Franz Steiner Verlag.

Sūtras

Aṣhṭasāhasrikāprajñāpāramitāsūtra, Shes rab kyi pha rol tu phyin pa brgyad stong pa'i mdo. P734.

Daśabhūmikasūtra, Sa bcu pa'i mdo. P761.3.

Laṅkāvatārasūtra, Lang kar gshegs pa'i mdo. P 775.

Mahāratnakūṭadharmaparyāyashatasāhasrikagranthasūtra, dKon mchog brtsegs pa chen po'i chos kyi rnam grangs le'u stong phrag brgya pa'i mdo. P760.

Prajñāhṛdaya/Bhagavatīprajñāpāramitāhṛdayasūtra, Shes rab snying po/bCom ldan 'das ma shes rab kyi pha rol tu phyin pa'i snying po'i mdo. P160.

Pitāputrasamāgamasūta, Yab dang sras mjal ba'i mdo. P760.

Ratnameghasūtra, dKon mchog sprin gyi mdo. P879.

Saṃdhinirmocanasūtra, dGongs pa nges par 'grel pa'i mdo. P774.

Śatasāhasrikāprajñāpāramitāsūtra, Shes rab kyi pha rol tu phyin pa stong phrag brgya pa'i mdo. P730.

Śālistabmasūtra, Sa lu'i ljang pa'i mdo. P876.

Śāstras

Āryavimuktisena. *Pañcavimśatisāhasrikāprajñapāramitopadeśaśāstrābhisamayālaṃkāravṛtti, Shes rab kyi pha rol tu phyin pa stong phrag nyi shu lnga pa'i man ngag gi bstan bcos mngon par rtogs pa'i rgyan gyi 'grel pa*. P5185.

Atiśa (Dipaṃkaraśrijñāna). *Bodhipathapradīpa, Byang chub lam gyi gron ma*. P5343.

______. *Bodhimārgapradipapañjikā, Byang chub lam gyi sgron ma'i dka' 'grel*. P5344.

______. *Madhyamakopadeśa, dBu ma'i man ngag ces bya ba*. P5324.

______. *Satyadvayāvatāra, bDen pa nyis la 'jug pa*. P5380.

Avalokitavrata. *Prajñāpradīpaṭīkā, Shes rab sgron ma'i rgya cher 'grel pa*. P5259.

Bhāvaviveka. *Prajñapradīpamūlamadhyamakavṛtti, dbU ma rtsa ba'i 'grel pa shes rab sgron ma*. P5253.

______. *Madhyamakahṛdayavṛttiarkajvālā, dbU ma'i snying po'i 'grel pa rtog ge 'bar ba*. P5255.

Buddhapālita. *Buddhapālitamūlamadhyamakavṛtti, dbU ma rtsa ba'i 'grel pa li ta*. P5242.

Candrakīrti. *Bodhisattvayogacaryācatuḥśatakaṭīkā, Byang chub sems dpa'i rnal 'byor spyod pa bzhi brgya pa'i rgya cher 'grel pa*. P5266.

______. *Madhyamakāvatāra, dbU ma la 'jug pa*. P5262.

______. *Madhyamakāvatārabhāṣya, dbU ma la 'jug pa'i bshad pa*. P5263.

______. *Prasannapadāmūlamadhyamakavṛtti, dbU ma rtsa ba'i 'grel pa tshig gsal ba*. P5260.

Dharmakīrti. *Pramāṇavārrttikakārikā, Tshad ma rnam 'grel gyi tshig le'ur byas pa*.P5709.

______. *Pramāṇaviniścayaḥ, Tshad ma rnam par nges pa*. P5710.

Dignāga. *Pramāṇasamuccaya, Tshad ma kun las btus pa*. P 5700.

______. *Ālambanaparīkṣā, dMigs pa brtag pa*. P5703.

Haribhadra. *Abhisamayālaṁkārāloka, mNgon par rtogs pa'i rgyan gyi snang ba*. P5192.

______. *Sphuṭārthā/ Abhisamayālaṃkāranāmaprajñapāramitopadeśaśāstravṛtti, 'Grel pa don gsal/ shes rab kyi pha rol tu phyin pa'i man ngag gi bstan bcos mngon par rtogs pa'i rgyal ces bya ba'i grel pa*. P5191.

Jetāri. *Sugatamatavibhaṅga, bDe bar gzhegs pa'i gzhung rnam par 'byed pa*. P5296.

Jñānagarbha. *Satyadvayavibhaṅgavṛtti, bDen pa gnyis rnam par 'byed pa 'grel pa*. Toh3882 (not in P).

______. *Satyadvayavibhaṅgakārikā, bDen pa gnyis rnam par 'byed pa*. Toh3881 (not in P).

Kamalaśīla. *Madhyamakālaṃakārapañjikā, dbU ma rgyan gyi dka' 'grel*. P5286.

______. *Tattvasaṃgrahapañjikā, De kho na nyid bsdus pa'i dka' 'grel*. P5765.

______. *Madhyamakāloka, dbU ma snang ba*. P5287.

______. *Bhāvanākrama, sGom pa'i rim pa*. P 5310-12.

______. *Sarvadharmaniḥsvabhāvasiddhi, Chos thams cad rang bzhin med par grub pa*. D, vol. Sa, 273a4-291a7.
Critical edition of the Tibetan by Seitetsu Moriyama in *An Annotated Translation of Kamalaśīla's "Sarvadharmaniḥsvabhāvasiddhi."* Part IV. Berkeley: Department of Oriental Languages, University of California, Berkeley, 1984.

Nāgārjuna. *Śūnyatāsaptativṛtti, sTong pa nyid bdun cu pa'i 'grel pa*. P5231.

______. *Yuktiṣaṣṭikākārikā, Rigs pa drug cu pa'i tshig le'ur byas pa*. P5225.

______. *Rājaparikathāratnāvalī, rGyal po la gtam bya ba rin po che'i phreng ba*. P5658.
Ngawang Samten, ed. *Ratnāvalī of Ācārya Nāgārjuna with the Commentary by Ajitamitra*. Sarnath: Central Institute of Higher Tibetan Studies, 1990.

______. *Madhyamakaśāstra/ Prajñānāmamūlamadhyamakakārikā, dbU ma rtsa ba'i tshig le'ur byas pa shes rab ces bya ba*. P5224.
J.W. de Jong, ed. *Mūlamadhyamakakārikāḥ*. Madras: Adyar Library and Research Center, 1977.

Śāntarakṣita. *Madhyamakālaṃkārakārikā, dbU ma rgyan gyi tshig le'ur byas pa*. P5284.
Masamichi Ichigō, ed. (critical edition) *Madhyamakālaṃkāra of Śāntarakṣita with his own commentary or Vṛtti and with the subcommentary or Pañjikā of Kamalaśīla*. Kyota: Buneido, 1985.
Sarnath: Pleasure of Elegant Sayings Press, 1976.
Edition printed from the wood blocks at Ka sbug, 1961.

_______. *Madhyamakālaṃkāravṛtti, dbU ma'i rgyan gyi rang 'grel pa*. P5285.
Masamichi Ichigō. ed., (critical edition). *Madhyamakālaṃkāra of Śāntarakṣita with His Own Commentary or Vṛtti and with the Subcommentary or Pañjikā of Kamalaśīla*. Kyoto:Buneido, 1985.
Śīlendrabodhi and Ye-shes-sde, trans., *dbU ma'i rgyan gyi 'grel pa*. D, dbu ma, vol Sa 56b4-84a1.
Edition printed from the woodblocks at Ka sbug, 1961.
Sarnath: Nyingma Students Welfare Committee, 1986.

_______. *Tattvasaṃgraha, De kho na nyid bsdus pa'i tshig le'ur byas pa*. P5764.
Embar Krishnamacharya, ed. *Tattvasaṃgraha of Śāntarakṣita with the Commentary of Kamalaśīla*. 2 vols. GOS 30-31. Baroda: Central Library, 1926. Reprinted Baroda,1984, 1988.

_______. *Vādanyāyavipañcitārthā, rTsod pa'i rigs pa'i 'grel pa don rnam par 'byed pa*. D vol. *Zhe*, 51a3-151a6.
Dwarikadas Shastri, ed. *Vādanyāyaprakaraṇa of Acharya Dharmakīrti with the Commentary Vipanchitārthā of Acharya Śāntarakṣita*. Varanasi: Bauddha Bharati, 1972.

_______ (attr.). *Satyadvayavibhangapañjikā, bDen pa gnyis rman par 'byed pa'i dka' 'grel*. P5283.

Śāntideva. *Bodhi[sattva]caryāvatāra, Byang chub sems pa'i spyod pa la 'jug pa*. P5272.

Vasubandhu. *Abhidharmakośakārikā, Chos mngon pa'i mdzod kyi tshig le'ur byas pa*. P5590.

_______. *Abhidharmakośabhāṣya, Chos mngon pa'i mdzod kyi bshad pa*. P5591.

Tibetan Sources

sBa gSal-snang (attr.). *sBa-bzhed* (*sBa bzhed ces bya ba las sBa gSal gnang gi bzhed pa bzhugs*). Beijing: Mi rigs dpe skrun khang, 1980.

Bu-ston-rin-chen-grub. *The Collected Works of Bu-ston*. New Delhi: International Academy of Indian Culture, 1966.

lCang-skya-rol-pa'i-rdo-rje. *Grub pa'i mtha'i rnam par bshag pa gsal bar bshad pa thub bstan lhun po'i mdzes rgyan*. Sarnath: Pleasure of Elegant Sayings Press, 1970.

'Gos-lo Gzhon-nu-dpal. *Deb ther sngon po*. 2 vols. Chengdu: Si khron mi rigs dpe skrun khang, 1984.

rGyal-tshab-dar-ma-rin-chen. *dbU ma rgyan gyi brjed byang*. Sarnath: Pleasure of Elegant Sayings Press, 1976.

_______. *Collected Works (gsuṅ 'bum) of Rgyal-tshab rje Dar-ma-rin-chen*. New Delhi: Ngawang Gelek Demo,1981.

_______. *dbU ma'i rtsa ba'i dka' gnas chen po brgyad. Collected Works (gsuṅ 'bum) of Rgyal-tshab rje Dar-ma-rin-chen*. New Delhi: Ngawang Gelek Demo, 1981.

_______. *mNgon rtogs pa'i rgyan gyi ba 'grel pa dang bcas pa'i rnam bshad snying po'i rgyan. Collected Works (gsuṅ 'bum) of Rgyal-tshab rje Dar-ma-rin-chen*. New Delhi: Ngawang Gelek Demo, 1981.

_______. *Tshad ma'i brjed byang chen mo. Collected Works (gsuṅ 'bum) of Rgyal-tshab rje Dar-ma-rin-chen*. New Delhi: Ngawang Gelek Demo, 1981.

rGyal-ba-dge-'dun-grub, Dalai Lama I. *mDsod-Tik Thar-Lam gSal-Byed*. Sarnath: dGe-lugs pa Student Welfare Committee, Central Institute of Higher Tibetan Studies, 1982.

'Jam-byangs-bzhad-ba. *Grub mtha'i rnam sbhad rang gzhan grub mtha'kun dang zab don mchog tu gsal ba kun bzang shing gi nyi ma lung rigs rgya mtsho skye dgu'i re ba kun skong*. Musoorie: Dalama, 1962.

rJe-btsun-chos-kyi-rgyal-mtshan. *bsTan bcos dbu ma la 'jug pa'i rnam bshad dgongs pa rab gsal gyi dka' gnad gsal bar byed pa'i spyi don legs bshad skal bzang mgul rgyan*. In *Collected Works*, vol. Ma. Bylakuppee: Sera Je College.

_______. *Grub mtha'i rnam bzhag bshad ba*. In *Grub don sa gsum*. Mundgod: Gajang Computer Input Center, 1999.

_______. *Phar phyin skabs dang po'i spyi don skal bzang klu dbang gi rol mtsho*. Bylakuppee: Sera Je Library Computer Project, 1999.

mKhas-drub-dge-legs-dpal-bzang. *sTong thun chen mo/Zab mo stong pa nyid rab tu gsal bar byed pa'i bstan bcos skal bzang mig 'byed*. In *Collected Works*, vol. Ka.

dKon-mchog-'jigs-med-dbang-po. *Grub pa'i mtha'i rnam par bzhag pa rin po che'i phreng ba*. Dharamsala: Tibetan Cultural Printing Press, 1995.

Mi-pham-'jam dbangs rnam rgyal rgya mtsho. *dbU ma rgyan gyi rnam bshad 'jam dbyangs bla ma dgyes pa'i zhal lung. Prints of the Writings of 'Jam-mgon 'Ju Mi-pham-rgya-mtsho,* ed. Dilgo Khyentse. Vol. 4, 787-820. Kathmandu, ca. 1990.

Ngag-dbang dbal ldan. *Grub mtha' chen mo'i mchan 'grel dka' gnad mdud grol blo gsal gces nor*. Sarnath: Pleasure of Elegant Sayings Press, 1964.

_______. *Grub mtha' bzhi'i lugs kyi kun rdzob dang don dam pa'i don rnam par bshad pa legs bshad dpyid kyi dpal moi' glu dbyangs*. In *The Collected Works of Chos-rje-ṅag-dbaṅ-dpal-ldan of Urga*, vol. 3. Delhi: Mongolian Lama Guru Deva, 1983.

Negi, J.S. *Bod skad dang legs sbyar gyi tshig mdzod chen mo*. 6 vols. Sarnath: Dictionary Unit, Central Institute of Higher Tibetan Studies, 1993-2000.

Thu'u-bkwan blo-bzang-chos-kyi-nyi-ma. *Grub mtha' thams cad kyi khungs dang 'dod tshul ston pa legs bshad shel gyi me long*. Sarnath: Kargyud Relief and Protection Committee, Central Institute of Higher Tibetan Studies, 1995-1996.

Tsong-kha-pa-blo-bzang-grags-pa. *dbU ma la 'jug pa'i rgya cher bshad pa dgongs pa rab gsal*. Sarnath: Pleasure of Elegant Sayings Press, 1973; Bylakuppee: Sera Je Library Project, 1999.

_______. *dbU ma rgyan gyi zin bris*. Sarnath: Pleasure of Elegant Sayings Press, 1976.

_______. *Byang chub lam gyi rim pa chen mo*. Sarnath: dGe-lugs pa Student Welfare Committee, 1991.

_______. *Byang chub lam rim 'bring ba*. Bylakuppee: Sera Je Library Computer Project, 1999.

_______. *Drang ba dang nges pa'i don rnam par phye ba'i bstan bcos legs bshad snying po*. Bylakuppee: Sera-Mey Computer Project Center (SMCPC Books), 1997.

_______. *dKa gnad brgyad gyi zin bris*. In *Khams gsum chos kyi rgyal po tsong kha pa chen po'i gSung 'bum,* vol. Ba, folios 567-601.

_______. *dbU ma rtsa ba'i tshig le'ur byas pa'i rnam bshad rig pa'i rgya mtsho*. In *The Complete Works of Tsong-kha-pa*, vol. Ba, 1-282. gTsang, Tibet: dGa' ldan phun tshogs gling woodblocks, n.d.

Ye-shes-sDe. *lTa ba khyad par*. P5847

Index